Journey to Adulthood: East Asian Perspectives

SAGE STUDIES IN INTERNATIONAL SOCIOLOGY

Series Editor Chaime Marcuello Servós (2016–ongoing)
Editor, Department of Psychology and Sociology,
Zaragoza University, Spain

Recent books in the series
Journey to Adulthood: East Asian Perspectives
Chin-Chun Yi & Ming-Chang Tsai

Power, Violence and Justice: Reflections, Responses and Responsibilities
Edited by Margaret Abraham

Sociologies in Dialogue
Edited by Sari Hanafi & Chin-Chun Yi

*Global Childhoods in International Perspective:
Universality, Diversity and Inequalities*
Edited by Claudio Baraldi & Lucia Rabello De Castro

Key Texts for Latin American Sociology
Edited by Fernanda Beigel

*Global Sociology and the Struggles for a Better World: Towards the
Futures We Want*
Edited by Markus S. Schulz

Sociology and Social Justice
Edited by Margaret Abraham

Facing An Unequal World: Challenges for Global Sociology
Edited by Raquel Sosa Elizaga

Journey to Adulthood: East Asian Perspectives

Edited by **Chin-Chun Yi &**
Ming-Chang Tsai

SSIS SERIES SAGE STUDIES IN INTERNATIONAL SOCIOLOGY: 68

Los Angeles I London I New Delhi
Singapore I Washington DC I Melbourne

Los Angeles | London | New Delhi
Singapore | Washington DC | Melbourne

SAGE Publications Ltd
1 Oliver's Yard
55 City Road
London EC1Y 1SP

SAGE Publications Inc.
2455 Teller Road
Thousand Oaks, California 91320

SAGE Publications India Pvt Ltd
B 1/I 1 Mohan Cooperative Industrial Area
Mathura Road
New Delhi 110044

SAGE Publications Asia-Pacific Pte Ltd
3 Church Street
#10-04 Samsung Hub
Singapore 049483

Library of Congress Control Number: 2022940354

British Library Cataloguing in Publication data

A catalogue record for this book is available from the British Library

Editor: Michael Ainsley
Assistant editor: Rhoda Ola-Said
Production editor: Vijayakumar
Copyeditor: Christobel Colleen Hopman
Proofreader: Benny Willy Stephen
Indexer: TNQ Technologies
Marketing manager: Ruslana Khatagova
Cover design: Sheila Tong
Typeset by: TNQ Technologies
Printed in the UK

ISBN 978-1-5296-0844-1
ISBN 978-1-5296-0843-4 (pbk)

Contents

List of Figures   *vii*

List of Tables   *xi*

About the Authors   *xv*

PART I   Introduction   1

1 Journey to Adulthood: East Asian Perspectives   3
   Chin-Chun Yi and Ming-Chang Tsai

**PART II   Family Formation in Young Adulthood:
             Getting Married or Remaining Single   25**

2 Marriage Intention and the Subsequent Marriage in Taiwan   27
   Chia-Hua Liu

3 Marrying Early or Remaining Single in Taiwan:
   The Choice of Young Adults   59
   Yung-Chen Yuan and Chin-Chun Yi

**PART III   From School-to-Work Transition: The Entry
              to Job Market   97**

4 Education-to-Work Transitions and Youth's Psychological
   Well-Being in Taiwan   99
   Michael Gebel

5 Landing a Middle-Class Position: College Degree,
   Occupational Status and Income of Young Adults
   in Taiwan   126
   Ming-Chang Tsai

**PART IV   Young Married Couples: Marital Adjustment
                at the Beginning Stage**   **153**

6   Domestic Labour Involvement of Young Taiwanese Couples
    in Different Partnership and Parenthood Statuses   155
    Tsui-o Tai, Yi-Fu Chen and Hsien-Chih Tu

7   Does Having a Grandchild Strengthen Intergenerational
    Solidarity? Financial, Instrumental and Emotional Support
    Exchanges in Taiwan   181
    Yi-Ping Shih

8   Childcare Arrangements Among Young Parents in Taiwan   210
    Wan-chi Chen and Hao-Chun Cheng

**PART V   The Longitudinal Effect From Early Adolescence
                to Young Adulthood**   **239**

9   Parent–Child Relationships From Adolescence to Early
    Adulthood: The Role of Conceptions of Adulthood   241
    Ju-Ping Lin, Chia-Wen Yu and Chiu-Hua Huang

10 Norms and Relations: Developmental Self-Esteem Trajectory
    and Its Determinants From Adolescence to Adulthood   266
    Yuh-Huey Jou

11 Early Delinquency Trajectory and Developmental Outcomes
    in Adulthood: Findings From the Taiwan Youth Project   289
    Yi-fu Chen and Chyi-In Wu

**PART VI   Transition to Adulthood in Japan, South Korea
                and China**   **321**

12 School-to-Work Transition Among High School Students in
    Japan: School-mediated System and Labour Market Outcomes   323
    Hiroshi Ishida

13 No More Gender Gaps? Gendered Employment Patterns of
    Young College Graduates in South Korea Since 2000   347
    Min Young Song and Ki-Soo Eun

14 Who Rises Higher in First Job Attainment? Trends and
    Patterns of School-to-Work Transition in Hong Kong   372
    Xiaogang Wu and Maocan Guo

Index   403

List of Figures

Figure 3.1   Taiwan's unmarried population by age and
              educational level in 2019   63
Figure 4.1   Outcome trajectories of treatment and matched
              control group   114
Figure 5.1   Employment status in 2011   133
Figure 5.2   Employment status in 2017   134
Figure 5.3   ISEI scores for groups J1 and J3 comparing those
              who have and those who do not have a college
              degree   135
Figure 8.1   The distributions of actual and ideal childcare
              arrangements   222
Figure 8.2   Actual childcare arrangements by family
              structure   225
Figure 8.3   Childcare arrangements by parents' education
              (intact families only)   225
Figure 8.4   Comparing the distributions of actual and ideal
              childcare arrangements   227
Figure 9.1   Output of mediation analysis   259
Figure 10.1   Analytical model   272
Figure 10.2   Four-class solution of freely estimated GMM   280
Figure 11.1   (A) Estimated probability of zero delinquency for
              trajectory groups. (B) Estimated probability of
              one delinquency for trajectory groups.
              (C) Estimated probability of two or more
              delinquency for trajectory groups   301
Figure 12.1   Destinations of high school graduates, 1950–2020   329
Figure 12.2   Rate of job openings to job applicants for high
              school graduates 1955–2019   330
Figure 12.3   School mediation rate among high school
              graduates by birth cohort (%)   333

Figure 12.4   School mediation and the timing of start of
               first job   334

Figure 12.5   School mediation and whether the first job was
               first preference   335

Figure 12.6   School mediation and firm size (percentage
               worked in large firms and public sector)   335

Figure 12.7   School mediation and employment status
               (percentage of students who obtained regular
               employment)   336

Figure 12.8   School mediation rate and high school grade
               by birth cohort   337

Figure 12.9   School mediation rate and high school types by
               birth cohort   338

Figure 12.10   Effect of school mediation on the timing of first
               job after various control   339

Figure 12.11   Effect of school mediation on first job preference
               after various control   339

Figure 12.12   Effect of school mediation on firm size
               after various control   340

Figure 12.13   Effect of school mediation on employment status
               after various control   341

Figure 12.14   Social background and the use of school
               mediation   342

Figure 13.1   Share of employees working fewer than 40 hours
               per week by gender (%), 2019, selected countries   352

Figure 13.2   Age-specific employment rates by level of
               educational attainment and gender (%), 2018,
               selected countries   353

Figure 13.3   Tertiary education rates of the South Korean
               population aged 25–34 by gender, 1998–2019   355

Figure 13.4   Age-specific employment rates of the
               South Korean population born in the 1970s
               and the 1980s by education level, birth
               cohort and gender   356

Figure 13.5   Patterns of college graduates' first employment
               over time: smoothed hazard rates of getting a
               non-part time job by gender and birth cohort   361

Figure 13.6   Patterns of college graduates' career break over
               time: smoothed hazard rates of leaving the
               labour market by gender and birth cohort   362
Figure 14.1   (A) Actual first-year-first-degree (FYFD) intake
               places of UGC-funded programmers, 1965–2019
               academic years, (B) Expansion of tertiary
               education in Hong Kong, 1971–2019   374
Figure 14.2   (A) Percentage of employment by industry in
               Hong Kong, 1993–2019, (B) Percentage of
               employment by occupation in Hong Kong,
               1993–2019   378
Figure 14.3   Percentage of female employment by industry in
               Hong Kong, 1993–2019   382
Figure 14.4   Predicted mean first job ISEI, by gender and
               education   389
Figure 14.5   Predicted logit for university vs. non-university
               education for selected first job occupational
               categories   394

List of Tables

Table 1.1   Age at first marriage, crude marriage rate, total
               fertility rate in Taiwan: 2000–2020   8
Table 2.1   Descriptive statistics   37
Table 2.2   Marital characteristics by desire to marry   45
Table 2.3   The effect of desire to marry on the probability
               of marriage in 2014   48
Table 2.A1   Definitions of variables for Table 2.2
               (all from TYP2014)   58
Table 3.1   Marital status of TYP samples (%)   67
Table 3.2   Marital status of interviewees by fertile status   68
Table 3.3   Marital and fertile status of interviewees,
               by education background   75
Table 3.4   Social demographic characteristics of interviewees   93
Table 4.1   Illustration of sample and treatment definition   105
Table 4.2   Descriptive statistics and balancing of control
               variables   110
Table 4.3   The effects of NEET on depressive symptoms,
               health and happiness   115
Table 4.4   Subgroup-specific effects of NEET, DID-PSM
               results   118
Table 5.1   Summary statistics J1 and J3   137
Table 5.2   ISEI Score for group J1 (SUR model)   139
Table 5.3   ISEI score for group J3 (SUR model)   141
Table 5.4   Income for group J1 (SUR model)   143
Table 5.5   Income for J3 group (SUR model)   144
Table 6.1   Distribution of individual and family
               characteristics by gender and partnership
               and parenthood statuses   168
Table 6.2   Individual and family effects on household
               labour: men's reports   172
Table 6.3   Individual and family effects on household labour:
               women's reports   173

Table 7.1 Descriptive statistics of the survey sample 188
Table 7.2 Descriptive statistics on intergenerational co-residence 190
Table 7.3 (A) Regression model of intergenerational financial support: G2 male vs. G1.
(B) Regression model of intergenerational financial support: G2 female vs. G1 193
Table 7.4 (A) Regression model of intergenerational instrumental support: G2 male vs. G1.
(B) Regression model of intergenerational instrumental support: G2 female vs. G1 196
Table 7.5 Regression model of intergenerational emotional support 199
Table 8.1 Descriptive statistics of socioeconomic backgrounds ($n = 663$) 220
Table 8.2 Descriptive statistics on parental leave, childcare subsidy and childcare expenditure 223
Table 8.3 Percentage of mismatch between ideal and actual childcare arrangements, by family structure 228
Table 8.4 Percentage of mismatch between ideal and actual childcare arrangements, by parents' education 228
Table 8.5 The ordinal logistic regression models: The association of childcare arrangements and parent's satisfaction to parent–child relationship 230
Table 9.1 Description of analytic variables ($N = 2,076$) 250
Table 9.2 Factor analysis of the importance of criteria for adulthood ($N = 2,076$) 253
Table 9.3 Importance of criteria for adulthood ($N = 2,076$) 254
Table 9.4 Comparison of perceived importance of criteria for adulthood by gender, education, marriage status and employment status of young adult ($N = 2,076$) 255
Table 9.5 Multiple regression analysis predicting young adults' conceptions of the transition to adulthood and intergenerational relationships ($N = 2,076$) 256
Table 10.1 Gender and family characteristics 276
Table 10.2 Mean and standard deviation of major variables 277
Table 10.3 Fit statistics for latent growth modelling (LGM) 278

Table 10.4   Fit statistics for latent class growth analysis
             (LCGA) and growth mixture modelling (GMM)   279
Table 10.5   Results of the three-step multivariate
             multinomial regression for self-esteem growth
             trajectories   281
Table 11.1   The developmental patterns of early delinquency   299
Table 11.2   Model selection process of the group-based
             modelling   300
Table 11.3   The delinquency and substance profile of the
             early delinquency trajectory groups   302
Table 11.4   The effects of the early delinquent trajectory
             groups on life-course transitions   305
Table 11.5   The effects of the early delinquent trajectory
             groups on social bonds   306
Table 11.6   The effects of the early delinquency trajectory
             groups on socio-economic attainment at age 30   307
Table 11.7   The developmental outcomes at age 30 of the
             early delinquent trajectory groups and the
             mediating role of life course transitions and social
             bonds during late adolescence and young
             adulthood   309
Table 12.1   Methods used for searching jobs by education for
             three countries (multiple answers)   326
Table 13.1   Characteristics of the analytic sample for the
             survival-time analysis   358
Table 13.A1   Structure of the survival-time dataset 1 concerning
             the timing of first employment   368
Table 13.A2   Structure of the survival-time dataset 2 concerning
             the timing of career break   370
Table 14.1   Percentage of employment by industry and
             occupation in Hong Kong, official statistics
             1995–2019   377
Table 14.2   Percentage of female employment by industry in
             Hong Kong, official statistics 1995–2019   380
Table 14.3   Summary statistics by cohort, HKPSSD 2011   385
Table 14.4   OLS estimates of the determinants of first job
             ISEI, HKPSSD 2011   388

Table 14.5 Marginal effects of the logit model estimates
of the determinants of first job occupational
status, HKPSSD 2011   391

Table 14.6 Coefficients of ordered logit model and
stereotyped ordered regression model estimates
of the determinants of first job occupational
status, HKPSSD 2011   393

About the Authors

Wan-Chi Chen is Professor of Sociology at National Taipei University, Taiwan. She is currently the Director of the Research Center for Education Systems and Policy, National Academy for Educational Research. Her research areas include education, family, gender and work, with a particular interest in how East Asian educational systems work. Her recent works include a number of projects evaluating college entrance policy and educational NPOs' intervention. Her efforts to advocate the use of administrative data facilitate evidence-based policy-making in education in Taiwan.

Yi-Fu Chen, PhD, is an Associate Professor with the Department of Sociology at National Taipei University. His main research areas include sociology of crime and deviance, sociology of the family and life course research. His research includes the efficacy of parenting programmes, gene-by-environment interaction effects on young adults' internalizing and externalizing problems and adolescent violence. He is also interested in topics such as adolescent sexting and the impact of SNS on adolescent physical and mental health.

Hao-Chun Cheng is originally from Taiwan and is currently a doctoral candidate at the Department of Sociology, University of Maryland, College Park. His research interests include demography and social stratification, especially the issues of first marriage and gender stratification. Hao-Chun has presented his projects in the Population Association of America (PAA) annual meetings.

Ki-Soo Eun is Professor of Sociology and Demography at Graduate School of International Studies as well as Director of Center for Transnational Migration and Social Inclusion, Seoul National University. He dedicates himself to helping people deal with care and care work from care economy perspective. His research lies in work-–life balance, low fertility and ageing, change of family values, gender, and development and Korean modernization. He was Vice President of International Association for Time Use Research from 2019 to 2013.

Michael Gebel is Full Professor of Methods of Empirical Social Research at the University of Bamberg (Germany) and Research Affiliate at the Leibniz-Institute for Educational Trajectories (LIfBi). He studied economics and social sciences at the University of Mannheim and UCL Louvain-la-Neuve and received his PhD in Sociology from the University of Mannheim. His main research interests are school-to-work transition, non-standard employment, unemployment, returns to education, longitudinal data analysis, causal inference and international comparative research.

Maocan Guo is a post-doc fellow at the Center for Applied Social and Economic Research at NYU Shanghai. He received his PhD in Sociology from Harvard University. His research spans the substantive fields of education, mobility, inequality, labour market processes and distributive justice. Broadly defined, he seeks to understand how different social groups are being incorporated or excluded in a variety of stratification processes and what mechanisms contribute to their respective outcomes, and how different social groups perceive, respond and make sense of the mobility and inequality at hand. He has published in both English and Chinese journals.

Chiu-Hua Huang is an Assistant Professor of the Department of Family Studies and Child Development at the Shih Chien University in Taiwan. Her research interests include intergenerational relationships in the aged society, and family life education programme development and evaluation.

Hiroshi Ishida is University Professor at the University of Tokyo. He received his PhD in sociology from Harvard University and held academic appointments at Columbia University and the University of Michigan. Ishida's research interests include comparative social mobility and social inequality over the life course. He is the author of *Social Mobility in Contemporary Japan* (Stanford) and the co-editor of

Social Class in Contemporary Japan (Routledge). He was the editor-in-chief of *Social Science Japan Journal* published by Oxford University Press, and he currently directs the Japanese Life Course Panel Surveys.

Yuh-Huey Jou is a research fellow and deputy director of the Institute of Ethnology, Academia Sinica, Taiwan. She received her PhD from Hiroshima University, Japan, in 1995. Her current research focuses on marital interaction and parent–child relationship. The research topics cover multi-dimensional personal interactions and mechanisms such as support, conflict, power, deception and humour. She also conducts long-term panel data to explore the transformation of intergenerational relations and values from the perspective of dyadic subsystems and life stages.

Ju-Ping Lin is a Professor of Human Development and Family Studies and director of Family Research and Development Centre at the National Taiwan Normal University. Her research focuses on ageing within the context of family life, such as intergenerational relationships and grandparenthood. Dr. Lin is vice president of Taiwan Association of Gerontology. She also served as member of 'Senior Citizens Welfare Promoting Group' of Ministry of Health and Welfare in Taiwan.

Chia-Hua Liu is an associate professor at Tamkang University, Taiwan. He received his PhD in Economics from the Texas A&M University. His research focuses on public policy with an emphasis on education and family related policies. His work in education has demonstrated how educational policy can alter students' learning behaviors, and shown that college quality is positively related to the future earnings. His work in family found that the Children and Youth Welfare Act can alter the intensity of child-parent interaction and thereby enhance children's non-cognitive skills such as prosociality evaluation.

Yi-Ping Shih, PhD, is an Associate Professor and Chair at the Department of Sociology, Fu Jen Catholic University, Taiwan. She received her PhD from the Department of Sociology, University of Buffalo, the State University of New York. Dr. Shih's research interests include studies of cultural capital, sociology of the family as well as studies regarding children's time use and playwork.

Min Young Song is a PhD candidate in Sociology at University of Warwick in the United Kingdom. Previously, she studied at Seoul National University and Stanford University for her BA and MA. She also worked for the Korea Institute for Health and Social Affairs (KIHASA). Her research revolves around gender, work and social inequality. In particular, her PhD research is about gender disparities in the labour market in the knowledge-based economy.

Tsui-o Tai is Associate Professor of Sociology at National Taipei University. She received her PhD in Sociology from the University of California, Irvine (UCI). Tsui-o Tai's research and teaching interests lie in family work, gender inequality, poverty and social welfare. She especially focuses on comparative family studies and international poverty research. She has published on these themes in such journals as *European Sociological Review*, *Journal of Family Issues*, *Social Forces* and *Social Science Research*.

Ming-Chang Tsai is a Research Fellow and Deputy Director of Research Center for Humanities and Social Sciences, Academia Sinica, Taiwan. He was former President of the International Society for Quality of Life Studies and Taiwanese Sociological Association. His current research focuses on the working experiences of youths in East Asia. His recent books include *Global Exposure in East Asia* (Routledge, 2015) and *Quality of Life in Japan: Contemporary Perspectives on Happiness* (coeditor, Springer, 2020).

Chyi-In Wu is a Research Fellow of the Institute of Sociology at Academia Sinica in Taiwan. Currently, he is the Principal Investigator of Taiwan Social Change Survey, 1985- and Taiwan Rural Social and Population Survey, 2018- . His research focuses on the outcomes of adolescent development in a life course perspective. His work has appeared in numerous journals including *Social Networks*, *Criminology*, *Developmental Psychology*, *Child Development*, *Social Psychology Quarterly*, *Journal of Research on Adolescence*, *Evolution and Human Behavior* and *International Sociology*.

Xiaogang Wu is Yufeng Global Professor of Social Science, and the Founding Director of Center for Applied Social and Economic Research (CASER) at NYU Shanghai, and Professor of Sociology at New York University. Wu joined NYU Shanghai in 2020 from the Hong Kong University of Science and Technology (HKUST), where he was Chair Professor of Social Science and Public Policy. His research interests include inequality and social stratification, social demography, survey and quantitative methods, and urban sociology. He has been the Chief Editor of the *Chinese Sociological Review* since 2011. He served as the President of International Chinese Sociological Association from 2018 to 2021.

Chin-Chun Yi is an adjunct research fellow at the Institute of Sociology, Academia Sinica, Taiwan. Dr. Yi has published extensively on changing families in Chinese and East Asian societies and the growth trajectories of youth from early adolescence to young adulthood. Chin-Chun Yi served as the president for the Committee on Family Research (RC06) in ISA (2014–2018) and was the ISA executive committee member of Research Council (2010–2014–2018). She has been in the editorial board and as guest editor for several journals. In addition, Dr. Yi is active in professional service for NGOs and the government.

Chia-Wen Yu is an Adjunct Assistant Professor of Human Development and Family Studies at the National Taiwan Normal University. Her research interest is intergenerational relationships, focussing on adolescent, parents and grandparent interaction in family life.

Yung-Chen Yuan is a Postdoctoral Fellow of Research Center for Humanities and Social Sciences, Academia Sinica, Taiwan. She received her PhD in Sociology from the University of Bristol. Her research interests include family relationships, intergenerational relationships, family formation, migration, and national and ethnic identity.

Part I

Introduction

1

Journey to Adulthood: East Asian Perspectives

Chin-Chun Yi and Ming-Chang Tsai

Transition to Adulthood

A major issue in research on young adults is how current social and economic changes have generated profound effects on their transition from school to work, family formation, personal relationships and subjective well-being. While this is a concern of academics globally, this book presents a collective effort to illustrate the special characteristics of young adulthood in East Asia. From the life course perspective, the transition from adolescence to adulthood is a critical life stage shaping the growth trajectory of individuals over time. In existing literature, a number of social markers during this transition period, such as leaving school, entering the labour force, getting married and becoming parents have been documented (Hogan and Astone, 1986; Park, 2013; Shanahan, 2000). By contrast, developmental psychology highlights the issue of maturity for this phase, such as including taking responsibility for oneself, developing a capability of making important decisions and becoming fully independent (Arnett, 2004). We propose that both social and developmental markers need to be incorporated in studying transition to adulthood.

Looking from a cross-cultural perspective, another important issue is the significant variations in defining adulthood by biological age across different societies. It is not a surprise that in East Asia the transition phase to young adulthood currently seems to have extended to age 30 and even to 35. This designated age range is adjustable, depending on research issues or social norms in focus (Arnett, 2000; Cepa and Furstenberg, 2021; Erikson, 1958; Furstenberg, 2010; Petry, 2002; Yi, 2015). Moreover, the ability to establish an independent life as young adults also varies in its importance across different cultural contexts (Buchmann, 1989; Shanahan, 2000). Earning sufficient income for economic independence, for instance, is emphasized in most societies. However, in societies where intergenerational co-residence and support of elderly parents are conventional familial practice, being independent financially as a vital adult milestone can be less emphasized in a successful transition to adulthood. Rather, being able to express filial attitudes to ageing parents may be perceived as a more critical social marker of becoming an adult (Lin and Yi, 2013).

In the East Asian context, a dominant feature of the changing growth trajectory of the young generation is their prolonged transition to adulthood. Many young people now have stayed in school longer, enter the labour market late, get married even later – in their mid-thirties – and find themselves financially constrained in supporting parents. This protracted young adulthood interacts with forces of tradition and modernization, the patterns and impacts of which clearly deserve research attention (Yi, 2013). One critical traditional value is inarguably educational degree, which has maintained its high importance even in the contemporary era (Hannum et al., 2019; Hsu, 1948; Yi et al., 2009). The continuing emphasis on higher education attainment as the sole means to future career success in this cultural area has resulted in a majority of youth spending more and more years in school despite a widespread concern of credential inflation (Liu, 2020b). Furthermore, a normative expectation of securing a stable job before getting married necessarily encourages a trend of delayed marriage and parenthood (Raymo et al., 2015; Yamada, 1999). A prolonged transition to adulthood hence appears inevitable. These overt behavioural patterns should not be considered separate events, but are intertwined and simultaneous. They to a large extent reflect the age-old influences of certain cultural prescriptions. Yet in some aspects, they are an emerging deviation from traditional values; that is, they do not closely follow what has been thought of as fulfilling a prescribed social role and responsibility in a timely manner and being ready for the next phase (Arnett, 2004). What the consequences of such protraction are for today's young generation is no doubt an urgent research issue.

This book aims at describing the particular growth context of the millennial generation in East Asia. Different from their Western counterparts, East Asian youths constantly face the challenge of conflicting normative demands from tradition and modernity, which imposes a necessity to accommodate, compromise or even concede in various spectrums of life (Yi, 2013). It is our intention to portray and to analyse the diverse developmental patterns which have occurred in their transition to adulthood. Family formation for some of them, as well as protracted singlehood for others, will be delineated with a deliberate attention to the interplay of norms and resources among this generation. On the other hand, their early career in a neoliberal economy which offers mostly precarious employment at entry level has grave impacts on their decision for union formation, having children and support for old parents. This book uses panel data to illustrate longitudinal processes from early adolescence to young adulthood for a wide range of issues on family relations, work experiences and individual well-being. Along with an intensive study of the Taiwan case, we also look at young people in Japan, Korea and Hong Kong in terms of their school-to-work transition as well as their different patterns of employment in a highly competitive labour market. These comparative findings allow an in-depth understanding of the unique structural and cultural mechanisms in operation affecting the journey to adulthood among East Asian youths.

East Asian Context

Competitive Educational System

The educational system in East Asia has a historical heritage, and its impact has become even more powerful nowadays. Among many ways that Confucianism encourages one to honour one's ancestors is to achieve a high educational attainment to qualify for the offices in the state (Hsu, 1948). This fundamental teaching remains influential today. To study hard and succeed in the competitive examination for better colleges has been the ultimate purpose of education for young people. While a strong desire to enter elite universities can also be seen elsewhere, high school students in this region are particularly trained to become hyper-competitive, with the only goal being to surpass others' scores in examinations (Chiang, 2018; Yi, 2013). In addition, in the annual entrance examination for universities, there is often a substantial proportion of re-examinees who did not receive good grades in the previous year. Their participation surely makes the test competition even tougher.

There is probably no better case to vividly illustrate the dominant value of educational achievement in society than the super-competitive educational system in East Asia which has propelled families to invest enormous resources to ensure young children's educational success in the first place. To excel in a college entrance examination is certainly a crucial stepping stone, but there are grave consequences. Previous literature on data from as early as the 1950s has documented that the fierce academic competition in East Asia caused high adolescent suicides (Zeng and LeTendre, 1998). The stressful high school years have produced long-term negative impacts on youth's well-being when moving into young adulthood (Ahn and Baek, 2013; Huang et al., 2021; Liu, 2019; Park and Chung, 2010; Tzeng and Yi, 2013; Yi et al., 2013). As a result, a young higher achiever also tends to be a person under high pressure (Lee et al., 2017; Lin and Gebel, 2021; Park, 2013). In our attempt to analyse significant mechanisms affecting the growth trajectory among young East Asian adults, educational competition and achievement in the earlier phase are key underlying factors which determine the subsequent evolution of life conditions in transition to adulthood among East Asian youths.

Persistent Cultural Norms

East Asian researchers have long noticed the co-existence of traditional and modern values in almost all spectrums of life (Cheng et al., 2000; Iwai and Yasuda, 2011; Miraz et al., 2017; Yi and Chang, 2008). The middle class, the rise of which has benefited from the rapid economic growth and educational expansion in this region, expresses a preference for the Western mode of life (Chen and Yi, 2021; Hsiao, 2013). On the other hand, conventional familial norms still exert significant influence on young people. While both marriage and fertility rates have declined, this has happened without a concomitant change of traditional attitudes towards the issue of acceptable childbirth (Jones and Yeung, 2014; Raymo et al., 2015; Yi and Jao, 2013). For most Taiwanese, bearing children (sons especially) after marriage is considered suitable. Birth out of wedlock should be avoided (Wu and Yi, 2003). The inseparable package of marriage and childbirth (or the marriage–childbirth package), rooted in the Confucius cultural tradition, remains almost intact and is partially responsible for low marriage, low fertility and a negligible proportion of premarital childbirth (Jones and Gubhaju, 2009; Tsuya et al., 2019; Yeung and Alipio, 2013).

In the family domain, cross-national comparison among Japan, South Korea, China and Taiwan has shown that despite some variations, traditional cultural norms have by and large maintained their impact on various aspects of family life (Iwai and Yasuda, 2011). For example, the majority of people in this region endorse traditional values such as the family's well-being having the priority over individual interests. It is popular belief that a three-generation household is a favourable arrangement for elderly parents. On the other hand, what is deemed 'modern' behaviours such as pre-marital cohabitation and divorce have been increasingly accepted by young people. It should be noted that in many family aspects, Japan reports higher conservative values, and China and Taiwan, in contrast, seem to embrace more non-traditional family attitudes (Lin and Yi, 2013). But overall, traditional cultural norms persist and exert a substantial influence in East Asia.

Specific evidence may best be illustrated by Table 1.1. As can be seen, son preference, especially having a 'Dragon son' (*long zi*), has been highly favoured (Hu and Chiang, 2021; Yi, 2019). Hence, while the total fertility rate has been gradually declining over the last few decades, once in every cycle of the Chinese Zodiac (i.e. a set of 12 animals for a cycle of 12 years), there is a sharp increase in births in each Dragon year (e.g. 2000, 2012). In contrast, a 'Tiger son' is not preferred. In the latest Year of the Tiger (2010), Taiwan had the lowest total fertility rate in the world (0.895). Similar demographic behaviours in accordance with cultural norms are also observed, such as the low marriage rate in the Lonely Year (*gu luan nian*) or inauspicious years for marriage (the crude marriage rate was 5.07‰ and 5.11‰ in 2009 and 2020). In addition, there was a sharp increase in the marriage rate in 2011 (7.1‰), which is the centennial year for the Republic of China and was considered a good year for marriage due to its homophony with 'hundred years of harmony' in Chinese. The year 2011 was followed by the favoured Year of the Dragon of 2012 which reached a high TFR of 1.27‰. The influence of the social timing is apparent in the statistics about marriage and fertility.

As the labour market has slackened, more young East Asian adults have become unemployed or work in precarious jobs (Heinrich and Galan, 2018; Sato and Imai, 2011). To rely on and to co-reside with

Table 1.1 Age at first marriage, crude marriage rate, total fertility rate in Taiwan: 2000–2020

Year	Social timing	Age at first marriage Male	Female	CMR(‰)	TFR (‰)
2000	Dragon	30.3	26.1	8.19	**1.680**
2001		30.8	26.4	7.63	1.400
2002		31.0	26.8	7.69	1.340
2003		31.2	27.2	7.60	1.235
2004		30.7	26.9	5.80	1.180
2005		30.6	27.4	6.21	1.115
2006		30.7	27.8	6.25	1.115
2007		31.0	28.1	5.89	1.100
2008		31.1	28.4	6.73	1.050
2009	Lonely Year	31.6	28.9	**5.07**	1.030
2010	Tiger	31.8	29.2	6.00	**0.895**
2011	100th Anniversary of the Republic of China	31.8	29.4	**7.13**	1.065
2012	Dragon	31.9	29.5	6.16	**1.270**
2013		32.0	29.7	6.32	1.065
2014		32.1	29.9	6.38	1.165
2015		32.2	30.0	6.58	1.175
2016		32.4	30.0	6.29	1.170
2017		32.4	30.0	5.86	1.125
2018		32.5	30.2	5.74	1.060
2019		32.6	30.4	5.70	1.050
2020		32.3	30.3	5.11	0.990

parents has become a prevalent lifestyle for many youths. They are often viewed with disapproval as 'parasite singles' (Yamada, 1999). The lack of economic independence is undoubtedly opposite to the normative expectation of Confucian teaching that a gentleman should be steadfast with regards to his own family and career at age 30 (*sanshi erli*). On the other hand, co-residence between generations is culturally supported as a filial act in East Asia. Not establishing an independent family in young adulthood seems to have gradually become acceptable, especially given the rising cost of housing and increasingly higher age at first marriage in this region (Lin and Yi, 2013; Yasuda et al., 2011; Yi, 2015).

Norms and Resources at Interplay in Transition to Adulthood: Illustrations From Taiwan Youth Project

Previous studies have highlighted a paradox in East Asian society, in which rapid social and economic changes parallel a limited change in familial norms and obligations (Raymo et al., 2015). This is perhaps an outcome out of young East Asian adults, whose protracted transition to adulthood is intertwined with constant challenges and tensions brought about by the interactions between modernity and tradition (Yi, 2013; Yi and Chang, 2019). While moving into adulthood implies following socially designated road maps for performing age-related normative roles (Salmela-Aro et al., 2007), young East Asians have spent more time in this phase before moving to mature adulthood. Those in their early thirties are expected to make important life decisions pertaining to family formation and career development, but with increased constraints. For example, the school-to-work transition and earnings from jobs in this phase have been determined largely by ranking, reputation and social networks possessed by both high schools and universities (Choi and Bae, 2020; Ishida, 1997, 2007; Liu, 2020a; Park and Kim, 2014). Those who lack educational credentials have encountered acute difficulties compared to past decades. With regard to the family formation decision, hypergamy or the mating gradient remains an important concern in the mate selection process for young adults (Tsutsui, 2013; Yi and Jao, 2013). Given the narrowed gender gap both in higher education and in labour force participation, assortative marriage on the basis of education or income leads to a lower probability of getting married or giving birth to children. Males with disadvantaged positions are especially perceived as not fulfilling the expected role of full-grown adults in this course.

What we suggest is that the Western model, with its greater emphasis on an individual's own decisions in this phase, does not fit the East Asian context very well (Yi and Chang, 2019). Hence, we argue that it is very important to focus on the continuing influence of cultural norms specific to East Asia in studying the transition to adulthood in this region. In order to achieve this goal, we advance two major focuses: one is to expound the potential strengths and/or constraints of the prevailing social norms and values shared among East Asian societies. It is important to observe how cultural norms such as filial piety continue to shape the developmental trajectory of young adults and even exert a determining influence on family behaviours. The other is to ascertain the longitudinal effects of the experiences of family, school and community since adolescence so that we can better delineate the effects of individual and family resources on the subsequent growth patterns among young East Asian adults.

Previous studies have documented the significance of both resources and norms in understanding the growth trajectory from early adolescence to emerging adulthood in East Asia (Park and Kim, 2014; Yi, 2013, 2015). A substantial proportion of three-generational households has characterized the family structure in this region. This living arrangement not only reflects a filial norm encouraging such a practice (Yi, 2014; Yi and Lin, 2009) but also is a way of resource pooling among multiple generations under the same roof. Filial piety and resource pooling combine to account for upward financial transfer to parents, which has been widely practiced in East Asia (Yi and Lin, 2019).

Different educational tracking also exerts a substantial influence on self-concept and labour market for young people, not to mention its impact on adopting deviant behaviours (Huang et al., 2021; Lin and Gebel, 2021). Education is correlated with the value they place on children, and their fertility intention (Chen and Yi, 2021; Hu and Chiang, 2021). All the existing literature suggests that the interplay of norms and resources continues to influence one life stage after another. Therefore, this book can be considered a continuing effort to uncover the hidden patterns of such interplay by looking at factors at structural, relational, normative and temporal levels. This multilevel approach promises effective capturing of the detailed features of the journey to young adulthood among East Asian youths.

Taiwan Youth Project (TYP)

There have been a few longitudinal panel studies on child and youth development in East Asia since early 2000. The Taiwan Youth Project (hereafter TYP) is perhaps the earliest large-scale youth panel survey in this region. The TYP investigates the trajectory of youths' growth in Taiwan from the life course perspective, which emphasizes the significance of social contexts, particularly family, school and community, in order to understand the targeted population. To focus on the developmental patterns as well as growth trajectories in this phase, the TYP focuses on collecting information about social structures, personal resources and cultural normative factors, in addition to conventional biological and psychological traits (Erikson, 1959).

Phase I Survey (2000–2009)

The TYP conducted surveys of youths in two phases from 2000 to 2020. In Phase I, the time frame was set from early adolescence to emerging adulthood. The linkage between life experiences during adolescence and the subsequent developmental outcomes during emerging adulthood was the major concern. Using a multistage stratified-cluster random sampling method, the TYP interviewed two cohorts (N=5600) of junior high school students in Taipei City (the capital in Taiwan), Taipei County (later called 'New Taipei City', a mixture of both agriculture and manufacturing industries) and Yi-Lan County (an agricultural region). The J1 cohort was the first-year junior high students with an average age of 13, and the J3 cohort the third-year students in junior high school, who were two years older. By the end of Phase I in 2009, our sample arrived at emerging adulthood (J1 aged 22, and J3 aged 24). After nine survey waves, the retention rate remained high at 65.8 per cent (N=3673).

It should be noted that during Phase I, homeroom teachers were also surveyed. In addition, parents participated in five waves of surveys conducted in the same year along with the main sample (e.g. for J1, Wave 1, Wave 3, Wave 6, Wave 8 and Wave 9). Overall, the research findings (Yi, 2013) confirm the significant influences of family, school and community on the developmental patterns of youths from their early adolescence to emerging adulthood. Meanwhile, early family experiences, the educational tracking system and entrance examinations for admission to competitive high schools and colleges, as well as leaving home and early work experiences, all generate important influences on the growth trajectory of Taiwanese youths.

Phase II (2011–2020)

In Phase II, the survey design focused on the experiences of the transition to adulthood. The original two cohorts (J1 and J3) were combined into one sample in the Phase II adult survey. Three waves of the survey were conducted in 2011, 2014 and 2017 with participants aged 25, 28 and 31 respectively. Family formation and labour market participation became the main theme, as most of them had left school and started to work. For young adults in this life stage, getting married, securing a job, having stable earnings and supporting parents appear to be salient markers of a successful transition to a fully mature adult. We are able to illustrate their variety of experiences in family as well as outside the family with our panel data. Not only was the information about universal markers such as finishing school, finding jobs and establishing a family collected, but data on beliefs and responses to social norms for adulthood were also gathered in the survey. Data from TYP Phase II provide a highly valuable source for scientific investigation of young adulthood in Taiwan.

Launch of the Spousal Survey (2013–2018)

After the completion of the TYP 2011 survey (or Wave 1 TYP adult survey), we noticed that 7 per cent of the sample were already married by age 25. Since the average age of first marriage in Taiwan in 2011 was 31.8 for males and 29.4 for females (see Table 1.1), this is clearly an early married group. The research team decided to launch a spousal survey to establish a new dataset containing information about their marriage and family formation, particularly their dyadic intimate relationships, family dynamics, normative practices and interpersonal conflicts at this particular life course. As the sampled respondents became older over time, their marriage rate increased as expected: in 2014, 20 per cent of young adults (with an average age of 28) were married; in 2017, 39.6 per cent were married (at age 31). It should be noted that the marriage rate of TYP samples corresponds well with the official statistics. The response rate of spousal surveys, which is 50.5 per cent, 73.7 per cent and 75.1 per cent for 2011, 2014 and 2017, respectively, is satisfactory. The preliminary findings provided by team members (Yi et al., 2019) show new patterns of the interplay of norms and resources in various family behaviours among young Taiwanese couples. In-depth qualitative interviews, another effort to solicit supplementary information on specific issues, were also performed on a small proportion of the sample. Benefiting from the qualitative data, this book is able to publish a special chapter to illustrate the persistent influence of cultural norms in young couples' marital decision on family formation.

In brief, TYP has made a strong effort to study Taiwanese youths with a special attention to the longitudinal effects generated by family, school and community. As our samples move into adulthood, the structural, relational and normative influences affecting the growth trajectories become the main concern. Because this book focuses on the transition to young adulthood, most chapters thus utilize the Phase II data, which allow the authors to delineate influences of specific life events originating from adolescence on subsequent experiences of young people in their early thirties. The diverse patterns of transition to young adulthood and their varied outcomes support our original argument that both resources and norms are influential factors in explaining the transitional process among contemporary youths in Taiwan.

Highlight of Chapters

This book is structured as follows. The second section that follows immediately illustrates how family is currently established and managed among young people in Taiwan. The third section focuses on their entry into the job market to delineate various outcomes from the school-to-work transition. To utilize data from the spousal surveys, the fourth section is devoted to research on young married couples' family dynamics pertinent for this life stage. Enabled by the panel data since 2000, the fifth section examines the longitudinal effect from early adolescence to young adulthood in family relations as well as in different aspects of well-being. To broaden the scope of analysis of youths, the sixth and last section includes three chapters on the transition to adulthood in Japan, South Korea and Hong Kong, with a shared focus on the school-to-work experiences and the outcomes for an individuals' status attainment and earnings.

The low marriage and fertility rates in East Asia have raised a question on why young people in this region either are postponing marriage or not getting married at all. In this book, we add one important issue which has received less attention from local researchers: early marriage. The first chapter links marriage intention reported at an earlier age to subsequent early marriages or remaining single by modelling quantitative data. Liu's chapter uses marriage intention at age 22 to predict whether actual marriage will take place by age 30. In addition to the expected positive correlation for both genders, he reports that early marriage is not necessarily associated with negative outcomes such as divorce. An important key is whether they have marriage intention in the phase of emerging adulthood. Since dating at age 22 is correlated with both marriage intention and actual marriage, motivation to find suitable partners at this phase can be considered helpful for the low marriage and low fertility problem in the region. This suggestion is further echoed by Yuan and Yi in their qualitative analysis of a number of respondents who have entered marriage and those who remain single (by early thirties). They report that few young people expressed a preference for being single for their whole life. Financial constraints and not having suitable partners are the main reasons for their delaying marriage. Unpleasant family experiences from earlier life stages also contribute to a lack of incentive to marry. As to early married Taiwanese, a marriage–childbirth package for every man and woman seems to have a pronounced influence, and it interacts with a set of structural and emotional factors in the decision to marry.

With the sample having an average age of 31 in 2017, their labour market experiences are rich enough to allow empirical analysis of the linkage between education, occupational status and income. The third section demonstrates the substantial effects of the educational system on early status attainment in Taiwan (the labour market outcomes of the educational system in other East Asian societies will be presented in the last section). Tsai's chapter observes youths from age 24 to 32 and confirms that a college degree (about 3/4 of the TYP samples) barely secured a middle-class position. The seemingly unrelated regression model he used reveals that graduates from national universities have a substantial advantage in terms of achieving a better occupational status. While college ranking and major significantly affect young adults' occupational status and earnings, their family background does not. Since East Asian societies are experiencing a declining rate of upward mobility between generations, Tsai's findings illustrate the enduring impact of the educational ranking system on job market entry, which in turn echoes a popular belief in the decisive importance of educational achievement for success in one's career.

The school-to-work transition is further investigated by evaluating its longitudinal influence on youths' psychological well-being. Gebel looks into this issue utilizing twelve waves of TYP datasets (2000–2017) and finds that the difference between the NEET (not in education, employment or training) and those having a job at the time of the interview is, in general, insignificant with regard to depressive symptoms, subjective health and happiness. While the transition from school to work does not produce salient effects on various aspects of psychological well-being for different groups of young people, leaving school in fact results in a marked decrease of depressive symptoms among Taiwanese youth. This interesting finding confirms that the educational institutions and the accompanying pressures weigh more heavily in the growth trajectory of youth in Taiwan (as elsewhere in East Asia) than in other parts of the world. It also points to the prolonged anxiety from low performance in school, not to mention nightmares due to endless tests and examinations for young people. Thus, leaving school seems to be a great relief for young people, and whether they work at a job or not right afterwards is less important as a risk factor for their subjective well-being in this region.

In the fourth section, three chapters describe the family dynamics among young married couples. Approximately 40 per cent of the sample had entered marriage by age 31. It is through observation on household division of labour, parenthood on intergenerational relations, and childcare arrangement that we can obtain a better understanding of how young couples manage their family life at the beginning of family formation. Tai, Chen and Tu examine differences in the division of labour at home by comparing three groups: married young parents, married young couples without children and young cohabiting couples (without children). Using institutional versus selection effects as their main theoretical argument, they show that no clear selection effect can be ascertained. Married mothers perform most housework, while married fathers do the least. Co-residing with their elderly parents also leads to young fathers' lower share in housework. Hence, they confirm that marriage and motherhood are responsible for Taiwanese couples' adoption of their specific patterns of housework labour. This study is one of the first to systematically investigate whether the division of housework can be attributed to the institutional or selection effect. The analyses clearly support the institutional argument, namely that cultural norms have prescribed certain behaviours in marriage and parenthood, which have forcefully shaped young Taiwanese couples' patterns of housework division of labour and probably the amount of leisure time each partner can have.

Parenthood is a new phase in the life course in which not only do young adults shoulder new responsibilities of caring for minor children, but also their relationship with parents evolves into new patterns. Among young couples participating in the TYP survey, those co-residing with parents constitute 46.2 per cent. Slightly more than one-third report grandparents as primary caregivers. Shih's chapter on intergenerational relationships explores how a grandchild brings about exchanges between young couples and their parents by focusing on the effect of co-residence and childcare arrangements. Findings confirm that there exist significant gendered outcomes from both factors. Specifically, co-residence is linked to upward financial support, the elderly parents being the main recipients. Additionally, more instrumental exchanges between generations have are reported. Grandparents who are responsible for childcare receive financial support in return, and they offer more instrumental help to these young parents. Young mothers are the principal coordinators regarding the give-and-take of resources, by which mutual bonds across generations are developed. Shih shows a patriarchal family in which young parent follow conventional norms of intergenerational exchange.

For young parents in Taiwan and in East Asia, the balance between work and family has been difficult due to inadequate welfare provisions and persistent normative expectations. Young couples frequently seek assistance from family members and kin for family care. Chen and Chen probe this issue by looking at the childcare arrangement for those having children under three years old. As expected, family care, especially a grandparent being a primary caregiver, exceeds the institutional and other forms of private care in Taiwan. The authors propose that the prevalence of childcare by grandparents is a form of familism. This chapter also investigates the gap between ideal and actual childcare arrangements of young parents. While the majority prefer to provide childcare on their own, the gap is larger for the more highly educated as well as single parents, with the latter often being constrained in financial resources. The authors suggest that family care with state support is an urgent priority. Providing accessible and affordable childcare services should be the primary goal of future policy.

The fifth section pays special attention to longitudinal influences from early adolescence on a number of social behaviours in young adulthood. Here three papers investigate parent–child relations, the development of self-esteem and the trajectory of delinquency with a longer time frame. Lin, Yu and Huang explore the concept of adulthood and examine its mediating role in giving financial supports for parents during young adulthood. As expected, parent–child affection in adolescence enhances young adults' identification with social role norms, which in turn, produces positive intergenerational upward support to elderly parents.

Jou's chapter places the growth trajectory of youth's self-esteem in focus. Using latent classification techniques, it is shown that the general trajectory of self-esteem from ages 15 to 32 is changing and can be distinguished into four groups: high and rising (constituting 53 per cent), curved and getting better (29 per cent), low and flat (12 per cent) and deteriorating (5 per cent). Evidence is found for the significant longitudinal influence of normative beliefs as well as of positive interpersonal relationships during adolescence on self-esteem development in young adulthood. Cultural norms are again evidenced with their salient effects on youth's psychological wellbeing over time.

Chen and Wu examine the consequences of adolescent deviance on the developmental outcomes in adulthood. From approximately 40 per cent of participants who reported delinquent behaviours during early adolescence, three trajectory groups are identified: high (9 per cent), moderate (15 per cent) and low (75 per cent). For the high delinquency group, their delinquent behaviours continue to be higher and they had less support from their family during early adulthood. However, with regard to social adjustment issues, the results seem to be mixed. While the high group a lower level of educational achievement and continued to use more substances (smoking and binge drinking), they became self-employed as owners of shops or food stands and had earnings no less than those of the other two groups at age 30. It implies that perhaps for some young people in Taiwan, early delinquency may be an expression of trying to be adults. It should be noted that most longitudinal studies focus on the continuity of delinquency, relatively few explore how early delinquency influences specific aspects of lives in later life courses. This chapter offers the first evidence of the early-later delinquency links in various adult outcomes in a non-Western context.

The final section includes three papers on young adults' occupational achievement in Japan, South Korea and Hong Kong. Hiroshi Ishida's chapter challenges a popular argument that the educational institutions in Japan no longer play a key role in reducing inequality. His research on high-school graduates from a longitudinal study provides evidence that school mediation in the labour market has helped students with disadvantaged origin to secure stable jobs in larger firms, which tend to provide more opportunities and benefits. The strong connection with corporations for high schools serves a critical buffer in the school-to-work transition, without which their graduates would become members of what is called the 'lost generation' (Brinton, 2011). This mechanism has often been misunderstood as the institutional interference in individuals' choice or responsibility. It is in fact particularly important in understanding why social inequality has not widened among Japanese young adults at their first jobs.

In contrast to the concern about the disparity between high school and college graduates in Japan, Song and Eun take on the gendered dualism in South Korea. More young females finish college degree and enter the labour market with the state policies being supportive of their labour participation. Yet, females still face enormous institutional discrimination in training, promotion and compensation. Even for young women born in the 1980s and afterwards are more likely to take a break from their career than men – a clear gender gap indicating a durable dualism on the basis of sex. It does not seem likely that having stable jobs is adequate in becoming mature, independent adult for young Korean females. They apparently face severe barriers in this aspect during their transition to adulthood and the institutional constrains are argued to be responsible.

Wu and Guo's study on the school-to-work transition in contemporary Hong Kong vividly tells another interesting story about how college graduates having their first jobs. In a context of higher educational expansion but a slow increase in managerial and professional positions in recent decades, the status attainment of the first job for college graduates reveals a substantial gender gap in favour of men, which is similar to what was found in South Korea in the preceding chapter. However, the disparity across sexes among those who have finished only a high-school education reveals a different pattern, in which women actually fare better than men on occupational status scores. In general terms, college graduates nowadays have landed their first jobs with a lower socioeconomic status than their previous cohorts. This means that it has become increasingly difficult for young cohorts to achieve a middle-class position in Hong Kong, echoing the finding provided by Tsai's chapter on the mobility of college graduates in Taiwan. As Wu and Guo have described, the transition to adulthood with regard to securing a stable job in the labour market is a bumpy road ahead rather than an effortless journey. How this experience affects their family and career in later life stages is an intriguing question.

Contribution to the Academic Community

This book provides a comprehensive profile of the developmental patterns of Taiwanese youths, juxtaposed with important studies on the young adults' experiences and achievements in the labour markets in Japan, South Korea and Hong Kong. Taiwan is considered an ideal research field to observe whether conventional Confucian culture continues to influence how youths behave and respond to various demanding life events in their journey to adulthood. Growing up in a society with a relatively stable political situation, remarkable growth records and strong familial norms, Taiwanese youths encounter distinctive challenges in the process of transition to adulthood. Parental expectation about children's educational achievement remains strong even in the phase of young adulthood. This is also true for the norm of the marriage and childbirth package. Indeed, numerous studies have documented a similar and persistent impact of traditional norms on contemporary East Asian youths (Park and Kim, 2014; Shek et al., 2014), presenting an interesting contrast to their Western counterparts. Our basic argument is that both individual and familial resources and cultural norms combine to affect the attitudes and behaviours in the transitional process which has been protracted to a great extent for the young generation in East Asian societies.

Benefiting from the valuable panel dataset of the Taiwan Youth Project (from 2000 to 2018), the research in this book has uncovered various longitudinal effects of the family, work and social institutions. The time frame covers from early adolescence to young adulthood, but special emphasis is placed on the *transition* to young adulthood for most chapters. This transition signifies important outcomes that can be partially explained by previous family investment, educational achievement and community support in earlier life stages. Since marriage starts to take place in young adulthood, the spousal survey of the TYP constitutes an invaluable addition to this book. Looking at both short-term and long-term outcomes of important life experiences from early adolescence to young adulthood promises a better understanding of the typical structural configurations that youths collectively represent, and thus enables meaningful policy suggestions on family dynamics, educational strategy, health and well-being issues on the basis of scientific evidence.

In brief, this book presents a general profile as well as specific analyses of youth transition to adulthood in East Asia by using Taiwan as an illustrative example along with comparative findings from East Asian neighbours. Chapter contributors have presented youths' transition in a general conceptual frame enabling direct comparison with their counterparts in advanced Western societies. Hence, this book allows global readers to understand how particular cultural contexts form and influence the challenging journey to adulthood in Taiwan and in East Asia. It is with this cross-cultural perspective in mind that we wish to inspire future theorization and research on youths across different regions of the world.

Acknowledgements

We would like to give our sincere thanks to the TYP research team for active and constructive contribution over the last 20 years. The great team spirit is a fond memory and shall always be treasured. Thanks also to the responsible and competent research assistants devoted to the completion of survey and data management. The participation of youth respondents, their parents and home teachers in junior high as well as interviewers' collaboration over the waves are deeply appreciated. We also give our special thanks to Dr. Yung-Chen Yuan for her great help in editing final chapters. This book marks a collective effort of our commitment to youth studies in Taiwan and in East Asia.

References

Ahn, S.-Y., & Baek, H.-J. (2013). Academic achievement-oriented society and its relationship to the psychological well-being of Korean adolescents. In C.-C. Yi (Ed.), *The psychological well-being of east Asian youth* (pp. 265–279). Dordrecht: Springer Publishing co.

Arnett, J. J. (2000). Emerging adulthood: A theory of development from the late teens through the twenties. *American Psychologist, 55*(5), 469–480.

Arnett, J. J. (2004). *Emerging adulthood: The winding road from the late teens through the twenties.* Oxford: Oxford University Press.

Brinton, M. C. (2011). *Lost in transition: Youth, work, and instability in postindustrial Japan.* Cambridge: Cambridge University Press.

Buchmann, M. (1989). *The script of life in modern society: Entry into adulthood in a changing world.* Chicago, IL: University of Chicago Press.

Cepa, K., & Furstenberg, F. F. (2021). Reaching adulthood: Persistent beliefs about the importance and timing of adult milestones. *Journal of Family Issues, 42*(1), 27–57.

Cheng, B.-S., Chou, L.-F., & Farh, J.-L. (2000). A triad model of paternalistic leadership: Constructs and measurement. *Indigenous Psychological Research in Chinese Societies, 14*, 3–64.

Chen, Y.-H., & Yi, C.-C. (2021). An exploration of individual, familial, and cultural factors associated with the value of children among Taiwanese young adults. *Child Indicators Research, 14*(2), 487–510.

Chiang, Y.-L. (2018). When things don't go as planned: Contingencies, cultural capital, and parental involvement for Elite University admission in China. *Comparative Education Review, 62*(4), 503–521.

Choi, J., & Bae, H. (2020). Changes in early labor market outcomes among young college graduates in South Korea. *The Annuals of the American Academy of Political and Social Science, 688*(1), 115–136.

Erikson, E. H. (1958). *Young man Luther: A study in psychoanalysis and history.* New York, NY: W. W. Norton.

Erikson, E. H. (1959). Identity and the life cycle: Selected papers. *Psychological Issues, 1*(1), 1–171. New York, NY: International Universities Press.

Furstenberg, F. (2010). On a new schedule: Transitions to adulthood and family change. *Future Child, 20*(1), 67–87.

Hannum, E., Ishida, H., Park, H., & Tam, T. (2019). Education in east Asian societies: Postwar expansion and the evolution of inequality. *Annual Review of Sociology, 45*, 625–647.

Heinrich, P., & Galan, C. (Eds.) (2018). *Being young in super-aging Japan: Formative events and cultural reactions.* London: Routledge.

Hogan, D. P., & Astone, N. M. (1986). The transition to adulthood. *Annual Review of Sociology, 12*, 109–130.

Hsiao, H.-H. M. (Ed.) (2013). *Chinese middle classes: Taiwan, Hong Kong, Macao and China.* Abingdon: Routledge.

Hsu, L. K. (1948). *Under the ancestors' shadow; Chinese culture and personality.* New York, NY: Columbia University Press.

Huang, F.-M., Chan H.-Y., & Tao, H.-L. (2021). The effect of high school entrance exam reform on adolescents' depressive symptoms in Taiwan: A closer look at gender differences. *School Psychology International, 42*(5), 465–485.

Hu, L.-C., & Chiang, Y.-L. (2021). Having children in a time of lowest-low fertility: Value of children, sex preference and fertility desire among Taiwanese young adults. *Child Indicators Research, 14*(2), 537–554.

Ishida, H. (1997). Educational credentials and labour-market entry outcomes in Japan. In W. Müller & Y. Shavit (Eds.), *From school to work: A comparative study of educational qualifications and occupational destinations* (pp. 287–309). Oxford: Oxford University Press.

Ishida, H. (2007). Japan: Educational expansion and inequality in access to higher education. In Y. Shavit, R. Arum & A. Gamoran (Eds.), *Stratification in higher education: A comparative study* (pp. 63–86). Stanford, CA: Stanford University Press.

Iwai, N., & Yasuda, T. (Eds.) (2011). *Family values in East Asia: A comparison among Japan, South Korea, China and Taiwan based on East Asian Social Survey, 2006.* Kyoto: Nakanishiya.

Jones, G. W., & Gubhaju, B. (2009). Factors influencing changes in mean age at first marriage and proportions never marrying in the low-fertility countries of East and Southeast Asia. *Asian Population Studies, 5*(3), 237–265.

Jones, G. W., & Yeung, W.-J. J. (2014). Marriage in Asia. *Journal of Family Issues, 35*(12), 1567–1583.

Lee, C.-T., Beckert, T. E., Nelson, L. J., Hsieh, C. H., Miller, R. B., & Wu, C.-I. (2017). Developing depressive symptoms over the adolescent years: The influence of affiliated cultural values among Taiwanese youth. *Journal of Child and Family Studies, 26*(11), 3102–3111.

Lin, W.-H., & Gebel, M. (2021). Education tracking and adolescent smoking: A counterfactual and prospective cohort study. *Addiction, 116*(7), 1871–1881.

Lin, J.-P., & Yi, C.-C. (2013). A comparative analysis of intergenerational relations in East Asia. *International Sociology, 28*(3), 297–315.

Liu, C.-H. (2019). The effect of cultivating art and talent skill on college outcomes: Evidence from Taiwan youth project. *Academia Economic Papers, 47*(4), 571–611.

Liu, C.-H. (2020a). The non-pecuniary returns of higher education: The associations between higher education and non-pecuniary-related job characteristics, health, well-being, and addictive behaviors. *Journal of Population Studies, 61*, 1–50.

Liu, C.-H. (2020b). The effect of diploma and major on earnings – evidence from the Taiwan youth project. *Taiwan Economic Review, 48*(4), 611–669.

Miraz, M. H., Habib, M. M., & Majumder, M. I. (2017). The effect of Korean culture and its impact on international business. *Frontiers in Management Research, 1*(1), 1–5.

Park, H. (2013). The transition to adulthood among Korean youths. *The Annals of the American Academy of Political and Social Science, 646*(1), 129–148.

Park, J.Y., & Chung, I.J. (2010). The effects of high school students' academic problems on suicidal ideation: Focusing on the mediation effects of individual-level risk and protective factors. *Journal of Child Welfare, 32,* 69–97.

Park, H., & Kim, K.-K. (Eds.) (2014). *Korean education in changing economic and demographic contexts.* Singapore: Springer Singapore.

Petry, N. M. (2002). A comparison of young, middle-aged, and older adult treatment-seeking pathological gamblers. *The Gerontologist, 42*(1), 92–99.

Raymo, J. M., Park, H., Xie, Y., & Yeung, W. J. (2015). Marriage and family in East Asia: Continuity and change. *Annual Review of Sociology, 41*(1), 471–492.

Salmela-Aro, K., Aunola, K., & Nurmi, J. E. (2007). Personal goals during emerging adulthood: A 10-year follow up. *Journal of Adolescent Research, 22*(6), 690–715.

Sato, Y., & Imai, J. (Eds.) (2011). *Japan's new inequality: Intersection of employment reforms and welfare arrangements.* Melbourne: Trans Pacific.

Shanahan, M. J. (2000). Pathways to adulthood in changing societies: Variability and mechanisms in life course perspective. *Annual Review of Sociology, 26,* 667–692.

Shek, D., Sun, R., & Ma, C. (2014). *Chinese adolescents in Hong Kong: Family life, psychological well-being and risk behavior.* Singapore: Springer Singapore.

Tsutsui, J. (2013). The transitional phase of mate selection in East Asian countries. *International Sociology, 28*(3), 257–276.

Tsuya, N., Choe, M. K., & Wang, F. (2019). *Convergence to very low fertility in East Asia: Processes, causes, and implications.* Tokyo: Springer.

Tzeng, S.-P., & Yi, C.-C. (2013). The effects of self-esteem on adolescent delinquency over time: Is the relationship linear?. In C.-C. Yi (Ed.), *The psychological well-being of East Asian youth* (pp. 243–261). Dordrecht: Springer.

Wu, M.-Y., & Yi, C.-C. (2003). A marriage is more than a marriage: The impacts of familial factors on marital satisfaction. *Journal of Population Studies, 26,* 71–95. (in Chinese).

Yamada, M. (1999). *The era of parasite singles.* Tokyo: Chikuma Shobo. (in Japanese).

Yasuda, T., Iwai, N., Yi, C.-C., & Xie, G. H. (2011). Intergenerational coresidence in China, Japan, South Korea and Taiwan: Comparative analysis based on the east Asian social survey, 2006. *Journal of Comparative Family Studies, 42*(5), 703–722.

Yeung, W.-J. J., & Alipio, C. (2013). Transitioning to adulthood in Asia: School, work, and family life. *The ANNALS of the American Academy of Political and Social Science, 646*(1), 6–27.

Yi, C.-C. (Ed.) (2013). *The psychological well-being of East Asian youth.* Dordrecht: Springer.

Yi, C.-C. (2014). Continuity and change of intergenerational relations in family of Taiwan region: The interplay of resources and norms. *Sociological Studies, 3,* 189–215. (in Chinese).

Yi, C.-C. (2015). Adolescents and transition to adulthood in Asia. In S. Quah (Ed.) *Handbook of families in Asia* (pp. 191–210). London: Routledge.

Yi, C.-C. (2019). Changing Taiwanese families: Research concerns of family sociologists. *Research on Women in Modern Chinese History, 34,* 219–254.

Yi, C.-C., & Chang, Y.-H. (2008). The continuity and change of patrilineal families: Family sociological research in Taiwan, 1960–2000. In G.-S. Hsieh (Ed.),

Interlocution: A thematic history of Taiwanese sociology, 1945–2005 (pp. 23–73). Taipei: Socio Publishing Co. (in Chinese).

Yi, C.-C., & Chang, C.-F. (2019). Family and gender in Taiwan. In J. Liu & J. Yamashita (Eds.), *Routledge handbook of East Asian gender studies* (pp. 217–235). London: Routledge.

Yi, C.-C., Fan, G.-H., & Chang, M.-Y. (2013). The developmental outcome of Taiwanese youth: Effects of educational tracking during adolescence. In C.-C. Yi (Ed.), *The psychological well-being of East Asian youth* (pp. 157–184). Dordrecht: Springer.

Yi, C.-C., & Jao, Y.-H. (2013). Changing mate selection and family values: Comparing Taiwan and Hong Kong. In W.-S. Yang & P.-S. Wan (Eds.), *Facing challenges: A comparison of Taiwan and Hong Kong* (pp. 97–134). Taiwan: Institute of Sociology, Academia Sinica.

Yi, C.-C., & Lin, J.-P. (2009). Types of relations between adult children and elderly parents in Taiwan: Mechanisms accounting for various relational types. *Journal of Comparative Family Studies, 40*(2), 305–324.

Yi, C.-C., & Lin, W.-S. (2019). Changing attitudes toward elderly parental support in Taiwan: Effects of individual resources and cultural norms. *Japanese Journal of Family Sociology, 31*(1), 45–64.

Yi, C.-C., Wu, C.-I., Chang, Y.-H., & Chang, C.-M. (2009). The psychological well-being of Taiwanese youth: School versus family context from early to late adolescence. *International Sociology, 24*(3), 397–429.

Yi, C.-C., Lin, W.-S., & Ma, K.-H. (2019). Marital satisfaction among Taiwanese young married couples: The importance of cultural norms. *Journal of Family Issues, 40*(14), 2015–2043.

Zeng, K., & LeTendre, G. (1998). Adolescent suicide and academic competition in East Asia. *Comparative Education Review, 42*(4), 513–528.

Part II

Family Formation in Young Adulthood: Getting Married or Remaining Single

2

Marriage Intention and the Subsequent Marriage in Taiwan

Chia-Hua Liu

Introduction

Many countries around the world have experienced a second demographic transition since the 1970s, with well-known demographic phenomena such as delaying first marriage, declining birth rates and rising divorce rates. Taking the Organization for Economic Co-operation and Development (OECD) countries as an example, in the past 30 years, the age of first marriage for males and females has risen by about 4.5 years. In 1990, the average age of first marriage for males and females was 27.7 years and 25.2 years, but by 2017 the average rose to 33.2 years and 30.8 years, respectively (OECD, 2020). Taiwan and other nearby East Asian countries also exhibit the same trend during this period. Over the same period, the age at first marriage for males and females in Taiwan, Japan and South Korea correspondingly increased by 3.4 and 4.2 years, 2.7 and 3.5 years, and 4.1 and 5.4 years. In the case of Taiwan, in 1990, the average age at first marriage for males and females was 29 and 25.8 years, but by 2017 it had risen to 32.4 and 30 years, respectively (Ministry of the Interior, 2020).

Theoretically, women's age at first marriage is negatively correlated with fertility due to their biological clock, and thus delaying their first marriage typically results in lower fertility. However, when a society has prevalent cohabitation and unmarried births, the delay in the age of first marriage does not necessarily imply a decline in fertility (Kiernan, 2001; Lichter et al., 2014). For example, Manning et al. (2014) indicated that the predominance of cohabitation in the US society directly postpones the age of first marriage, but at the same time, also increases the possibility of children growing up in cohabiting families. According to the Pew Research Center, the proportion of American children living with unmarried parents has more than doubled from 13 per cent in 1968 to 32 per cent in 2017. Among these children, 22 per cent live in a cohabiting couple family (Livingston, 2018).

Although cohabitation and unmarried pregnancy are common experiences in most Western societies, they are rarer in Taiwan. According to Yang (2013), the estimated cohabitation rate among people aged 20 to 34 was only 4 per cent in 2010 in Taiwan, which is much lower than the 11 per cent in the United States (Copen et al., 2012), 28.6 per cent in Denmark and 21.8 per cent in France (OECD, 2020). Furthermore, childbirth mainly occurs after marriage in Taiwan and other East Asian countries. This cultural norm means that any unexpected pregnancy spurs couples to enter marriage to legitimize the childbirth (Raymo and Iwasawa, 2008). In Taiwan, the proportion of children born out of wedlock was 3.4 per cent in 1998 and only marginally rose to 3.9 per cent by 2018 (Ministry of Interior, 2020).

The above-mentioned data show that people in Taiwan are less likely to choose either non-marital cohabitation or non-marital childrearing than most Western societies. Since age at first marriage is a key determinant of fertility, in cases where non-marital pregnancy is not widespread, delaying marriage or not getting married will eventually cause a decline in the fertility rate, thereby slowing population growth. Thus, it is necessary to understand why modern people are postponing marriage or choosing not to enter marriage. The unique features of Taiwan's family formation suggest a good case for analysing factors that may push people to enter marriage at an earlier age. This chapter examines the effect of the desire to marry in emerging adulthood on the probability of marriage in early adulthood.

Fishbein and Ajzen (1975) argued that behavioural expectations help us understand subsequent behaviours at the individual level, suggesting that individuals' wish to marry or societal expectations about marriage should be powerful predictors of subsequent family formation. When individuals' desire to marry can be viewed as the tendency to enter the marriage market, the economic theory predicts that the desire to marry is positively correlated with the timing of marriage (Keeley, 1977). However, subject to data limitations, which refer to cross-sectional data, a disproportionally large part of the research has focused on factors associated with the desire to marry among young adults. Although understanding determinants of the desire to marry allows one to recognize current family formation and family changes, as suggested by Manning et al. (2007), further research should explore the relationship between the desire to marry and marital behaviour – that is, whether the desire to marry in emerging adults relates to subsequent marriage. Unfortunately, to the best of our knowledge, only a few studies applied longitudinal data drawn from the United States and Nepal to present that the desire to marry is associated with the likelihood of entering a marriage (Allendorf et al., 2019; Lichter et al., 2004).

Studies on early marriages in the United States and Taiwan have shown that compared with single people, those who got married early are more likely to come from disadvantaged families and have a relatively low level of education (Tai et al., 2019; Uecker and Stokes, 2008). Thus, those married early may have a higher probability of divorce relative to those married at the average age (e.g., Lehrer, 2008; Rotz, 2016). Despite the potential higher divorce risk for early marriages compared to other marriages, among early marriages, those with the desire to marry may entail different characteristics from those without such a desire to marry because those with a desire to marry are more likely from higher socioeconomic status families than those without such a desire (Lichter et al., 2004; Manning et al., 2019).This pattern implies that with a similar age at the first marriage, there may be differences in marital characteristics (such as premarital pregnancy or economic stability), leading to variations in marital quality between marriage with and without a desire to marry. If the differences in marital characteristics between the two are the factors that can enhance marital stability, the desire to marry is not only positively correlated with probability of getting married but also that of marital stability. Taking the first cohabitation as an example, Guzzo (2009) points out that almost half of all first cohabitations begin with intentions to marry. Furthermore, among all first cohabitors, those with intentions to marry are more likely to evolve the cohabiting relationship into marriage (Guzzo, 2009). This result implies that planning to marry may be a facilitating factor for union formation as well as union stability.

Given insufficient evidence on the relationship between the desire to marry and actual marriage, this chapter examines the effect of the desire to marry in emerging adulthood on the probability of marriage before age 30. We base the analysis on a longitudinal panel survey of Taiwan Youth Project (TYP), taking the desire to marry at the age of

22 as a binary variable. It is coded 1 if respondents reported that they want to get married at a certain age and 0 if they reported not wanting to get married or having yet thought about the matter. Marital status in 2014 (meaning getting married before age 30) is also a binary variable with a value of 1 if respondents were married in 2014 (including widowed or divorced) and otherwise 0. The average age of the respondents in 2014 was about 28 years, and the medium age at first marriage is 31.8 years for men and 29.6 years for women (Ministry of the Interior, 2020). Thus, the married respondents in this chapter can be viewed as getting married early – that is, those who got married at an early age than the remainder of the population.

The chapter first compared background factors between those with and without a desire to marry to see whether those with a desire to marry are more likely to be from economically advantaged families. It then located several factors known to affect marital stability to gauge whether differences in factors facilitate the risk of divorce between marriages with and without a desire to marry. Finally, a regression analysis was used to examine whether there is a positive correlation between the desire to marry and marriage. The analyses may provide insight into relationships between marriage intention in emerging adulthood and marriage in young adulthood and potential divorce risk. The analytical result for the relationship between the desire to marry and the probability of marriage not only enhances our understanding of how individuals' wish to marry is tied to actual actions but also provides an opportunity to see whether the relationship remains consistent under different cultural settings.

Literature Review

Factors in Determining the Probability of Marriage

The major demographic transition challenges in East Asian societies (including Taiwan and nearby other Asia countries) are the delayed first marriage and the low fertility rate (Jones, 2007). From being single to having a spouse is indeed an important life-course transition. The decision to marry and the timing of marriage for young adults can be affected by many factors, including the desire to marry, educational attainment, work status, family background, cultural norms and more. The main purpose of the chapter is to examine the relationship between the desire to marry in emerging adulthood and the likelihood of marriage in young adulthood. Thus, the literature review of factors associated with entering into marriage will begin with the relationship between the two.

In economics, Keeley (1977) suggested that a person's decision to marry can be regarded as taking place in two stages. In the first stage, people decide to enter the marriage market, and during the second stage, they search for a mate in the market. Within this framework, the age of first marriage depends on the determinants of entering the marriage market and the search time for a spouse in the market. The expected benefits of marriage and search costs both affect the decision to enter the marriage market and the time spent searching for a mate in the market. By assuming that individuals' desire to marry can be viewed as the tendency to enter the marriage market, this theory predicts that compared to those without any expectation to marry, individuals with such an expectation are more likely to marry at an earlier age. Related studies have shown that the desire to marry is positively related to the likelihood of marriage and the timing of marriage (Allendorf et al., 2019; Lichter et al., 2004).

In her seminar work, Oppenheimer (1988) pointed out that educational attainment and work status are important factors in determining the timing of marriage. On the one hand, spending more time in school will delay the timing of marriage. On the other, education is the key to job stability and thus can be viewed as one factor that promotes entering into marriage. These patterns, however, are different between the binary genders. Men need resources to enter into marriage as men traditionally are expected to form a family after completing their studies and having a stable job, but women need not. Women thus enter into marriage at a younger age than men (Lundberg and Pollak, 2014).

This resource explanation for entries into marriage suggests that both education and job stability are the factors that discourage women from getting married. The prevalence of higher education, thus, is the key factor for women to delay marriage or forego marriage (Lundberg and Pollak, 2014; Raymo, 2003) because women gain less than men from marriage, resulting in less incentive to enter into marriage.

Family background is a significant factor in determining children's educational attainment. Those who have gotten married earlier are likely to be less educated (Sassler and Goldscheider, 2004). Moreover, compared to singles, the early married are more likely from economically disadvantaged families (Tai et al., 2019; Uecker and Stokes, 2008). Family structure such as non-intact family as the indicator of less resource or bad family cohesion or lack of good supervision on behaviours may be a driver that pushes individuals to marry at younger ages (Axinn and Thornton, 1992; Carlson et al., 2004; Musick and Bumpass, 1999; Wolfinger, 2003). For example, those who have grown from broken families may feel the uneasy family atmosphere and want to leave the family sooner (Carlson et al., 2004; Wolfinger, 2003) than those who have grown from intact families. They also are more likely to have early sexual experience, which increases the likelihood of early marriage or unmarried pregnancy (Musick and Bumpass, 1999). Tai et al. (2019) showed that among those who marry early, more than 60 per cent report the birth of a child within the first eight months of marriage; in other words, they form post-conception 'shotgun' marriages.

A closely related factor to education is the change in cultural norms, specifically the concept of gender roles and gender equality. The improvement of women's educational level and earning capacity has changed the traditional gender roles within a household (that is, men are breadwinners, and women are homemakers), which changes the pattern of the gendered division of labour in the family (Lundberg and Pollak, 2007). However, married women still bear most housework and childcare responsibilities (Aguiar and Hurst, 2007; Lu and Yi, 2005). Therefore, the opportunity cost of entering into marriage for highly educated women is much higher than that of other women, encouraging their willingness to remain single.

In addition to the concept of gender role, the concept of gender equality often appears to highly educated, young, and employed people in urban residents. People who live in urban areas as an indicator of gender equality or liberality have a lower likelihood of marriage or are often married at an older age than those in other areas (Leonhardt and Quealy, 2015). Moreover, the change in social norms may contribute to delaying marriage. For example, premarital sex and premarital cohabitation are less stigmatized in the modern society. People can enjoy the benefits of living together without marriage commitment and are thus more likely to postpone marriage or even complete forgo marriage (Lundberg and Pollak, 2014).

Factors Associated With the Desire to Marry

The literature has accumulated a wide range of results discussing the factors that affect marriage expectations, which can be divided into two aspects. The first one covers personal characteristics, including gender, age, personal attractiveness, religion, experiences with heterosexual interaction and sexual behaviour. The second aspect is family backgrounds that include parental marital status and parent–child relationships.

There is a gender difference in forming the desire to marry (Crissey, 2005; Popenoe, 2005). Age is expected to positively correlate with the desire to marry, as older people have a lower degree of uncertainty about the future than their younger counterparts. The former is more likely to form an expectation to marry. Physical attractiveness and non-physical attractiveness also correlate with expectations to marry. According to Gecas and Seff (1990), those with stronger capabilities (such as academic achievement) herald a stable future, and so they are more likely to be favoured in the marriage market, as they signal good preparation for the future. Thus, we expect a positive relationship between the ability and the desire to marry. Using longitudinal data from the National Longitudinal Survey of Youth 1997 cohort (NSLY97), Arocho and Kamp Dush (2016) found that the expectation to marry negatively correlates with minor delinquent activity. Evidence from Crissey (2005) suggests that although both females' and males' GPA (grade point average) is unrelated to marital expectations, females' BMI (body mass index) negatively relates to marriage expectations.

Religion is also a critical factor in forming the desire to marry. Since most religions emphasize the importance of family, it is reasonable to believe that those with religious beliefs are more likely to hold pro-marriage attitudes. Moreover, religious organizations are a kind of social network like a marriage market, and it is easier for single adults to search for partners within them. Therefore, it is easier for people with religious beliefs to find people with similar characteristics, and they are more likely to have a positive marriage attitude than those without religious beliefs (e.g., Ellison et al., 2011; Heaton and Pratt, 1990).

One of the most important factors associated with the desire to marry is dating experiences. Related studies found that dating experience is positively associated with the desire to marry as well as positive attitudes towards the transition into a union (Crissey, 2005; Willoughby and Carroll, 2010).

In addition to those findings above, family background factors influence individuals' expectations to marry. According to the social learning theory, children first learn things from their biological parents, and hence their parents influence their family values. It is not difficult to imagine that adolescents who experienced parental divorce or separation may be particularly sensitive to marital instability, and so they have a lower likelihood of forming any marital expectations and a lower propensity to actually marry. In addition, parents' marital attitudes may also influence a child's marital attitude, especially when the parents' attitudes towards marriage are traditional in the sense of emphasizing the positive attitude towards marriage or viewing 'marriage' as an important institution (Axinn and Thornton, 1996; Willoughby et al., 2012). In that case, compared with those whose parents are less traditional, individuals whose parents are more traditional should have a more positive attitude towards entering marriages.

The literature supports the intergeneration transmission of marital attitude and has pointed out that children from an intact family are more likely to have the desire to marry than those from a non-intact family (Amato, 1988; Axinn and Thornton, 1996). Amato (1988) used an Australian sample and found that respondents who experienced parental divorce hold a negative attitude towards forming a family relative to their counterparts. Results of a US survey showed that those from intact families have a higher expectation to marry (Crissey, 2005). Tasker and Richards (1994) argued that poor parent–child relationships are associated with negative attitudes towards marriage. Based on a sample of Taiwan, Pan (2014) found that the father–child relationship is more critical in determining a child's expectation to marry.

Data

The Data Source

The chapter uses data from the TYP, conducted by the Institute of Sociology, Academia Sinica, Taiwan, which began to collect samples from 7th grade (J1) and 9th grade (J3) students from two cities (New

Taipei City and Taipei City) and one county (Yilan County) in northern Taiwan in 2000. The three selected areas cover about one-third of Taiwan's population (Ministry of the Interior, 2016). The average age for J1 and J3 are 13 and 15 years old, respectively. In addition to student samples, TYP also conducts parallel surveys on students' parents and their homeroom teachers. These students constitute a fixed sample in the panel survey. The survey has been divided into teenage (2000–2009) and adulthood (2011–2017) stages. In the first stage, starting from 2000, a nine-year follow-up survey was conducted on the J1 and J3 samples; in 2011, the research team launched the second stage, when the average age of the J1 and J3 samples reached 24 and 26 years, at which stage the research team combined the two samples and began to collect information about them entering early adulthood. The survey has been conducted every three years since 2011 and has collected three waves of adult data (TYP2011, TYP2014 and TYP2017).

TYP adopts 'multi-stage stratified cluster sampling', with county or city as the first stratification and township as the second stratification. After that, two-stage cluster sampling is conducted in the second stratification. At the first stage, 'school' is used as the sampling unit, while class is used as the sampling unit at the second stage. Forty schools and a total of 162 classes were selected, with 81 classes for 7th grade and 9th grade. The completed interviews are 2,690 and 2,851, respectively (Tai et al., 2019).

This chapter uses data collected in both the first and second stages. After deleting respondents with missing information for the variables and those who got married before age 22, the final analytical sample is 2,443, of which 1,286 are males and 1,157 are females.

Definitions of Variables

The main dependent variable is respondents' marital status in 2014 (married = 1, non-married = 0). This binary variable, married in 2014, is created based on a question in TYP2014: What is your marital status? In the TYP2014, there were 466 married, accounting for about 20 per cent of the analytical sample. The mean and median age at first marriage are, respectively, 26.8 and 27. Among them, 203 are male (mean and median age at marriage are both 27), and 263 are females (mean and median age at marriage are 26.7 and 27), accounting for

44 per cent and 56 per cent of the married sample, respectively. The median ages of first marriage for men and women in Taiwan in 2014 were 31.8 and 29.6 years old (Ministry of the Interior, 2020), which are 4.8 years and 2.6 years higher than the analytical sample of married men and women, respectively. Therefore, those married in this chapter can be viewed as having entered early marriages.

The main independent variable in this chapter is respondents' desire to marry at the age of 22, which is a binary variable. This variable was taken from the 9th wave of the J1 sample and the 7th wave of the J3 sample (the respondents were at age 22). The questionnaire asked respondents: When do you want to get married? The answers included (1) am already married, (2) want to get married at a certain age, (3) do not want to get married and (4) never thought about getting married. Since this study aims to analyse the influence of the desire to marry in emerging adulthood on the likelihood of marriage in early adulthood, the discussion of marriage is limited to marriages between 22 and 30 years old (respondents' oldest age of marriage in 2014 was 30 years old). The samples married before the age of 22 were deleted (30 marriage samples, accounting for about 5 per cent of all marriage samples). Accordingly, the analysis may not be directly applicable to marriages before the age of 22. The proportions for those who want to marry, do not want to marry and never thought of getting married are 37.5 per cent, 9 per cent and 53.6 per cent, in that order. A binary variable for the desire to marry at age 22 is created with a value 1 if participants reported they want to get married at some certain age and a value 0 if participants reported they do not want to get married or never thought about getting married.

The respondents' key demographic characteristics in 2014 are reported at the top of Table 2.1, including gender, year of birth, educational attainment, work status, marital status. The respondents' gender was coded as male (=1) and female (=0). Educational attainment was classified into high school or below (reference group), junior college, college, master or above. Three dummy variables were used. The respondents' work status was dichotomized into employed (=1) and not employed (=0). Finally, marital status was a binary variable: married (=1) and not married (=0).

Along with the desire to marry, the present study also controls for personal characteristics and family background. The personal characteristics include religion, dating status at the age of 22, sexual

Table 2.1 Descriptive statistics

Variable (The wave of the survey)	Full sample				Male sample				Female sample			
	Mean	Desire to marry		Mean Diff.	Mean	Desire to marry		Mean Diff.	Mean	Desire to marry		Mean Diff.
		No	Yes			No	Yes			No	Yes	
	(1)	(2)	(3)	(4)	(5)	(6)	(7)	(8)	(9)	(10)	(11)	(12)
Key demographic variables from TYP2014												
Female	0.474	0.436	0.536	0.100**								
Year of birth	1985.7	1985.7	1985.7	0.072	1985.7	1985.7	1985.7	0.080	1985.7	1985.6	1985.7	0.068
Education level: high school or below	0.130	0.139	0.115	−0.025+	0.167	0.167	0.167	−0.000	0.089	0.104	0.069	−0.034*
Education level: junior college	0.080	0.084	0.073	−0.011	0.082	0.087	0.071	−0.017	0.078	0.080	0.075	−0.004
Education level: college	0.582	0.589	0.570	−0.020	0.519	0.534	0.489	−0.045	0.652	0.661	0.640	−0.021
Education level: master or above	0.208	0.187	0.242	0.055**	0.232	0.211	0.273	0.062*	0.182	0.156	0.216	0.060*
Currently employed (1=yes)	0.888	0.885	0.893	0.008	0.914	0.907	0.927	0.020	0.859	0.856	0.864	0.008
Married in 2014	0.195	0.147	0.275	0.128**	0.163	0.120	0.249	0.130**	0.232	0.183	0.297	0.114**

(Continued)

Table 2.1 Descriptive statistics (Continued)

Variable (The wave of the survey)	Full sample				Male sample				Female sample			
	Mean	Desire to marry		Mean Diff.	Mean	Desire to marry		Mean Diff.	Mean	Desire to marry		Mean Diff.
		No	Yes			No	Yes			No	Yes	
	(1)	(2)	(3)	(4)	(5)	(6)	(7)	(8)	(9)	(10)	(11)	(12)
Desire to marry at age 22 (J1W9; J3W7)	0.375				0.330				0.424			
Religion: Catholic/Protestant (J1W9; J3W7)	0.043	0.037	0.053	0.017+	0.040	0.037	0.045	0.008	0.047	0.036	0.061	0.025+
Religion: other religions	0.468	0.439	0.515	0.076**	0.448	0.438	0.468	0.030	0.490	0.441	0.556	0.115**
Dating someone at age 22 (J1W9; J3W7)	0.386	0.319	0.498	0.179**	0.365	0.301	0.496	0.196**	0.409	0.342	0.499	0.157**
Having sex before marriage (J1W9; J3W7)	0.317	0.270	0.396	0.126**	0.383	0.334	0.482	0.148**	0.244	0.186	0.322	0.136**
Parents' education level: junior college or above (J1W1; J3W1)	0.279	0.265	0.303	0.039*	0.278	0.266	0.304	0.038	0.280	0.263	0.303	0.041

Monthly income: 30k–50k (NTD) (PJ1W1; PJ3W1)	0.274	0.283	0.260	−0.023	0.255	0.257	0.252	−0.005	0.296	0.317	0.267	−0.050+
Monthly income: 50k–80k	0.368	0.375	0.356	−0.019	0.385	0.389	0.376	−0.013	0.348	0.356	0.338	−0.018
Monthly income: 80k–120k	0.194	0.176	0.224	0.048**	0.210	0.193	0.245	0.052*	0.175	0.153	0.206	0.053*
Monthly income: over 120k	0.061	0.060	0.061	0.001	0.054	0.055	0.054	−0.000	0.067	0.068	0.067	−0.000
Number of sibling (J1W1; J3W1)	2.698	2.719	2.662	−0.057	2.594	2.621	2.539	−0.083	2.812	2.845	2.768	−0.078
Parents' marriage being happy in 9th grade (J1W3; J3W1)	0.755	0.749	0.765	0.017	0.773	0.758	0.802	0.044+	0.735	0.736	0.733	−0.003
Family cohesion in 9th grade (J1W3; J3W1)	21.8	21.8	21.6	−0.174	21.7	21.7	21.6	−0.131	21.8	22.0	21.7	−0.255
Parents' marital status in 9th grade: separation or divorce (J1W3; J3W1)	0.066	0.064	0.071	0.007	0.066	0.060	0.078	0.017	0.067	0.068	0.065	−0.002
Parents' marital status in 9th grade: One of them passed away	0.033	0.036	0.028	−0.008	0.040	0.046	0.028	−0.018+	0.025	0.023	0.029	0.006

(Continued)

Table 2.1 Descriptive statistics (Continued)

Variable (The wave of the survey)	Full sample				Male sample				Female sample			
	Mean	Desire to marry		Mean Diff.	Mean	Desire to marry		Mean Diff.	Mean	Desire to marry		Mean Diff.
		No	Yes			No	Yes			No	Yes	
	(1)	(2)	(3)	(4)	(5)	(6)	(7)	(8)	(9)	(10)	(11)	(12)
Location in 9th grade: New Taipei city (J1W3; J3W1)	0.386	0.382	0.393	0.011	0.372	0.359	0.400	0.041	0.401	0.411	0.387	−0.024
Location in 9th grade: Yilan county	0.252	0.257	0.243	−0.014	0.257	0.264	0.245	−0.019	0.246	0.249	0.242	−0.007
Observations	2,443	1,527	916		1,286	861	425		1,157	666	491	

Note: The waves of survey are indicated in parentheses. J1, J3 and W stand for J1 cohort, J3 cohort and Wave, respectively. The PJ1W1 and PJ3W1 stand for the wave 1 of parental survey for J1 and J3 cohorts, respectively. The reference groups for these variables are: 'no religion' for religion; 'lower than junior college' for parents' education level; 'below 30K' for monthly income; 'intactness' for parental marital status; 'Taipei City' for location. **p<0.01, *p<0.05, +p<0.1.

experience before marriage and residence at the time of sampling. Religion was divided into three categories: no religion (reference), Catholic/Protestant or other religions. Dating status at the age of 22 as well as sexual experience before marriage were dichotomized variables. Residence at the time of sampling includes Taipei City (reference), New Taipei City and Yilan County, which represent different levels of urbanization (from more to less urban).

Family background includes parents' education level, monthly family income during adolescence, the number of siblings, happiness in parents' marriage, family cohesion and parental marital status. Parents' education level was dichotomized into father's or mother's education level being junior college or above ($=1$) and not being junior college or above ($=0$). The monthly family income categories were below 30k (NT\$), 30–50k, over 50–80k, over 80–120k and over 120k, with below 30k as the reference group. The number of siblings is based on respondents' self-report at wave 1, ranging from 1 to 6. The happiness in parents' marriage was based on respondents' self-report and was coded 1 if respondents thought that their parents' marriage was happy. For family cohesion, it was measured at 9th grade for both J1 and J3 samples, which was based on the summation of six items that captured mutual family help and emotional attachment: (1) when making decisions, I will discuss them with my family; (2) our family members all enjoy our family time; (3) when there is a family activity, our family members will join; (4) our family members will accept each other's friends; (5) when I am down, I can receive comfort from my family and (6) when I need help or advice, I can receive help or advice from my family. Each item was based on a 4-point Likert scale ('strongly disagree' to 'strongly agree'). Higher scores indicated higher family cohesion. Parental marital status was classified into three categories: intact (reference), separate or divorced, and one or both parents passed away.

Since the marriages discussed in this chapter are restricted to ages 22–30, they can be viewed as earlier marriages in the same birth cohort in Taiwan. Studies have shown that people who marry earlier are more likely to come from disadvantaged families (Tai et al., 2019; Uecker and Stokes, 2008), and there is a negative relationship between the ages of marriage and divorce (Lehrer, 2008; Rotz, 2016). Despite the potential higher divorce risk for early marriages, among early marriages, there may be differences in marital characteristics (such as premarital conception or economic stability) between those with a desire to marry and those without because those who have a desire to marry are more likely to come from higher socioeconomic families. If those with a desire to marry entail marital characteristics that may enhance marital stability, this means that given the similar age of marriage, early marriages with the desire to marry will be more stable than those without such a desire to marry.

Several factors that may foster marital stability are considered: age at first marriage, conception before marriage, household economic stability (measured by spouse's job status), division of labour (measured by that the wife is responsible for the daily expense for the family), matching characteristics (measured by that the spouses are similar in ages and levels of education), objective and subjective marital quality. The higher the age at first marriage, the longer it takes to find a spouse in the marriage market, implying a lower probability of mismatch. Therefore, the age at first marriage is negatively related to chances of divorce (Lehrer, 2008; Rotz, 2016). Premarital conception means that the individual entered into marriage because of pregnancy but not finding the most suitable partner; in that sense, premarital pregnancy would have a positive relationship with divorce (Weiss and Willis, 1997). Economic stability, division of labour and similar characteristics of husbands and wives have enhanced marital stability (Becker et al., 1977; Lundberg and Pollak, 2014; Weiss and Willis, 1997). The objective quality of marriage is measured by the number of activities that the couple does together, including whether the couple can have a heart-to-heart talk, walk, engage in outdoor activities and discuss family affairs together. The subjective quality of marriage is based on the respondents' self-assessment of whether they are satisfied with their spouses. These factors are expected to have a negative relationship with divorce. For the sake of convenience, Table 2.A1 in the appendix presents all the detailed information about these variables.

The Descriptive Statistics

Table 2.1 contains the sample means based on the full sample, male sample and female sample, which are listed in columns (1) to (4), columns (5) to (8), and columns (9) to (12), respectively. Column (1) is the mean, column (2) and column (3) are the means based on the respondents' having the desire to marry, and column (4) is the mean difference between respondents with and without the desire to marry. The same presentation is used for males and females.

In column (1), about 47 per cent respondents are females. In 2014, the average age of respondents was 28 years (born in 1985–1986), closed to 80 per cent respondents have a bachelor degree (58.2 per cent college and 20.8 per cent master degree), about 90 per cent respondents are currently employed and 20 per cent were married.

About 38 per cent of the sample has the desire to marry at the age of 22. Around one-half of the respondents has a religious belief, of which 4 per cent believe in Catholicism or Christianity, and 47 per cent believe in other religions. The percentages of dating someone by age 22 and premarital sexual experience are, respectively, about 39 per cent and 32 per cent. For family background, the proportion of parents' education level being junior college or above is around 28 per cent. Monthly family income (in NT$) below 30k, 30k–50k, over 50k–80k, over 80k–120k and over 120k is 10.3 per cent, 27.4 per cent, 36.8 per cent, 19.4 per cent and 6.1 per cent of respondents, respectively. The average number of siblings is 2.7. About three quarters of respondents reported that their parents are happy in marriage. About one in ten had a non-intact family at respondents' age of 15 (6.7 per cent for parents' divorce or separation, and 3.5 per cent for one or both parents passed away). The proportion of respondents from Taipei City, New Taipei City and Yilan County is 36.2 per cent, 38.6 per cent and 25.2 per cent, respectively.

As shown in column (4), compared to those without the desire to marry, respondents with the desire to marry are more likely to be female, have a master degree, be married, be religious, have a dating partner at the age of 22, have sexual experience before marriage, have parents' education level being junior college or above and come from a family with a monthly family income in the over NTD80k–120k range. These results indicate that people who expect to marry are less likely to come from economically disadvantaged families.

Column (5) shows in 2014 that the proportion of married men is about 16 per cent. About one-third of men have a desire to marry. Similar to the results of column (4), column (8) reveals that men with the desire to marry are more likely to have a master degree, have gotten married, have dated someone at the age 22, have sex experience before marriage, have parents' education level being junior college or above and have family income in the over NTD80k–120k range than relative to those without such a desire. Their parents' marriages are also more likely to be happy and intact.

Column (9) shows that the proportion of women who are married is 23.2 per cent, which is about 7 per cent higher than for men. Nearly 42 per cent of women have the desire to marry, which is about 10 per cent higher than that of men. Moreover, column (12) indicates that compared with women without the desire to marry, women who hope to marry have higher percentages of a master degree, being married, being religious, dating someone by age 22, premarital sexual experience and family income in the over 80k–120k range.

Women collectively are not only likely to wish to marry but are more likely to get married. Apart from that, regardless of gender, there are positive and significant differences in the proportions of getting a master's degree, getting married, dating someone, having premarital sexual experience and having over NTD80k–120k range between those with and without the desire to marry.

Marital Characteristics for the Married

In this subsection, we examine differences in marital characteristics between those with the desire to marry and those without among those who are married. The results are in Table 2.2. Following the same presentation as Table 2.1, columns (1) to (4), columns (5) to (8), and columns (9) to (12) are the results of the full sample, males and females, respectively.

In column (1), the average age at first marriage is about 27 years. About 31 per cent of brides have conceived before marriage. The percentage of having a job, spouse having a job and both husband and wife having jobs is 84.1 per cent, 85.6 per cent and 71.5 per cent, respectively. Only about one-third of wives are responsible for household expenses. Sixty-three per cent of couples have an age gap within two years, and 48 per cent of couples have similar levels of education. The average number of activities done together is 3.6. More than 90 per cent indicated that they are satisfied with their spouses; this is perhaps because these respondents have not been married for too long and are still in their honeymoon period.

Column (4) shows that compared with those without the desire to marry, respondents wishing to marry are slightly younger and less likely

Table 2.2 Marital characteristics by desire to marry

	Full sample				Male sample				Female sample			
		Desire to marry				Desire to marry				Desire to marry		
		No 48%	Yes 52%			No 50%	Yes 50%			No 46%	Yes 54%	
	Mean	Mean	Mean	Mean Diff.	Mean	Mean	Mean	Mean Diff.	Mean	Mean	Mean	Mean Diff.
	(1)	(2)	(3)	(4)	(5)	(6)	(7)	(8)	(9)	(10)	(11)	(12)
Timing of marriage:												
Age at the first marriage	26.9	27.1	26.7	−0.339+	27.1	27.4	26.9	−0.552*	26.7	26.7	26.6	−0.146
Conceived before marriage	0.313	0.370	0.264	−0.106*	0.340	0.429	0.257	−0.171*	0.293	0.322	0.269	−0.053
Stable economic condition:												
Have a job	0.841	0.833	0.848	0.015	0.970	0.980	0.962	−0.018	0.741	0.712	0.766	0.054
Spouse has a job	0.856	0.819	0.888	0.069*	0.744	0.663	0.819	0.156*	0.943	0.949	0.938	−0.011
Both spouses have jobs	0.715	0.662	0.760	0.098*	0.734	0.653	0.810	0.156*	0.700	0.669	0.724	0.055
Division of labour and matching sorting:												
The wife is responsible for the daily expense for the family	0.313	0.282	0.340	0.058	0.320	0.327	0.314	−0.012	0.308	0.246	0.359	0.113*

(Continued)

Table 2.2 Marital characteristics by desire to marry (Continued)

	Full sample				Male sample				Female sample			
	Mean	Desire to marry		Mean	Mean	Desire to marry		Mean	Mean	Desire to marry		Mean
		No 48%	Yes 52%	Diff.		No 50%	Yes 50%	Diff.		No 46%	Yes 54%	Diff.
	(1)	(2)	(3)	(4)	(5)	(6)	(7)	(8)	(9)	(10)	(11)	(12)
Matching characteristics between the husband and the wife:												
Age gap between −2 and 2 years	0.633	0.625	0.640	0.015	0.729	0.714	0.743	0.029	0.559	0.551	0.566	0.015
Same level of education	0.479	0.426	0.524	0.098*	0.448	0.388	0.505	0.117+	0.502	0.458	0.538	0.080
Marital quality (objective and subjective measures):												
Number of activities that the spouse do together	3.6	3.6	3.6	0.069	3.7	3.6	3.8	0.257**	3.5	3.5	3.5	−0.065
Satisfied with the spouse	0.940	0.944	0.936	−0.008	0.941	0.959	0.924	−0.035	0.939	0.932	0.945	0.013
	466	216	250		203	98	105		263	118	145	

Note: Only married sample is used. All variables are from TYP2014. **$p < 0.01$, *$p < 0.05$, +$p < 0.1$.

to form a shotgun marriage. Their economic conditions tend to be more stable as they and their spouses are more likely to have jobs. In addition, these spouses are more likely to have similar levels of education.

The chapter also compared the selected marital characteristics between those with and without the wish to marry for married men and married women, respectively. For married men, column (8) points out highly similar relations as in column (4) except for the number of activities done together. In column (8), it can be seen that the number of activities done together for men who wish to marry is higher compared to those without the desire to marry. However, for married women, column (12) indicates that among the selected factors, women with the desire to marry are only more likely to be in charge of family daily expenses relative to those without the desire to marry. Thus, the differences in marital characteristics between married women with and without the desire to marry are less evident.

Overall, those with the desire to marry are less likely to get married due to pregnancy. They and their spouses both are likely working and have a similar educational level. Although these results only hold true for men, these results extend our understanding of marital stability regarding early marriages by showing that those who had the desire to marry might have a lower divorce risk relative to those without such a wish.

The Empirical Strategy

Before presenting the empirical results, this chapter describes the empirical methods. As mentioned, marital status is a binary variable. The chapter uses a linear probability model (LPM) to examine the effect of the desire to marry on the subsequent probability of marriage before age 30. Although logit or probit models are more commonly used in the literature for a binary dependent variable, the reasons for the use of LPM are as follows. First, Hellevik (2009) pointed out in most applications that the results of LPM are very similar to the logit model, but LPM has the advantage that its coefficients are easier to explain. Second, although the disadvantage of LPM is that its prediction probability may be negative or greater than one, the main focus in this chapter is on the relationship between an explanatory variable and the dependent variable rather than the predicted probability. Therefore, the regression analysis uses LPM for the convenience of comparison and intuition so as to convey the coefficients' meaning.

Results

Desire to Marry and Probability of Marriage

Table 2.3 shows the regression results that affect the probability of marriage. The dependent variable is 'married in 2014', which is a binary variable. The variable is coded 1 if the respondent was married at the time of the interview in 2014 and 0 if otherwise. Models (1) to (3) are results for the full, male and female samples, respectively.

Table 2.3 The effect of desire to marry on the probability of marriage in 2014

	Full sample	Male sample	Female sample
	(1)	(2)	(3)
Desire to marry	0.100**	0.096**	0.107**
	(0.017)	(0.022)	(0.025)
Female	0.061**		
	(0.015)		
Year of birth	−0.036**	−0.028*	−0.045**
	(0.009)	(0.012)	(0.014)
Education level: junior college	−0.048	−0.046	−0.029
	(0.039)	(0.051)	(0.062)
Education level: college	−0.142**	−0.136**	−0.124**
	(0.027)	(0.033)	(0.047)
Education level: master or above	−0.215**	−0.187**	−0.209**
	(0.030)	(0.036)	(0.053)
Currently employed	−0.106**	0.063**	−0.229**
	(0.025)	(0.024)	(0.037)
Religion: Catholic/Protestant	0.031	0.079	−0.002
	(0.037)	(0.051)	(0.055)
Religion: other religions	0.008	0.012	0.005
	(0.015)	(0.020)	(0.024)
Dating someone at age 22	0.156**	0.130**	0.187**
	(0.018)	(0.024)	(0.028)
Having sex before marriage	0.050**	0.081**	−0.003
	(0.019)	(0.024)	(0.033)

Table 2.3 The effect of desire to marry on the probability of marriage in 2014 (Continued)

	Full sample	Male sample	Female sample
	(1)	(2)	(3)
Parents' education level: junior college or above	−0.031+	−0.044*	−0.027
	(0.017)	(0.021)	(0.028)
Monthly income: 30k–50k (NTD)	0.045	0.055	0.037
	(0.028)	(0.036)	(0.044)
Monthly income: 50k–80k	0.052+	0.061+	0.047
	(0.028)	(0.036)	(0.043)
Monthly income: 80k–120k	0.057+	0.107**	0.000
	(0.031)	(0.040)	(0.048)
Monthly income: over 120k	0.095*	0.117*	0.073
	(0.041)	(0.054)	(0.061)
Number of sibling	0.001	0.004	0.001
	(0.009)	(0.012)	(0.013)
Parents' marriage being happy in 9th grade	0.010	−0.002	0.022
	(0.020)	(0.027)	(0.031)
Family cohesion in 9th grade	0.004**	0.004+	0.005*
	(0.002)	(0.002)	(0.002)
Parents' marital status in 9th grade: separation or divorce	−0.019	−0.025	0.011
	(0.033)	(0.042)	(0.052)
Parents' marital status in 9th grade: One of them passed away	0.048	0.033	0.091
	(0.044)	(0.050)	(0.084)
Location in 9th grade: New Taipei city	0.085**	0.065**	0.098**
	(0.017)	(0.022)	(0.027)
Location in 9th grade: Yilan county	0.108**	0.114**	0.099**
	(0.020)	(0.026)	(0.031)
Constant	2.785**	1.985*	3.590**
	(0.720)	(0.960)	(1.086)
Observations	2,443	1,286	1,157
R-squared	0.161	0.173	0.175

Note 1: The mean of the married is 19.5%, 16.3%, 23.2% for full sample, male sample, female sample, respectively.
Note 2: The reference groups for these variables are the same as indicated in Table 1.1. Robust standard errors in the parentheses clustered at the junior high school. **$p<0.01$, *$p<0.05$, +$p<0.1$.

Model (1) shows that the desire to marry positively correlates with the probability of marriage ($p<0.001$). Therefore, the desire to marry during emerging adulthood can predict the subsequent probability of marriage. Consistent with the literature, there is a gender difference in marriage. Women's probability of marriage is higher than men's, while the year of birth negatively relates to the probability of marriage. Educational attainment and having a job are negatively correlated with the probability of getting married. Those who have a college or above degree are more likely to follow the traditional career path – pursuing a higher degree to find a good job, and then forming a family – and thus are less likely to be the early married. As can be seen later, the negative correlation between employment status and marriage is entirely driven by females and could be explained by resource and cultural norm explanations (see below). This pattern is consistent with the theory of marriage in Oppenheimer (1988).

Those dating someone by age 22 and having premarital sexual experience are more likely to marry before age 30. The estimate of dating someone is about 16 per cent with *t*-statistic 8.7, suggesting a high correlation between dating during emerging adulthood and the probability of marriage in young adulthood. Parents' education level being junior college or above is negatively related to the probability of marriage, but monthly family income positively correlates with the likelihood of marriage. Highly educated parents care more about children's education and enable their children to pursue higher education, which delays entry into marriage. Family income, as an indicator of family resource, not only affects children's opportunity to pursue educational attainment but also the likelihood of getting married. These patterns suggest that family income is more important in determining family formation than educational achievement. As can be seen later, the results hold only for men. Not surprisingly, family cohesion is positively correlated with the probability of marriage. There are differences in probability among different regions. Individuals who live in New Taipei City or live in Yilan County are more likely to enter marriage than those who live in Taipei City. The results may reflect that people from an urban area like Taipei City are more educated, have more job opportunities and hence would be likely to postpone marriage relative to other areas. These results can also be explained by the difference in the cultural norms such as the concept of gender roles or gender equality among different urbanized areas. People from urban areas are more liberal and thus value indi-vidualism more.

As can be seen in Model (2), the Model (1) results are preserved for men, except for employment status. However, it is not the case for women. As shown in Model (3), only correlations between marriage and the desire to marry, education level, dating someone, family cohesion and living locations are the same as in Model (1). Factors of premarital sex, parents' education level and family monthly income are not the same in Model (1) as they are all uncorrelated with the probability of marriage. The gender-specific significance results, including work status, premarital sex, parents' education level and family monthly income, thus may be worth discussing. Some of these results can be easily understood by the overarching theoretical argu-ment of 'the interplay of norm and resources'.

For men, having a job is positively correlated with the probability of marriage, but it is the opposite for women. This gender difference in correlation between work status and marriage can be understood either by resource or cultural norm perspectives. From a resource explanation, for men having a job represents personal resource, and thus having a job is positively related to the probability of marriage. However, for women, having a job indicates higher personal economic independence, and thus work status is negatively related to marriage (especially early marriage). The cultural norm perspective will rein-force this gender difference. Men are often the breadwinner in a family, while women are more likely to quit their jobs after marriage.

The positive correlation between premarital sex and marriage hold only for men not for women. This chapter finds that premarital sexual behaviour and dating someone are highly correlated for women. Controlling both variables at the same time will make premarital sexual behaviour insignificant; however, this is not true for men. These patterns may mean that women are more likely to enter into marriage through stable relationships, while men may do so either through stable relationships or sexual behaviour. Men thus are more likely to get married relative to women because of unplanned pregnancy. In Table 2.2, the proportion of premarital pregnancy in the male sample is 34 per cent, which is higher than the 29.4 per cent in the female sample.

There is a gender difference in the relationship between the parents' education level and marriage, as well as the one between monthly

family income and marriage. The result indicates that parents' education and monthly family income are correlated with marriage only
for men. In terms of resource explanation, higher educated parents are
more able to help their children pursue their educational attainment
and are more likely to view education as an important pathway to
accumulate resources. From the cultural standpoint, pursuing
educational attainment is the primary goal for men in a patriarchal
society, as men need to sustain their economic power, and education is
the way to do so. Thus, higher parents' education level would be
negatively related to men's likelihood of early marriage. Family
income, on the other hand, is positively related to marriage for men
only, which can be explained by the interplay of cultural norm and
resources. For the cultural norm, especially in a patriarchal society,
family resource is more likely to be disproportionally distributed to
sons rather than girls. The economic resource is positively related to
marriage; hence, family economic resource can be positively related
to the men's likelihood of marriage.

Discussion and Conclusion

The above analyses reveal a positive correlation between the desire to
marry as expressed during emerging adulthood and subsequent marriage before age 30. The result holds for males and females, and the
effect of the desire to marry on the probability of marriage is similar.
In addition, as shown in Table 2.1, individuals with a desire to marry
at the age of 22 have parents' education level and family income level
between 80k and 120k higher than those without such desire.
Furthermore, their final educational attainments are more likely to be
a master's degree or above than their counterparts. These patterns
suggest that individuals with a desire to marry are less likely to be
from a lower socioeconomic status. The finding aligns with the US
studies, in which they found that young adult women who are from
disadvantaged families (such as a non-intact family) report lower
expectations to marry (Lichter et al., 2004; Manning et al., 2019).
Moreover, as Table 2.2 shows, among those married, individuals with
a desire to marry are less likely to have conceived before marriage,
also known as forming a shotgun marriage. These couples' economic
conditions (measured by spouse's job status) are more stable and
likely have similar levels of education. Since the differences in these

factors will facilitate marital quality. These patterns thus imply that among all early marriages, marriages with a desire to marry will be more stable than marriages without such a desire.

An increase in the desire to marry at an early age thus may be helpful in promoting the likelihood of marriage. More importantly, those who married early due to a stronger desire to marry are less likely to divorce than those who did without such a desire (such as premarital pregnancy). With the cultural norm whereby a child is typically born within marriage in Taiwan and other East Asian countries (Jones and Gubhaju, 2009; Raymo et al., 2015), an increase in the marriage rate will help increase the overall fertility rate. The results in this chapter offer an important empirical reference for the formulation and promotion of related social policies, especially for countries with less social support for out-of-wedlock birth.

Other factors associated with the probability of marriage include gender, year of birth, educational attainment, work status, dating a partner by age 22, premarital sexual experience, family income, family cohesion and living in New Taipei City or Yilan County relative to living in Taipei City. The effect is also found regardless of gender, including the year of birth, educational attainment, dating a partner by age 22, family cohesion and living in New Taipei City or Yilan County. Implications of these results are triple. First, given that dating a partner strongly correlates with both the desire to marry (see Table 2.1) and marriage for both genders, the issue of not getting married or delaying marriage in Taiwan is closely related to whether the youth generation can easily find a suitable partner. Second, the happy and easy family life perceived or experienced by respondents during their adolescence as measured by family cohesion can positively contribute to the willingness of marrying. Last but not least, results that educational attainment and the level of urbanization are negatively correlated with marriage suggest that the prevalence of higher education and the subsequent changes in social norms such as gender role attitudes and gender equality are important factors in delaying marriage.

Some limitations for the empirical results need to be stated. First, TYP's sampling population is from northern Taiwan with two cities and one county, namely Taipei City, New Taipei City and Yilan County. The results may be inapplicable to the rest of Taiwan. However, Tai et al. (2019, p. 2009) noted:

Yet the three areas—Taipei City, New Taipei City, and Yi-Lan County—were selected for data collection because they represent essential regional differences in Taiwan in terms of urbanization levels, economic production modes, and population composition. Thus, our research based on the TYP data still portrays important dimensions of family formation in Taiwan.

In addition, society and social policy in Taiwan are less supportive of cohabitation and extramarital childbirth. Therefore, the results in this chapter are at best applicable to countries with limited support for non-marital childbirth and not to Western countries such as the United States and those in Western Europe.

Nonetheless, the findings further our understanding of early marriage. Forming a desire to marry in emerging adulthood is positively related to entering marriage before age 30. In addition, among those married at similar ages of the first marriage, the desire to marry tends to result in a lower divorce risk than otherwise. Further research can extend this analysis by using a survival model to examine whether the desire to marry in emerging adulthood is positively related to subsequent marriage in early adulthood, and compare marital satisfaction and marital stability between married individuals with and without the desire to marry.

References

Aguiar, M., & Hurst, E. (2007). Measuring trends in leisure: The allocation of time over five decades. *The Quarterly Journal of Economics, 122*(3), 969–1006.

Allendorf, K., Thornton, A., Mitchell, C., & Young-DeMarco, L. (2019). The influence of developmental idealism on marital attitudes, expectations, and timing. *Journal of Family Issues, 40*(17), 2359–2388.

Amato, P. R. (1988). Parental divorce and attitudes toward marriage and family life. *Journal of Marriage and the Family, 50*(2), 453–461.

Arocho, R., & Kamp Dush, C. M. (2016). Anticipating the ball and chain reciprocal associations between marital expectations and delinquency. *Journal of Marriage and the Family, 78*(5), 1371–1381.

Axinn, W. G., & Thornton, A. (1992). The influence of parental resources on the timing of the transition to marriage. *Social Science Research, 21*(3), 261–285.

Axinn, W. G., & Thornton, A. (1996). The influence of parents' marital dissolutions on children's attitudes toward family formation. *Demography, 33*(1), 66–81.

Becker, G. S., Landes, E. M., & Michael, R. T. (1977). An economic analysis of marital instability. *Journal of Political Economy, 85*(6), 1141–1187.

Carlson, M., McLanahan, S., & England, P. (2004). Union formation in fragile families. *Demography, 41*(2), 237–261.

Copen, C. E., Daniels, K., Vespa, J., & Mosher, W. D. (2012). First marriages in the United States: Data from the 2006–2010 national survey of family growth. *National Health Statistics Reports, 49*, 1–21.

Crissey, S. R. (2005). Race/ethnic differences in the marital expectations of adolescents: The role of romantic relationships. *Journal of Marriage and Family, 67*(3), 697–709.

Ellison, C. G., Burdette, A. M., & Glenn, N. D. (2011). Praying for Mr. Right? Religion, family background, and marital expectations among college women. *Journal of Family Issues, 32*(7), 906–931.

Fishbein, M., & Ajzen, I. (1975). *Belief, attitude, intention and behavior*. Reading, MA: Addison-Wesley.

Gecas, V., & Seff, M. (1990). Social class and self-esteem: Psychological centrality, compensation, and the relative effects of work and home. *Social Psychology Quarterly, 53*(2), 165–173.

Guzzo, K. B. (2009). Marital intentions and the stability of first cohabitations. *Journal of Family Issues, 30*(2), 179–205.

Heaton, T. B., & Pratt, E. L. (1990). The effects of religious homogamy on marital satisfaction and stability. *Journal of Family Issues, 11*(2), 191–207.

Hellevik, O. (2009). Linear versus logistic regression when the dependent variable is a dichotomy. *Quality and Quantity, 43*(1), 59–74.

Jones, G. W. (2007). Delayed marriage and very low fertility in Pacific Asia. *Population and Development Review, 33*(3), 453–478.

Jones, G. W., & Gubhaju, B. (2009). Factors influencing changes in mean age at first marriage and proportions never marrying in the low-fertility countries of East and Southeast Asia. *Asian Population Studies, 5*(3), 237–265.

Keeley, M. C. (1977). The economics of family formation. *Economic Inquiry, 15*(2), 238–250.

Kiernan, K. (2001). The rise of cohabitation and childbearing outside marriage in western Europe. *International Journal of Law, Policy and the Family, 15*(1), 1–21.

Lehrer, E. L. (2008). Age at marriage and marital instability: Revisiting the Becker–Landes–Michael hypothesis. *Journal of Population Economics, 21*(2), 463–484.

Leonhardt, D., & Quealy, K. (2015). *How your hometown affects your chances of marriage*, The New York Times. Retrieved from https://tinyurl.com/4hax8rr8

Lichter, D. T., Batson, C. D., & Brown, J. B. (2004). Welfare reform and marriage promotion: The marital expectations and desires of single and cohabiting mothers. *Social Service Review, 78*(1), 2–25.

Lichter, D. T., Sassle, S., & Turner, R. N. (2014). Cohabitation, post-conception unions, and the rise in nonmarital fertility. *Social Science Research, 47*, 134–147.

Livingston, G. (2018). *About one-third of U.S. children are living with an unmarried parent*. Pew Research Center. Retrieved 4 July 2020, from https://tinyurl.com/ya66llyv

Lundberg, S., & Pollak, R. A. (2007). The American family and family economics. *Journal of Economic Perspectives, 21*(2), 3–26.

Lundberg, S., & Pollak, R. A. (2014). Cohabitation and the uneven retreat from marriage in the United States, 1950–2010, In L. P. Boustan, C. Frydman &

R. A. Margo (Eds.), *Human capital in history: The American record* (pp. 241–272). University of Chicago Press.

Lu, Y.-H., & Yi, C.-C. (2005). Conjugal resources and the household division of labor under Taiwanese social change: A comparison between the 1970s and 1990s social-cultural contexts. *Taiwanese Sociology, 10,* 41–94. (in Chinese).

Manning, W. D., Brown, S., & Payne, K. K. (2014). Two decades of stability and change in age at first union formation. *Journal of Marriage and Family, 76*(2), 247–260.

Manning, W. D., Longmore, M. A., & Giordano, P. C. (2007). The changing institution of marriage: Adolescents expectation to cohabit and to marry. *Journal of Marriage and Family, 69,* 559–575.

Manning, W. D., Smock, P. J., & Fettro, M. N. (2019). Cohabitation and marital expectations among single millennials in the US. *Population Research and Policy Review, 38*(3), 327–346.

Ministry of the Interior. (2016). *The 2015 statistical yearbook of the Republic of China.* Taipei, Taiwan: Ministry of the Interior.

Ministry of the Interior. (2020). *Median and average age at marriage, and births by status and nationality of biological mother and father.* Retrieved 4 July 2020, from https://www.ris.gov.tw/app/portal/346

Musick, K., & Bumpass, L. (1999). How do prior experiences in the family affect transitions to adulthood? In A. Booth, A. C. Crouter & M. J. Shanahan (Eds.), *Transitions to adulthood in a changing economy: No work, no family, no future* (pp. 69–102). London: Praeger.

Oppenheimer, V. K. (1988). A theory of marriage timing. *American Journal of Sociology, 94*(3), 563–591.

Organization for Economic Co-operation and Development. (2020). *OECD family database.* Retrieved from http://www.oecd.org/social/family/database.htm

Pan, E.-L. (2014). Timing of parental divorce, marriage expectations, and romance in Taiwan. *Journal of Comparative Family Studies, 45*(1), 77–92.

Popenoe, D. (2005). *The state of unions 2005: The social health of marriage in America.* Piscataway, NJ: National Marriage Project.

Raymo, J. M. (2003). Educational attainment and the transition to first marriage among Japanese women. *Demography, 40*(1), 83–103.

Raymo, J. M., & Iwasawa, M. (2008). Bridal pregnancy and spouse pairing patterns in Japan. *Journal of Marriage and Family, 70*(4), 847–860.

Raymo, J. M., Park, H., Xie, Y., & Yeung, W.-J. (2015). Marriage and family in East Asia: Continuity and change. *Annual Review of Sociology, 41*(8), 1–22.

Rotz, D. (2016). Why have divorce rates fallen?: The role of women's age at marriage. *Journal of Human Resources, 51*(4), 961–1002.

Sassler, S., & Goldscheider, F. (2004). Revisiting Jane Austen's theory of marriage timing: Changes in union formation among American men in the late 20th century. *Journal of Family Issues, 25*(2), 139–166.

Tai, T.-O, Yi, C.-C., & Liu, C.-H. (2019). Early marriage in Taiwan: Evidence from panel data. *Journal of Family Issues, 40*(14), 1989–2014.

Tasker, F. L., & Richards, M. P. M. (1994). Adolescents' attitudes toward marriage and marital prospects after parental divorce: A review. *Journal of Adolescent Research, 9*(3), 340–362.

Uecker, J. E., & Stokes, C. E. (2008). Early marriage in the United States. *Journal of Marriage and Family, 70*(4), 835–846.

Weiss, Y., & Willis, R. J. (1997). Match quality, new information, and marital dissolution. *Journal of Labor Economics, 15*(1, Part 2), S293–S329.

Willoughby, B. J., & Carroll, J. S. (2010). Sexual experience and couple formation attitudes among emerging adults. *Journal of Adult Development, 17*(1), 1–11.

Willoughby, B. J., Carroll, J. S., Vitas, J. M., & Hill, L. M. (2012). When are you getting married? The intergenerational transmission of attitudes regarding marital timing and marital importance. *Journal of Family Issues, 33*(2), 223–245.

Wolfinger, N. H. (2003). Family structure homogamy: The effects of parental divorce on partner selection and marital stability. *Social Science Research, 32*(1), 80–97.

Yang, C.-L. (2013). Potential problems in estimating the number of cohabitants in Taiwan based on census and household registration data. *B.A.S. Coordination and Development Society, 691*, 28–35. (in Chinese).

Appendix

Table 2.A1   Definitions of variables for Table 2.2 (all from TYP2014)

Variable	Definition
Timing of marriage:	
Age at first marriage	R's age at first marriage
Conceived before marriage	=1 R had conceived before marriage
Stable economic condition:	
Have a job	=1 R is currently working
Spouse has a job	=1 R's spouse is currently working
Both spouses have jobs	=1 Husband and wife are currently working
Division of labour and mating of likes:	
The wife is responsible for daily expenses for the family	=1 The wife is responsible for the family's daily expense
Matching characteristics between the husband and the wife:	
age gap between −2 and 2 years	=1
same level of education	=1
Marital quality (objective and subjective measures):	
Number of activity together that spouse do together (from 0 to 4)	Spouse will do the following activity together: (1) walking, (2) heart-to-heart talking, (3) going outside for leisure and (4) discussing things related to the household.
Satisfied with the spouse	=1 R is satisfied with the spouse

3

Marrying Early or Remaining Single in Taiwan: The Choice of Young Adults

Yung-Chen Yuan and Chin-Chun Yi

Introduction

Marriage is a significant life-course event in Chinese societies. Globally, getting married is one of the crucial indicators of the transition to adulthood (Hsu, 1948; Park, 2013). Due to drastic social changes over the past few decades, there is an increasing trend of late marriage, bachelorism and postponed fertility in Taiwan. Neighbouring East Asian societies have also been experiencing a similar trend. According to the Ministry of the Interior of Taiwan, the average ages of first marriage for men and women were 32.6 and 30.3 years old, respectively, in 2019. Between 2009 and 2019, the population of unmarried 30- to 34-year-olds increased from 52.3 to 63.0 per cent for men and from 35.9 to 47.7 per cent for women. These phenomena have seriously changed Taiwan's demographic structure, producing challenging consequences such as declining birth rates and a rapidly growing elderly population.

Marriage and mate selection fall in the private sphere. For young Taiwanese couples, however, marriage is not an individual event, but a family matter constrained by social norms and practice (Wu and Yi, 2003; Yi et al., 2019). It is well documented in studies of mate preferences that cultural norms continue their significant influence in the decision process (Glick et al., 2006; Hu and Chiang, 2021). In addition to marriage and fertility values, family structure and family relations also produce pronounced effects (Wolfinger, 2003). Therefore, it is proposed that structural, relational, as well as normative factors must be considered when analysing marriage, family, and gender issues in Taiwan (Yi and Chang, 2019).

This chapter explores Taiwanese young adults' marital decision-making through in-depth interviews in order to delineate reasons for the declining marriage rate. By doing so, we study the majority of young adults who have marriage intention but remain single in their early 30s. We also include young adults who have no interest in getting married at the time of the interview. Furthermore, a small minority who entered into marriage early (by mid-20s) will be compared to illustrate mechanisms affecting various marriage decisions. It is expected that analysing these three different groups in terms of their marital decisions will help illuminate the current family formation process in Taiwan.

Structural, Normative and Emotional Factors

Previous studies on marriage decisions have mostly focused on the impact of structural factors, with relatively fewer concerns for normative aspects. Such research has pointed out that marriage behaviour is strongly associated with the educational system (Moffitt, 2000), family and personal socioeconomic status (Moffitt, 2000; Oppenheimer, 1988) and cultural norms and gender role ideology (Bumpass et al., 1991).

The impact of education and economic status on family formation has been the focal subject in most studies. Gary Becker (1981) explored marriage through the concept of 'rational choice' from an economic perspective, which has been widely influential. He argues that the division of gender roles and the reciprocal relations in marriage are the main motivations for men and women in marriage decision-making (Becker, 1981). Given women's entry into the labour market and greater economic autonomy, the benefits from marriage and the incentives for marriage have relatively reduced. However, scholars who oppose the above argument claim that women's participation in the labour force reduces men's advantage in the employment environment and leads to a significant delay of men's first marriage (Oppenheimer et al., 1997). In contrast, the marriage rate of employed women has increased gradually. This implies that women with higher education and economic status are more favoured by men in the marriage market (Oppenheimer, 1988).

While structural factors dominate the research on marital timing, normative perspectives have gained increasing attention as well. Research emphasized that traditional social norms and values have loosened, resulting in changes in gender relations, family formation and family function (Bumpass et al., 1991). Blossfeld (1995) also stated that the degree and speed of variation in marriage and child-bearing behaviour are associated with the cultural norms, traditions and policies of different societies. In other words, marriage timing is inevitably affected by normative factors imposed by the social context in which individuals are situated.

Furthermore, the emotional aspect of the family undoubtedly has a significant influence on marriage decisions. Previous family relationships, such as parental relationships and parent–child relationships, have been shown to produce long-term effects on adult children's intimacy and marriage formation (Amato et al., 1995; Pan, 2014). Therefore, the emotional experiences within the family certainly ought to be considered in studying marriage decisions.

This study incorporates structural, normative and emotional factors to examine the marital decision-making of Taiwanese young adults and uses marital timing to delineate how marriage decision is made. In the following, we first highlight empirical findings from the Eastern and Western societies about important mechanisms accounting for the marriage transition from structural, normative and emotional factors, followed by an empirical analysis of Taiwanese youth.

Structural Factors

Family Status

The characteristics of an individual's family of origin are significantly associated with the timing of marriage; people from high socioeconomic status families are less likely to marry young (Axinn and Thornton, 1992; Uecker and Stokes, 2008). Greater parental resources for supporting children's higher education result in the children's delayed labour force entry, which in turn significantly delays the subsequent life-course developments, such as marriage (Waite and Spitze, 1981).

In addition, family structure transitions are also vital to young adults' marital timing. Family disruption, such as parental divorce or death, is often accompanied by reduced economic resources and inconsistent parenting styles, which can prompt young adults to leave home in order to escape from the unpleasant home environment (Wolfinger, 2003). Consequently, these young adults are more likely to get married earlier than their peers (Axinn and Thornton, 1992;

Goldscheider and Goldscheider, 1998). In contrast, other studies have argued that parental divorce is associated with negative attitudes and lower expectations of marriage (Axinn and Thornton, 1996; Tasker and Richards, 1994). Scholars have indicated that children of single-parent families are more likely to be afraid of establishing intimate relationships or more likely to worry that their marriage, like their parents' marriage, will end up in divorce (Wallerstein et al., 2000), leading to their delayed marriage or singleness (Glick et al., 2006; South, 2001).

Relevant studies on Taiwanese youth have echoed this negative outcome. Compared to children of two-parent families, young adults who experienced parental divorce in adolescence are more likely to have lower marital expectations (Pan, 2014). However, with regard to the actual marital behaviour, young adults who experienced parental divorce in early adolescence have higher likelihood of getting married earlier than their peers (Tai et al., 2019).

Individual Resources

From the structural perspective, the expansion of higher education and the increase in female employment have driven the second demographic transition in Western society and resulted in delayed age of first marriage, lower marriage rates and fertility rates (Becker, 1981; Lesthaeghe, 1983). Young adults tend to postpone their marriage in order to pursue higher education and career development or to enter marriage after acquiring stable employment (Oppenheimer, 1988; Sweeney, 2002). Similar phenomena also occur in East Asian societies (Jones and Gubhaju, 2009; Yang et al., 2006). The non-marriage rate has been shown to be positively correlated with the improvement of Asian women's education between 1960 and 2000 (Jones, 2005).

In contemporary societies, differences in personal resources are likely to lead to various marriage partner choices. Generally, homogamous marriage, or marriage between people of similar educational and economic status, remains the most preferred mating pattern (Kalmijn, 1998; Moffitt, 2000). In Taiwan, the composition of marriage used to be consistent with the homogamy hypothesis (Tsai, 1994). However, recent studies point out that mating patterns tend to follow the marriage gradient (Yang et al., 2006).

It should be noted that the preference to follow either the mating gradient or mating homogamy falls in the domain of normative expectations, which are often evaluated by mating partners' individual human capital or personal resources. In this regard, educational background and economic status are considered significant in marriage timing and may reveal gender variation, as discussed in the following section.

Education Status. In Asia, the educational gradient in marriage is a common phenomenon. Educated Asian men are more likely to marry women who have lower educational levels (Jones, 2005). In Taiwan, since the expansion of higher education in 1985, women's educational level has significantly increased, and the educational gap between men and women has narrowed accordingly (Yi and Chang, 2019). As a consequence, women of higher educational level and men of lower educational level are more likely to be marginalized in the marriage market, resulting in an outcome of higher unmarried rates (Yang et al., 2006). In 2019, over half of Taiwanese men and women aged 30–34 were unmarried, and the figures for those with higher educational degrees are even higher (64.8 per cent for men and 53.2 per cent for women) (Figure 3.1, Ministry of the Interior, 2020a). While the proportion of unmarried people with higher education drops after age 35, highly educated unmarried women still outnumber unmarried men

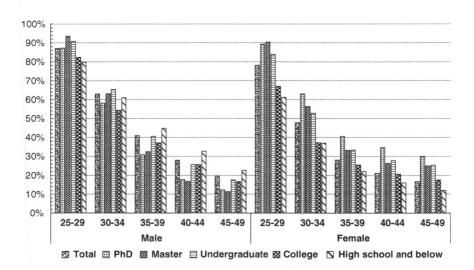

Figure 3.1 Taiwan's unmarried population by age and educational level in 2019 (Ministry of the Interior, 2020a)

within the same age and education group. Conversely, less educated men – those with junior high school degrees and below – are less likely to be married. In other words, the marriage gradient in education is common in the Taiwanese context.

An empirical study concurs with the above mating pattern, showing that since 1990, higher educated women tend to stay single instead of 'marrying down' (Yang et al., 2006). Therefore, if Taiwan continues to follow the same marriage gradient pattern, non-marriage rates will likely continue to increase with the expansion of higher education in the future (Yang et al., 2006).

Economic Condition. With the rise in women's educational attainment, women's employment opportunities and career advancement have also improved. This change has inevitably affected women's marriage decisions and seems to reduce their willingness to marry (Jones, 2005; Ono, 2003). Stable employment and economic independence allow women to obtain financial security without marriage (Ono, 2003; Raymo and Iwasawa, 2005), and have changed women's view of gender roles in the family (Yang et al., 2006). In addition, the difficulty of balancing family and work also contributes to delayed marriage (Ono, 2003; Raymo and Iwasawa, 2005). Compared to wife and mother's roles in the family, education and career provide women self-fulfilment, and ultimately economic independence (Jones, 2005). Therefore, more women postpone marriage plans or prefer to enjoy single life rather than getting married (Westley et al., 2010). Also, the traditional division of gender roles remains influential in that men are still expected to be the main economic providers of the family. Thus, men in young adulthood are less likely to enter marriage if they have not achieved stable employment (Thompson and Walker, 1989). It appears that having economic resources produces opposite effects on men and women, with resourceful women more likely to delay family formation.

Normative or Ideological Factors

Marriage is an important milestone in the process of transitioning to adulthood (Furstenberg, 2010; Park, 2013). For centuries, Chinese young adults are expected to get married, have a child and continue the family name (Hsu, 1948). Nowadays, the role of marriage and traditional family values has been challenged. In the West, being single, cohabitation, divorce and engaging in non-traditional intimate relationships are becoming more common and are no longer considered violations of social norms and morality, making marriage just one of the options, not a necessary life event (Blossfeld, 1995).

However, this is not the current situation in either Taiwan or the rest of East Asia. In Taiwan, marriage and childbirth remain the dominant cross-generational value (Cheng and Yang, 2021; Yang, 2004). Childbirth within wedlock, considered a normative sequence (Hu and Chiang, 2021; Jones and Gubhaju, 2009), has restricted the practice of non-traditional marriage patterns. The growing trend of marriage delay may serve as an evidence of such normative expectation. Indeed, cultural tradition has been shown to precipitate marriages – a typical outcome of the inseparable'marriage and childbirth packages' in East Asia (Jones and Gubhaju, 2009; Wu and Yi, 2003). It is suggested that pregnancy and childbirth after marriage have become crucial factors in young adults' marriage decisions.

Moreover, gender role values also affect marriage formation. Previous reports indicate that in countries with a non-traditional division of gender roles, such as the United States and Northern European countries, women's economic autonomy is conducive to marriage formation (Ono, 2003; Sweeney, 2002). However, gender roles remain clearly divided in East Asia, and women are still expected to be the primary caregivers of the family, even women with full-time jobs (Jones, 2005). Furthermore, value differences between men and women in marriage expectations seem to reinforce the delay in marriage (Bumpass and Choe, 2004). In Taiwan, with economic development and the rise of women's movements since the 1990s, society has become more inclusive and liberal, leading Asia in women's rights and gender equality (Yi and Chang, 2019). Gender role attitudes in Taiwan have undergone fast changes, as higher educated people become more supportive of gender equality, especially females (Lu and Jou, 2015). It will be interesting to see how the emerging ideological shift towards gender equality interacts with conventional normative expectations in family formation decision-making between genders.

Emotional Factors

As mentioned in the previous section, emotional factors also need to be examined, especially the impact of family relations on young adult children's marital timing. Prior research has reported the negative influence parental divorce and family disruption have on children's future family formation. In particular, parental conflict that occurs during family disruption is likely to cause a decrease in parents' parenting function and emotional support (Amato et al., 1995), ultimately damaging the parent–child relationship (Erel and Burman, 1995). As a result, children from disrupted families are more likely to leave home early (Goldscheider and Goldscheider, 1998) and/or to engage in early romantic and sexual relationships (Cavanagh et al., 2008), in order to build a sense of intimacy and belonging from outside of their family (Gabardi and Rosen, 1992). A continuous marital conflict between parents may have as serious an impact on children's development as a parental divorce (Chen, 2014; Hines, 1997). Exposure to family conflict during adolescence is shown to be associated with lower expectations of future marriage (Axinn and Thornton, 1996; Pan, 2014), while better parent–child relationships reduce the likelihood of having no marriage expectations (Pan, 2014; Tasker and Richards, 1994).

On the other hand, research has shown that poor parent–child relationships caused by inappropriate parenting style and discipline may increase the possibility of adolescents engaging in romantic relationships and sexual involvement (Miller et al., 1986), and as a consequence, increase the potential of early family formation (Tai et al., 2019). In other words, poor parent–child relationships during adolescence are likely to produce negative marriage attitudes in the long run, even as they may result in early marriage in reality. The seemingly oppositional effects require more systematic study to delineate possible psychological and emotional factors operating in the dating and family formation processes.

Therefore, this study argues that the parent–child relationship during adolescence plays an essential role in affecting the timing of children's marriage. In order to better capture the interplay between family structure and family relations, young adults from both intact families and divorced or high-conflict families will be compared to show how emotional factors from parents' and parent–child relationships during adolescence contribute to young adults' marriage decision-makings.

To summarize the aforementioned discussion on mechanisms affecting marriage formation, we assert that structural, normative and emotional factors have an important influence on marriage timing at the individual, family and social levels. In addition, these factors may interact with each other to determine the marriage timing of Taiwanese young adults. Our research aims to explore the influence of family structure and family relations during adolescence, as well as individual resources and normative expectations on family formation in the transition to young adulthood in the Taiwanese context.

Research Method

Samples

This study utilizes in-depth qualitative interviews of 41 young adults chosen from the Taiwan Youth Project (TYP). The qualitative data were collected via in-depth interviews since 2003, with 60 representative samples based on J1 samples and stratified by father's occupation, place of residence and other individual characteristics, in order to understand adolescents' families and the experiences of schools and communities of different socioeconomic backgrounds. Four subsequent waves of follow-up in-depth interviews have been conducted until 2019. This study mainly used data collected between 2011 and 2019.

   As respondents grew up and entered young adulthood, TYP started the third wave of in-depth interviews in 2011, in order to delineate the expectations and practices of young adults' marriage and childbirth. The main focus of this wave is on the data collection of early married young adults. The average ages of TYP's male and female respondents were 25.4 and 25.4 years old, respectively, in the TYP2011 survey. Data (Table 3.1) show that only about 7 per cent of respondents were married in the TYP2011 survey; the corresponding figure in 2014 was

Table 3.1 Marital status of TYP samples (%)

	TYP2011	TYP2014	TYP2017
Unmarried	92.94	79.43	60.41
Married	6.94	20.57	39.59
Refuse to answer	0.03		
Missing	0.03		
Total	*N* = 3,129	*N* = 2,752	*N* = 2,551

20 per cent; in 2017, the majority of young adults were still single (60.4 per cent).

Unlike previous studies defining people who married during adolescence (under the age of 18 years) as the early-married, TYP uses a different indicator (Tai et al., 2019). Those who reported having entered their first marriage by 2011 are defined as the early married group due to their much lower average age of first marriage of 25 years old (compared to their peers of 31.8 for men and 29.4 for women). Hence, the respondents who reported marriage experience (first marriage, remarriage, divorce and death of spouse) by 2011, were selected from the TYP2011 and TYP2014 surveys. Criteria for sample selection included their fertility status (pre-marital pregnancy, post-marital pregnancy or childlessness), coresident status (living with their parents, with spouse's parents or non-coresidence with parents) and childbearing status. A total of 22 early married young adults were interviewed, 3 of which are from follow-up samples.

In 2017, the fourth wave of follow-up interviews was conducted. For comparison, TYP interviewed 12 unmarried young adults and 7 non-early married respondents (referring to those who married at aged 28 or above) to solicit their marriage decision experiences. Because these interviews were conducted between 2012 and 2019, samples of the latter two groups vary in age, as shown in Table 3.2.

In-Depth Interviews

Semi-structured in-depth interviews were mostly conducted in coffee shops or restaurants, and each interview lasted for approximately 1.5–2 hours. The content of the interviews consisted mainly of

Table 3.2 Marital status of interviewees by fertile status

	Early marriage Married by 2011	Non-early marriage Married after 2011	Unmarried
Pre-marital pregnancy	13	1	–
Post-marital pregnancy	3	2	–
Married with no child	6	4	–
Total	22	7	12

individuals' family relationships, career development, dating experiences, marriage and childbearing experiences (for married respondents), expectations of marriage and perceptions of singlehood (for unmarried respondents) and attitudes towards social and cultural norms of marriage and childbearing. The sequence of questions and the follow-up questions were adjusted according to the responses of the interviewees. The in-depth interviews were conducted by six research team members. Most of the interviews were completed by two interviewers; only five were one-on-one interviews. All interviews were audio-recorded with the consent of the interviewees and transcribed for analysis.

Analysis

Grounded theory (Strauss and Corbin, 1998) was applied to analyse data and build the emerging concepts into categories. We used NVivo software to code the passages and content related to marriage, childbirth and singlehood in the transcripts, and to mark relevant information on the participants' feelings, views and attitudes associated with the concepts. Data were then re-examined, and concepts generated were revised and refined to more accurately reflect the data. Then, concepts were grouped into categories such as 'values and norms of marriage and childbirth', 'personal economic and education background', 'family relationships', 'singlehood', 'romantic relationships', 'expectations and planning of marriage and childbirth', to name a few. Finally, these categories were generalized into three dimensions: 'culture and norms', 'social structural factors' and 'relational factors'.

Research Findings and Discussion

According to the in-depth interview data, not only are individuals' life experiences different, but the extent of each factor's relative influence on marriage timing also varies. The decision of marrying early and remaining single may be affected by the interaction of two or more factors. The analysis in the following section consists of two parts: the first part will explore factors affecting marriage formation of the early married (married by mid-20s); the second part will focus on the reasons why young adults in their early 30s remain single (delayed marriage and with no intention to marry).

Early Marriage

Conforming to Cultural Norms

Postconception Marriage ('Shotgun Marriage')

The previous research suggests that the expectation of children being born in the wedlock is undoubtedly the prevailing cultural norm in Taiwan (Yi, 2013). If premarital pregnancy occurs, getting married appears to be the only or the most reasonable solution, to prevent their offspring become an illegitimate child.

Our research concurs with this observation. Among 13 out of 22 early married young adult interviewees had premarital conception, and all of them confirm that premarital conception was their primary reason for entering marriage at a relatively early age. This echoes quite well the results from our survey data. According to the TYP2011 survey, those who have experienced premarital childbearing or pre-marital conception accounted for 59.9 per cent of all early married samples. In other words, around 60 per cent of early married young adults fall into the category of postconception marriages. For women experiencing premarital pregnancy, shotgun marriage seems to be the only consequence. PM6 is a typical example. She explained that she and her parents were worried about marrying her boyfriend at the time, but she eventually decided to get married because she was pregnant.

> It was a shotgun marriage. ... I was worried about our future at that time. In fact, his financial situation is not very well, ... Actually, they (my parents) had opposed my marrying my ex-husband (boyfriend at the time). ... Just because I have a baby in my belly, as a matter of course, we had no choice but to get married. (PM6, female, first married at age 20, with premarital pregnancy)

Furthermore, the postconception marriage can be regarded as a manifestation of traditional values because men are expected to take responsibility for the premarital conception. Thus, when premarital pregnancy occurs, men often react by getting married so that the baby will be born in wedlock. Many male interviewees mention that the pregnancy of their girlfriends was the key reason for them to marry early. For example, PM8, now a father of three girls, cohabited with his girlfriend before marriage. He made his marriage decision after his girlfriend became pregnant. He said,

I, personally, abortion... it is not an option for me. I really can't do this kind of thing. ..... I said I would be responsible (for the baby), and my wife also agreed, so we got married. After her pregnancy, we started preparing for marriage. (PM8, male, first married at age 24, with girlfriend having premarital pregnancy)

Despite the fact that social values in Taiwan have become more inclusive and open-minded in recent years, the long-standing cultural norms make the public generally have a low acceptance of childbirth out of wedlock (Yi and Jao, 2013). Therefore, for unmarried pregnant women and their partners, in order to give birth to a child, marriage is a practical and reasonable option.

In cases of premarital conception, the timing of wedding is crucial and is not always determined by young adults, but by their parents. Some parents are very involved in the timing of children's marriage when premarital pregnancy occurs (PM1, PM2). Parents mostly prefer having the wedding ceremony before the baby is born. Young couples also tend to comply with parents' expectations by marrying early. It is obvious that parental opinions still have a salient influence on their children's marriage decision-makings. As an early married woman with premarital pregnancy, PM1 shared her father's insistence on the marriage timing:

My dad wanted to hold the wedding ceremony before the baby arrived. We (PM1 and her husband) actually wanted to wait until after the baby was born to hold the wedding. But my dad said, 'No, the wedding must take place before the baby arrives.' I preferred to do it after giving birth because I would be tired with that big pregnant belly. (PM1, female, first married at age 23, with premarital pregnancy)

It is clear that there may be opposing ideas about marriage timing between parents and adult children in the context of premarital pregnancy. Young adults do not necessarily prefer to get married before childbirth. However, parents tend to follow cultural norms and insist that their children marry before the baby arrives so as to protect the family's reputation and ensure the establishment of a legitimate parent–child relationship.

Reproductive Intention

For those with post-marital pregnancy, marriage is also affected by the sequence of life events, and reproduction appears to be a strong motivation for getting married early. Some young adults think that childbearing is the main purpose of marriage. For them, the timing of women's 'best childbearing years' is the most essential concern for getting married. MB4, for example, after six years of dating with her boyfriends, decided to get married in order to have a baby early.

> I thought it would be better to have a baby early, and so we got married in 2010. (MB4, female, first married at age 25)

Another interviewee also expressed his concern about giving birth with a higher maternal age. He explained:

> At that time, we just wanted to have a child quickly, because we have pressure. Everyone knows that the older a woman is, the harder it is to bear a child. (MB1, male, first married at age 26)

Thus, he decided that having a baby early would be easier, as they would still be energetic enough to take care of the newborn. In other words, due to the self-imposed age-related pressure, they decided to get married. In Taiwan, women's average age of first birth continues to rise from 26.7 years old in 2000 to 31.01 years old in 2019 (Ministry of the Interior, 2020b). The dominant cultural value of childbearing within marriage, coupled with the public idea of reproductive risks of advanced age, appear to prompt couples who are willing to have children to enter into marriage early.

Structural Factors

The Deficiency of Family Functions

Although premarital conception is the most direct and vital reason for early marriage, this result may be complicated by family malfunctions. In our early married group, 3 out of 22 interviewees experienced parental divorce, and 5 out of 22 experienced parental death in childhood or adolescence. Among 8 early married young adults who experienced family disruption during their childhood or adolescence, 7 of them married after premarital pregnancy.

Our interview data demonstrate that parental divorce or the death of parents may lead to changes in the family's economic condition and parenting styles, which accelerates both cohabitation and early employment for children, and consequently increases the occurrence of early marriage. For example, PM12's financial hardship was affected by parental divorce. She started cohabiting with her boyfriend from high school and got married at the age of 21 due to premarital pregnancy.

> Since my parents divorced, we (PM12 and her brother) moved out, and I started working since high school, ... So we were self-sufficient and didn't get a dime from the family at all. .... I had a boyfriend at the time, he did take care of me, if I didn't meet him, I couldn't graduate from senior high school. .... I lived in his home, and his family also took care of me. He also offered assistance in terms of money. (PM12, female, first married at age 21, with premarital pregnancy)

PM12's experience suggests that early marriage can be attributed to the impact of cultural norms and family structure. Her premarital pregnancy may seem to be from cohabitation, but it is actually due to the decline of family functions resulting from family disruption.

Moreover, changes in parenting quality caused by family disruption also indirectly affect the marriage timing. PM4 and PM13 both rebelliously dropped out of school because of family disruption, cohabitated with girlfriends and got married when premarital pregnancies occurred. PM4 explained why he was rebellious in school:

> I probably rebelled when they (my parents) divorced (when I was 10 years old). My brother and I lived with my father, no one disciplined us, and I was slacking off, so I did whatever I wanted. Because my dad had to work, he didn't have time to take care of me.... I rarely went home since junior high school, and lived with my friends. (PM4, male, first married at age 17, with girlfriend having premarital pregnancy)

It should be noted that family disruption does not inevitably cause an accelerated life-course transition; instead, it decreases family function, which indirectly leads to early marriage. In this study, the decrease of family function includes family economic downturn and decline in parenting quality.

Previous research has documented that parental divorce can make children distrustful of marriage and afraid of establishing close relationships (Wallerstein et al., 2000). Our study, in contrast, found that some young adults who experienced parental divorce in childhood were more eager to build their own family. PM11, whose parents divorced when she was seven years old, always wanted to have a complete family of her own. At the age of 19, she lived with her boyfriend and boyfriend's parents, and married at age 24 due to premarital pregnancy. As she recalled,

> I feel that his home is more like a so-called 'home'. I was able to have a steaming hot meal in his home at that time, which I felt terrific about, and I was so envious! ... I was wholeheartedly asking for marriage, because I grew up in a single parent family. Therefore, I always wanted to have a family, and I wish to have a complete family. (PM11, female, first married at age 24, with premarital pregnancy)

As can be seen, family disruption weakens family functions, which likely cause children to leave schools early, or leave their original family to cohabit with their partners, and eventually marry early because of premarital conception. Although the main reason for early marriage is the normative expectation that the child should be born in wedlock, it is actually an outcome of poor parenting quality and economic situation.

The economic disadvantage has also associated with the decrease in family function even in intact families. Getting married becomes an option to leave the family hardship. For example, due to her family's economic problem, M6 applied for student loans and borrowed money from relatives to pay for high school tuition fees. She described the financial situation of her family at the time:

> My family didn't give me money, or just gave me 1,000 NTD (around 35 USD), but it was all my allowance for two weeks. My dad doesn't take care of family. He doesn't have much income, and he was drinking and living it up with friends when he received salary on the payday. (M6, female, first married at age 26)

Due to the poor dwelling environment of her house, M6's boyfriend suggested her to live with him. Since then, M6 started cohabiting with her boyfriend, who also offered her pocket money when she was 19 years old. Although her father objected to her cohabitation at that time, she still insisted on moving out from home. Congruent with the findings by Meier and Allen's research (2008), our data provide an explanation to show why young adults expect to escape from disadvantaged family conditions by marrying early.

Educational Status

Overall, the early married young adults in our study have lower educational attainment, especially those young adults with premarital conception (see Table 3.3). Thirteen of 22 early married interviewees have less than a college degree. Among these 13 respondents, 6 women had premarital pregnancy and 6 men had wives who had premarital pregnancy.

For lower educated, there are various reasons for dropping out of school: unfavourable family financial situation (PM11, PM12), personal health condition (MB3) or no interest in continuing studying (PM3, PM4, PM7, PM8, PM9, PM13). PM4, who started working after graduating from junior high school, met his ex-wife. He stated:

> I was expelled from junior college after a month of studying because I was involved in a fight. I used to be rebellious and naughty. I didn't like studying since I was a kid in elementary school..... I met her (PM4's ex-wife) in a tattoo shop where I worked, she was the customer of the shop. We started dating after I graduated from junior high school. (PM4, male, first married at age 17, with partners having premarital pregnancy)

It is evident that leaving school early does not directly result in early marriage, but through early entry into the labour force, romantic

Table 3.3 Marital and fertile status of interviewees, by education background

	Pre-marital pregnancy	Post-marital pregnancy	Married with no child	Unmarried
Postgraduate	-	-	4	5
Undergraduate/ College	3	4	5	6
Incomplete Undergraduate/ College	4	-	1	-
High School and Incomplete	5	1	-	1
Junior High School and below	2	-	-	-
Total	14	5	10	12

involvement and premarital sex, the process of transition to adulthood is likely to be expedited. This is particularly acute for females. Because in East Asian society, the emphasis on prescribed order of life-course events does not leave much room for premarital pregnancy. Hence, pregnant female students often drop out from school, which ultimately makes them have lower education than their unmarried peers (PM1, PM2, PM6, PM9, PM10). In other words, lower educational attainment is the result, not the reason, for early married young women who were forced to interrupt their studies due to premarital pregnancy.

Moreover, the inability to balance childcare and study after marriage becomes a barrier for early married couples to resume their schooling. For women, the attitude of her husband's family also affects whether they can return to school. PM6 shared the reason why she abandoned her studies:

> I suspended my studies in my first year of college, and I was planning to go back to school after giving birth to my child.... But, my mother-in-law told me to go to work. Since then, I felt I could never go back to school because of economic pressure, and I didn't want to take a loan, that's too tiring. Thus, I have been working until now. (PM6, female, first married at age 20, with premarital pregnancy)

Ostensibly, early married young adults drop out from school owing to premarital pregnancy. However, after marriage and childbirth, the life plans of married couples are often forced to become child-centred, and their careers must be adjusted to suit the needs of children and family. As a result, personal educational attainment is no longer as important, which makes it less likely for early married young adults to complete their studies and obtain a higher level of education.

Emotional Factors

Strained Family Relationships

According to TYP survey data, negative family relationships tend to give rise to early marriage; in particular, conflict-ridden parent–child relationships cause young adults to marry early to leave their original family (Tai et al., 2019). This is confirmed by our qualitative interviews. For example, with a strict mother and a busy working father who had no time for communication, M9 yearned for the heart-warming atmosphere of her boyfriend's family. As a result, she ended up by marrying early. M9 stated:

Our family has financial security but not much emotional communication.... I was looking for the part which I didn't have.... I am yearning for my mother and I to be like sisters. However, the relationship between me and my mother has never been like that. I have been in conflict with my mother for a long time. That's why I was so eager to leave home at that time.... That was the only reason to get married, I just want to live with him legally. If you don't have a spousal status, it makes people feel like a casual girl. (M9, female, first married at age 27)

M9's experience shows that the expectation of a harmonious family prompted her to leave the strained family relationships via marriage. Her case also highlights the importance of normative influence. Even when escaping from the original family, young adults still prefer to have family formation in accordance with the sequence of life-course and cultural practices.

Excessive interference from parents also results in tension between parents and children. Growing up in such an atmosphere makes young adults feel restricted when staying at home. Therefore, getting married is an escape from parental control. M7 shared her experience as follows:

My dad told me that the only way I could leave this home was to get married. So next month, I got married in a civil ceremony, and then I moved out of the house. ...The point is that I would rather take a bet on the rest of my life than remain stuck in that house! (M7, female, first married at age 27)

The influence of emotional factors on the marriage timing is one of the critical findings of this study. Our interviews demonstrate that even in an intact family with favourable socioeconomic conditions, emotional experience, particularly the parent–child relationship, significantly impacts the child's marriage timing. The lack of close parent–child communication and the presence of parent–child conflict are likely to push young adults to enter into marriage early. The desire to leave the natal family and establish their own family produces strong incentives for young couples to marry earlier than their peers, especially those with poor parent–child relationships.

Romantic Experience and Love Impulse

A driving motivation for early marriage is, of course, the love impulse in a relationship. Romantic experience or impulsive love are compelling reasons for getting married early. During the infatuation stage, young adults tend to get married impulsively, in part out of the fear that they will otherwise 'miss their opportunity'. PM10, a single mother who got married at age 21, before she finished her under-graduate study, is a typical case. Triggered by the impulse of love, she also found she was pregnant at the time. However, the couple divorced three years later. PM10 said,

> Honestly, from dating to marriage, it was about 7 or 8 months, and we had a shotgun wedding.... We had a flash marriage, and it was a whirlwind romance. ... It was just a love impulse! .... In fact, I feel we were immersed in married life for only over a year. Later on, my husband had an affair and started gambling. Then we separated, and then got divorced. (PM10, female, first married at age 21, with premarital pregnancy)

In contemporary Taiwan, most young adults' impulsive decisions still need to be approved by parents or elderly family members. Marriage is not just up to the young couple, for parents of both sides have powerful influence on the marriage. For example, M5 married at age 23. He met his wife when he travelled abroad. Because his wife is a foreigner, it was difficult to maintain a long-distance relationship at the time. Therefore, they decided to marry for love. M5 explained the circumstances of their marriage decision:

> There must be an impulse to get married. ... I feel that it's not only up to me, that the families on both sides must feel OK, and then we can have a wedding....I didn't think too much at that time. I felt very stable and confident – I wouldn't have any regrets. I think that some things are determined, and there are things that you don't really need to think too much to make a decision. (M5, male, first married at age 23)

As can be seen, even for love impulse marriages, when Taiwanese young adults embark on a marriage decision, it is expected that they will submit to their parents' advice and ask for their approval.

The Interaction Between Normative, Structural and Emotional Factors

From the previous discussion, an interaction of three factors on early marriage appears. To begin, family economic disadvantage and family disruption often lead to a declining family function. As a consequence, the inadequate family function or disharmonious family relationships are likely to impel young adults to move out from natal family and to engage in romantic relationships early in order to seek for reliance and support. If premarital pregnancy takes place, then young couples usually end up in early marriage. Our analyses suggest that the occurrence of early marriage resulted from multiple factors.

To reiterate, PM11 is a typical example, who experienced parental divorce, the family financial hardship caused by her mother's invest-ment failure, parent–child conflict, early school leaving and early labour force entry. In pursuit of a warm family atmosphere, she began to cohabitate with her boyfriend and his family, and then got pregnant and married at the age of 24. PM11's transitional experience reveals the profound impact of family structure, emotional relationships and cultural norms on the specific marriage timing.

Another noticeable feature is that young adults who married early tend to pursue the ideal family characterized by a warm and harmo-nious family relationship, stable financial support and the feeling of home. Their early marriage decisions reflect the significant influence of East Asian cultural norms regarding the sequence of a subscribed life course. Even with different family backgrounds and life experiences, these early married young couples seek to build a consummate family by following the sequential practice that conforms to cultural norms.

Remaining Single

Overall, only a few interviewees made it clear that they have no intention of marriage (S2, S3, S6, S8), while the majority still wanted to be married at some point in the future but temporarily delayed their entry into marriage. It should be noted that the average age of our respondents was 31 years old at the time of the interview, which corresponded to the average age of first marriage in Taiwan in 2018. Hence, they may be considered falling into the category of the marriageable age. Nevertheless, our analyses focus on their current singlehood and the reasons accounting for their delaying marriage.

In the following, we divide young adults who remain single in early 30s into two groups. The first group is termed 'delaying marriage', which refers to the majority of young adults who have the marriage intention but are not yet married for different reasons. The second group focuses on young adults who indicate having no marriage intention as of the interview day. We delineate factors contributing to delaying mar-riage and why they are not interested in marriage in their early 30s.

Delaying Marriage

Emotional Factors

Absence of Romantic Experience and Suitable Partner

The primary reason young adults remain single in their early 30s is the lack of romantic experience or having no relationship partner. Among all unmarried samples in the TYP2017 survey, 'Not having a suitable partner' was the most reported reason for their singlehood (32.2 per cent). For those not engaged in relationships, delaying marriage appears to be more realistic for their plans for both genders. S5 and S10 who are not in relationship are typical examples.

> I don't have [a girlfriend] for now, ... I am not unwilling to get married, but I'm also not tempted to get married. For me, getting married is not something you can achieve even if you treat it seriously. I think I might as well devote myself to work at this stage. It will be more rewarding! (S5, male, unmarried, age 31)

> If I meet the right person, I will get married; if I can't find a suitable partner, I will not get married. I don't want to get married just for the sake of marriage. (S10, females, un married, age 30)

Hence, having no dating partner or suitable partner becomes the upfront reason for singlehood and can thus be considered the main obstacle to marriage encountered by single young adults in Taiwan.

A note needs to be made that since most youths have marriage intention, once suitable mates appear, active planning of marriage will take place (S4 and S11). S11 and his girlfriend have known each other for around 13 years. Although they had only been dating for half a year, they decided to settle down. He explained his marriage decision:

> I think she is the right person. She is suitable for me, ...we are happy and getting along well with each other, over the half year of dating. As we have known and familiar with each other for years, then we can actually discuss the next stage, and whether we should start doing it (to get married). (S11, male, unmarried, age 30)

These examples reveal the reluctance to get married blindly and imply that delaying marriage is a manifestation of the value of marriage. For young adults who have marriage intention, once a suitable mate appears, the single status may change.

Lack of Marriage Consensus Between the Couple

Our interviews with unmarried young adults found that some who are in relationships actually intend to get married, but the couple has different ideas about marriage. S7 had a stable relationship with his ex-girlfriend for years but cannot reach a consensus on marriage between them. He broke up with her and then looked for a new partner, so the marriage timing was delayed. As he explained:

> There is no consensus on marriage. I want to get married, but she doesn't. ...I just can't wait any longer, I think it's been delayed for so long. ...I started thinking of getting married two or three years ago. I should say that I wanted to get married since I was young, because I've been longing for the feeling of forming a family of my own. (S7, male, unmarried, age 31)

Marriage is the start of family formation that requires both parties to be committed. If the couple does not have a consensus on marriage, delaying the marriage timing is unavoidable. As different attitudes towards marriage are emerging in Taiwan, there is an increasing endorsement of marriage being not necessarily the end of all relationships. Thus, the lack of marriage consensus may be regarded as the outcome of the changing marriage values upheld by the young generation. As a result, delaying marriage among young adults may continue for some time.

Insufficient Economic Resources

Disadvantageous family economic condition is vital for entering into early marriage. However, for unmarried young adults, family financial situation was not generally mentioned as the out-front consideration. If finance is a concern, the personal economic situation may influence the marriage decision, especially among male interviewees. Insufficient financial ability (S12), unstable employment (S9) or financial pressure of buying property (S5, S11) are often reported. Let us take S12, a car salesman who lost money in investments, for example:

> My income is not really stable, so how can I get married? ... The definition of richness is broad, in my opinion, but I must have at least 10 million (New Taiwan Dollar) in my account. Then I will feel relieved. ...if I have the ability, then I really hope that my future wife will have a better life. That is if I married her, she doesn't have to work. (S12, male, unmarried, age 30)

The excerpt shows that traditional gender ideology for men to bear the financial responsibility and women to take care of home maintains its effect among young Taiwanese men. The worry expressed by S12 clearly indicates the impact of personal resources and cultural norms on young adults' marriage timing. Young males assert that good economic status and material possessions are essential for them to enter into marriage.

In contrast, none of our female interviewees raised their own insufficient economic resources as the factor in delaying marriage. One female interviewee stated, 'I will find someone who already has a house to marry, and he should earn more than me' (S10). The hypergamy marriage preference among females reinforces men's concern about accumulating assets to qualify for marriage. Our analyses are congruent with Fukuda's research (2020) that stable employment and income accumulation are essential factors in family formation in East Asian societies.

It is worth noting that although females discuss less of their own economic situation as a factor leading to delayed marriage, woman's earning ability has actually become an important mate selection criterion for men. When asked about his criteria for choosing a spouse, S9 replied:

> Having money and possessing rich life experiences (are important). I have financial ability and my partner must also have financial ability. Marriage must have bread (money) to support it. Just having love is not enough.... In fact, if you want to have a good life, a well-fed and well-clad life, you cannot afford to live on one income. (S9, male, unmarried, age 31)

This echoes the emerging trend of double-earner family in which couples share financial responsibility (Lu and Jou, 2015). Women's economic ability is thus favoured by men in their male selection. Overall, insufficient economic resources affect males more in the marriage decision process.

No Intention of Marriage

Approximately 60 per cent of Taiwanese young adults aged 31 are not married. Their single status may be temporary if the current situation is only to delay marriage. However, if singlehood becomes a personal choice and a feasible long-term plan, not entering marriage will be the ultimate outcome. Given Taiwan's patriarchal culture and the male advantage in the age gradient, to deviate from the normative path of family formation often produces harsher consequences for women. In this section, we will focus on women who plan to remain single in their future life. We will start by delineating significant mechanisms accounting for this unconventional choice.

Challenge Cultural Norms

From a normative perspective, marriage paves the way for bearing children, especially sons, for the paternal family line (Hsu, 1948). If this traditional norm is not followed, and reproduction is not taken into consideration as the main purpose of life, a serious challenge to cultural practice occurs.

Enabled by their earning ability, our seven female interviewees stated that they can financially support themselves without getting married, and they do not want to get married just for the purpose of reproduction. These women exhibited resistance to the patriarchal culture and strongly believed that women ought not to rely on men for economic security or fulfilment. S2, for example, has a master's degree and a good job in the financial services industry. Although she has been in a stable relationship with her boyfriend for two years, she has no intention of getting married. Her father, however, has been urging her to get married, which often makes her furious. In her own words,

> My dad, he always says, 'you should get married soon. Never mind if you don't pass the exam (civil service exam), just go and get married quickly.' Every time he says this it really pisses me off. I told him I don't want to get married. Every time he tells me to get married, I feel humiliated. I wonder why girls must marry to make her life – it seems that only through marriage can one feel a sense of stability and safety. Why is that so? (S2, female, unmarried, age 32)

S3, who also has no marriage intention, had a conversation with her mother about marriage and childbearing. She does not agree with getting married for the sake of having children. She defended her attitudes as follows:

> My mom told me, marriage is because you have to reproduce, and take responsibility for your life. I told my mom, 'Alright! But if I want to have a baby, why do I have to get married? If you just want me to have a child,

I could give birth to a baby.'... I just can't figure out why I have to get married. If you just want to have a baby, you can have a baby without getting married. If I am capable of raising a child, I can just find a boyfriend. I don't need to get married, and I still can give birth to a child. (S3, female, unmarried, age 32)

Women in these examples present a clear challenge to traditional cultural norms. Although patriarchal norms and the marriage–childbearing package are still mainstream values, the marital values of young adults, especially females, have changed. It is evident that careers and financial independence make it possible for women to realize their choice of remaining single. For these women, marriage and childbirth have become an option rather than a necessity.

Emotional Factors

Family Disharmony

Negative family relationship not only affects young adults' entry into early marriage, it also reduces their marriage intention. However, while poor parent–child relationship is likely to lead to early marriage, conflicting parental relationships may make young adults' marriage intention foregone (Tai et al., 2019). S6 has experienced long-term parental conflict since childhood and is hesitant to enter into marriage. He preferred to remain single for life, as he explained:

My mom kept asking me to find someone. I told her I want to be single for life... I don't want to get married.... Ever since I can remember, when I was in elementary school, my parents quarreled. Sometimes they fought fiercely. When looking back, I found they have influenced me, and they affected me gradually, like what I have just mentioned, that I don't want to get married. I can't find someone who can tolerate my personality, someone I can also tolerate. I think I can't find someone like that. (S6, male, unmarried, age 31)

For young adults, the distrust of marriage may arise from observing parents' frequent quarrels and conflicts in their early family experiences. The worry to replicate parents' failed marriage often destroys their marriage intention. This finding is consistent with Axinn and Thornton's research (1996). Our analysis confirms with the quantitative analysis that negative parent–child relations and parental conflicts lead to opposite effects on young adults' timing of marriage, with parental conflict having long-term consequences on the children's decision to remain single.

Lack of Incentive to Marry: Freedom and Affection

Obviously, the lack of incentives to marry contributes to the increase of singlehood in Taiwan. It is not unusual to hear unmarried young adults saying that 'there is no need to get married just for the sake of marriage'. Values on marriage and family formation are facing apparent challenges. From our interviews, enjoying the freedom of being single is a crucial factor for no marriage intention. S6 and S8 are two representative examples. They explained as follows:

> I would like to be single for a lifetime, I really want to stay single. I don't want to get married, I really want to have freedom. (S6, male, unmarried, age 31)

> I think [marriage] is very troublesome, it means you have to cooperate with another person. But, I'm too lazy to date, I'm a bit too lazy to leave my comfort zone.... I used to want to get married when I was in school, when my classmates were getting married one after another. I didn't have the feeling of envy at all, because I know the situations of their families quite well. So I didn't feel like getting married, because it doesn't seem to have freedom. (S8, female, unmarried, age 30)

For young adults who do not yearn for marriage, being single means freedom without compromise. Both men and women feel comfortable with the current status, and there is no need to change. The unpleasant marriage experiences of others also contribute to their lack of desire for marriage.

On the other hand, the lack of marriage incentive may result from the insistence on mutual affection. S2 and S3 are both in stable relationships for more than two years. While they enjoy the quality of their relationships with their boyfriends, they have also expressed that they have no intention of getting married. S2 explained:

> I feel that the affection between two people is more important than anything else, and as for the consideration of economic conditions and parents on both sides, those are secondary. Because I think if you want to maintain a marriage, of course, it is based on affection, and if you don't have an affectionate foundation, then why do you want to marry? (S2, female, unmarried, age 32)

It is clear that marriage is not regarded as the end goal of long-term relationships. Apart from the attraction of freedom, no intention of marriage also reflects changing marriage values in Taiwan. The unfettered single life and unmarried couple relationship are gradually being accepted by the society; those who fall into the category are not being discriminated against nor being labelled negatively. Marriage has gradually become an option in life for these young adults, not a necessary life-course event.

The Interaction Between Normative and Structural Factors

In our previous discussion on economic resources as a salient concern that produces delaying effects on marriage decisions, gender difference was reported. Men are more likely to follow the traditional gender norm by accumulating better economic resources before marriage, thus tending to delay their marriage timing. Women care less about their own economic situation in the marriage decisions, but consider men's adequate financial ability as an essential criterion for future spouses. It is contended that gender difference in reasons for delaying marriage is a result of the interaction of structural and normative factors.

In the past, the normative expectation from the traditional gender division tended to propel women to leave the workplace for family after marriage, and consequently, women lost their economic autonomy. These women's plight in marriage has become the best vigilance for their daughters so that female young adults are more likely to value their economic independence. For example, S2, who has a stable relationship but is not interested in getting married, explained her mother's situation:

> She (S2's mother) has become a full-time housewife for children, everything depends on my dad's whims. ... My mom has no economic autonomy. When she spends money, my dad just keeps nagging her and controls her spending. Therefore, I will never give up my job for the sake of family. ... I really have never thought about depending on my husband to support my life. (S2, female, unmarried, age 32)

For S2, the lack of economic autonomy makes her mother rely on her father, a path she does not want to replicate. Our discussions above show that economic self-sufficiency not only empowers women to remain single but also enables them to resist the subordinate position in the family. In other words, singlehood has become a feasible choice among young adults, especially females with financial ability.

Clearly, the interaction of normative and structural factors in producing the singlehood status among young adults is possible due to the changing social context. In Taiwan, the gender gap in education between men and women is narrowed, which in turn enhances women's labour force participation and economic independence. On the other hand, the dominant influence of patriarchal family norms sustains, restricting women's life opportunities after entering into the marriage. Our study suggests that the inconsistent development of gender equality in the public and private spheres, as well as the inconsistent change in modern attitudes and traditional practices towards gender roles have led to the trend of delaying marriage and remaining single. This finding is worthy of reference for future studies in delaying marriage and permanent singlehood in other East Asian societies that share similar cultural heritage.

Conclusion

This study examines reasons why the majority of Taiwanese young adults remain single in their early 30s, in comparison to their counterparts who married in their mid-20s. We intend to offer an East Asian perspective in delineating significant mechanisms that affect the marriage formation of the young generation. By doing so, we incorporate the impact of structural, normative and emotional aspects on the marriage formation process in Taiwan.

To briefly recap, while most Taiwanese young adults have marriage intention, for those who have delayed marriage in their early 30s, the lack of a suitable partner with marriage consensus and economic difficulty are two main reasons for remaining single. Moreover, the anxiety caused by the cultural norm that pressures young adults to bear the brunt of their family's financial responsibility affects young men with economic disadvantages in their family formation decisions.

On the other hand, for the minority of young adults with no intention to marry in their early 30s, previous experience of family disharmony and the freedom enjoyed being unmarried result in remaining single as a preferred life choice. The endorsement of marriage not for reproduction, accompanied by the increasing economic ability, also enables women to resist the normative trajectory of entering into marriage.

As for the small proportion of early married youth, the prevalent practice of shotgun marriage confirms the continuing influence of normative expectation. The desire to establish one's own harmonious family so as to leave the original conflict-ridden family is an impetus for some young adults to marry earlier than their peers. Marriage decision based on the love impulse also requires family approval. It is asserted that marriage is not merely a matter of two young adults, but a matter of two families.

Overall, our study supports the continuing importance of cultural norms in the family formation process in Taiwan. The most obvious example is that for young couples with premarital pregnancy, normative influence is likely to produce postconception marriage because only babies born in wedlock are accepted. However, cultural norms are confronted by various challenges with regard to family formation, and significant gender difference and the interaction of cultural norms and personal resources can be observed. To be specific, women with higher human capital tend to express their disobedience to the traditional path of family formation, and their choice of remaining single presents clear challenges to traditional cultural norms. In contrast, men with lower economic resources are likely to remain single. The normative expectations for men to be the economic providers of the family and the preference to follow the marriage gradient in Taiwan jointly led to men with insufficient personal resources having little marriageability.

In terms of family relations, negative parent–child relations and parental conflicts are likely to present opposite effects on young adults' timing of marriage. While conflicting parent–child relationship prompts young adults to enter into marriage early, parental conflicts cause young adults to lose confidence in marriage and thus lower their marriage intention. This finding is consistent with previous studies on the timing of parental divorce, which point out that young adults whose parents divorced during adolescence, compared to childhood, are more likely to remain single (Pan, 2014; Tai et al., 2019). Future studies encompassing the timing of parental divorce are needed.

For structural mechanisms, our analyses show that unfavourable family conditions, such as the death of parents, parental divorce or family economic disadvantages, result in a decrease in family function.

Inadequate family functions tend to cause early home leaving, cohabitation and premarital pregnancy, which directly or indirectly result in the occurrence of early marriage. Our study thus suggests that the interaction of cultural norms, resources and family function produces a salient influence on the family formation process in Taiwan.

More empirical research is required to verify whether or not identical processes occur in other East Asian societies with similar cultural contexts. In addition, the unmarried young adults of this study are between 30 and 32 years old and are still in the suitable marriage age bracket. Therefore, whether they will remain single or enter late marriage remains to be explored when they exceed the 'appropriate marriage age' in their late 30s and early 40s.

In brief, studying delayed marriage among young adults in Taiwan is a timely issue that allows us to clarify trends in family formation in a changing East Asian society. Compared with the early married, a greater impact of negative family experience and normative prescription are observed among unmarried young adults. Therefore, this study proposes that in addition to structural and emotional factors, the normative factor also assumes a significant role in the family formation process of Taiwanese young adults.

References

Amato, P., Loomis, L., & Booth, A. (1995). Parental divorce, marital conflict, and offspring well-being during early adulthood. *Social Forces, 73*(3), 895–915.

Axinn, W. G., & Thornton, A. (1992). The influence of parental resources on the timing of the transition to marriage. *Social Science Research, 21*, 261–285.

Axinn, W. G., & Thornton, A. (1996). The influence of parents' marital dissolutions on children's attitudes toward family formation. *Demography, 33*(1), 66–81.

Becker, G. S. (1981). *Treatise on the family* (2nd ed., 1991). Cambridge, MA: Harvard University Press.

Blossfeld, H. P. (1995). Changes in the process of family formation and women's growing economic independence: A comparison of nine countries. In H. P. Blossfeld (Ed.), *The new role of women: Family formation in modern societies* (pp. 3–32). Boulder, CO: Westview.

Bumpass, L. L., & Choe, M. K. (2004). Attitudes relating to marriage and family life. In N. O. Tsuya and L. L. Bumpass (Eds.), *Marriage, work, and family life in comparative perspective: Japan, South Korea, and the United States* (pp. 19–38). Honolulu: University of Hawaii Press.

Bumpass, L., Martin, T. C., & Sweet, J. A. (1991). The impact of family background and early marital factors on marital disruption. *Journal of Family Issues, 12*(1), 22–42.

Cavanagh, S., Crissey, S., & Raley, K. (2008). Family structure history and adolescent romance. *Journal of Marriage and Family, 70*(3), 698–714.

Chen, W.-C. (2014). For the sake of the children? Re-evaluating the consequences of parental divorce in Taiwan. *Taiwanese Journal of Sociology, 54*, 31–73.

Cheng, Y.-H., & Yang, C.-L. (2021). Continuity and changes in attitudes toward marriage in contemporary Taiwan. *Journal of Population Research, 38*(2), 139–167.

Erel, O., & Burman, B. (1995). Interrelatedness of marital relations and parent-child relations: A meta-analytic review. *Psychological Bulletin, 118*(1), 108–132.

Fukuda, S. (2020). Marriage will (continue to) be the key to the future of fertility in Japan and East Asia. *Vienna Yearbook of Population Research, 18*, 71–79.

Furstenberg, F. (2010). On a new schedule: Transitions to adulthood and family change. *Future Child, 20*(1), 67–87.

Gabardi, L., & Rosen, L. A. (1992). Intimate relationships: College students from divorced and intact families. *Journal of Divorce and Remarriage, 18*, 25–56.

Glick, J., Ruf, S., White, M., & Goldscheider, F. (2006). Educational engagement and early family formation: Differences by ethnicity and generation. *Social Forces, 84*(3), 1391–1415.

Goldscheider, F. K., & Goldscheider, C. (1998). The effects of childhood family structure on leaving and returning home. *Journal of Marriage and Family, 60*(3), 745–756.

Hines, A. M. (1997). Divorce-related transitions, adolescent development, and the role of the parent–child relationship: A review of the literature. *Journal of Marriage and Family, 59*(2), 375–388.

Hsu, L. K. (1948). *Under the ancestors' shadow: Chinese culture and personality.* New York, NY: Columbia University Press.

Hu, L.-C., & Chiang, Y.-L. (2021). Having children in a time of lowest-low fertility: Value of children, sex preference and fertility desire among Taiwanese young adults. *Child Indicators Research, 14*(2), 537–554.

Jones, G. (2005). The 'flight from marriage' in South-East and East Asia. *Journal of Comparative Family Studies, 36*(1), 93–119.

Jones, G. W., & Gubhaju, B. (2009). Factors influencing changes in mean age at first marriage and proportions never marrying in the low-fertility countries of East and Southeast Asia. *Asian Population Studies, 5*(3), 237–265.

Kalmijn, M. (1998). Intermarriage and homogamy: Causes, patterns, trends. *Annual Review of Sociology, 24*, 395–421.

Lesthaeghe, R. (1983). A century of demographic and cultural change in Western Europe: An exploration of underlying dimensions. *Population and Development Review, 9*(3), 411–435.

Lu, Y.-C., & Jou, Y.-H. (2015). The gender-role attitudes construction from adolescence to young adulthood in the 21th century's Taiwan. *Taiwanese Journal of Sociology, 58*, 95–155.

Meier, A., & Allen, G. (2008). Intimate relationship development during the transition to adulthood: Differences by social class. *New Directions for Child and Adolescent Development, 119*, 25–39.

Miller, B. C., McCoy, J. K., Olson, T. D., & Wallace, C. M. (1986). Parental discipline and control attempts in relation to adolescent sexual attitudes and behavior. *Journal of Marriage and Family*, *48*(3), 503–512.

Ministry of the Interior (Taiwan). (2020a). *Dataset of Population aged 15 and over by age, sex and marital status*. Retrieved 1 July 2020, from http://www.ris.gov.tw/app/portal/346

Ministry of the Interior (Taiwan). (2020b). *Dataset of Median age and mean age at marriage*. Retrieved 1 July 2020, from http://www.ris.gov.tw/app/portal/346

Moffitt, R. (2000). Female wages, male wages, and the economic model of marriage: The basic evidence. In L. Waite, C. Bacrach, M. Hindin, E. Thomson & A. Thornton (Eds.), *The ties that bind: Perspectives on marriage and cohabitation* (pp. 126–146). New York, NY: Aldine de Gruyter.

Ono, H. (2003). Women's economic standing, marriage timing, and cross-national contexts of gender. *Journal of Marriage and Family*, *65*(2), 275–286.

Oppenheimer, V. K. (1988). A theory of marriage timing. *American Journal of Sociology*, *94*(3), 563–591.

Oppenheimer, V. K., Kalmijn, M., & Lim, N. (1997). Men's career development and marriage timing during a period of rising inequality. *Demography*, *34*(3), 311–330.

Pan, E. (2014). Timing of parental divorce, marriage expectations, and romance in Taiwan. *Journal of Comparative Family Studies*, *45*(1), 77–92.

Park, H. (2013). The transition to adulthood among Korean youths. *The Annals of the American Academy of Political and Social Science*, *646*(1), 129–148.

Raymo, J., & Iwasawa, M. (2005). Marriage market mismatches in Japan: An alternative view of the relationship between women's education and marriage. *American Sociology Review*, *70*(5), 801–822.

South, S. J. (2001). The variable effects of family background on the timing of first marriage: United States, 1969–1993. *Social Science Research*, *30*(4), 606–626.

Strauss, A., & Corbin, J. (1998). *Basics of qualitative research: Techniques and procedures for developing grounded theory*. Los Angeles, CA: SAGE.

Sweeney, M. (2002). Two decades of family change: The shifting economic foundations of marriage. *American Sociological Review*, *67*(1), 132–147.

Tai, T.-O., Yi, C.-C., & Liu, C.-H. (2019). Early marriage in Taiwan: Evidence from panel data. *Journal of Family Issues*, *40*(14), 1989–2014.

Tasker, F., & Richards, M. (1994). Adolescents' attitudes toward marriage and marital prospects after parental divorce: A review. *Journal of Adolescent Research*, *9*(3), 340–362.

Thompson, L., & Walker, A. J. (1989). Gender in families: Women and men in marriage, work, and parenthood. *Journal of Marriage and Family*, *51*(4), 845–871.

Tsai, S.-L. (1994). Assortative mating in Taiwan. *Journal of Social Sciences and Philosophy*, *6*(2), 335–371.

Uecker, J. E., & Stokes, C. E. (2008). Early marriage in the United States. *Journal of Marriage and Family*, *70*(4), 835–846.

Waite, L. J., & Spitze, G. D. (1981). Young women's transition to marriage. *Demography*, *18*(4), 681–694.

Wallerstein, J. S., Lewis, J. M., & Blakeslee, S. (2000). *The unexpected legacy of divorce. A 25-year landmark study*. New York, NY: Hyperion.

Westley, S., Choe, M., & Retherford, R. (2010). Very low fertility in Asia: Is there a problem? Can it be solved?, *Asia Pacific Issues*, *94*, 1–12.

Wolfinger, N. (2003). Parental divorce and offspring marriage: Early or late?. *Social Forces*, *82*(1), 337–353.

Wu, M.-Y., & Yi, C.-C. (2003). A marriage is more than a marriage: The impacts of familial factors on marital satisfaction. *Journal of Population Studies*, *26*, 71–95.

Yang, C.-L. (2004). Fertility implication and estimate of cohabitation in Taiwan. *Taiwanese Journal of Sociology*, *32*, 189–213.

Yang, C.-L., Li, T.-C., & Chen, K.-J. (2006). Assortative mating in Taiwan: Changes and persistence. *Journal of Population Studies*, *33*, 1–32.

Yi, C.-C. (2013). Changing East Asian families: Values and behaviors. *International Sociology*, *28*(3), 253–256.

Yi, C.-C., & Chang, C.-F. (2019). Family and gender in Taiwan. In J. Liu & J. Yamashita (Eds.), *Routledge handbook of East Asian gender studies* (pp. 217–235). London: Routledge.

Yi, C.-C., & Jao, Y.-H. (2013). Bianqianzhong de zeouyujiatingjiazhiguan: Taiwan he xianggang de bijiao [Changing mate selection and family values: Comparing Taiwan and Hong Kong]. In W.-S. Yang & P.-S. Wan (Eds.), *Facing challenges: A comparison of Taiwan and Hong Kong* (pp. 97–134). Taipei: Institute of Sociology, Academia Sinica.

Yi, C.-C., Lin, W.-H., & Ma, K.-H. (2019). Marital satisfaction among Taiwanese young married couples: The importance of cultural norms. *Journal of Family Issues*, *40*(14), 2015–2043.

Appendix:

Table 3.4 Social demographic characteristics of interviewees

Marital status	Interviewee	Sex	Education	Family status	Cohabitation before marriage	Age of first marriage	First marriage year	Interview age
Pre-marital pregnancy	PM1	F	Incomplete Undergraduate		Y	23	2006	32
	PM2**	F	Undergraduate		Y	27	2014	28
	PM3	M	Junior High School	Father's death	Y	21	2007	30
	PM4	M	Incomplete College	Parental divorce	N	17	2003	26
	PM5	F	High School	Parents' death	Y	21	2008	25
	PM6	F	Incomplete Undergraduate		N	20	2004	28
	PM7	M	Incomplete High school		N	22	2006	28
	PM8	M	College		Y	24	2009	31
	PM9	M	High School	Father's death	Y	21	2006	31

(Continued)

Table 3.4 Social demographic characteristics of interviewees (Continued)

Marital status	Interviewee	Sex	Education	Family status	Cohabitation before marriage	Age of first marriage	First marriage year	Interview age
	PM10	F	Incomplete Undergraduate		N	21	2006	31
	PM11	F	Incomplete High school	Parental divorce	Y	24	2010	29
	PM12	F	High School	Parental divorce	Y	21	2008	29
	PM13	M	Junior High School	Father's death	Y	20	2007	29
	PM14	M	Undergraduate		Y	25	2011	31
Post-marital pregnancy	MB1**	M	Undergraduate		N	26	2013	29
	MB2**	F	Undergraduate		N	28	2014	30
	MB3	F	Incomplete High School		Y	25	2010	28
	MB4	F	Undergraduate		Y	25	2010	28
	MB5	M	Undergraduate		Y	25	2010	31
Married with no child	M1**	M	College		N	32	2019	32
	M2**	M	Undergraduate		N	29	2015	30
	M3**	M	College		Y	28	2015	30
	M4**	M	Postgraduate		Y	31	2018	31

ID	Gender	Education	Life event	Marriage Y/N	Age	Year	Age
M5	M	Postgraduate		N	23	2010	26
M6	F	College		Y	25	2011	29
M7	F	Postgraduate		Y	27	2011	31
M8	F	Undergraduate		Y	25	2010	31
M9	F	Postgraduate		Y	27	2011	32
M10	F	Incomplete Undergraduate	Father's death	N	22	2008	31
Unmarried							
S1	F	Undergraduate		Y			32
S2	F	Postgraduate					32
S3	F	College					32
S4	F	Postgraduate	Father's death				31
S5	M	Undergraduate					31
S6	M	Undergraduate					31
S7	M	High School		Y			31
S8	F	Postgraduate					30
S9	M	Postgraduate					31
S10	F	Undergraduate	Parental divorce				30
S11	M	Postgraduate					30
S12	M	Undergraduate					30

**Non-early married respondents, who got married after 2011.

Part III

From School-to-Work Transition:
The Entry to Job Market

4

Education-to-Work Transitions and Youth's Psychological Well-Being in Taiwan

Michael Gebel

Introduction

Across the globe, many youths experience a problematic education-to-work transition, particularly episodes of being not in employment, education or training (NEET). Even though youth unemployment is low in East Asia in worldwide comparison, youth joblessness still represents an urgent topic of social inequality as youths are more affected than prime-aged workers (ILO, 2017). This study focuses on Taiwan, which experienced an increase in youth unemployment over the last decades (Craig et al., 2019; Huang, 2013). After long periods of economic growth and a successful transition to a service economy, Taiwan suffered from economic turmoil in the 1990s. Despite a quick recovery after the 1997 financial crisis there was an increase in unemployment rates in the 2000s (Hsiao, 2013). For example, for 15–24-year-old Taiwanese, the unemployment rate increased from 5 per cent in the early 1990s to 11–15 per cent in the 2000s (National Statistics, Republic of China, 2020). Similarly, for 25–29-year-olds, there was an increase from 2 per cent to 5–8 per cent in the 2000s. After 2010 unemployment slightly declined again, particularly for 15–19-year-olds.

Against this background the question arises what the consequences of being NEET after leaving education are for the young persons who experience it. This has received limited attention in research on Taiwan despite the increasing prevalence of NEET (Chen, 2011). Specifically, this study investigates the consequences of being NEET for psychological well-being, which allows for building upon previous Taiwanese studies that investigated the relationships between education, non-employment and psychological well-being.

There is already much research on the consequences of non-employment for psychological well-being for the general working-age population (e.g. see the review of Paul and Moser, 2009). Studies also exist for Taiwan. For example, using data from the 1994 Taiwan Social Change Survey (TSCS), Tsou and Liu (2001) found for 20–64-year-old Taiwanese that past unemployment experience reduced subjective well-being, in terms of happiness and satisfaction, even after controlling for income, health and social contacts. Using survey data collected on Taiwanese aged 20 or over in 2012, Lin et al. (2014) found a negative association of unemployment with various measures subjective well-being. Drawing on TSCS2009 data, Tsai et al. (2016) showed that unemployment reduced subjective well-being even after controlling for income, debt and financial assistance from kin, friends and banks.

There are only few youth-specific studies (e.g. Högberg et al., 2019; Jongbloed and Giret, 2021). This applies especially to Taiwan, where studies on youth psychological well-being mainly focused on the situation in education. For example, using Taiwan Youth Project (TYP) data, Yi et al. (2009) discovered peaks in depressive symptoms in the last year before education tracking in junior and senior high school, what they related to the strong pressures to perform in the two competitive entrance exams. They also highlighted the relevance of family and school factors for differential growth curves of depressive symptoms. In a follow-up study, Yi et al. (2013) showed that educational tracking into general and vocational high school tracks affected youths' psychological development next to gender, family context and early school experiences. In contrast, also based on TYP data, Wang et al. (2018) found that education transitions had little impact as most youths kept a low level of depressive symptoms across junior and senior high school. So far, there is only one study on Taiwan that extended this research on education-to-work transitions. Based on TYP Sample J3, Huang and Chien (2013) investigated for 16–24-year-olds the effect of schooling, working, combining work and study, and NEET on mental disorder, physical disorder and sleep disorder using random effect models.

Building on this pioneering study our study makes the following contributions. Compared to Huang and Chien (2013) the sample is extended by investigating both TYP Samples J1 and J3 and including the three most recent TYP waves 2011, 2014 and 2017. This shifts the focus more to labour market experiences after leaving education because more education-to-work transitions could be observed. Our study focuses on the situation at the first interview after leaving education, which captures the short-term effects of being NEET versus having a job on psychological well-being, measured in terms of depressive symptoms, subjective health and happiness. But it should be already noted that our study neither looks at the duration of being NEET, nor at job quality or long-term effects. These possible extensions will be discussed later as avenues for future research. In terms of methodology a difference-in-differences approach combined with propensity score matching is applied, which eliminates individual fixed effects and common time trends that potentially biased results from previous studies using cross-sectional regression or random effects panel/growth curve models (Brüderl and Ludwig, 2015; Gangl, 2010). Though, it must be emphasized that our identification strategy also rests on assumptions that can be disputed. Another extension done in this study is the investigation of whether effects differ between gender, education and age groups, which should give some first insights into effect heterogeneities.

Theory and State of the Art

Leaving Education and Psychological Well-Being

The transition from education to work is a central stage in the individual life course, which is expected to have a substantial influence on the psychological well-being of young people (Arnett, 2000). From a theoretical perspective the expected effect of leaving education on well-being is ambiguous. Being enrolled in education may reduce well-being due to pressure to perform, the feeling of subordination and coercion as well as experiences of failure. This is documented especially for Taiwan, where exams play a crucial role for the education and work career because of credentialism and the emphasis on academic merit (Huang and Chien, 2013; Wang et al., 2018; Yi, 2013; Yi et al., 2009). Performance demands arise from parents, teachers and classmates. Taiwanese students also face exhaustion from long hours of study at school, additional cram school and home, which leaves little time for relaxation (Shih and Yi, 2014; Yi et al., 2009, 2013). When leaving education, school leavers are freed from these pressures and they can develop in the world of work by unfolding their talents, earning money and becoming more autonomous from their parental home. Accordingly, leaving education should increase psychological well-being.

On the other hand, entering the labour market may not run as smooth (Tsai, 1998). A problematic transition process may have detrimental effects on subjective well-being. Previous literature on subjective well-being showed that it is particularly relevant to investigate whether education leavers become NEET or are able to get a job (Jongbloed and Giret, 2021). In the following, the important distinction of being NEET versus having a job after leaving education is considered in detail.

The Effect of Being NEET Versus Having a Job on Psychological Well-Being

Synthesizing and extending previous theoretical models such as the one of Jahoda (1981) and Fryer (1986), Nordenmark and Strandh (1999) highlight the economic and psychosocial rewards of employment. Becoming NEET induces a loss of economic rewards in terms of income, which requires young people to adjust their standard of living and which also restricts their control over their own situation and ability to plan ahead (Strandh, 2000). This may act as a stressor negatively affecting youths' psychological well-being. Joblessness is also thought to deprive individuals of psychosocial (i.e. non-monetary) rewards. Next to the loss of psychosocial rewards there might be psychological impairment due to the social stigma of being non-employed.

How are these mechanisms expected to be moderated by the specific societal context of Taiwan? In the Taiwanese society, where employment is the norm and represents the main source of income, work is central to individuals' identity and participation in society. Accordingly, the loss of psychosocial rewards should be particularly strong in Taiwan, which should intensify the negative effects of being NEET on psychological well-being. Furthermore, comparative research suggests that in countries characterized by education systems with tracking, a high share of vocational schools and low track mobility, such as Taiwan (Yi et al., 2013), the capabilities of youth unemployed to control their situation and, hence, their psychological well-being may be lowered (Högberg et al., 2019). Moreover, comparative research showed that in countries with limited welfare provision for jobless people, such as in Taiwan (Yu and Chiu, 2014), the negative effects of unemployment on well-being effects are expected to be stronger (Voßemer et al., 2018).

In contrast, there are also arguments why the negative effects of being NEET on psychological well-being should be less severe in Taiwan. Comparative research showed that the well-being gap between NEET and employed youth is relatively small in welfare regimes, in which support is largely given by the family (Jongbloed and Giret, 2021). This is expected to apply also to Taiwan because Taiwan is characterized by a familistic welfare regime with liberal elements, in which the family substitutes the state by providing support for their off-springs in need (Ochiai, 2009). In this regard, previous research on Taiwan found that financial assistance from kin moderates the negative effect of indebtedness on well-being and health (Tsai et al., 2016). However, even if the family can compensate the loss of economic rewards, the feeling of economic dependence may put psychological pressures on young people (Yi, 2013).

Furthermore, in the Taiwanese context the negative effect of NEET might be mitigated by the activation turn of labour market policies and deregulation of the labour market that aimed at a faster reintegration of unemployed into work via activation measures (Kim and Shi, 2020). Moreover, deteriorating youth labour market conditions in Taiwan might have weakened employment rewards. Yu and Chiu (2014) found a decline in first occupational attainment in Taiwan over cohorts. There was also an increase in nonstandard and precarious work, which has low pay. For the whole working population, Hsiao (2013) reported that narrowly defined nonstandard employment such as part-time work, fixed-term work, and dispatched workers quadrupled from 2.3 per cent in 2001 to 8.8 per cent in 2010. But also informal and self-employment/own-account work forms, which can also be categorized as nonstandard and precarious work, are common in Taiwan (Hsiao, 2013). As in other countries, it can be expected that particularly young people are affected by nonstandard and precarious work.

Also theoretically, one could derive a general counterargument based on theories of job search and the conception of emerging adulthood (Arnett, 2000). Accordingly, being NEET after leaving education is seen as integrative part of the formative and explorative early labour market career, which should not harm psychological well-being. It is often argued that the negative effects of non-employment are stronger in mid-life when responsibilities and financial obligations are higher due to parenting (Broomhall and

Winefield, 1990), which is often postponed beyond the education-to-work transition period in Taiwan (Chen and Chen, 2014). One may also argue that the negative effects of NEET on psychological well-being are less pronounced among young people as being NEET is quite common after leaving education and a shared experience of peers, which should reduce the stigmatization.

Research Design

Data and Sample

Data from all twelve waves of the TYP2000–2017 were used (for a description, see, Yi, 2013). Both cohorts J1 (first year junior high school students, ~13-year-old in 2000) and J3 (third year junior high school students, ~15-years-old in 2000) were investigated. The TYP offers panel data for nine waves that were conducted in roughly one-year intervals in the period 2000–2009.[1] Wave 10 followed in 2011, i.e. two years after Wave 9. Waves 11 and 12 were conducted in a three-year cycle in 2014 and 2017.

It is often emphasized that it is difficult to define the education-to-work transition as the labour market entry process has become less clear (Arnett, 2000). However, this problem is less severe in Taiwan because rates of returning to education are relatively low and youth usually complete education before entering the labour market (Yu and Chiu, 2014). The process of leaving education was reconstructed based on the information that was provided at the date of every interview.[2] For every wave, it was determined whether the respondents still attended education or not (see Table 4.1). Our definition of attending education includes all kind of formal education, including vocational school, college and university education. Cram school and military service were also counted as education like in previous Taiwanese studies (Yu and Chiu, 2014). Students combining education with part-time work were defined as being in education because the focus of this paper is on the first job after leaving education and not on an evaluation of the combination of study and work.

Leaving education is defined when a person was in education at $t - 1$ but not in education at t. No restrictions were imposed on the time after t because the focus was on the immediate effects of the transition process. The gap between $t - 1$ and t was allowed to be up to three years long, which correspondents to the gap between Waves 10–12. For

Table 4.1 Illustration of sample and treatment definition

	$t - 1$	t
Sample definition	In education	Not in education (for the 1st time)
Treatment group definition		No job
Control group definition		job

Notes: The sample definition applies both for the treatment and the control group. No sample conditions imposed for periods after *t*.
Source: Own illustration.

consistency reasons, gaps of up to three years were also allowed for Waves 1–9 if there was missing information. As the transition process from education to work is not linear and some persons return to education, there were a few multiple events of leaving education observed for one person. In order to create harmonized analysis the analyses were restricted to the first event of leaving education for each person.

Overall 3,522 first entrants (J1: 1,660 persons; J3: 1,862 persons) into the labour market were observed. Around 12 per cent of these persons entered the labour market at age 18 or younger.[3] 27 per cent were aged 18 or 19 and 6 per cent were aged 20 or 22. A great proportion (39 per cent) entered the labour market at ages 23 to 25. The remaining 16 per cent of labour market entrants were 26 years old or older when leaving education for the first time.

Treatment Variable

For the sample of first-time education leavers the treatment group is defined as being NEET at *t* (see Table 4.1). Next to unemployed youth this includes the group of inactive youth, i.e. persons not actively seeking for a job. This broader definition is seen as an advantage compared to the narrow unemployment definition but it has also the drawback of resulting in a rather heterogeneous group (Chen, 2011). Unfortunately, TYP data do not allow a clear differentiation of NEET subgroups across all waves. For that reason and reasons of sample size we analyse NEET as one group.

For the sample of first-time education leavers the control group is defined as having a job at *t* (see Table 4.1). This includes employment, self-employment and work in the family business. Whereas in Waves 1–9 there were no restrictions, i.e. including job of any duration and working hours, the questionnaires of Waves 10–12 restricted the definition of a job to paid work of more than 15 hours each week for more than four months. Unfortunately, it was not possible to fully harmonize the definition of the first job because there is no information on job duration in Waves 1–9 and because working time information was only collected starting in Wave 5 (Sample J3)/Wave 6 (Sample J1). However, we tried to address the issue of working time, differentiating between part-time and full-time work, in terms of subgroup analyses.

Descriptive analysis of the analytical sample show that 26 per cent of labour market entrants were NEET and 74 per cent had a job at the first interview after leaving education for the first time. The NEET share is much higher than in official statistics because the latter includes NEET irrespectively of the timing of leaving education. In contrast, this study focuses on NEET at the very beginning of the labour market career, when the NEET incidence is usually the highest.

Outcome Variables

This study considers various measures of psychological well-being. This should account for the complexity of the concept of psychological well-being as much as possible given the available longitudinal measures in the TYP data. Three outcome variables were considered:

1. Index of depressive symptoms: Adopted from the short version of the Symptom Checklist-90-Revised (SCL-90-R) (Derogatis, 1986) the TYP data contain an item battery of depressive symptoms (Yi et al., 2013). We focused on seven items (5-point-intensity scales) that were most often available: headaches, loneliness, depressed mood, insomnia, feeling numb or punctured in certain parts of the body, feeling congestion in the throat, and weakness in certain parts of the body. A mean index of all the items that were available in a wave was created. It ranges from 1 to 5, with higher values indicating higher levels of depression.
2. Self-rated health: It can be seen as a general health measure, capturing not only the psychological health but also a self-assessment of physical health.
3. Happiness: In contrast to the cognitive component of well-being (i.e. global judgements of life satisfaction), happiness represents a positive affective component of well-being (Diener et al., 1999). Studies show for Taiwan that both components are correlated but conceptually different (Tsou and Liu, 2001). The TYP offers a longitudinal measure of happiness only.

Both the health and the happiness scale were normalized to a 0-to-1-scale to account for different answer scales (4-point scale versus 5-point scale) in different TYP waves. Higher values on the scale mean better health/higher happiness.

Changes in outcomes between $t - 1$ and t were analysed. Analyses were restricted to the waves in which information on the respective outcome measure were available, which resulted in different sample sizes for the three outcome variables. The sample size declined from 3,522 to 3,156 for depression (Wave 5 missing for Sample J3), to 2,709 for health (Wave 4 missing for Sample J1, Waves 2–4 missing for Sample J3) and to 1,619 for happiness (Waves 4, 8 missing for Sample J1, Waves 2, 3, 4, 6, 7 missing for Sample J3).

Method: Difference-in-Differences Propensity-Score Matching (DID-PSM)

A Difference-In-Differences Propensity Score Matching (DID-PSM) design was applied (Heckman et al., 1997). This is theoretically rooted in the potential outcome framework that defines, both for the treatment ($D = 1$) and control group ($D = 0$), two potential outcomes at each time point (Y^0, Y^1), of which one is observed and one is unobserved/counterfactual (Rubin, 2005).

According to the Difference-In-Differences (DID) approach (Lechner, 2011), the Average Treatment Effect on the Threated (ATT), i.e. the effect of being NEET for the group of NEET, is identified by comparing the change in well-being $E(Y_t^1 - Y_{t-1}^0 | D = 1)$ of the treatment group between period $t - 1$ and t to the counterfactual trend in well-being $E(Y_t^0 - Y_{t-1}^0 | D = 1)$ they would have hypothetically experienced if they had found a job. According to the common baseline trend assumption this counterfactual trend is approximated by the actual change in the well-being $E(Y_t^0 - Y_{t-1}^0 | D = 0)$ of the control group. Changes are measured at the individual level as individual panel data are available. These within-person comparisons eliminate unobserved individual fixed effects. Further, the between-comparison with the trend of a control group additionally removes common time trends (e.g. period or ageing effects) that affect the treatment and control group in the same way.

To make the common baseline trend assumption more plausible, the control group in the DID design was formed via Propensity Score

Matching (PSM) (Gangl, 2015) using the Stata ado kmatch (Jann, 2017). Similarity was measured in terms of the propensity score $P(D = 1/X)$, estimated in a logistic regression, which measures the probability of being NEET versus getting a job after leaving education, conditional on a set of control variables X. A common support condition was imposed to guarantee that there is overlap of the range of propensity scores between the treatment and control group. Applying several algorithms produced rather consistent results, yet Epanechnikov kernel matching (bandwidth: 0.02) was chosen as it showed the best balancing properties. Standard errors were bootstrapped with 1,000 repetitions because there are no analytical standard errors for kernel matching and because recent research showed that bootstrapping performs rather well (Bodory et al., 2020).

Control Variables

It should be noted that, compared to cross-sectional estimators or random effects panel/growth curve models, DID-PSM is not subject to the usual confounding bias because the within-comparison elimi-nates individual effects (Brüderl and Ludwig, 2015; Gangl, 2010). Control variables X are only needed that are expected to influence both changes in well-being and employment transitions in order to make the common baseline trend assumption more plausible. These variables were measured before the treatment (at $t - 1$) in order to avoid overcontrol bias (Elwert and Winship, 2014). Following Lechner (2011), we did not condition on the pre-treatment outcome itself, as that might induce an endogenous selection bias by conditioning on a collider (Elwert and Winship, 2014).

Specifically, we controlled for age (in a quadratic form) and gender, which is expected to influence employment (Sakaguchi, 2016) and well-being trajectories (Yi et al., 2013). We accounted for the sample affiliation (J1 vs. J3) to capture sample-related differences. We addressed prevailing regional differences and the multistage-stratified clustering of data collection by controlling for the three sample regions Taipei City, Taipei County and Yilan County (Yi, 2013).

Parental background, which is assumed to be relevant for labour market success (Tsai, 1998) and well-being trajectories (Yi et al., 2009, 2013) was measured by various variables that were collected when the respondent was around 15 years old (Wave 1 of Sample J3; Wave 3 of

Sample J1, if missing, information from Wave 2 or Wave 1 was used). Three levels of parents' highest education level were distinguished as a measure of cultural capital: (1) low: no parents, never received formal education, elementary education or junior high school; (2) medium: senior high school, vocational senior high school; (3) high: junior college, university or graduate school. Four group dummies of parents' highest occupation position, accounting for social capital were included: (i) legislators, senior officials, managers, professionals (ISCO major groups 1 + 2); (ii) technicians, associate professionals, clerks (ISCO major groups 3 + 4); (iii) service, shop, market sales workers (ISCO major group 5); (iv) skilled agricultural fishery, craft and related trades workers, plant and machine operators and assemblers, elementary occupations (ISCO major groups 6–9), armed forces and non-employed parents. As a measure of economic capital parents' average monthly income was included, grouped into the three categories low income (<50,000 TWD), medium income (50,000–90,000 TWD) and high income (>90,000 TWD). The number of siblings were incorporated as a measure for resource competition in the family of origin.

Family intactness was included, distinguishing (i) whether respondents lived with two parents, (ii) whether one parent deceased or (iii) whether the parents divorced or were separated. Family cohesion was measured based on questions on family-level cohesive behaviour (Yi et al., 2009, 2013). Six statements with 4-point answer scale were combined in a mean index, with a higher value representing higher cohesion: (i) 'Family members discuss matters with each other before making a decision', (ii) 'Family members like to spend their free time together', (iii) 'Every family member participates in family activities', (iv) 'Family members accept each other's friends', (v) 'I can get comfort from my family when I experience setbacks in life', and (vi) 'I can rely on my family when I need help or advice'.

The last level of education attainment as an important determinant of employment (Tsai, 1998; Tsai and Xie, 2008) and well-being trajectories (Yi et al., 2013) was differentiated into the categories junior/senior high school, vocational high school, junior college, technical college and university.

Finally, time-varying binary indicators for being married and for having children in the post-treatment period were incorporated. This should account for potential confounding by family formation. These are the only two control variables that were measured in the post-treatment period to account for the anticipatory nature of family formation. This bears the risk of overcontrol bias if the labour market entry process affects family formation and not vice versa. However, sensitivity checks confirmed that the results did not substantially differ when excluding the potentially endogenous control variables.

Listwise deletion was applied for missing control variables, which further slightly reduced the sample size from 3,156 to 2,954 for depression, from 2,709 to 2,558 for health and from 1,619 to 1,538 for happiness.

Empirical Results

Descriptive Statistics and Balancing of Control Variables

Table 4.2 shows the balancing of control variables before and after matching. The unmatched comparison also provides bivariate

Table 4.2 Descriptive statistics and balancing of control variables

	Before matching			After matching		
	Treated (NEET)	**Control (job)**	**% Bias**	**Treated (NEET)**	**Control (job)**	**% Bias**
Age	19.21	20.97	−62.5	19.24	19.21	1.0
Age squared	376.63	447.72	−62.1	377.60	376.96	0.6
Female	0.40	0.52	−23.7	0.41	0.38	4.5
Sample J1	0.48	0.55	−13.3	0.48	0.49	−1.2
Region						
Taipei City	0.35	0.35	−0.3	0.35	0.34	1.8
Taipei County	0.41	0.39	3.9	0.41	0.40	0.7
Yilan	0.25	0.26	−4.0	0.25	0.26	−2.8
Parental education						
Low	0.33	0.34	−2.8	0.33	0.34	−2.4
Medium	0.41	0.41	0.1	0.42	0.41	1.0
High	0.26	0.25	2.9	0.25	0.25	1.5
Parental occupation						
ISCO 1–2	0.25	0.25	0.4	0.25	0.24	1.5
ISCO 3–4	0.23	0.23	−0.8	0.23	0.22	2.1
ISCO 5	0.20	0.23	−7.2	0.20	0.21	−1.2
ISCO 6–9, armed forces, inactive	0.31	0.28	6.9	0.31	0.32	−2.2

Table 4.2 Descriptive statistics and balancing of control variables (Continued)

	Before matching			After matching		
	Treated (NEET)	**Control (job)**	**% Bias**	**Treated (NEET)**	**Control (job)**	**% Bias**
Parental income						
Low	0.40	0.42	−3.6	0.40	0.41	−2.3
Medium	0.43	0.40	7.4	0.43	0.42	2.4
High	0.17	0.18	−4.9	0.17	0.17	0.0
Number of siblings	1.65	1.72	−7.3	1.66	1.68	−2.4
Family intactness						
Two parents reside together	0.90	0.89	4.5	0.90	0.90	0.6
One parent deceased	0.03	0.03	−3.7	0.03	0.03	−0.1
Parents divorced/ separated	0.07	0.08	−2.9	0.07	0.07	−0.6
Family cohesion	2.81	2.86	−8.0	2.82	2.81	1.4
Last level of education attainment						
Junior/senior high school	0.23	0.08	41.4	0.23	0.22	1.4
Vocational high school	0.21	0.14	17.1	0.21	0.23	−4.7
Junior college	0.07	0.05	11.2	0.08	0.08	−2.5
Technical college	0.21	0.28	−17.1	0.21	0.20	3.3
University	0.28	0.44	−35.1	0.28	0.27	1.0
Being married (at t)	0.02	0.02	−2.1	0.02	0.02	0.1
Having a child (at t)	0.01	0.01	−1.9	0.01	0.01	0.9
N	721	2,233		716[a]	2,232[b]	

Notes: Exemplified for the analytical sample for the outcome variable 'index of depression symptoms'. Means are displayed in the first two columns of each panel. In the third column of each panel, % bias denotes the standardized percentage bias, defined for each control variable as the difference in means normalized by the square root of the averaged variances (Gangl, 2015).
[a] 5 treated excluded after matching due to no common support.
[b] 1 control excluded after matching due to no common support.
Source: TYP2000−2017; own calculations.

descriptive statistics describing the composition of the treatment (NEET) and control group (job). The balancing in Table 4.2 is displayed for the sample of the outcome 'index of depression symptoms', which had the largest sample size. The balancing was also checked for the smaller samples of other outcome variables but it is not reported due to space restrictions.

For example, the mean age was much lower in the treatment group (19.21 years) than in the unmatched control group (20.97 years) before matching (Table 4.2, left panel). This resulted in a mean standardized bias of −62.5 per cent. Via matching (Table 4.2, right panel), this difference was substantially reduced to a mean standardized bias of 1.0 per cent because the treated and the matched controls had on average almost an equal age (treated: 19.24 years; matched controls: 19.21 years). Just 40 per cent of the NEET were women compared to 52 per cent women among the first job holders. This resulted in a mean standardized bias of −23.7 per cent before matching, which decreased to 4.5 per cent after matching.

In the following, we briefly highlight the major differences in mean values of the control variables between treatment and control group before matching. Compared to the control group of first job holders, persons who became NEET were more likely to be younger, male and from Sample J3. There is not much variation in the geographical origins showing that the regional differences are of limited importance for the chances of getting a job instead of becoming a NEET.

Interestingly, NEET and jobholders had rather similar characteristics of the family of origin in terms of parental highest level of education and occupation, parental income, number of siblings, family intactness and family cohesion. This shows a limited influence of the parental background on the probability of finding a job directly after leaving education in Taiwan.

There were strong differences in terms of the education background of the respondents. Students from junior/senior high school, vocational high school and junior college tended to be overrepresented among NEET, whereas students from technical college and university college were overrepresented among job holders. Despite strong educational expansion in Taiwan (Huang and Chien, 2013), receiving higher education still generates relative advantages in finding a first job. The finding that vocational high school graduates were overrepresented among NEET is in line with previous research that highlighted that vocational education does little in easing the education-to-work transition (Yu and Chiu, 2014), which is related to the limited links between vocational schools and businesses in Taiwan (Tsai, 1998). However, it should be noted that vocational high school students still performed relatively better than the lowest educated group of junior/senior high school students. There were no substantial difference in the experience of own family formation (being married or presence of children) at labour market entry between the two groups.

After matching (Table 4.2, right panel), the mean standardized bias (in per cent) was below the threshold of 5 per cent for all control variables, which is often seen as the standard in matching analysis (Gangl, 2015). Imposing the common support condition only led to the exclusion of few persons.

The Effects of NEET on Depressive Symptoms, Health and Happiness

Figure 4.1(a)–(c) visualize the DID-PSM results for all three outcomes and Table 4.3(a)–(c) provides detailed estimation results. At $t - 1$, i.e. at the last interview before leaving education, the treatment group (i.e. those who were NEET at t) already had a slightly higher average mean index of depressive symptoms (1.542) compared to the matched control group (i.e. those who had a job at t) (1.510) (see Figure 4.1(a)). The difference between the two values (Coef. $= 0.032$, $p = 0.267$) represents the cross-sectional matching estimator at $t - 1$ (see Table 4.3(a)). A similar group difference was obtained at t. Those who were NEET at t had on average depressive symptoms of 1.482 compared to 1.449 for those who had a job at t (see Figure 4.1(a)). Again, the difference between the two groups (Coef. $= 0.033$, $p = 0.238$) is the cross-sectional matching estimator at t (see Table 4.3(a)). Interestingly, both groups had a small and statistically significant decline in depressive symptoms. After leaving education the persons who become NEET at t had a decline in the depression index (Coef. $= -0.059$, $p = 0.023$). The decline is almost the same in the matched control group of persons who find a job at t (Coef. $= -0.061$, $p = 0.002$). Both comparisons are equivalent to a before-after estimator, which takes a 'within'-comparative perspective that eliminates individual fixed effects. Hence, leaving education slightly improves the depressive symptoms, irrespectively of having found a job or being

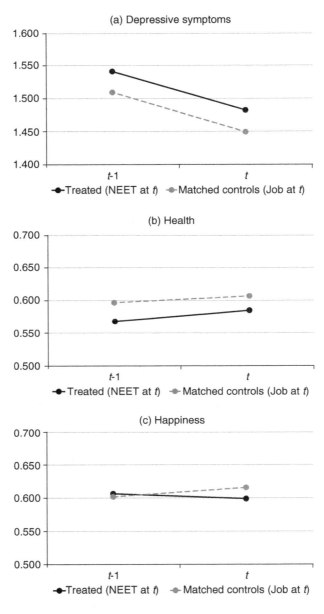

Figure 4.1 Outcome trajectories of treatment and matched control group. *Notes:* When comparing Figure (a) to Figures (b) and (c) the different scaling of outcome variables and zooming of the vertical axes should be taken into account. Number of cases: (a) Depressive symptoms ($N_{Treated} = 716$, $N_{Controls} = 2,232$); (b) Health ($N_{Treated} = 552$, $N_{Controls} = 1,999$); (c) Happiness ($N_{Treated} = 234$, $N_{Controls} = 1,275$)
Source: TYP2000–2017; own calculations.

Table 4.3 The effects of NEET on depressive symptoms, health and happiness

	Coef.	b.s.e.	z-statistic	p-value
(a) Depressive symptoms $(N_{Treated} = 716, N_{Controls} = 2,232)$				
Cross-sectional matching estimator at $t - 1$	0.032	0.028	1.110	0.267
Cross-sectional matching estimator at t	0.033	0.028	1.180	0.238
Before-after estimator for treated (t vs. $t - 1$)	−0.059	0.026	−2.270	0.023
Before-after estimator for matched controls (t vs. $t - 1$)	−0.061	0.020	−3.070	0.002
DID-PSM estimator	**0.002**	**0.033**	**0.050**	**0.962**
(b) Health $(N_{Treated} = 552, N_{Controls} = 1,999)$				
Cross-sectional matching estimator at $t - 1$	−0.028	0.012	−2.400	0.017
Cross-sectional matching estimator at t	−0.021	0.012	−1.800	0.072
Before-after estimator for treated (t vs. $t - 1$)	0.016	0.012	1.400	0.161
Before-after estimator for matched controls (t vs. $t - 1$)	0.009	0.009	1.010	0.312
DID-PSM estimator	**0.007**	**0.014**	**0.520**	**0.603**
(c) Happiness $(N_{Treated} = 234, N_{Controls} = 1,275)$				
Cross-sectional matching estimator at $t - 1$	0.003	0.017	0.170	0.865
Cross-sectional matching estimator at t	−0.017	0.018	−0.940	0.349
Before-after estimator for treated (t vs. $t - 1$)	−0.007	0.016	−0.430	0.670
Before-after estimator for matched controls (t vs. $t - 1$)	0.013	0.013	1.000	0.317
DID-PSM estimator	**−0.020**	**0.020**	**−0.990**	**0.324**

Notes: Coef.=coefficient; b.s.e.= bootstrapped standard error. The cross-sectional matching estimator at $t - 1$ is equal to the difference in outcomes between the treated and matched controls at t. The cross-sectional matching estimator at $t - 1$ is equal to the difference in outcomes between the treated and matched controls at $t - 1$. The before-after estimator for the treated is equal to the outcome at t minus the outcome at $t - 1$ for the treated. The before-after estimator for the treated is equal to the outcome at t minus the outcome at $t - 1$ for the matched controls. The DID-PSM estimator is described in the Section 'Method' in detail.
Source: TYP2000–2017; own calculations.

NEET at the first interview after leaving education. The difference in the group-specific changes in depression index yields the ATT based on the DID-PSM estimator (Coef. = 0.002; p = 0.962). Thus, according to our DID-PSM estimator we do not find evidence that becoming NEET after leaving education has an effect on depressive symptoms. The difference in the temporal changes of depressive for the two groups is statistically insignificant and very small in magnitude.

In terms of subjective health it can be seen in Figure 4.1 (b) that there was a mean difference in subjective health at t, i.e. at the first interview after leaving education. Among the NEET the subjective health is 0.585 and lower than the subjective health of the matched control group, i.e. those who found a job at t (0.606). The mean difference represents the cross-sectional matching estimator at t (Coef. = -0.021, p = 0.072) (see Table 4.3(b)). The difference is small in size. From a cross-sectional perspective, we would conclude that being NEET slightly reduces the subjective health. However, when taking the pre-treatment period $t-1$ into account we can see that a similar difference already existed between the two groups prior to leaving education. At $t-1$, i.e. the last interview before leaving education, the treatment group has on average a subjective health of 0.568, which is lower than the value of the matched control group (0.597). This is equivalent to a cross-sectional estimator of -0.028 (p = 0.017) at $t-1$. Thus, the mean difference that is observed at t can be fully attributed to the pre-existing health differences of the two groups. Across time, one can observe an increase in subjective health for both groups. Those who become NEET at t experienced an increase in subjective health (Coef. = 0.016, p = 0.161) and those who get a job at t also experience an increase in subjective health (Coef. = 0.009, p = 0.312). But increases in health are small and not statistically significant. As the change over time is very similar for the two groups the DID-PSM estimator for the ATT is very small and statistically insignificant (Coef. = 0.007, p = 0.603). Thus, according to our DID-PSM estimator we do not find evidence that becoming NEET after leaving education has an effect on subjective health. This finding underlines the importance of implementing the longitudinal design via the DID-PSM because the cross-sectional PSM at t would give the wrong impression that being NEET reduces subjective health.

In terms of happiness, Figure 4.1(c) shows that both groups had almost an identical level of happiness at the last interview before leaving education at $t - 1$ (treated: 0.607; controls: 0.604). Therefore, the cross-sectional matching estimator is very small at $t - 1$ (Coef. = 0.003, $p = 0.865$) (Table 4.3(c)). Over time there were slightly divergent trends in the level of happiness (see Figure 4.1(c)). Becoming NEET reduced the mean value of the happiness indicator from 0.607 at $t - 1$ to 0.600 at t. In contrast, the matched control group, i.e. persons getting a job, experienced a slight increase in the level of happiness from 0.604 at t to 0.617. However, both before-after estimators are small and statistically insignificant (treated: Coef. = −0.007, $p = 0.670$; matched controls: Coef. = 0.013, $p = 0.317$). The DID-PSM estimator for the ATT, which is the difference in between the two before-after estimators, yielded a small and statistically insignificant effect of −0.020 points ($p = 0.324$). Thus, according to our DID-PSM estimator we do not find evidence that becoming NEET after leaving education has an effect on happiness.

Subgroup-Specific Analyses

One concern could be that the analyses included both part-time and full-time workers. Therefore, we conducted sensitivity analyses in which we excluded part-time workers from the control group such that there was only the comparison between NEET and full-time workers. Part-time work was defined as working less than 40 hours[4] (including overtime work) based on working time information that was available since Wave 6 (Sample J1) and Wave 5 (Sample J3). Persons with a job but with missing information on working time were excluded from the analyses. Overall, just around 11 per cent of the first jobs with working time information were part-time jobs. This is in line with previous studies that found a relatively low share of part-time work in Taiwan (Hsiao, 2013; Yu, 2009). Table 4.4 shows that the DID-PSM results based on the full sample (including both part-timers and full-timers in the control group) and the DID-PSM results based on the full-timers as a control group do not substantially differ. The effects are still small in size and statistically insignificant when focusing on the contrast between NEET and full-time workers.

Based on various theoretical arguments, it could be expected that the effects of being NEET versus having a job on psychological well-being varies between subgroups. This section will give some first insights into this topic of effect heterogeneity. Due to the limited

Table 4.4   Subgroup-specific effects of NEET, DID-PSM results

	(a) Depressive symptoms		(b) Health		(c) Happiness	
	ATT	p-value	ATT	p-value	ATT	p-value
Definition of work						
Full sample	0.002	0.962	0.007	0.603	−0.020	0.324
Excluding part-timers	−0.046	0.299	0.012	0.431	−0.008	0.696
Gender						
Men	−0.063	0.145	−0.008	0.703	−0.003	0.900
Women	0.076	0.194	0.023	0.326	−0.045	0.284
Education						
Low educated	−0.001	0.991	−0.058	0.061	−0.072	0.179
High educated	−0.018	0.689	0.022	0.200	0.005	0.822
Age (at t)						
≤22 years old	−0.021	0.644	−0.032	0.218	−0.041	0.449
>22 years old	−0.009	0.836	0.028	0.108	0.016	0.443

Notes: ATT= Average Treatment Effect on the Treated (as estimated by DID-PSM).
Source: TYP2000–2017; own calculations.

sample size and the specific demands of the DID-PSM approach, this analysis was restricted to binary comparisons. The DID-PSM approach was implemented separately for each group. This stratified approach yields the highest flexibility because each parameter is allowed to vary across subgroups. It also guarantees that matched pairs are only formed within one group and not across groups as it happens when estimating one joint model. The focus is on differences in gender, education and age as three major lines of social stratification and inequality.

Theoretically, one may argue that men and high educated persons are more negatively affected by being NEET (versus having a job) than women and low educated persons. This is because men and high educated persons are privileged in the labour market and, thus, may have more economic rewards to loose when being NEET. Furthermore, individual and societal expectation might be higher such that 'failure' in the labour market may entail a stronger loss of psychological rewards for men and high educated persons. In contrast, one may also expect the reverse relation in terms of women and low educated being more affected by being NEET. For them, the NEET status might be a more enduring phenomenon and more difficult to gain employment. One may also assume that effects differ by age as age is strongly related to the education such that the previous arguments on the moderating role of education apply. Another argument might be that younger NEET are less negatively affected because they may have still better support by their family of origin. In addition, the experience of being NEET might be seen as part of the early working career of young education leavers, whereas such an event might be more critical to young people who spent many years in education.

Overall, Table 4.4 shows that 17 out of the 18 subgroup-specific effects for gender, education and age were statistically insignificant and that all effect sizes are small. Effects were rather similar for men and for women with regard to health and happiness. There was just the tendency in the point estimates that becoming NEET increased depressive symptoms for women (Coef. $= 0.076$, $p = 0.194$) but decreased it for men (Coef. $= -0.063$, $p = 0.145$). The small difference in the opposing effects was statistically significant at the 5 per cent level ($p = 0.049$ for test of equality of coefficients). Point estimates for depressive symptoms were quite similar for both education groups. But point estimates showed for low-educated negative effects of NEET on health (Coef. $= -0.058$, $p = 0.061$) and happiness (Coef. $= -0.072$, $p = 0.179$) in contrast to small positive effects for high educated (health: Coef. $= 0.022$, $p = 0.200$; happiness: Coef. $= 0.005$, $p = 0.822$). Likewise, rather similar patterns were found for age, with younger ones showing stronger and negative point estimates for health and happiness but all of them being small size and statistical insignificance.

Conclusions

Based on TYP data we investigated how becoming NEET compared to having a first job after leaving education for the first time is related to youth's psychological well-being, measured in terms of depressive symptoms, subjective health and happiness.

Our descriptive analyses showed that around one quarter labour market entrants were NEET at the first interview after leaving education for the first time. This high share of NEET could be explained by the study focus on the very beginning of the labour market career, at which the NEET incidence is usually the highest. Compared to the control group of first job holders, persons who became NEET at the beginning of their labour market career were on average more likely to be younger, male and lower educated students. On average, NEET and first jobholders did not differ much in characteristics of their family of origin, such as parental education, occupation, income, family intactness and family cohesion as well as own family formation.

DID-PSM analyses did not show any statistically significant average effects of becoming a NEET versus having a job on depressive symptoms, subjective health and happiness at the first interview after leaving education. It should be mentioned that the sample of NEET was relatively small for the health and especially the happiness analysis. However, it should be noted that next to statistical insignificance the effect sizes were also very small. Overall, it seems like the binary distinction of being NEET or having a job after leaving education is, on average, not of great relevance for depressive symptoms, subjective health and happiness when investigating the immediate effects at the first interview date after leaving education for the first time. This conclusion is limited to the contemporaneous effects because only the situation at the first interview after leaving education was investigated, which does not allow any conclusions about potential medium or long-term effects and the effects of further career dynamics that may take place afterwards. This conclusion is also limited to the average effect of the binary distinction of being NEET versus having a job at the first interview after leaving education for the first time. This ignores any kind of potential heterogeneity of the treatment or the counterfactual situation.

An interesting side finding of this study was that the event of leaving education slightly decreased on average the level of depressive symptoms for education leavers in Taiwan, irrespective of being NEET or having a job at the first interview after leaving education for the first time. This fits well to previous findings that highlighted the strong psychological pressures in the Taiwanese education system due to strong performance demands and exhaustion from long hours of study at school, additional cram school and at home (Shih and Yi, 2014; Yi et al., 2009, 2013). Similarly, there was an increase in the subjective health for both groups when leaving education. But the increase was small and not statistically significant.

Subgroup-specific analyses confirmed that the results were not due the inclusion of part-time workers. Also when comparing NEET to full-time first job holders there were no substantially or statistically significant effects of being NEET on the psychological well-being. Likewise, despite one exception, we did not find any statistically significant effect of NEET on psychological well-being for any gender, education or age group we considered. However, it should be noted that sample sizes of the treatment group in the subgroup-specific analyses were low, particularly in the case of health and happiness. Hence, we like to mention that our findings indicated the tendency in the point estimates that becoming NEET slightly increased depressive symptoms particularly for women and reduced health and happiness particularly for low-educated and for younger persons. The negative NEET effect on health was statistically significant for the low-educated persons.

Next to the mentioned problem of small sample sizes in some analyses, we would like to emphasize further limitations of our study and outline ideas for future research. First, our results should not be interpreted as the true causal effects. Our DID-PSM approach eliminated individual fixed effects and common trends in baseline outcomes but it is biased if the common baseline trend assumption was violated. Although we tried to make this assumption more plausible by conditioning on a rich set of potentially confounding variables, bias might remain due to neglected confounders. Moreover, we argued that education-to-work transition affects psychological well-being but there might be a problem of reverse causality.

Second, as previously mentioned, using a simplified binary indicator of being NEET versus having a job neglects the heterogeneity that may exist both within the group of NEET and the group of persons having a job. The NEET group is composed of diverse groups such as unemployed youth searching for a job, discouraged or idle youth not looking for a job as well as inactive persons who fully engage in housework, childcare or care for elderly. The control group of persons having a job is composed of a diverse array of types and quality of work. This dichotomization was primarily done due to limited longitudinal information on the subgroups in the TYP data and sample size consideration. Revealing the heterogeneity of the two groups could be an interesting avenue of future research.

Third, as previously mentioned, the definition of the treatment only takes the labour market status at the first interview after leaving education into account. This does neither account for any longer-term effects nor for any employment dynamics that may take place during the early career. Future research could investigate how the effects differ with the duration of NEET, career dynamics as well as the longer-term implications for psychological well-being. The TYP data provide an interesting data source in this respect because, starting in Wave 10, retrospective job history calendar were collected for the period 2006–2017. This could also be a promising avenue for future research.

Notes

1   Wave 9 was not conducted for J3.

2   Starting in 2011 monthly job histories were collected with retrospective information dating back to 2006. But this information is not available for previous waves, which would lead to an underrepresentation of early, low-educated education leavers. Another reason for not using this monthly information was that the monthly job history did not distinguish whether in jobless periods the respondent was in education or unemployed/inactive, which was crucial for the analysis.

3   The age refers to t and does not always coincide with the exact age of labour market entry because of the gap of up to three years between $t - 1$ and t.

4   Forty hours has been the normal working hours threshold in Taiwan since the early 2000s (Chen et al., 2003).

References

Arnett, J. J. (2000). Emerging adulthood. A theory of development from the late teens through the twenties. *American Psychologist, 55*(5), 469–480.

Bodory, H., Camponovo, L., Huber, M., & Lechner, M. (2020). The finite sample performance of inference methods for propensity score matching and weighting estimators. *Journal of Business & Economic Statistics, 38*(1), 183–200.

Broomhall, H. S., & Winefield, A. H. (1990). A comparison of the affective well-being of young and middle-aged unemployed men matched for length of unemployment. *The British Journal of Medial Psychology, 63*(Pt 1), 43–52.

Brüderl, J., & Ludwig, V. (2015). Fixed-effects panel regression. In H. Best & C. Wolf (Eds.), *The SAGE handbook of regression analysis and causal inference* (pp. 327–357). Los Angeles, CA: SAGE.

Chen, Y.-W. (2011). Once a NEET always a NEET? Experiences of employment and unemployment among youth in a job training programme in Taiwan. *International Journal of Social Welfare, 20*(1), 33–42.

Chen, Y.-H., & Chen, H. (2014). Continuity and changes in the timing and formation of first marriage among postwar birth cohorts in Taiwan. *Journal of Family Issues, 35*(12), 1584–1604.

Chen, S.-J., Roger Ko, J.-J., & Lawler, J. (2003). Changing patterns of industrial relations in Taiwan. *Industrial Relations*, *42*(3), 315–340.

Craig, L., Churchill, B., & Wong, M. (2019). Youth, recession, and downward gender convergence: Young people's employment, education, and homemaking in Finland, Spain, Taiwan, and the United States 2000–2013. *Social Politics*, *26*(1), 59–86.

Derogatis, L. R. (1986). *SCL-90-R: Administration, scoring & procedures manual-II for the revised version and other instruments of the psychopathology rating scale series*. Towson, MD: Clinic Psychometric Research.

Diener, E., Suh, E. M., Lucas, R. E., & Smith, H. L. (1999). Subjective well-being: Three decades of progress. *Psychological Bulletin*, *125*(2), 276–302.

Elwert, F., & Winship, C. (2014). Endogenous selection bias: The problem of conditioning on a collider variable. *Annual Review of Sociology*, *40*, 31–53.

Fryer, D. (1986). Employment deprivation and personal agency during unemployment: A critical discussion of Jahoda's explanation of the psychological effects of unemployment. *Social Behaviour*, *1*(3), 3–23.

Gangl, M. (2010). Causal inference in sociological research. *Annual Review of Sociology*, *36*(1), 21–47.

Gangl, M. (2015). Matching estimators for treatment effects. In H. Best & C. Wolf (Eds.), *The SAGE handbook of regression analysis and causal inference* (pp. 251–276). Los Angeles, CA: SAGE.

Heckman, J. J., Ichimura, H., & Todd, P. E. (1997). Matching as an econometric evaluation estimator. Evidence from evaluating a job training programme. *Review of Economic Studies*, *64*(4), 605–654.

Högberg, B., Voßemer, J., Gebel, M., & Strandh, M. (2019). Unemployment, well-being, and the moderating role of education policies: A multilevel study. *International Journal of Comparative Sociology*, *60*(4), 269–291.

Hsiao, H.-H. M. (2013). Precarious work in Taiwan. *American Behavioral Scientist*, *57*(3, 373–389.

Huang, L.-W. W. (2013). The transition tempo and life course orientation of young adults in Taiwan. *The Annals of the American Academy of Political and Social Science*, *646*(1), 69–85.

Huang, F.-M., & Chien, Y.-N. (2013). Working, schooling, and psychological well-being: Evidence from longitudinal data for Taiwanese youth. In C.-C. Yi (Ed.), *The psychological well-being of East Asian youth* (pp. 185–207). Dordrecht: Springer Netherlands.

ILO. (2017). *Global employment trends for youth 2017*. Geneva: ILO.

Jahoda, M. (1981). Work, employment, and unemployment: Values, theories, and approaches in social research. *American Psychologist*, *36*(2), 184–191.

Jann, B. (2017). *KMATCH: Stata module for multivariate-distance and propensity-score matching, including entropy balancing, inverse probability weighting, (coarsened) exact matching, and regression adjustment*. Retrieved from https://ideas.repec.org/c/boc/bocode/s458346.html

Jongbloed, J. and Giret, J.-F. (2022) Quality of life of NEET youth in comparative perspective: Subjective well-being during the transition to adulthood, *Journal of Youth Studies*, *25*(3): 321–343.

Kim, W.-S., & Shi, S.-J. (2020). East Asian approaches of activation: The politics of labor market policies in South Korea and Taiwan. *Policy and Society*, *39*(2), 226–246.

Lechner, M. (2011). The estimation of causal effects by difference-in-difference methods. *Foundations and Trends in Econometrics*, *4*(3), 165–224.

Lin, C.-C., Cheng, T.-C., & Wang, S.-C. (2014). Measuring subjective well-being in Taiwan. *Social Indicators Research*, *116*(1), 17–45.

National Statistics, Republic of China. (2020). *Labor force. Statistical tables. Unemployment rate by age.* Taipei: National Statistics, R.O.C. Retrieved from https://eng.stat.gov.tw/ct.asp?xItem=15761&ctNode=1609

Nordenmark, M., & Strandh, M. (1999). Towards a sociological understanding of mental well-being among the unemployed: The role of economic and psychosocial factors. *Sociology*, *33*(3), 577–597.

Ochiai, E. (2009). Care diamonds and welfare regimes in East and South-East Asian societies. Bridging family and welfare sociology. *International Journal of Japanese Sociology*, *18*(1), 60–78.

Paul, K. I., & Moser, K. (2009). Unemployment impairs mental health: Meta-analyses. *Journal of Vocational Behavior*, *74*(3), 264–282.

Rubin, D. B. (2005). Causal inference using potential outcomes: Design, modeling, decisions. *Journal of the American Statistical Association*, *100*(469), 322–331.

Sakaguchi, Y. (2016). Gender difference in unemployment risk in the face of globalization. Effects of institutional factors in the case of Japan and Taiwan. In H. Tarōmaru (Ed.), *Labor markets, gender and social stratification in East Asia: A global perspective* (pp. 32–51). Leiden; Boston, MA: Brill.

Shih, Y.-P., & Yi, C.-C. (2014). Cultivating the difference: Social class, parental values, cultural capital and children's after-school activities in Taiwan. *Journal of Comparative Family Studies*, *45*(1), 55–75.

Strandh, M. (2000). Different exit routes from unemployment and their impact on mental well-being: The role of the economic situation and the predictability of the life course. *Work, Employment & Society*, *14*(3), 459–479.

Tsai, S.-L. (1998). The transition from school to work in Taiwan. In Y. Shavit & W. Müller (Eds.), *From school to work. A comparative study of educational qualifications and occupational destinations* (pp. 443–470). Oxford: Clarendon Press.

Tsai, M.-C., Dwyer, R. E., & Tsay, R.-M. (2016). Does financial assistance really assist? The impact of debt on wellbeing, health behavior and self-concept in Taiwan. *Social Indicators Research*, *125*(1), 127–147.

Tsai, S.-L., & Xie, Y. (2008). Returns to college education reexamined. Individual treatment effects, selection bias, and sorting gain. *Population Review*, *47*(1), 1–20.

Tsou, M.-W., & Liu, J.-T. (2001). Happiness and domain satisfaction in Taiwan. *Journal of Happiness Studies*, *2*(3), 269–288.

Voßemer, J., Gebel, M., Täht, K., Unt, M., Högberg, B., & Strandh, M. (2018). The effects of unemployment and insecure jobs on well-being and health: The moderating role of labor market policies. *Social Indicators Research*, *138*(3), 1229–1257.

Wang, Y.-C.L., Chan, H.-Y., & Chen, P.-C. (2018). Transitions of developmental trajectories of depressive symptoms between junior and senior high school among youths in Taiwan: Linkages to symptoms in young adulthood. *Journal of Abnormal Child Psychology*, *46*(8), 1687–1704.

Yi, C.-C. (2013). Introduction to the psychological well-being of East Asian youth. The transiton from early adolescence to young adulthood. In C.-C. Yi (Ed.), *The psychological well-being of East Asian youth* (pp. 1–26). Dordrecht: Springer Netherlands.

Yi, C.-C., Fan, G.-H., & Chang, M.-Y. (2013). The developmental outcome of Taiwanese youth: Effects of educational tracking during adolescence. In C.-C. Yi (Ed.), *The psychological well-being of East Asian youth* (pp. 157–184). Dordrecht: Springer Netherlands.

Yi, C.-C., Wu, C.-I., Chang, Y.-H., & Chang, M.-Y. (2009). The psychological well-being of Taiwanese youth. *International Sociology*, *24*(3), 397–429.

Yu, W. (2009). *Gendered trajectories. Women, work, and social change in Japan and Taiwan*. Stanford, CA: Stanford University Press.

Yu, W., & Chiu, C.-T. (2014). Off to a good start: A comparative study of changes in men's first job prospects in East Asia. *Research in Social Stratification and Mobility*, *37*, 3–22.

5

Landing a Middle-Class Position: College Degree, Occupational Status and Income of Young Adults in Taiwan[1]

Ming-Chang Tsai

College degree has been a ticket to middle-class status in contemporary societies. In the post-war era, the expansion of the middle class in Western countries benefited from a Fordist mode of production, in which increased manufacturing proficiency, strong regulation of labour markets, the collective bargaining of strong unions and institutionalized social insurance combined to support an expanding middle class (Ikeler and Limonic, 2018). In Taiwan, the origin of the middle class was an offspring of a successful export-oriented sector that was the engine of fast growth and wealth generation (Su, 2008; Tsai et al., 2014). Like rich democracies, this expansion of the middle class lasted until recently, when a neoliberal regime dominated the global economy and constricted the opportunity for social mobility (Ikeler and Limonic, 2018). In Taiwan's version of neoliberal transition, increased flexibility of capital mobility has meant massive investment moving out towards China and Southeast Asian countries, uprooting otherwise numerous local jobs at both the managerial-professional and semi-skilled levels. Economic growth has been slow, although not quite stagnating: the GDP growth rate has been at an average of 2.72 per cent during 2008–2018. However, the increase of wages has been much more limited, registering at 1.57 per cent in the private sector.[2] The labour market for new entrants seems to have offered fewer positions than decades ago that promised a middle-class career through accumulating knowledge and skills in a tenured job. The youth in Taiwan, as those elsewhere, are dubbed 'a collapsed generation' (Lin et al., 2011), parallelling a prevailing argument that youths in higher income countries are 'lost in transition' or the 'lost generation' (Bell and Blanchflower, 2011; Brinton, 2011; Furlong et al., 2018).

While the current descriptive account of youths in Taiwan paints a dismal picture of their prospective mobility, there are surprisingly few empirical findings depicting the patterns and mechanisms underlying their attainment of occupational status at present. Without detailed investigation of the process and dynamics of the early career of young workers it is hard to evaluate to what extent the argument of the lost generation is valid in Taiwan's context. Thus, it is worth a focused effort to examine the occupational status among youths, mobilizing recent survey data that depict how they have arrived at certain types of occupational status that offer a ticket to join the middle class at present or in the near future.

In highlighting the trajectory of occupational status attainment of Taiwanese young adults, this chapter is particularly interested in understanding the influence of young adults' postsecondary educational experience and an array of their employment characteristics on their occupational status and earnings. Using panel data collected from the Taiwan Youth Project which allows longitudinal observation of young people from youth to early adulthood, I perform a generalized least squares model of standardized occupational status scores from three observation periods. Because the research issue is mobility towards a middle-class status, I select only those with a college degree for analysis. This chapter provides important findings for understanding the status attainment processes of youths in Taiwan from a longitudinal approach.

Educational Expansion and Occupational Status in Early Career

A first job (or early job) in one's early career has been seen as a summary of young workers' background resources and influences. Parents' substantial support and a family's cultural climate (cultural capital, parental encouragement, resultant inspiration and motivation, and so on) help youths accomplish a desired educational degree and get off to a good start (Duncan et al., 1972; Sewell et al., 1970). The occupational status at which males or females begin their career carries high importance for understanding the process of social stratification over their life course. Jobs in one's early career serve as a stepping stone to higher occupational attainment and decent pay (Scherer, 2004). The first job or jobs not only are predictive of future mobility, they can be highly, although not perfectly, correlated with job status even before retirement (Duncan et al., 1972, p. 207). Earlier studies from Taiwan suggest that the likelihood of achieving a middle-class position has been high for young people with a college education (Tsai, 1998; Tsai et al., 2014).

One main issue in policy debates about young people is the upward trend of mismatch between education and employment for college students, whose numbers have been expanding tremendously in the past two decades owing to an expansion of higher education (Weng and Chang, 2011). As Taiwan upgraded to a knowledge-based economy at the end of the last century after decades of export-oriented manufacturing industrialization, extended education has become required for young people. During 2007–2016, approximately 2,293,000 students graduated from four-year colleges[3] and entered job markets, expecting to work at jobs that offer decent pay and a promising career. The increased number of entrants with a college degree leads to what has been called 'credential inflation'. Studies in other East Asian societies have also raised such concerns (Sandefur and Park, 2007; Yu and Chiu, 2014). Gerber and Cheung (2008) documented a similar trend in wealthy Western societies, in which race and gender differences in access to postsecondary education have decreased. However, horizontal stratification appears to have influenced more forcefully the career opportunities and earnings of young people. Horizontal stratification, in contrast to ascriptive origins such as race, ethnicity or gender, refers to distinctions in education and labour market. College education is highly diverse in giving human capital training, social capital provision and prestige branding, which all have significant implications for landing different class positions when starting to work. Sectors and firms in the labour market similarly constitute a constellation of various offerings and pathways of mobility towards desirable occupations and class positions.

In the Taiwan context, earlier studies observed that college education was a key to prestigious occupational status when there was 'excess demand' for workers with higher education in a fast-growing economy before the 1990s in Taiwan (Tsai, 1998). Nowadays, devaluation of the college degree might prevent a new generation of college graduates from landing even those occupations in the lower-middle stratum. Against the trend of devalued college degrees, many young people have turned to strengthen their human capital by entering elite universities so that they can be distinguished with a clear signal in the labour market. Signal theory would argue that educational expansion leads to a problem of 'insufficient information' for employers when they are not capable of differentiating workers in terms of potential productivity, as most of them have a college degree (Spence, 1973). To secure a better job, young people in Taiwan, as has been observed in many other societies, compete fiercely for the limited admissions offered by elite universities that would provide a clear signal of better capability or higher productivity when they enter the labour market. Unlike in the United States, public universities in Taiwan are considered prestigious and elite, as the government provides tremendous resources to support research activities and offer a generous pension system for the faculty in retirement (Chen, Chuang and Yan, 2015). Public universities have outperformed private ones in terms of research grants and journal publications (Tsai, 2010). The media regularly provide survey results that show Taiwan's employers favour entrants with a degree from a public university.

This consideration of where degrees are from echoes a set of recent research findings that asserts the effect of alma mater (Borgen, 2015; Brunello and Cappellari, 2008; Jung and Lee, 2016; Thomas and Zhang, 2005; Witteveen and Attewell, 2017). Although this effect of selective colleges is reported across societies, the significance and duration of its effects on wages and other job premiums varies. While researchers have noted a striking influence in the case of the United States (Witteveen and Attewell, 2017), findings from Italian college graduates reveal that it does not persist for a long time and does not trigger substantial mobility towards better performing firms. Signaling theory (1974) might interpret these findings as college competitiveness or prestige ranking functioning merely as selection devices which make admission or graduation difficult to obtain, while being irrelevant to employment. It may help a graduate enter a favoured firm, yet it may lose importance for career mobility over time (Witteveen and Attewell, 2017). Despite these context-specific outcomes, it can be hypothesized that in Taiwan, young workers with a degree from a public university should obtain a higher-status occupational stratum early in their career, but the effect is expected to decrease in the longer term.

Additionally, college major is a consideration which has been found to generate substantial effects on employment and pay, but this has been infrequently investigated in Taiwan. In a study of graduates from the University of Texas system, architecture, engineering, computers, statistics, mathematics and health majors are among the highest earners (measured at age 24–28). In contrast, arts, psychology and social work, biology and life sciences rank lower. This gap is not very different from that among average college graduates in the United States (Carnevale et al., 2017). Witteveen and Attewell (2017) report from longitudinal observation of US college graduates that a college major indeed predicts future earnings effectively. Ten years after graduation, health, business and management, and the math-related majors are associated with higher average earnings. In contrast, those majoring in education earn the least. However, their analysis maintains that college selectivity is more important than a major in affecting earnings. In light of these research insights, this study incorporates one's major as a potential factor in estimating occupational status for young workers in Taiwan.

Sectors, Firm Characteristics and the Internal Labour Market

The education credential, or human capital approach to youths' early career, concentrates on personal training, resources and skills for getting good jobs. It pays less attention to firm-level structural features in promoting mobility. For the structural theory of mobility, occupational mobility is largely a consequence of position allocation in a specific firm. While this structural perspective does not belittle the importance of educational credentials, strong motives or adroit entrepreneurship, it places heavy emphasis on the process a person enters a specific firm and is 'pipelined' towards the highest possible position before retirement. This concern brings up a classic debate on socialization versus allocation in the status attainment literature (Kerchhoff, 1976). The socialization perspective is very interested in the evolution of an individual's abilities and aspirations that help in climbing the social ladder, the main elements of which are parental influences and familial cultural milieus. For the allocation perspective, these social psychological factors are minimized, with a focus instead on social structural forces which identify, select, classify and assign job seekers. Occupational attainment processes demonstrate allocation of status and privileges by way of mechanisms often externally constrained or activated. In sum, it is the firm and employment status which gives a position, from which young workers are tagged with a ranked status. The specific internal labour market built in these working environments can function as stepping stones for future mobility. It can also operate as a hurdle that slows one's mobility. These firm-level characteristics are critical in understanding different mobility outcomes even for young workers who are starting to accumulate working experience.

The structural argument proposes a number of important factors in determining occupational status obtainment which are incorporated in this analysis. A number of factors are worth considering as suggested in the literature on occupational status attainment. First, in Taiwan, the state sector tends to provide quality- (or capability-) matched jobs in the labour market as long as entrants can pass a competitive national examination and become public officers, starting a lifetime career from the lowest rank. Alternatively, entrants can be hired by the government as contract workers with a fixed term, in which positions they usually work quite stably for a length of time, although with lower salaries and less generous pensions. Moving up the career ladder in Taiwan's government, in general, is tremendously slow due to a strict system of seniority with complex bureaucratic regulations (Huang and Fang, 2013; Pan and Lee, 2015). It often is affected by personal relationships rather than by merits. It can be predicted that having a government job helps land a better occupational status and payment for the entrants but these advantages diminish in later phases of career.

The second factor this study examines is concerned with job stability. Because firms increasingly adopt flexible policies in hiring new, young workers, more and more jobs offered are not standard full-time jobs, but are temporary jobs or jobs with a short-term contract (one or two years). From a dualist labour market perspective, these workers rarely enter an internal labour market and benefit from the social closure of resources and opportunities that are available only for workers who have long committed to a firm. Part-timers usually fill positions that require less skill and lower pay, and they receive less social respect from the work they perform. Straightforwardly, it can be hypothesized that a full-time contract, compared to a part-time one, renders a higher occupational status for entrants in the labour market.

Third, an individual's occupational mobility is closely linked to specific characteristics in a firm (Granovetter, 1988; Kalleberg and

Mouw, 2018; Rosenfeld, 1992). A successful enterprise raises employees' salary and occupational status rapidly. These firms tend to hire more employees and structure the firm in a hierarchical way that results in recruiting more highly educated employers and provides more room for workers to move up the career ladder. In contrast, a small firm tends to provide fewer promotion opportunities even for long-time employees. As firms expand in size, various sets of job ladders are added and an internal labour market is likely to exist, which allows a higher ceiling of salary grade (Oi and Idson, 1999). The firm size wage effect argument additionally suggests that large firms hold monopolistic positions that allow them to earn excess profits to share with workers through higher wages (Hollister, 2004).

Finally, as firm size increases in modern firms, a class appears between capital and labour which has supervising authority over other wage labourers (Erikson and Goldthorpe, 1992). The Marxist approach has highlighted an intermediate class which features a function of authority and control over lower-ranked workers in class relationships (Wright, 2005). This issue also brings in the idea of the gradations between non-manual and manual workers as well as those in between in the Weberian approach to the class system (Breen, 2005). It has been found that incumbents of service class positions obtain more prestigious positions and earn higher incomes (Kurz and Muller, 1987).

Data and Methods

For entrants in the labour market, reaching the middle class cannot be realized quickly even if they are equipped with a college degree, as was observed in a time of fast economic growth (Tsai, 1998). Even for the most successful, nowadays it is a long process, perhaps requiring 10 years or so. This has a critical implication for research design and data collection. A suitable design should observe young people at work when they enter the labour market after graduation from college and trace their trajectories over a reasonably long period of time. The Taiwan Youth Project (TYP) provides longitudinal data on respondents from two groups who were first interviewed when in grades 7 and 9 in 2000 and were followed up every one or two years. They at present have entered early adulthood. These panel data fit the study's aim well. The current study uses data from the second phase of the survey, conducted in 2011, 2014 and 2017 for participants who continued to be approached by the survey team. Only four-year college graduates are included in order to investigate their initial occupational career. This attention does not imply that those having lower than college degrees are not eligible to achieve a middle-class position. Because this study is particularly interested in horizontal stratification concerning postsecondary education and its influence on social mobility for young adults; it thus is reasonable to analyse a special subpopulation for this goal. Endogenous selection bias due to a subgroup being discarded in analysis (Elwert and Winship, 2014) is therefore not a threat to our research design, which seeks to ascertain a causal influence on occupational status and income in early adulthood of the experiences of postsecondary education in particular, rather than education in general. The first group (interviewed when in the first year of junior high school, J1) was observed during age 24–30 ($n = 785$), and the second group (interviewed when in the third year of junior high school, J3) was observed during age 26–32 ($n = 805$). They were in the phase of emerging adulthood.

Figure 5.1 shows the employment status in the J1 and J3 groups as observed in 2011 (ages 24 and 26). Most respondents (73 per cent and 85 per cent, respectively) were already in the labour market. This

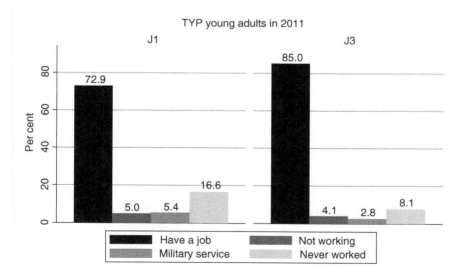

Figure 5.1   Employment status in 2011

figure increased to 91 per cent in 2017 for both groups. However, the unemployment rate in 2011 and 2017 was 9.0 per cent and 8.5 per cent, respectively, which is slightly higher than the official figures.[4] Among the TYP young adults, very few reported having 'never worked' (for various reasons, like taking care of family members, participating in job training courses or just finishing military service) when they were around age 30, this category remaining a large one at age 24 (see Figures 5.1 and 5.2).

Measurement of occupational status. The interest of this chapter to observe whether young college-educated workers can land a middle-class position, and the big-class concepts (for instance, a set of categories like capitalist, petit bourgeoisie, intermediate class and proletariat) are ideal indicators (Jonsson et al., 2011). However, given their relatively short career time in the labour market and the smaller probability in achieving upper-class positions, I decided to use a gradational approach in order to see where they stand in the system of stratified positions by way of their occupational status score. This approach does not adopt a system of big class categories that places a young worker in a situation of being either middle class or not. It employs a continuous measure which can show how close a young worker is to the middle class by illustrating where they started their

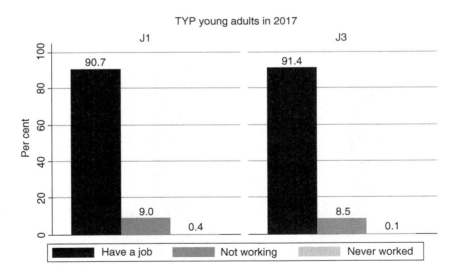

Figure 5.2 Employment status in 2017

career and how fast they have climbed the social ladder with the help of the factors of horizontal stratification.

In practice, for young adults who reported having a job when interviewed, their occupational information was initially coded according to the Taiwan Standard Classification of Occupation, developed by the Directorate General of Budget, Accounting and Statistics. I matched the four-digit codes with those of the International Standard Classification of Occupations, which were then translated to the widely used standard international socio-economic index (ISEI) of occupational status developed by Ganzeboom and Treiman (2019; Ganzeboom et al., 1992). Figure 5.3 reports the average ISEI scores for the J1 and J3 groups. Those who did not hold a four-year college degree are included here for comparison. In the J1 group, those who have a college degree or more scored 47 in 2011 (age 24) and moved up to 51 in 2017 (age 30). Because J3 are two years older than J1, their scores are slightly higher, with an average of 51 in 2011 (age 26) and 52 in 2017 (age 32). The magnitude of mobility for this group was trivial. As J1 caught up with J3 at age 30, the difference between them was small at roughly one point. With an ISEI score slightly above 50, the typical jobs include engineering science

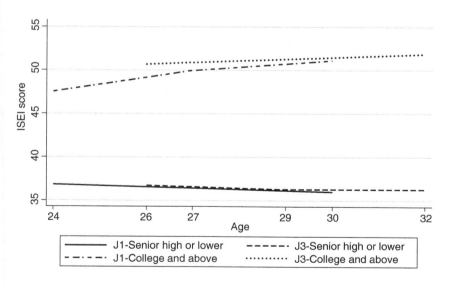

Figure 5.3 ISEI scores for groups J1 and J3 comparing those who have and those who do not have a college degree

technicians, paramedical practitioners or government social benefits officials. These jobs can be considered a position slightly *lower* than the middleclass. But it is definitely *not* a lower class. Tsai (1998, p. 456) reported a score of 63 for the first jobs in the early 1990s, which is much higher than either J1 or J3 as observed at age 30. Tsai's (1998) measurement might not be fully comparable with mine, yet with such a substantial gap, it still suggests that today's youths appear to have started their jobs at a lower status compared to their counterparts who entered the labour market when Taiwan was an economic tiger.

Note that for those with a senior high school diploma or lower, the occupational status scores are much lower, roughly at 37. Typical jobs at this level include truck and lorry drivers, metal molders and hotel receptionists. Both groups, because of limited educational credentials, seem to have experienced very limited mobility in this life phase, as shown by their flat lines during early adulthood.

Two major sets of important factors are considered for their potential influences on occupational status obtained by young people. The first one relates to whether young workers graduated from public or private universities (see Table 5.1 for summary statistics). A binary dummy design was used (public = 1, private = 0). As for the respondents' college majors, I classify all majors into four main categories: finance-economics, technology and applied science, pure science, and humanities and social service, with the latter being the reference group in the dummy design. Admittedly, these basic measures remain somewhat sub-optimal and fall short in representing resources, training capacities and prestige at the university level, as well as experiences in the *field* (specific skills learned, feminized majors, performance, etc.) (Gerber and Cheung, 2008). This limitation in measurement is noted.

The second set of predictors concerns the characteristics of the sector and firm with which a young worker is affiliated. With regard to the sectors, three categories are identified: working in the government sector, in the private sector (used as a reference) and the self-employed. In addition, permanent job is also coded into a dummy variable to compare with temporary jobs. To assess the firm's influence on occupational status, firm size is measured by the total of employees. As for authority in work, the TYP provides a simple measure of whether a respondent has authority over others when working. Having and lacking such authority are designed into a dummy for comparison.

Table 5.1 Summary statistics J1 and J3

	J 1 sample				J 3 sample			
	Age 24		Age 30		Age 26		Age 32	
	Mean	SD	Mean	SD	Mean	SD	Mean	SD
Male (=1)	0.60				0.65			
Father's education	11.15	3.28			11.27	3.31		
Father's ISEI	40.27	13.87			40.66	15.14		
Married	0.02		0.33		0.05		0.43	
Graduates of public university	0.26				0.27			
Major								
Humanities and social service	0.27				0.28			
Finance-econ	0.27				0.23			
Technology	0.32				0.37			
Science	0.14				0.13			
Company								
Private	0.14		0.15		0.17		0.16	
State	0.81		0.77		0.76		0.72	
Self-employed	0.04		0.08		0.07		0.12	
Tenured	0.59		0.82		0.68		0.82	
Firm size	14.93	12.76	16.83	13.09	16.82	13.06	16.49	13.22
Supervising others in job	2.18	8.27	3.11	10.21	2.22	9.03	3.47	10.90

A number of background variables are considered in the estimation. In addition to gender (male = 1), the education (in years) and occupation of the father are included for assessing the influence of family background. Being married (=1, otherwise = 0 at time when interviewed) is considered, as the literature suggests that marriage is likely to stimulate young adults to work hard to get ahead in their career (Gorman, 2000). The three regions in which they studied when in junior high school, that is, Taipei City, New Taipei City and I-Lan County (used as a reference), were not incorporated in the analysis, because preliminary analysis did not reveal any substantial effects.

That is, whether one grew up in urban or rural regions has trivial influences on occupational status in young adulthood.

As this study is interested in occupational status observed in three periods, I decided to estimate a respondent's status scores simultaneously in a system of equations. It is likely that there exist unobserved variables that affect the three observations simultaneously over time. Thus I assume that the residuals of the three occupational status scores are mutually correlated. The residuals' correlations are considered in the estimation. This consideration is equivalent to what has been called the seemingly unrelated regression (SUR) model or the correlated residuals model (Fiebig, 2003), which is favoured for its better efficiency in estimation. This estimation approach also has the merit of allowing cross-comparison of an identical predictor in operation across different times. A comparison as such would not be feasible in multilevel analysis which assumes that a predictor tends to have the same magnitude of effect over time. I did not choose to use the latent growth curve model for two reasons, because there are only three observations in seven years in the panel data used, and much speculation is needed to gauge the incremental changes over time. With such limited observations, the maximum likelihood estimation in fact encountered difficulty in producing the structure of observed data in my preliminary trials. In what follows I present the findings from the SUR models. The full information maximum likelihood method is used for handling missing data, with an assumption of missing at random.[5]

Results and Analysis

Table 5.2 reports the results from the SUR models of the ISEI scores for J1 group at three observations (ages 24, 27 and 30). Males and females in their early career do not show difference in occupational status when an array of controls are considered. With regard to family background, both the education and occupation of the father produce no appreciable net effects for young people's occupational status, except that a positive correlation is found between the father's education and the young person's status at age 26. Marital status does not have a notable influence.

Graduates from a public university, compared to those from a private one, clearly have an advantage on the first observation of

Table 5.2 ISEI Score for group J1 (SUR model)

	Age 24		Age 27		Age 30	
	b	s.e.	*b*	s.e.	*b*	s.e.
Male	−0.799	(1.267)	0.144	(1.269)	−1.312	(1.354)
Fa-edu	0.017	(0.197)	0.692***	(0.186)	0.342	(0.195)
Fa-occ	0.085	(0.048)	0.016	(0.046)	0.026	(0.049)
Married	1.180	(3.679)	0.539	(1.217)	−1.552	(0.887)
Public Univ.	4.468**	(1.441)	4.837***	(1.289)	6.256***	(1.346)
Major (ref: Humanities and social service)						
Finance-econ	−1.387	(1.536)	−0.614	(1.485)	0.007	(1.569)
Technology	4.266**	(1.547)	6.435***	(1.434)	5.248***	(1.532)
Science	1.785	(1.970)	2.208	(1.752)	3.601	(1.860)
Sector (ref: Private)						
State	4.929**	(1.556)	1.170	(1.327)	3.438*	(1.345)
Self-employed	−1.903	(2.642)	−3.536	(1.824)	−3.279	(1.742)
Tenured	3.133*	(1.325)	1.626	(1.181)	1.940	(1.256)
Firm size	0.018	(0.038)	0.094**	(0.034)	0.062	(0.035)
Supervising	0.095	(0.058)	0.093*	(0.046)	0.049	(0.040)
Constant	39.559		34.969		40.552	
R^2	0.102		0.153		0.127	
r among residuals			0.573			
N			639			

*$p < 0.05$; **$p < 0.01$; ***$p < 0.001$

occupational status across equations. Compared to graduates from private universities, those having a degree from public ones on average scored 4.8 points higher at age 24, and 6.9 points higher at age 30. Because its effect is more substantial as young workers reach age 30, which indicates a continuing effect of the alma mater even after having graduated quite a long time earlier. This result differs from other studies that observed only its signal effect mostly at the beginning of a career (Ishida et al., 1997). Young people with different majors also vary in obtaining an occupational status. Those with a major in 'technology and applied sciences' enjoyed a better kick-off by 4.3 points at age 24, compared to those with a major in humanities or social service. This advantage persisted, with a larger magnitude, at age 30. However, a finance-economics or science major does not facilitate occupational status for J1 at this phase, which is different from what was found in rich economies (Witteveen and Attewell, 2017). This probably can be explained by an oversupply of graduates with finance- and business-related majors, even those equipped with specialty certifications. Researchers (Chen, Cheng, Lai and Hsiao, 2015) suggest further exploring the specific sub-sectors in which these graduates get employed for potential differences in wage earning. Surprisingly, the coefficient of pure science majors does not display a sizable benefit at the starting point. But at age 30, this major generates favourable effects.

The lower part of Table 5.2 estimates the influences of a number of sectoral and firm-level factors. A set of dummies is designed to compare three groups: working in the public sector (that is, in the government, public schools or public-funded institutes), being self-employed and being hired in the private sector. Working in the public sector, compared to the private sector, appears to enhance occupational status, although this effect is less obvious in estimation for age 27. Noteworthy are the self-employed, whose scores are not significantly lower statistically, despite the negative coefficients. A possible interpretation is that young people working as self-employers at this age might in fact have little capital. Many of them are engaged in online retailing, getting from the ISEI a score lower than technician or managerial positions. Holding a permanent job, not surprisingly, helps obtain a prestigious occupational status, despite its decreased influence later on. Firm size and having authority over other workers do not have consistent, appreciable effects in the estimation: only in the equation for age 27 do they have significant influence.

The model fit statistics are satisfactory in estimation for the J1 group, with R^2 for each equation ranging from 10 per cent to 15 per cent. The average correlation among the residual factors is 0.573, justifying the choice of the SUR model. On the basis of the likelihood ratio statistics, there is a significant improvement of the analysed model: χ^2 for the current model vs. saturated model is 78.9 (df = 36), while the baseline model is 835.5 (df = 78). In addition, the coefficient of determination is 26 per cent. RMSEA is a low 0.043 and the comparative fitness index (CFI) is 0.943, showing a good model fit.

Table 5.3 shows the outcomes for the J3 group. The model fit statistics are satisfactory. R^2 for each equation, which ranges between 14 and -18 per cent, indicates good performance. The residual factors now have an average correlation at 0.557. RMSEA and CFI are about the same. A substantial gender gap in occupational status starts to show at age 32. This finding is important for understanding how early, rather than how persistent, the gender gap in occupational status begins from a life-course perspective. Father's education appears influential for occupational status measured at ages 26 and 29; however, it diminished at age 32. Father's occupation does not have any notable effect. Like group J1, public college graduates on average

Table 5.3 ISEI score for group J3 (SUR model)

	Age 26		Age 29		Age 32	
	b	s.e.	*b*	s.e.	*b*	s.e.
Male	1.450	(1.245)	1.436	(1.243)	3.107*	(1.239)
Fa-edu	0.671***	(0.179)	0.408*	(0.181)	0.261	(0.180)
Fa-occ	0.029	(0.040)	0.068	(0.041)	0.046	(0.040)
Married	1.113	(2.080)	−0.341	(0.955)	−1.269	(0.826)
Public Univ.	2.880*	(1.296)	3.565**	(1.297)	4.650***	(1.290)
Major (ref: Humanities and social service)						
Finance-econ	−4.608**	(1.578)	−1.537	(1.598)	−3.330*	(1.594)
Technology	2.045	(1.467)	2.775	(1.463)	2.056	(1.455)
Science	3.553	(1.910)	6.315***	(1.890)	5.275**	(1.895)
Sector (ref: Private)						
State	1.591	(1.427)	−0.989	(1.290)	−1.065	(1.327)
Self-employed	1.321	(2.179)	−3.775**	(1.462)	−5.609***	(1.447)
Tenured	4.431**	(1.357)	3.356**	(1.220)	1.279	(1.272)
Firm size	0.095*	(0.037)	0.087*	(0.034)	0.140***	(0.035)
Supervising	−0.018	(0.048)	0.032	(0.045)	−0.016	(0.036)
constant	35.225		36.715		40.842	
R^2		0.141		0.129		0.169
r among residuals			0.557			
N			666			

*$p < 0.05$; **$p < 0.01$; ***$p < 0.001$

obtain advantageous positions over time, when compared to their counterparts with private college degrees. Those with a major in technology or applied science do not secure better status, but those with pure science majors appear to have advanced in mobility, when compared to majors in humanities and social service. Study of the finance and economics fields continue to bring a lower score of occupational status.

Unlike the result for J1, working in the public sector does not accelerate the upgrading of occupational status. Being a self-employed person, however, continues to hinder the level of occupational status. Job tenure continues to produce favourable effects at ages 26 and 29. Similarly, working in a larger firm consistently has a positive effect during emerging adulthood. Authority over other workers is not a strong predictor, a replication of what was observed in analysis of group J1.

Effects on Income: Occupational Status and Firm-Level Characteristics

To what extent is income of the analysed young adults determined by their human capital and firm characteristics in Taiwan? The regression estimation for the J1 group is displayed in Table 5.4. Income is measured by their earnings in ten thousand Taiwanese dollars (TWD) monthly. The means for the three observation periods are 2.9, 4.0 and 4,8, respectively (the exchange rate is about 31 TWD to one US dollar). Income at this level is low when compared to those in Japan, South Korea or even coastal China, even though the magnitude of increase in this observed period seems to be substantial (90 per cent).

The models in Table 5.4 include all predictors in Tables 5.2 and 5.3 and add the socio-economic score of occupation to capture its specific effect on income.[6] With regard to the family background's influence, it is found that father's education has an influence at age 27 and 30, while his occupation is not a facilitating factor. Marital status does not boost the income level for J1 throughout. Public university graduates do not have an observable effect in three equations. This result does not change even when occupation is dropped from the equation (not shown to save space). Thus, a public university degree has only an indirect effect on income by way of landing a better occupation. It does not necessarily increase the earnings for young

Table 5.4 Income for group J1 (SUR model)

	Age 24		Age 27		Age 30	
	b	s.e.	*b*	s.e.	*b*	s.e.
Male	0.175	(0.104)	0.162	(0.193)	0.506*	(0.242)
Fa-edu	0.032	(0.016)	0.066*	(0.029)	0.119***	(0.035)
Fa-occ	0.002	(0.004)	0.001	(0.007)	0.012	(0.009)
Married	−0.290	(0.289)	−0.017	(0.194)	0.156	(0.168)
Public Univ.	−0.185	(0.125)	0.077	(0.204)	0.244	(0.242)
Major (ref: Humanities and social service)						
Finance-econ	0.010	(0.133)	0.241	(0.233)	0.192	(0.276)
Technology	−0.114	(0.134)	0.203	(0.228)	0.191	(0.273)
Science	0.078	(0.172)	0.104	(0.275)	0.258	(0.329)
Sector (ref: Private)						
State	0.574***	(0.126)	−0.151	(0.216)	−0.464	(0.251)
Self-employed	0.884***	(0.214)	0.111	(0.299)	1.026**	(0.332)
Tenured	0.666***	(0.104)	0.301	(0.195)	0.610*	(0.240)
Firm size	0.011***	(0.003)	0.014*	(0.005)	0.017*	(0.007)
Supervising	0.012**	(0.005)	0.018*	(0.008)	0.019*	(0.008)
Occupation	0.013***	(0.003)	0.028***	(0.005)	0.056***	(0.006)
constant	1.001		1.049		−1.275	
R^2	0.147		0.093		0.197	
r among residuals			0.594			
N			639			

$p < 0.05$; $^{**}p < 0.01$; $^{***}p < 0.001$

adults. Majors do not have notable influence, either. Those employed in the state sector are better paid at the beginning of their career. Yet, this wage effect is reduced substantially in a few years (when at age 30), probably because the state sector practices a system of seniority under which increases of salary are slower than in private firms. Those who are self-employed, despite their lower scores on occupational status (see previous discussions), appear to earn more at ages 24 and 30 (nearly 9,000 TD more per month), but not at age 27. Their earnings might not be as stable but in general stay above that of public sector workers or those hired in private firms. Permanent job, firm size and a supervising position all contribute to a better income. Not surprisingly, occupational status is a strong predictor. What is noteworthy is that when working experience has accumulated over time, moving up the ladder of occupational status produces more returns in earnings.

Table 5.5 displays the estimation outcomes for the J3 group, the average monthly income of which is 3.4, 4.5 and 5.2 ten thousand TD, respectively. Like what was found previously for J1, family background measured by father's education shows a substantial influence at age 30. A degree from a public university appears to produce notable income effects. College majors in technology, pure science, and finance and economics, compared to humanities and social

Table 5.5   Income for J3 group (SUR model)

	Age 26		Age 29		Age 32	
	b	**s.e.**	**b**	**s.e.**	**b**	**s.e.**
Male	0.062	(0.125)	−0.041	(0.217)	0.116	(0.266)
Fa-edu	−0.000	(0.019)	0.049	(0.031)	0.077*	(0.035)
Fa-occ	0.004	(0.004)	0.002	(0.007)	−0.004	(0.008)
Married	−0.079	(0.203)	0.036	(0.165)	0.161	(0.176)
Public Univ.	0.504***	(0.133)	1.219***	(0.232)	1.018***	(0.259)
Major (ref: Humanities and social service)						
Finance-econ	0.155	(0.164)	0.395	(0.297)	0.630*	(0.320)
Technology	0.133	(0.150)	0.695*	(0.271)	0.993***	(0.291)
Science	0.305	(0.198)	0.685	(0.353)	1.117**	(0.380)
Sector (ref: Private)						
State	0.276	(0.146)	−0.282	(0.222)	−0.700*	(0.275)
Self-employed	0.309	(0.220)	0.580*	(0.262)	0.779*	(0.311)
Tenured	0.593***	(0.135)	0.510*	(0.212)	0.642*	(0.269)
Firm size	0.012**	(0.004)	0.021***	(0.006)	0.033***	(0.007)
Supervising	0.008	(0.005)	0.017*	(0.008)	0.009	(0.008)
Occupation	0.018***	(0.004)	0.025***	(0.006)	0.042***	(0.007)
constant	1.276		0.993		0.097	
R^2	0.146		0.145		0.189	
r among residuals			0.551			
N			666			

*$p < 0.05$; **$p < 0.01$; ***$p < 0.001$

service, clearly produce a better return in terms of income at age 32, when the young people have accumulated more experience in the labour market. Pay in the state sector is comparable to that in the private sector, but at age 32, it is clearly surpassed by the other two types of employment. Firm-level characteristics this chapter considers as well as occupational status all produce income effects as expected, except that having a supervising position at this phase of one's career does not have a consistent influence.

Parking Lot or Hurdle Race? Concluding Remarks

The main findings from panel analysis of occupational status and earnings for young adults in Taiwan can be summarized as follows. First, college graduates had nearly approached a middle-class position when they reached 30 years old. Their status gap with those with a high school diploma increased, as is observed through the ISEI index. College graduates seem to have approached a position close to the middle class, while their status appears to be lower than their counterparts who entered the labour market two decades ago in a period of rapid economic growth (Tsai, 1998). After some more years in their career, the young adults this chapter studies should be able to land a middle-class position. Second, the distance the youths moved along the occupational ladder appears to be insubstantial. Despite a slightly upward trend, the speed of mobility into higher occupational positions is slow, which foretells that to advance beyond a middle-class position surely takes much more time than before. Third, the different level of occupational status among college graduates in the initial phase of their career is highly correlated with their alma mater and their majors. As they accumulated more working experience over time, these influences remained, while the effects of their affiliated firms become more substantial. Indeed, at age 30 their future mobility additionally to depend greatly on which sector they work in as well as how large the firm is and how stable the job is. These institutional characteristics, however, do not suppress or replace the alma mater effect after having left college nearly a decade ago. Last, the earnings of young adults are determined by various factors, including their alma mater, majors, and sector and firm-level characteristics. These various factors combine to affect income among young adults with a college degree. In broad terms, the influence of family background on personal income has diminished, while the influence of specific skill training in college and the sector or firm in which young adults are employed, which are two main elements in horizontal stratification, appear to be substantial in their moving up in the hierarchical stratification as either indicated by occupational status or income level. Young adults across many societies have experienced increased difficulty in getting a job after leaving school, even with fine educational credentials. Even in high-income countries, slack demand in the labour market leaves them unemployed for quite a length of time and accelerates their feeling of being excluded. They seem to stall in a large 'parking lot' when they finish education from college (Furstenberg, 2013). When they can enter the labour market and be offered a decent job cannot be foretold. In contrast to this parking lot model, the finding of this chapter reveals that young adults in Taiwan are more likely to participate in a 'hurdle race'. They can enter the labour market shortly after graduation from college and start to compete for prestigious social status with peers. However, what they enter is a hurdle race, in which speed of mobility has been slowed. Compared to the young cohorts two or three decades earlier, their barriers are apparently higher, as it takes a longer time to secure a middle-class or even upper-middle position. Other add-on requirements might be needed, such as graduate degree, extra skills or training, or stronger social capitals. Yet the evidence gathered also suggests that they are not very far from that destination.

Future research may pay attention to the different patterns of social mobility for young workers across societies and develop theoretical explanations for observed similarities and divergences. While this concern lies beyond the scope this chapter, I provide some tentative accounts for the hurdle race model for the youth of Taiwan. One major reason is the low cost of higher education. The government policy effectively generates a cap on the fee of higher education, such that it is affordable for most families in Taiwan. The yearly fee for a college student is approximately about US$4,000 for science and technology majors (slightly lower for majors in humanities and social sciences). With new colleges increased in large number in the past two decades such that admission to college has become less difficult for most high-school graduates, more young workers with college degrees have entered the labour market each year. These entrants have been absorbed into the labour market in the context of a low minimum wage policy. Given the moderate economic growth in Taiwan and massive outward-oriented investment into China, the unemployment rate for young cohorts would be much higher if not for their relatively low wages, about US$1,100 monthly as of 2018.[7] College graduates have entered a labour market that offered a position close to the middle class. Yet it is not a position with which to earn high income that allows a decent life quality, not to mention owning a house in urban areas where most jobs are located.

The findings of this chapter might bring some gloomy news for both scholars and policymakers. The young adults in Taiwan have indeed encountered a hurdle in their mobility, which has slowed their speed of advancing towards the middle class. This also has an implication that their transition to adulthood is prolonged before they become financially viable by way of obtaining a decent job and fair wage in the labour market. This situation means that many policy incentives for young people, especially those with a college degree, to get married and have offspring might not effectively achieve one main targeted goal, which is to boost the super-low fertility that has been a societal concern for the past two decades (Wang et al., 2013). However, this does not mean that securing a middle-class position and identity is not feasible. Despite a much protracted process, their prospective mobility remains promising given that they have already nearly reached the middle class. Our study provides perhaps the only evidence of young people's working conditions and occupational status for responding to a prevalent dismal view of life for youths.

Youths in Japan and the United Kingdom seem to be stuck in the predicament of the above-mentioned parking lot model. Increasingly, jobs at the entry level are mostly temporary, casual and seasonal ones, with less prestige than permanent contracts (Brinton, 2011; Furlong et al., 2018; Mitani, 2008; Schmelzer, 2008). Instability in one's early career affects occupational class in young generations more than before. It is speculated that their mobility upward may be slower than what was observed in Taiwan in this chapter; thus, it seems appropriate to call for more cross-country studies by concerned researchers. Clear specification of these two as well as other unexplored models to understand how young adults are constrained in different manners at entry into the labour market is a research priority. It is hoped that when these research results are available, public policy can come up with effective measures to not merely adjust weak labour institutions but also reduce inequality in the early career phase.

Notes

1   The authors thanks two anonymous reviewers for their helpful comments on the draft of this chapter.

2   The Directorate General of Budget, Accounting and Statistics (DGBAS) of Executive Yuan (www1.stat.gov.tw)

3   Department of Statistics, Ministry of Education (https://eds.moe.gov.tw/edust/webmain.aspx?sys=210&funid=edufld&clear=1).

4   The unemployment rate for age 25–29 as of 2017 was 6.6 per cent. See National Statistics, ROC (https://www.stat.gov.tw/ct.asp?xItem=37135&ctNode=517&mp=4). Accessed 20 October 2021.

5   Those who participated only once in any of the three follow-ups were not included in the analysis in order to obtain reliable estimation from the imputation procedures. This reduces participants by about 12 per cent in the SUR regression tables.

6   The inclusion of occupational status, essentially a socio-economic index of a job position, might incur a potential overcontrol bias in estimation (Elwert and Winship, 2014), that is, unnecessarily conditioning on occupational status in assessing the effect of social backgrounds, major and firm-level characteristics on income. To check this possibility, I conducted additional estimation by excluding the occupational status from all models in Tables 5.4 and 5.5. I found that the results remained similar. Therefore, overcontrolling is not an issue herein.

7   Source: Ministry of Labor. www.mol.gov.tw/announcement/2099/41533. Accessed 18 December 2019.

References

Bell, D. N. F., & Blanchflower, D. G. (2011). *Young people and the great recession*, Discussion paper no. 5674. Bonn: The Institute for the Study of Labor (IZA).

Borgen, N. T. (2015). Changes in the economic returns to attending prestigious institutions in Norway. *European Societies*, *17*(2), 219–241.

Breen, R. (2005). Foundations of a neo-Weberian class analysis. In E. O. Wright (Ed.), *Approaches to class analysis* (pp. 31–50). Cambridge: Cambridge University Press.

Brinton, M. C. (2011). *Lost in transition: Youth, work, and instability in postindustrial Japan*. Cambridge: Cambridge University Press.

Brunello, G., & Cappellari, L. (2008). The labour market effects of alma mater: Evidence from Italy. *Economics of Education Review*, *27*(5), 564–574.

Carnevale, A. P., Fasules, M. L., Bond Huie, S. A., & Troutman, D. R. (2017). *Major matters most: The economic value of bachelor's degrees from the University of Texas System*. Washington, DC: Georgetown University Center on Education and the Workforce.

Chen, C.-P., Cheng, P.-W., Lai, H.-M., & Hsiao, H.-C. (2015a). Exploring the relationship between certifications and wages among university graduate students:

A propensity score-matched analysis. *Contemporary Educational Research Quarterly, 23*(1), 71–111. (in Chinese).

Chen, K.-J., Chuang, W.-C., & Yang, C. (2015b). Factors influencing gradual retirement among middle-aged and older workers in Taiwan. *Journal of Human Resource Management, 15*(1), 87–108. (in Chinese).

Duncan, O. D., Featherman, D. L., & Duncan, B. (1972). *Socioeconomic background and achievement.* New York, NY: Seminar Press.

Elwert, F., & Winship, C. (2014). Endogenous selection bias: The problem of conditioning on a collider variable. *Annual Review of Sociology, 40,* 31–53.

Erikson, R., & Goldthorpe, J. H. (1992). *The constant flux: A study of class mobility in industrial societies.* New York, NY: Oxford University Press.

Fiebig, D. G. (2003). Seemingly unrelated regression. In B. H. Baltagi (Ed.), *A companion to theoretical econometrics* (pp. 101–121). Dordrecht: Springer.

Furlong, A., Goodwin, J., O'Connor, H., Hadfield, S., Hall, S., Lowden, K., et al (2018). *Young people in the labour market: Past, present, future.* London: Routledge.

Furstenberg, Jr., F. F. (2013). Transitions to adulthood: What we can learn from the west. *The Annals of the American Academy of Political and Social Science, 646*(1), 28–41.

Ganzeboom, H. B. G., De Graaf, P. M., & Treiman, D. J. (1992). A standard international socio-economic index of occupational status. *Social Science Research, 21*(1), 1–56.

Ganzeboom, H. B. G., & Treiman, D. J. (2019). *International stratification and mobility file: Conversion tools.* Amsterdam: Department of Social Research Methodology. Retrieved 4 January 2019, from http://www.harryganzeboom.nl/ismf/index.htm

Gerber, T., & Cheung, S. Y. (2008). Horizontal stratification in postsecondary education: Forms, explanations, and implications. *Annual Review of Sociology, 34,* 299–318.

Gorman, E. H. (2000). Marriage and money: The effect of marital status on attitudes toward pay and finances. *Work and Occupation, 27*(1), 64–88.

Granovetter, M. (1988). The sociological and economic approaches to labor market analysis. In G. Farkas & P. England (Eds.), *Industries, firms, and jobs* (pp. 233–263). Boston, MA: Springer.

Hollister, M. N. (2004). Does firm size matter anymore? The new economy and firm size wage effects. *American Sociological Review, 69*(5), 659–676.

Huang, H.-R., & Fang, K.-H. (2013). Taiwanese civil servants' gender differences in human capital, job choice/career goal, and career advancement: A case of the TGBS, 2008. *Taiwan Political Science Review, 17*(2), 231–282. (in Chinese).

Ikeler, P., & Limonic, L. (2018). Middle class decline? The growth of professional-managers in the neoliberal era. *The Sociological Quarterly, 59*(4), 549–570.

Ishida, H., Spilerman, S., & Su, K.-H. (1997). Educational credentials and promotion chances in Japanese and American Organizations. *American Sociological Review, 62*(6), 866–882.

Jonsson, J., Grusky, D., Pollak, R., di Carlo, M., & Mood, C. (2011). Occupations and social mobility: Gradational, big-class, and micro-class reproduction in comparative perspective. In T. Smeeding, R. Erikson & M. Jäntti (Eds.), *Persistence, privilege, and parenting: The comparative study of intergenerational mobility* (pp. 138–171). New York, NY: Russell Sage Foundation.

Jung, J., & Lee, S. J. (2016). Influence of university prestige on graduate wage and job satisfaction: The case of South Korea. *Journal of Higher Education Policy and Management, 38*(3), 297–315.

Kalleberg, A. L., & Mouw, T. (2018). Occupations, organizations, and intragenerational career. *Annual Review of Sociology, 44*, 283–303.

Kerchhoff, A. C. (1976). The status attainment process: Socialization and allocation. *Social Forces, 55*(2), 368–381.

Kurz, K., & Muller, W. (1987). Class mobility in the industrial world. *Annual Review of Sociology, 13*, 417–442.

Lin, T.-H., Hung, C.-S., Lee, C.-H., Wang, C.-C., & Cheng, F.-Y. (2011). *Generation of collapse: Crises of capital monopoly, poverty, and the lowest fertility in Taiwan.* Taipei: Taiwan Labor Front. (in Chinese).

Mitani, N. (2008). Youth employment in Japan after the 1990s bubble burst. In G. DeFreitas (Ed.), *Young workers in the global economy* (pp. 109–134). Cheltenham: Edward Elgar.

Oi, W. Y., & Idson, T. L. (1999). Firm size and wages. In O. Ashenfelter & D. Card (Eds.), *Handbook of labor economics* (Vol. 3, pp. 2165–2214). Part. B. Amsterdam: Elsevier.

Pan, Y.-J., & Lee, L.-S. (2015). An Investigation of new mid-level civil servants' public service motivation and its antecedents. *Journal of Civil Service, 7*(1), 35–69. (in Chinese).

Rosenfeld, R. A. (1992). Job mobility and career processes. *Annual Review of Sociology, 18*, 39–61.

Sandefur, G. D., & Park, H. (2007). Educational expansion and changes in occupational returns to education in Korea. *Research in Social Stratification and Mobility, 25*(4), 306–322.

Scherer, S. (2004). Stepping-stone or traps? The consequences of labor market entry positions on future career in West Germany, Great Britain and Italy. *Work, Employment and Society, 18*(2), 369–394.

Schmelzer, P. (2008). Increasing employment instability among young people? Labor market entries and early careers in Great Britain since the 1980s. In H.-P. Blossfeld, S. Buchholz, E. Bukodi & K. Kurz (Eds.), *Young workers, globalization and the labor market* (pp. 181–205). Cheltenham: Edward Elgar.

Sewell, W. H., Haller, A. O., & Olendorf, G. W. (1970). The educational and early occupational status attainment process: Replication and revision. *American Sociological Review, 35*(6), 1014–1027.

Spence, M. (1973). Job market signaling. *Quarterly Journal of Economics, 87*(3), 355–374.

Su, K.-H. (2008). Trends of income distribution and social mobility in Taiwan. In H.-Z. Wang, K.-C. Li, & I.-C. Kung (Eds.), *Step in forbidden zones: Twenty years social transformation in Taiwan, 1987–2008* (pp. 187–217). Taipei: Socio Publishing.

Thomas, S. L., & Zhang, L. (2005). Post-baccalaureate wage growth within 4 years of graduation: The effects of college quality and college major. *Research in Higher Education, 46,* 437–459.

Tsai, S.-L. (1998). The transition from school to work in Taiwan. In Y. Shavit & W. Müller (Eds.), *From school to work: A comparative study of educational qualifications and occupational destinations* (pp. 443–470). Oxford: Clarendon.

Tsai, M.-C. (2010). Evaluating sociologists in Taiwan: Power, profession and passers-by. In S. Patel (Ed.), *The ISA handbook of diverse sociological tradition* (pp. 313–323). Los Angeles, CA: SAGE.

Tsai, M.-C., Fan, G.-H., Hsiao, H.-H.M., & Wang, H.-Z. (2014). Profiling the middle class in Taiwan today. In H.-H. M. Hsiao (Ed.), *Chinese middle class: Taiwan, Hong Kong, Macao and China* (pp. 15–35). London: Routledge.

Wang, T.-M., Dong, Y.-J., & Chen, J.-R. (2013). The spatial pattern of fertility in Taiwan: A diffusion approach. *Taiwanese Journal of Social Welfare, 11*(1), 31–67. (in Chinese).

Weng, K., & Chang, F. (2011). Mismatch between education and work: School to work transition after higher education expansion. *Social Science Review, 5*(1), 1–38. (in Chinese).

Witteveen, D., & Attewell, P. (2017). The earnings payoff from attending a selective college. *Social Science Research, 66,* 154–169.

Wright, E. O. (2005). Foundations of a neo-Marxist class analysis. In E. O. Wright (Ed.), *Approaches to class analysis* (pp. 4–30). Cambridge: Cambridge University Press.

Yu, W.-H., & Chiu, C.-T. (2014). Off to a good start: A comparative study of changes in men's first job prospects in East Asia. *Research in Social Stratification and Mobility, 37,* 3–22.

Part IV

Young Married Couples: Marital Adjustment at the Beginning Stage

6

Domestic Labour Involvement of Young Taiwanese Couples in Different Partnership and Parenthood Statuses

Tsui-o Tai, Yi-Fu Chen and Hsien-Chih Tu

Introduction

Prior research has revealed that two major life transitions – to an intimate union and to parenthood – are strongly associated with time spent on domestic work and other family arrangements. According to most empirical studies based on cross-sectional data, married women undertake more domestic labour than cohabiting or single women do, and cohabiting men contribute more time to household labour than married men do (Baxter, 2005; Davis et al., 2007; Horne et al., 2017; Pepin et al., 2018; Shelton and John, 1993; South and Spitze, 1994). The allocation of household labour among cohabiting couples is more egalitarian than it is among married couples (Domínguez-Folgueras, 2012). Further, parents with dependent children have a more traditional division of housework than couples without children (Fuwa, 2004; Kluwer et al., 2002; Treas and Tai, 2012). However, some studies based on American and Australian longitudinal data arrive at mixed findings, showing that the time spent on domestic work by women and men does not change with the transition from cohabitation to marriage (Baxter et al., 2008; Gupta 1999). Meanwhile, while most longitudinal studies show that women substantially increase their time on housework after childbirth, especially after having the first child, fatherhood usually does not affect the amount of time that men spend on housework.

Scholars have identified two competing hypotheses – the selection and institution perspectives – to account for the disparities in domestic work involvement among couples of different partnership and parenthood statuses. The selection perspective argues that the factors leading to variations in housework involvement may also affect individuals' likelihood of making certain transitions or obtaining certain statuses (Baxter, 2005; Davis et al., 2007; Domínguez-Folgueras, 2012). For instance, women who enter a cohabitation union rather than a marriage may be less inclined to endorse conventional marriage and traditional gender roles. In this sense, these women may be reluctant to perform a large share of household tasks. Along the same vein, women who choose to raise children may identify with the traditional values of motherhood and role-associated responsibilities. On the contrary, the institution argument suggests that social institutions shape individuals' attitudes and behaviours (Cherlin, 1978). Distinctive family statuses involve different role responsibilities and create different kinds of institutional contexts. Couples arrange their household tasks according to these contexts and statuses (Baxter, 2005).

Although scholars have theorized the selection and institution processes to explain differences in the performance of household labour across statuses, few studies have empirically tested whether the impact of partnership and parenthood status on the distribution of household labour comes from one or both effects. Furthermore, despite much research on the association of partnership and parenthood statuses with domestic arrangements in Western societies, very few studies have examined the patterns in Taiwan or other East Asian countries. It is important to note that the connections between individuals' involvement in housework and their union types as documented in Western societies may not explain the situation in Taiwan. In terms of partnership formation, despite an increase in the number of nonmarital unions and out-of-wedlock births in Western societies (Batalova and Cohen, 2002; Sobotka and Toulemon, 2008), in Taiwan, unmarried co-residence and nonmarital parenthood are much less common than in Nordic or Western European countries, partly reflecting the social disapproval of nonmarital unions and child-bearing(Hwong et al., 2012; Yang et al., 2006; Wang and Chen, 2017). Although young adults tend to be more accepting of unions outside of marriage, most young cohabitors intend to marry their partners, which indicates that cohabitation is usually a precursor for marriage for young Taiwanese adults (Chien, 2018).

Taiwan has experienced substantially postponed first marriage and decreasing fertility. In 2010, the total fertility rate was less than 1, becoming the country with the lowest fertility rate in that year (The Ministry of Interior, ROC, 2020). Because of extremely low unmarried cohabitation and fertility rates, union types and parenthood status may have different meanings in Taiwan (Domínguez-Folgueras, 2012; Heuveline and Timberlake, 2004; Tai et al., 2014). In light of these phenomena, the effects of marital status and parenthood on domestic work may not be the same in Taiwan as in Western societies.

Due to a lack of systematic investigation of the effect of partnership and parenthood status on the distribution of household labour in previous studies, plus the unique patterns of family formation in Taiwan, this study extends the scope of the literature to examine whether an institution or a selection effect contributes to these differences in individuals' engagement in housework across distinctive partnerships and parenthood statuses in Taiwan. Our research questions are: (1) Do individuals' involvements in housework vary among partnership unions or parenthood statuses? (2) If they do, are these variations attributable to an institution and/or to a selection effect?

Explaining Household Labour

Several theories have been applied to the division of household labour and personal involvement in domestic work. Based on Becker's (1981) neo-economic approach, the human capital perspective associates gender specialization in human capital with the division of paid and unpaid work. Conventionally, boys are raised to concentrate on market success; girls are socialized to prioritize family work. The human capital approach assumes that due to men's and women's differential investment in human capital, gender specialization is a rational economic strategy to maximize household utility.

The time availability and relative resource/exchange perspectives also assess household labour from a rational and instrumental standpoint (Coltrane, 2000). The time availability assumption is more straightforward. Because time is limited, the spouse who is not employed in the labour market can devote more time to housework. The relative resource/exchange approach, in contrast, hypothesizes housework to be so tedious that both men and women want to avoid it. To escape endless domestic chores, the spouse with more resources (education, income, occupational prestige, etc.) will bargain his or her way out of them (Baxter and Tai, 2016; Coltrane, 2000; Lundberg and

Pollak, 1996). Because women usually have fewer of these economic resources, they undertake most of the household tasks.

While some empirical studies are consistent with these economic and gender-neutral models, others have limited statistical support. For example, some studies show that even when wives earn more or hold more prestigious positions than their husbands, they still spend more time on housework and perform a larger share of household labour (Brines, 1994; Coltrane, 2000). To address the persistence of gendered domestic arrangements, feminist scholars provide a gender perspective that originates from West and Zimmerman's concept of *doing gender*. According to West and Zimmerman, gender is 'a routine accomplishment embedded in everyday interaction' (1987, p. 125). In line with this argument, instead of considering the gendered division of labour as a result of rational calculation or efficient arrangement, Berk (1985) frames the marital household as a gender factory where, in addition to goods and services, gender is produced through the arrangements of everyday domestic work. In other words, the daily practices of domestic chores and care work at home produce women's submission to patriarchal norms.

Women are found to undertake the majority of domestic work in all documented societies (Kan et al., 2011; Lachance-Grzela and Bouchard, 2010; Treas and Lui, 2013). However, the way in which couples share household tasks and the amount of time that each partner devotes to domestic labour vary considerably across countries. The following section discusses the patterns of domestic labour arrangements in Taiwan.

Housework Patterns in Taiwan

Most studies of housework patterns in Taiwan focus on married couples and parents. Very few studies have investigated the variations in domestic work among singles, cohabitors and marrieds. Partially due to data limitations, no panel studies have examined whether Taiwanese individuals adjust their engagement in household labour following their transitions to an intimate relationship or parenthood. According to cross-national data, the division of household labour is generally more traditional in Taiwan than in many Western societies. According to a study of 27 countries (Baxter and Tai, 2016), in 2012, married Taiwanese women's share of housework time was more than

65 per cent, a percentage which was higher than that of women in 21 other countries. In terms of the absolute amount of time spent on housework, partially because of outsourcing (including hired domestic help and eating out) or assistance they received with domestic chores and childcare from older generations (Hsiao, 2005), married Taiwanese women dedicated less time to domestic work than their counterparts in many countries (Baxter and Tai, 2016). In addition, the number of children in the household is positively associated with women's share of total housework time; the presence of more preschool children in the household is negatively correlated with men's percentage of total housework time (Hsiao, 2005).

Similar to patterns observed in Western societies, the gender gap in housework time in Taiwan has narrowed over the past several decades, mainly as a result of women's substantially reduced time spent on household labour. Between 1987 and 2000, the amount of time coupled Taiwanese women allocated to housework decreased from 33.25 to 22.63 hours per week, while coupled men's housework hours increased slightly from 2.8 to 4.08 hours per week (Hsiao, 2005). While the gender difference in housework time has declined, women continue to undertake a disproportionate part of domestic work, and the gender segregation in household labour persists. Taiwanese women are still responsible for most routine household tasks, such as laundry, cooking and cleaning (Chang and Li, 2007).

These factors accounting for individuals' involvement in housework are generally applied to the domestic labour arrangements among Taiwanese couples. More equal income contributions within couples and their liberal gender attitudes lead to a more egalitarian division of housework (Hsiao, 2005; Lu and Yi, 2005).

As noted, the division of domestic work is more gendered in Taiwan. Economic models and gender perspectives are two major explanations for the variation in housework involvement between men and women. In actuality, more factors complicate the gendered distribution of housework. The following section reviews research on the connection between housework and partnership and parenthood status.

Distribution of Housework, Partnership Status and Parenthood

Involvement in household tasks differs not only between men and women but also across life stages. Partnership formation and parenthood are two major life transitions that bring considerable changes to domestic arrangements. Cross-sectional studies show that married women contribute to housework more than cohabiting or uncoupled women do, and that cohabitors distribute household tasks more equally than married people (Baxter, 2005; Davis et al., 2007; Horne et al., 2017). Furthermore, mothers are found to spend more time on housework than do child-free women, whereas fathers spend less time on housework than men without children do (Bianchi et al., 2012; Dribe et al., 2009). At the same time, according to a few panel studies (Baxter et al., 2008; Gupta, 1999; Haynes et al., 2015), women increase their time spent on housework when they move from singlehood to marriage or cohabitation, whereas men do not. There are no significant differences, however, in the increased amount of time women spend on housework after they enter either a cohabitation union or a marriage, nor does the transition from cohabitation to marriage affect the amount of time women and men spend on domestic work. Moreover, motherhood (especially after the first childbirth) increases women's time on domestic work and leads to a more traditional division of housework between spouses (Baxter et al., 2008; Gupta, 1999; Kluwer et al., 2002; Sanchez and Thomson, 1997; Schober, 2013). However, men either do not change their time on domestic work after the first birth or slightly reduce their time on housework after having an additional child (Baxter et al., 2008; Gupta, 1999; Sanchez and Thomson, 1997).

Between the two mechanisms of housework division, the selection perspective posits that people who make certain life transitions or establish certain family types (such as parenthood, marriage, cohabitation) possess distinctive characteristics (Nock, 1995). These characteristics are likely associated with their involvement in household tasks. Many studies have investigated the individual and family traits that predict the probability of entering marriage, cohabitation, remaining single, or becoming a parent. In terms of demographic and socioeconomic characteristics, individuals with lower SES and who come from fragmented or disadvantaged families of origin are more likely to enter nonmarital relationships or become unmarried parents (Dush et al., 2018; Ishizuka, 2018; Nock, 1995). Ideo-culturally, cohabitors are less religious, express less commitment to marital permanence, and are less likely to endorse traditional gender roles (Axinn and Thornton, 1992; Clarkberg et al., 1995; Dush et al., 2018;

Eggebeen and Dew, 2009; Nock, 1995; Raymo et al., 2009). In line with the selection argument, women who choose to marry and then have children may espouse traditional family values, and thus accept the traditional division of housework and family care (Haynes et al., 2015).

In contrast, the institution perspective suggests that social institutions shape individuals' external behaviours and inner thoughts (Cherlin, 1978). The traditional family that consists of married parents and their biological children provides social control of reproduction and childrearing. It defines role rights and responsibilities and sets guidelines for proper behaviour. In other words, varying family processes and outcomes happen in response to people's changes in their family statuses. Compared to traditional legally married parents with children, some alternative family forms, such as blended families (e.g. stepfamilies) and nonmarital cohabitation unions, are considered incomplete institutions (Cherlin, 1978; Nock, 1995). The notion of 'incomplete institutionalization' suggests these alternative union types lack legal protection for the durability of commitment, and are short of normative prescriptions for role performance (Baxter, 2005; Heuveline and Timberlake, 2004; Ishii-Kuntz and Coltrane, 1992; Musick and Michelmore, 2018). For instance, due to the more ambiguous norms for cohabitation, partners probably have the space to negotiate a more equitable division of paid and unpaid work but legally married couples do not (Baxter, 2005). Also, because of the instability of unmarried unions, to maintain economic security, cohabitors may avoid concentrating on housework (Brines and Joyner, 1999).

From the perspective of the human capital theory, wives who specialize in family care in a stable marital household are at lower risk of losing financial support from their spouses than are women in a cohabiting union. Married women, therefore, have an incentive to concentrate on family work. In addition, because of legal sanctions and normative standards for marriage, spouses may be more committed to a marital relationship and identify with traditional family roles, such as a breadwinning husband and a stay-at-home wife. Along with the idea of gender display, a strong commitment to marital roles motivates women to assume a wife's traditional role through their daily dedication to family work and encourages men to display the appropriate behaviours of a husband by investing more time in paid work.

Parenthood also involves certain culturally defined responsibilities and behaviours. Conventionally, a good mother is devoted to family work, and a good father earns enough to support the family. To take care of their children, some mothers reduce their work hours or even leave the paid workforce. Thus, parenthood is usually connected with an enhanced gender display, wherein women assume a nurturing role and allocate more time to family work, and men reduce their involvement in household labour and invest more time in paid work, possibly to make up for the loss of their spouses' earnings (Baxter et al., 2008).

Previous studies have revealed the effect of partnership and parenthood status on the distribution of housework. In terms of the effect of partnership status, based on a study of five Western countries by Domínguez-Folgueras (2012), while cohabiting women contribute to housework less than married women do, the difference is more pronounced in Spain and Italy than in the UK. According to Domínguez-Folgueras' argument, in societies like those in Scandinavian countries, where nonmarital cohabitation is widespread or even indistinguishable from marriage, the effect of cohabitation on domestic labour arrangements is expected to be negligible. In contrast, in conservative societies such as Italy and Spain, where cohabitation is rare, people tend to conform to conventional marital norms, and unmarried co-residence seems limited to highly educated and employed women. In these societies, cohabitors tend to have a more egalitarian relationship and a less gendered division of housework than married couples. In comparison, the association between parenthood status and household labour is relatively consistent across societies. As mentioned, mothers tend to spend more time on domestic work than do women without children, based on both cross-sectional and panel data (Baxter et al., 2008; Hsiao, 2005; Treas and Tai, 2012). Cross-sectional data also reveals that fathers spend less time on domestic work than child-free men. Panel studies, however, show men's stable involvement in domestic work over the life course (Baxter et al., 2008; Baxter and Tai, 2016; Gupta, 1999).

As noted, no panel studies have examined how the transition to partnership and parenthood affects Taiwanese men's and women's involvement in household labour. Given the divergent patterns of family formation in Taiwan, the findings observed in Western societies may not account for conditions in Taiwan. Thus, it is critical to investigate whether the link between partnership and parenthood statuses and housework involvement and its associated mechanisms in Taiwan may also differ from what is observed in Western societies.

Methodological Issues

The mixed findings for the association between partnership and parenthood statuses and the distribution of housework may result from the less clear specification of the two effects in analyses: selection and institutional effects. In related cross-sectional studies, the information on family status, housework arrangements, gender attitudes and other individual and family characteristics is collected at one time point, which may confound the results statistically. It is difficult to clarify the temporal ordering of partnership formation or parenthood and housework involvement with a cross-sectional design. In other words, it is unclear as to whether the variations in dedication to housework across these statuses result from a selection effect of predisposing characteristics of couples or from the impact of an institution.

Studies using longitudinal data collect information on individuals' entry into and exit from intimate unions, their transition to parenthood and their changes in domestic labour engagement. Therefore, the causal link between partnership or parenthood status and housework involvement is less ambiguous (Gupta, 1999). More precisely, when one examines the partnership or parenthood transitions of those individuals, the selection bias or the unmeasured interindividual heterogeneity is already controlled; thus, whether there are changes in domestic labour arrangements after the entry into, or exit from, an intimate relationship, such as from cohabitation to marriage, can be attributable to an institution effect. However, for instance, for the partnership transition of different individuals, when one compares the household arrangements of individuals moving from singlehood to marriage with those moving from singlehood to cohabitation, the two effects are likely to mingle if the predisposing characteristics associated with the selection into union status are not controlled.

Inverse probability of treatment weighting (IPTW) is widely used to take the selection effect into account when estimating the causal order (Hernán et al., 2000; Robins et al., 2000; Sampson et al., 2006). The selection into partnership or parenthood status can be controlled by conducting a weighted estimation, assigning each subject's data a weight inversely proportional to their probability of being selected. For instance, we give greater weight to respondents who were at lower risk of forming a cohabitation relationship, which would adjust the potential selection bias. Once the selection into a specific union status is taken into account with a weighting factor, the differences in housework dedication between married couples and cohabitors can be attributable to the influence of partnership status or parenthood status. This method enables us to evaluate the effect of selection through the comparison of weighted and unweighted estimates. That is, this study assesses both the selection and institution effects simultaneously using IPTW.

In summary, despite much research on differences in domestic labour engagement across union forms, very few studies have systematically investigated whether these disparities stem from a selection process or an institution effect. To address this limitation, this study will use IPTW and test the effects of the two mechanisms on the connection between partnership and parenthood statuses and domestic labour arrangements. Due to data constraints, this study focuses on married parents, child-free married couples and child-free cohabiting couples.

Methods

This study relies on data from the Taiwan Youth Project (TYP). Since 2000, the TYP panel survey has followed two cohorts (J-1, the first year of junior high school and J-3, the third year of junior high school) when members of these cohorts were 13 and 15 years old, every two to three years. The first survey consists of 1,592 J-1 respondents and 1,537 J-3 respondents. The most recent wave was conducted in 2017 when the J-1 cohort reached an average age of 30 years and the J-3 reached 32 years. Due to a loss of some cases, 2,550 respondents were recruited in 2017.

Our analyses were restricted to married or cohabiting respondents.

To investigate the distribution of domestic work across partnership and parenthood statuses, this study combines the first and most recent waves (2017) of data. The 2017 wave is the only one to collect measures of domestic work arrangements from both married and cohabiting respondents. Wave 1 provides essential data on respondents' adolescence. With missing data deleted, the final analytic sample consists of 425 coupled women (married or cohabiting) and 499 coupled men.

The dependent variable is the frequency of doing housework, assessed by the average score of four items measuring the respondents' frequency of doing four household tasks per week that are traditionally done by women: laundry, meal preparation, cleaning and washing dishes. The original coding was reversed to range from 1 = *never* to 7 = *almost every day*. Higher scores reflect more frequent involvement in housework. The spouse's/partner's domestic involvement is measured in the same way.

The key independent variable is partnership and parenthood statuses. Given that there are too few stepfamilies or cohabiting respondents with children (only two, which were excluded from the final analysis) to form other union categories, our study combines partnership and parenthood statuses to divide respondents into three categories: married parents, married respondents without children and cohabiting respondents (without children) (omitted group).

This study evaluates respondents' gender attitudes by estimating the mean scores of the following six statements: (1) A man should have the final word about decisions in his home; (2) A preschool child is likely to suffer if his or her mother works; (3) A man's job is to earn money and a woman's job is to look after the family; (4) It is acceptable for married women to be laid off before men during an economic recession; (5) Men make better leaders than women; (6) A woman should choose the family over work when there is a conflict between family and work responsibilities (Overall Cronbach's alpha = 0.78; For men: 0.75; For women: 0.75). The responses range from *strongly agree* (=1) to *strongly disagree* (=4). Higher values suggest more egalitarian attitudes towards gender roles.

The demographic and socioeconomic variables that predict the respondent's involvement in domestic work include the respondent's age (in years), educational attainment (in years), work status (working = 0, nonworking = 1) and monthly household income (in thousands of NT dollars). In addition, we construct the measure of relative education (the respondent has more years of education, the respondent and spouse/partner have the same amount of education and the spouse/partner has more years of education) to test the relative resource hypothesis in our models. Due to missing data of the work status and income of spouses/partners, this study did not add the measure of a spouse's/partner's work status or the distribution of income between spouses/partners. Finally, given that multigenerational coresidence and intergenerational support of finance and services may affect the respondents' involvement in domestic work, the intergenerational living arrangements of respondents are coded as living with the parents of male spouses/partners, living with the parents of female spouses/partners and living with spouses/partners only (omitted group). Because 91 respondents did not reveal information on the living arrangements of their spouses' or partners' parents, we add a category of missing data to measure intergenerational living arrangements to keep as many cases as possible in the analyses.

To test the selection effect on the frequency of doing housework, we construct a weighting factor to adjust estimates. Specifically, we conduct a multinomial logistic regression to obtain the probability of an individual being married with children, being married without children or cohabiting without children in 2017 using covariates including the respondent's age, gender, the SES of the family of origin, family structure (nonintact = 1, intact = 0), gender attitudes, geographic location during adolescence (at wave 1) and later educational achievement (in years). The study then analyses the respondent's frequency of doing domestic tasks, weighting subjects by the inverse of their probability of being married with children, being married without children or cohabiting without children (inverse probability treatment weight, IPTW) (Bartlett, 2012). To avoid the influence of extreme values in the weights, the study follows Robins et al (2000) suggestion to calculate the stabilized weights, which were used in the final regression models.

Result

Descriptive Statistics

Table 6.1 summarizes the distribution of individual and family characteristics by gender and partnership and parenthood statuses. Among 499 men, about 53 per cent of male respondents are married fathers, 28 per cent are married without children and almost 19 per cent are child-free cohabitors; among 425 women, 54 per cent are married mothers, 29 per cent are married without children and nearly 17 per cent are in a nonmarital cohabitation relationship without children.

Not surprisingly, women report higher rates of doing housework than men (5.2 vs. 4.4, once a week vs. once a month). Probably because of the commonness of eating out of home, hiring domestic help and receiving assistance with housework from older generations in Taiwan, the frequency of doing housework by these young respondents is not high. In terms of the distribution of domestic labour involvement among partnership and parenthood statuses, married mothers are more involved in housework than child-free women. There are no significant differences in domestic labour involvement among men in different partnership and parenthood statuses.

On average, both male and female respondents have obtained college or university degrees (15–16 years). Married fathers and mothers have lower levels of educational attainment than nonparents. As expected, many more women than men are not in the labour market (18 per cent vs. 3 per cent). Interestingly, a smaller proportion of cohabiting men are employed than married fathers, whereas a larger percentage of cohabiting women are at work than married mothers. In terms of financial resources, men reported higher household income than women. Married, and child-free women report higher levels of household income, followed by mothers and cohabiting (child-free) women.

In regards to gender attitudes, the women expressed more egalitarian attitudes towards gender roles than the men did (3.2 vs. 2.8). Married fathers are more traditional than men without children, while married mothers hold more traditional gender attitudes than child-free women. Finally, leading an independent household is the most common living arrangement among young couples, followed by co-residence with the parents of the male partner.

Multivariate Analysis

Tables 6.2 and 6.3 present the multivariate analyses that assess the individual and family effects on coupled men's and coupled women's involvement in household tasks. Model 1 tests the effect of partnership and parenthood statuses on the frequency of doing domestic work without other predictors in consideration. Model 2 estimates a full model with all individual and family variables included. Model 3 adjusts the estimates of Model 2 with a weighting factor.

Table 6.1 Distribution of individual and family characteristics by gender and partnership and parenthood statuses

Variable	Men				t test/ Bonferroni/Chi-squared
	(a) All	(b) Married fathers	(c) Married, w/o children	(d) Cohabiting w/o children	
Frequency of Doing Household Tasks by Respondent	4.40	4.29	4.46	4.48	e>a
Respondent's Age (in years)	31.91	32.01	31.89	31.65	b>d
Respondent's Education (in years)	15.33	14.76	16.01	15.90	e>a, c>b, d>b
Education Relative to Spouse/ Partner (%)					
Same Levels of Education	51.90	51.32	56.03	47.31	
Respondent with Higher Education	27.66	24.53	29.08	34.41	
Spouse/Partner with Higher Education	20.44	24.15	14.89	18.28	
Monthly Household Income (in thousand)	104.12	101.49	106.43	108.10	a>e
Respondent's Work Status (%)					
Working	96.79	98.11	97.16	92.47	a>e, b>d
Respondent's Gender Attitudes	2.83	2.76	2.89	2.94	e>a, c>b, d>b
Intergenerational Coresidence (%)					$p < 0.001$

	(e) All	(f) Married Mothers	(g) Married, w/o children	(h) Cohabiting w/o children	t test/ Bonferroni/ Chi-squared
Couples only	40.28	43.77	56.03	6.45	
Living with the Parents of Male Spouses/Partners	43.69	48.68	35.46	41.94	
Living with the Parents of Female Spouses/Partners	5.01	5.66	2.84	6.45	
Missing	11.02	1.89	5.67	45.16	
Sub-N		265	141	93	
Total N			499		

	Women				t test/
Variable	(e) All	(f) Married Mothers	(g) Married, w/o children	(h) Cohabiting w/o children	Bonferroni/ Chi-squared
Frequency of Doing Household Tasks by Respondent	5.19	5.41	5.04	4.75	e>a, f>g, f>h
Respondent's Age (in years)	31.82	31.88	31.81	31.65	
Respondent's Education (in years)	15.72	15.49	16.23	15.58	e>a, g>f, g>h
Education Relative to Spouse/ Partner (%)					
Same Levels of Education	50.47	51.32	56.03	47.31	
Respondent with Higher Education	27.70	24.53	29.08	34.41	
Spouse/Partner with Higher Education	21.83	24.15	14.89	18.28	

(Continued)

Table 6.1 Distribution of individual and family characteristics by gender and partnership and parenthood statuses (Continued)

| Variable | Women | | | | t test/ |
	(e) All	(f) Married Mothers	(g) Married, w/o children	(h) Cohabiting w/o children	Bonferroni/ Chi-squared
Monthly Household Income (in thousand)	92.00	88.03	104.75	82.75	a>e, g>f, g>h
Respondent's Work Status (%)					
Working	82.39	75.65	88.71	93.06	a>e, g>f, h>f
Respondent's Gender Attitudes	3.17	3.07	3.28	3.32	e>a, g>f, h>f
Intergenerational Coresidence (%)					$p < 0.001$
Couples only	51.17	43.77	56.03	6.45	
Living with the Parents of Male Spouses/Partners	25.35	48.68	35.46	41.94	
Living with the Parents of Female Spouses/Partners	15.02	5.66	2.84	6.45	
Missing	8.45	1.89	5.67	45.16	
Sub-N		230	124	72	
Total N			425		

Based on men's reports (Table 6.2), when other variables are not held constant, there are no significant differences in domestic involvement between married and cohabiting men. Model 2 investigates the effect of partnership and parenthood statuses on housework with other predictors controlled. When all other characteristics are held constant, cohabiting men report higher rates of doing household tasks than married men, whether there are children in the household or not ($p < 0.01$ and $p < 0.05$). As the findings suggest, it is marital, rather than parenthood status, that affects men's involvement in household labour. Meanwhile, men with higher educational attainment ($p < 0.01$), who hold more egalitarian gender attitudes ($p < 0.001$), and those whose spouses/partners do more housework ($p < 0.001$), report higher levels of domestic engagement. In line with the relative resource perspective, men with less education than their spouses/partners also do more domestic work ($p < 0.001$). In addition, men living with their own parents or parents of their spouses/partners do less family work ($p < 0.05$).

The estimates in Model 3 are adjusted with a weighting factor to account for selection into different union types. According to Model 3, the effect of partnership and parenthood statuses is similar to what is suggested in Model 2, although the coefficients and significance levels are slightly reduced, suggesting little evidence of the selection effect on men's participation in domestic labour. In other words, the institution effect accounts for the difference in the frequency of doing domestic work across partnership and parenthood statuses. At the same time, relative educational attainment becomes non-significant. All other effects remain similar to those in Model 2.

Turning to women's reports in Table 6.3, when other explanatory variables are not controlled (Model 1), compared to cohabiting women without children, married women with and without children report higher rates of doing household tasks ($p < 0.001$ and $p < 0.10$). According to Model 2, all else being equal, married mothers are still more involved in housework ($p < 0.05$), but there is no significant difference in domestic involvement between married women without children and cohabiting women. That is, when one compares women with similar individual and family characteristics (e.g. gender attitudes, work status), being a mother increases a woman's involvement in domestic labour. At the same time, non-employed women are more engaged in domestic work ($p < 0.001$), whereas women who live with

Table 6.2 Individual and family effects on household labour: men's reports

Variable	Model 1		Model 2 Non-adjusted		Model 3 Adjusted	
Intercept	4.478	***	1.692		1.591	*
Partnership and Parenthood Statuses						
(Cohabiting, without children=ref)						
Married fathers	-0.191		-0.635	**	-0.589	*
Married, without Children	0.078		-0.497	*	-0.487	+
Respondent's Age			-0.038		-0.024	
Respondent's Education			0.099	**	0.079	+
Education Relative to Spouse/Partner						
Respondent with Higher Education			-0.009		-0.174	
Spouse/Partner with Higher Education			0.569	***	0.344	
Same Levels of Education (ref)						
Monthly Household Income			0.001		0.001	
Respondent's Work Status (Working=ref)						
Non-working			0.156		0.234	
Respondent's Gender Attitudes			0.532	***	0.507	***
Domestic Involvement by Spouse/Partner			0.255	***	0.277	**
Intergenerational Coresidence (W/O Parents=ref)						
Living w/Parents of Male Spouses/Partners			-0.296	*	-0.246	+
Living w/Parents of Female Spouses/Partners			-0.588	*	-0.647	*
Missing			-0.305		-0.284	
N			499			
R-squared	0.010		0.132		0.116	

$+p < 0.1$, $^*p < 0.05$, $^{**}p < 0.01$, $^{***}p < 0.001$

Variable	Model 1		Model 2 Non-adjusted		Model 3 Adjusted	
Intercept	4.739	***	3.934	**	5.413	**
Partnership and Parenthood Statuses						
(Cohabiting, without children)						
Married Mothers	0.669	***	0.590	*	0.737	*
Married, without Children	0.303	+	0.318		0.476	
Respondent's Age			0.041		-0.029	
Respondent's Education			-0.021		0.000	
Education Relative to Spouse/Partner						
Respondent with Higher Education			0.059		-0.128	
Spouse/Partner with Higher Education			0.022		-0.039	
Same Levels of Education (ref)						
Monthly Household Income			0.001		0.000	
Respondent's Work Status (Working=ref)						
Non-working			0.656	***	0.698	***
Respondent's Gender Attitudes			-0.188		0.024	
Domestic Involvement by Spouse/Partner			0.075		0.015	
Intergenerational Coresidence (Couples only=ref)						
Living w/Parents of Male Spouses/Partners			-0.173		-0.262	
Living w/Parents of Female Spouses/Partners			-0.294	+	-0.332	
Missing			0.434	+	0.234	
N			425			
R-squared	0.061		0.156		0.144	

+$p < 0.1$, *$p < 0.05$, **$p < 0.01$, ***$p < 0.001$

their parents report lower rates of doing housework ($p < 0.10$). Other predictors are not statistically significant.

Based on the weighted analyses shown in Model 3, the effect of partnership and parenthood statuses on domestic involvement is, once again, similar to the results in Model 2. Married mothers remain more involved in domestic work ($p < 0.05$). Similar to the analyses on male respondents, the results do not present clear patterns of selection effect on women's domestic involvement across different partnership and parenthood statuses. Motherhood is the determinant of women's engagement in household labour. Furthermore, nonworking women report higher rates of doing household tasks ($p < 0.001$). Finally, additional analyses that combine both females and males show that married mothers perform more domestic work than child-free women and men in the three statuses (results available upon request).

In summary, consistent with previous studies, married mothers report higher frequencies of performing household labour than child-free women, whereas cohabiting men contribute significantly more to domestic work than married men do. The weighted analyses produce similar effects of partnership and parenthood statuses for both men and women. Thus, our findings support the presence of an institution effect on the varying involvement in housework in responding to partnership types and parenthood status. For men, marital status is a key influence on their performance of housework. For women, motherhood appears to be the essential factor.

Discussion

This study uses the method of IPTW to examine whether an institution effect or a selection process contributes to the disparities in domestic labour involvement across three partnership and parenthood statuses: married with children, married without children and cohabiting without children. Based on men's reports, which show similar findings with most cross-sectional studies, with all things held constant, married fathers report the lowest rates of doing housework. However, different from the Western longitudinal studies, which show no significant differences in domestic work time between cohabiting and married men, Taiwanese cohabiting men are more involved in domestic work than married men. For women, consistent with

Western studies, motherhood is associated with a higher frequency of performing housework. In addition, there are no significant differences between married and cohabiting child-free women.

Importantly, as the adjusted analyses that take selection effects into consideration show similar estimates to the unadjusted results, the differences in the frequency of doing housework can be attributable to the institution hypothesis for both men and women. In terms of partnership status, unmarried cohabitation may have different meanings and thus affect domestic arrangements through varying selection or institutional processes in many societies. For instance, in societies where legal marriage is indistinguishable from unmarried cohabitation, there may be no apparent differences in domestic arrangements between married and unmarried couples.

Our expectation was that the rarity of cohabitation in Taiwan may yield a strong selection influence as well as an institution effect on the distribution of household labour. However, a selection effect appears absent in our findings, and we consider some possibilities for this outcome. First, this study is restricted to young adults aged 25–36. Young adults are more accepting of cohabitation and other nontraditional relationships (Hwong et al., 2012; Wang and Chen, 2017). Thus, young cohabitors may be less selective than cohabitors in older cohorts. Second, the majority of young cohabitors expressed their intention to marry their partners (Chien, 2018). For young Taiwanese adults, cohabitation is usually a precursor to marriage. Hence, a selection process might have already taken place when these young adults began cohabiting. The factors leading to the absence of a selection effect in our analyses are expected to be different from those in Nordic and Western European societies.

For the net of gender attitudes, work status and relative educational attainment, an institutional process accounts for the differences between cohabiting men and married men and between mothers and child-free women. As discussed in the introduction section, social institutions provide guidelines for proper status-associated responsibilities and behaviours. Our results show that marriage and motherhood socialize Taiwanese couples to behave in particular ways, including the housework they perform. Low rates of nonmarital cohabitation and childbirth suggest that Taiwanese continue to see marriage, especially a married household with biological children, as an essential or even sacred institution and conform to its traditional norms (Davis et al., 2007). The less prevalent unmarried co-residence among our respondents suggests that unmarried cohabitation, in which couples are allowed to negotiate alternative roles, responsibilities and family arrangements, is an incompletely institutionalized union in the Taiwanese society.

The findings also suggest parenthood as a major status that has a substantial effect on men's and women's family arrangements. It is plausible that men and women are inclined to accept the culturally prescribed parenthood responsibilities after having children. The prevalence of multigenerational households and grandparental childcare may reinforce a traditional division of household labour (Hsiao, 2005). It is also possible that a more gendered division of housework is a compromise, as the presence of children in the household increases the amount of family work. In order to undertake more household labour, mothers may need to reduce their time of paid work or even withdraw from the labour market to concentrate on family work, given the dearth of affordable childcare facilities in Taiwan. In contrast, men may dedicate more time and efforts to paid work if they have several children and/or decreased income from their spouses.

In addition to partnership and parenthood statuses, some of our findings align with previous studies. Consistent with the gender perspective, men who adopt more egalitarian gender attitudes are more likely to perform domestic work. As for the relative resource perspective, the unadjusted results show that men with more educated spouses are more engaged in housework. Meanwhile, nonworking women report higher rates of doing housework, potentially because they have more time for family and less earned income. Finally, multigenerational households are also found to affect individuals' domestic arrangements. Due to the additional help from parents or parents-in-laws – who reinforce the traditional gender and parenthood roles – men living with their own or their partners' parents are less engaged in household tasks.

Conclusion

This study provides insight into the study of family work. It extends the scope of literature by examining the differences in domestic labour involvement across Taiwanese partnership and parenthood statuses. It is also one of the first to systematically investigate whether these differences stem from an institution influence or a selection effect by using an IPTW weighting method. This study concludes by suggesting that the institution mechanism mainly explains the differences in domestic labour involvement across partnership and parenthood statuses. Our results indicate that in Taiwan, where nonmarital family behaviours are less common and less socially accepted, a married household with children continues to be the dominant institution for family formation, and a site for the production and reinforcement of traditional gender roles (Berk, 1985).

In the end, this study is not without limitations. First, the TYP study did not provide data on the respondents' involvement in domestic work in previous waves; therefore, our study cannot examine individuals' levels of engagement in housework over their life stages. Second, because there are too few stepfamilies and cohabiting respondents with children, observation of domestic arrangements in these families is fruitless. Third, the measurement of domestic work involvement is assessed by the frequency of doing household tasks (e.g. cooking, cleaning) per week by the respondent and the spouse/partner separately. It is difficult to create a variable to measure the division of housework within couples. Our study, therefore, examines the rates of performing household tasks by individuals in different partnership and parenthood statuses with their spouses' involvement in housework controlled. Fourth, the TYP data did not provide information on the work status, work hours or earnings of cohabitors' partners, and therefore we cannot construct the respondents' income relative to their cohabiting partners in our analysis. Finally, the TYP did not have data on the frequency of dining out or using purchased help, which hinders the examination of the way in which the outsourcing of domestic work affects individuals' engagement in housework.

Despite these limitations, this study sheds additional light on previous findings. This research is one of the first to examine differences in domestic work across Taiwanese partnership and parenthood statuses, whether those differences stem from an institution effect or a selection process. Given the growth in alternative family formation, future studies should examine the distribution of household labour and other gender relationships in a wide range of family types.

References

Axinn, W., & Thornton, A. (1992). The relationship between cohabitation and divorce: Selectivity or causal influence? *Demography, 29*(3), 357–374.

Bartlett, J. (2012). *Handling missing data in Stata: A whirlwind tour', presentation presented at the 2012 Italian Stata Users Group Meeting.* Bologna. Retrieved from https://www.stata.com/meeting/italy12/abstracts/materials/it12_bartlett.pdf

Batalova, J., & Cohen, P. N. (2002). Premarital cohabitation and housework: Couples in cross-national perspective. *Journal of Marriage and Family, 64*(3), 129–144.

Baxter, J. (2005). To marry or not to marry: Marital status and the household division of labor. *Journal of Family Issues, 26*(3), 300–321.

Baxter, J., Hewitt, B., & Haynes, M. (2008). Life course transitions and housework: Marriage, parenthood, and time on housework. *Journal of Marriage and Family, 70*(2), 259–272.

Baxter, J., & Tai, T. (2016). Unpaid domestic work. In S. Edgell, H. Gottfried & E. Granter (Eds.), *The SAGE handbook of the sociology of work and employment* (pp. 444–466). Los Angeles, CA: SAGE Publications.

Becker, G. (1981). *A treatise on the family.* Chicago, IL: University of Chicago.

Berk, S. F. (1985). *The gender factory.* New York, NY: Plenum.

Bianchi, S. M., Sayer, L. C., Milkie, M. A., & Robinson, J. P. (2012). Housework: Who did, does or will do it, and how much does it matter? *Social Forces, 91*(1), 55–63.

Brines, J. (1994). Economic dependency, gender, and the division of labor at home. *American Journal of Sociology, 100*(3), 652–688.

Brines, J., & Joyner, K. (1999). The ties that bind: Principles of cohesion in cohabitation and marriage. *American Sociological Review, 64*(3), 333–355.

Chang, C.-F., & Li, Y.-H. (2007). Women's housework, men's housework: Explanations for the continuing gender division of housework. *Journal of Social Sciences and Philosophy, 19*(2), 203–229.

Cherlin, A. (1978). Remarriage as an incomplete institution. *American Journal of Sociology, 84*(3), 634–650.

Chien, C.-C. (2018). *Cohabitation equals marriage? A comparison of relationship quality among cohabitors and marrieds.* Master's thesis. Taiwan: National Taipei University.

Clarkberg, M., Stolzenberg, R. M., & Waite, L. J. (1995). Attitudes, values, and entrance into marital unions. *Social Forces, 74*(2), 609–634.

Coltrane, S. (2000), Research on household labor: Modeling and measuring the social embeddedness of routine family work. *Journal of Marriage and Family, 62*(4), 1208–1233.

Davis, S. N., Greenstein, T. N., & Marks, J. (2007). Effects of union type on division of household labor: Do cohabiting men really perform more housework? *Journal of Family Issues, 28*(9), 1246–1272.

Domínguez-Folgueras, M. (2012). Is cohabitation more egalitarian? The division of household labor in five European countries. *Journal of Family Issues, 34*(12), 1623–1646.

Dribe, M., Stanfors, M., & Buehler, C. (2009). Does parenthood strengthen a traditional household division of labor? Evidence from Sweden. *Journal of Marriage and Family, 71*(1), 33–45.

Dush, C. M. K., Jang, B., & Snyder, A. R. (2018). A cohort comparison of predictors of young adult union formation and dissolution in the US. *Advances in Life Course Research, 38*, 37–49.

Eggebeen, D., & Dew, J. (2009). The role of religion in adolescence for family formation in young adulthood. *Journal of Marriage and Family, 71*(1), 108–121.

Fuwa, M. (2004). Macro-level gender inequality and the division of household labor in 22 countries. *American Sociological Review, 69*(6), 751–767.

Gupta, S. (1999). The effects of transitions in marital status on men's performance of house-work. *Journal of Marriage and the Family, 61*(3), 700–711.

Dribe Haynes, M., Baxter, J., Hewitt, B., & Western, M. (2015). Time on housework and selection into and out of relationships in Australia: A multiprocess, multilevel approach. *Longitudinal and Life Course Studies, 6*(3), 245–263.

Hernán, M. Á., Brumback, B., & Robins, J. M. (2000). Marginal structural models to estimate the causal effect of zidovudine on the survival of HIV-positive men. *Epidemiology, 11*(5), 561–570.

Heuveline, P., & Timberlake, J. (2004). The role of cohabitation in family formation, The United States in comparative perspective. *Journal of Marriage and Family, 66*(5), 1214–1230.

Horne, R., Johnson, M., Galambos, N., & Krahn, H. (2017). Time, money, or gender? Predictors of the division of household labor across life stages. *Sex Roles, 78*(11), 731–743.

Hsiao, Y.-L. (2005). The division of household labor in Taiwan: Economic dependence and gender. *Taiwanese Journal of Sociology, 34*, 115–145.

Hwong, S.-L., Lee, S.-H., & Chao, Y.-C. (2012). Sexual attitudes and values in Taiwan differences among gender, cohort, and three cluster groups. *Formosan Journal of Sexology, 18*(1), 83–114.

Ishii-Kuntz, M., & Coltrane, S. (1992) Remarriage, stepparenting, and household labor, *Journal of Family Issues, 13*(2), 215–233.

Ishizuka, P. (2018). The economic foundations of cohabiting couples' union transitions. *Demography, 55*(2), 535–557.

Kan, M. Y., Sullivan, O., & Gershuny, J. (2011). Gender convergence in domestic work: Discerning the effects of interactional and institutional barriers from large-scale data. *Sociology, 45*(2), 234–251.

Kluwer, E. S., Heesink, J. A. M., & Van De Vliert, E. (2002). The division of labor across the transition to parenthood: A justice perspective. *Journal of Marriage and Family, 64*(4), 930–943.

Lachance-Grzela, M., & Bouchard, G. (2010). Why do women do the lion's share of housework? *Sex Roles, 63*(11), 767–780.

Lundberg, S., & Pollak, R. A. (1996). Bargaining and distribution in marriage. *Journal of Economic Perspectives, 10*(4), 139–158.

Lu, Y.-H., & Yi, C.-C. (2005). Conjugal resources and the household division of labor under Taiwanese social change: A comparison between the 1970s and 1990s social-cultural contexts. *Taiwan Sociology, 10*, 41–94.

Ministry of Interior, ROC. (2020). *Statistical yearbook of interior.* Retrieved from https://www.moi.gov.tw/files/site_stuff/321/2/year/year.html

Musick, K., & Michelmore, K. (2018). Cross-national comparisons of union stability in cohabiting and married families with children, *Demography*, *55*(4), 1389–1421.

Dribe Nock, S. L. (1995). A comparison of marriages and cohabiting relationships. *Journal of Family Issues*, *16*(1), 53–76.

Pepin, J. R., Sayer, L. C., & Casper, L. M. (2018). Marital status and mothers' time use: Childcare, housework, leisure, and sleep. *Demography*, *55*(1), 107–133.

Raymo, J. M., Iwasawa, M., & Bumpass, L. (2009). Cohabitation and family formation in Japan. *Demography*, *46*(4), 785–803.

Robins, J. M., Hernán, M. Á., & Brumback, B. (2000). Marginal structural models and causal inference in epidemiology. *Epidemiology*, *11*(5), 550–560.

Sampson, R. J., Laub, J. H., & Wimer, C. (2006). Does marriage reduce crime? A counterfactual approach to within-individual causal effects. *Criminology*, *44*(3), 465–508.

Dribe Sanchez, L., & Thompson, E. (1997). Becoming mothers and fathers: Parenthood, gender and the division of labor. *Gender and Society*, *11*(6), 747–772.

Dribe Schober, P. S. (2013). The parenthood effect on gender inequality: Explaining the change in paid and domestic work when British couples become parents. *European Sociological Review*, *29*(1), 74–85.

Shelton, B., & John, D. (1993). Does marital status make a difference? Housework among married and cohabiting men and women. *Journal of Family Issues*, *14*(3), 401–420.

Sobotka, T., & Toulemon, L. (2008). Changing family and partnership behaviour: Common trends and persistent diversity across Europe. *Demographic Research*, *19*(6), 85–138.

South, S. J., & Spitze, G. (1994). Housework in marital and nonmarital households. *American Sociological Review*, *59*(3), 327–347.

Tai, T., Baxter, J., & Hewitt, B. (2014). Do co-residence and intentions make a difference? Relationship satisfaction in married, cohabiting, and living apart together couples in four countries. *Demographic Research*, *31*, 71–104.

Treas, J., & Lui, J. (2013). Studying housework across nations. *Journal of Family Theory and Review*, *5*(2), 135–149.

Treas, J., & Tai, T. (2012). Apron strings of working mothers: Maternal employment and housework in cross-national perspective. *Social Science Research*, *41*(4), 833–842.

Wang, W.-P., & Chen, M.-H. (2017). Gendered attitudes toward non-conforming sexual practices in Taiwan: The impacts of male sexual privileges, sexual division of labor, and familism. *Journal of Women's and Gender Studies*, *40*, 53–105.

West, C., & Zimmerman, D. H. (1987). Doing gender. *Gender and Society*, *1*(2), 125–151.

Yang, C.-L., Li, T.-C., & Chen, K.-J. (2006). Assortative mating in Taiwan: Changes and persistence. *Journal of Population Studies*, *33*, 1–32.

7

Does Having a Grandchild Strengthen Intergenerational Solidarity? Financial, Instrumental and Emotional Support Exchanges in Taiwan

Yi-Ping Shih

Introduction

Becoming a parent is a significant event associated with dramatic changes affecting social and familial lives. Having children also brings a sense of pride or recognition from others as a rite of adulthood (Cherlin, 2010). In this way, having a parenthood status alters one's social roles or expectations either at home or in the public sphere. As a primary small group, the lives of all family members are linked and altered if the dynamic changes. How do young parents with preschool children manage their relationship and support with their older parents? How, in return, do grandparents handle their support to their adult children with newborns? Using an analysis of survey data from the Taiwan Youth Project (TYP) 2017, this chapter addresses these dynamics in the Taiwanese context by examining how young couples experience parenthood, a critical transition in their life course, and how it influences their intergenerational support and exchanges.

The current study is inspired by life-course theory (Elder, 1994) and the intergenerational solidarity perspective (Silverstein and Bengtson, 1997). The fundamental concept of these two approaches is the notion that family lives are interdependent (Elder et al., 2003; Macmillan and Copher, 2005). Young parents may experience different types of intergenerational support than their childless peers. Parents, compared with nonparents in general, 'Have higher stress and strain in balancing work, childcare, and financial matters' than nonparents (Huss and Pollmann-Schult, 2020, p. 385). The transition to parenthood is often associated with declines in marital satisfaction, especially after having a couple's first child (Birditt et al., 2010; Kluwer, 2010). Scholarship on parental well-being has demonstrated that the first year of parenthood is the most demanding and challenging period (Nomaguchi and Milkie, 2004).

In this way, how do the elders exchange their resources, labour and emotion with their adult children when they have become grandparents? The answer to this question is demanded among ageing East Asian societies, including Taiwan. For the past decade, Taiwan has experienced a rapid decline in its birth rate and emergent ageing issues. The conventional family norms such as filial piety have been democratized (see Yeh, 2009). Women's status has been greatly improved with long years in education than before. As an ageing society with patrilineal convention and lack of public childcare/eldercare, how do Taiwanese people manage their relationships or exchanges across generations? Taiwan is a unique case to explore. To fully address the relationship between parenthood status and intergenerational exchange, the next section will review the scholarship of intergenerational support.

Intergenerational Support and Parenthood Status

Previous studies show that as young adults navigate new roles following marriage, becoming parents or even divorce, the resource exchanges between them and the older generation often shift (Bucx et al., 2012; Min et al., 2021). On the one hand, the responsibility of parenthood generally leads to decreased time for leisure and work, resulting in smaller social networks (Kalmijn and De Graff, 2012) and potentially diminishing couples' intergenerational contacts. On the other hand, studies also found that young adults with children receive more financial or instrumental support from their parents than their childless siblings, with the birth of the first child causing the biggest bump (Bucx et al., 2012).

From the perspective of ageing parents, intergenerational supports are more than just an issue of resources exchange; they significantly affect the social, psychological and even physical well-being of family members (Bengtson and Roberts, 1991). Research has found that grandparenthood is meaningful for seniors as well. Spending time with a grandchild provides a sense of building a family legacy (Moore and

Rosenthal, 2016). In patrilineal Taiwan, it may be crucial that ageing adults have a grandson to carry family descent.

In order to understand how parenthood status makes an impact on intergenerational exchanges, this study utilizes available questions from the TYP 2017 survey and decided to focus on three forms of support flow between generations: financial, instrumental and emotional support.

Intergenerational Financial Support

Monetary resources constitute an essential social function shared across generations. Contemporary parents might consider financial support as an investment or stake in their family's future (Giarrusso et al., 2005). From the social stratification perspective, parents secure their family's socioeconomic status across generations through financial support (Albertini and Radl, 2012). Indeed, parents from higher social classes make larger financial transfers than their lower-class counterparts (Albertini and Radl, 2012).

The welfare regime also alters how families transmit their economic resources across generations. For example, downward transfers from parents to children are more frequent in southern European countries than in Nordic welfare states (Albertini et al., 2007). In western European societies, financial support is even a net downward flow from the older to the younger generations. Institutional context as well as local family culture are essential when one considers intergenerational economic supports in local society.

Local culture regarding their concepts around kinship and value on family also changes the dynamics of intergenerational exchanges. Intergenerational transfers usually include adult children offering financial support to their ageing parents. For people in societies steeped in the Confucian tradition, such as Taiwan, China, Hong Kong and Singapore, giving elderly parents money and care is a widespread way to express filial piety (Zimmer et al., 2008). Upstream transfers are usually found among East Asian societies, where families serve as a source of old-age support, as these populations are ageing rapidly (Kinsella, 2000; Knodel and Debavalya, 1997). Scholars have argued that adult children may transfer material resources to their ageing parents, particularly if they were socialized with a strong sense of filial responsibility in their culture, primarily out of altruism (Lee et al., 1994).

Others describe intergenerational financial exchanges as a type of long-term contract. Parents might consider their financial support for children in early adulthood as a long-term investment that will mature years later and make it easier for their children to support them as their needs increase. For example, in a study of parents in Indonesia, Frankenberg and his colleagues (2002) found that parents consider their investment in their children's education partly as a loan their children would someday repay from an income boosted by that investment.

If financial support is an essential resource that family members share, does having a parenthood status facilitate or hinder intergenerational economic exchanges? Is it altruism or pragmatism that leads older generations to give more resources to their offspring? A longitudinal study of German households found that ageing parents see downward financial support as a way of expressing emotional support during their adult children's parenthood transitions (Min et al., 2021). In line with the German study, a study in Britain shows, ageing parents give more money to their married adult children if the adult children have more children (Grundy, 2005). On the contrary, adult children are less likely to transfer money to their elder parents if they have children (Bucx et al., 2012). The presence of a grandchild tends to promote downward financial support and inhibit upward giving.

Moreover, research shows some interdependence between different types of support, which are exchanged, between generations. For example, ageing parents who provide financial support to their adult children expect to receive physical or emotional aid from their children when they become ill (Lin and Wu, 2014). Such reciprocity indicates that intergenerational relationships might look like altruism today but function as a mutual back-and-forth exchange in the long term.

Intergenerational Instrumental Support: Domestic Help

Having an effective family network is seen by many parents as essential for successful childrearing (Hansen, 2005; Hogg and Worth, 2009). In this study, instrumental supports refer to various bits of help at home, no matter if it happens in or out of the respondent's house. Among all domestic help, childcare is our central focus, which is confirmed by research in Taiwan likely because it lacks public childcare for preschool and younger children (Shih, 2019). Grandparents' assistance plays a crucial part in contemporary childrearing. More and more ageing parents have become the major child care providers even after they are retired (Komter and Vollebergh, 2002); such help is centred around care for grandchildren (Cong and Silverstein, 2012). In other words, the presence of a grandchild might facilitate downward supports.

Childcare by grandmothers has been a widespread practice in contemporary East Asia, where public childcare is scarce and working hours are long. Caring for grandchildren might provide a new way of distributing responsibilities within the extended family (Silverstein et al., 2006; Yang, 1996). Studies in Taiwan also show that instrumental support is a way for seniors to show their support to their children's families in their early stages (Lee et al., 1994). Research conducted in South Korea suggests that, with financial support, instrumental support may have a reciprocal component, as grandmothers who take care of grandchildren have frequent labour exchanges with the younger generation (Lee and Bauer, 2013). The perspective of kin-keeper theory argues that women receive more support but are also offered more help across generations. Korean qualitative study further reveals that grandmothers identify as responsible for providing logistical support for their adult children. Indeed, it may work in much the same way as financial investments in a child's education; young parents can dedicate more time to developing their careers if their parents provide childcare support, thus becoming better financially able to help their parents later (Lee and Bauer, 2013). This may be why grandparents support their daughters instrumentally more than their sons (Min et al., 2021).

In sum, the transition to parenthood is not merely an issue for new parents but also a significant life event for grandparents, especially the grandmother, as they might anticipate a shift in their instrumental support for their adult sons, daughters or in-laws.

Intergenerational Emotional Support

Much as with financial and instrumental support, parenthood status seems to strengthen the downward flow of emotional support and diminish its upward flow. Each generation contributes its relative surplus to other family members (Rossi and Rossi, 1990). A recent study demonstrates that new parents, especially mothers, are less likely to provide emotional and instrumental support to the older generation after having the first child (Min et al., 2021). Diminishment of energy, time, material resources and mental well-being may explain this change.

A longitudinal interview study in the United States demonstrates that adult children with kids receive greater emotional support from their ageing parents, and first-time parenthood signals the greatest increase (Belsky and Rovine, 1984). Ageing parents and adult children who are emotionally close to one another may be more willing to provide and receive other kinds of support (such as instrumental and economic ones) as family roles undergo reorganization during transitions (Elder, 1985; Settersten, 2017). However, in another more recent longitudinal quantitative study conducted in Germany, older women continue to provide emotional support at a high level after the birth of a grandchild, whereas the grandfathers increase their emotional support significantly only after a grandchild is born (Min et al., 2021). Other studies have found no association between parenthood status and changes in intergenerational emotional support (Bucx et al., 2012; Fingerman et al., 2009). In sum, there is no strong, consistent results regarding how parenthood makes an impact on intergenerational emotional support.

Gender and Intergenerational Support

The life-course theory imparts that women and men develop different social relations over time, both at work and home (Elder, 1994). The dynamics of intergenerational support in the transition to parenthood may reflect this change.

As most literature examining the impact of gender on intergenerational support indicate, women tend to give and receive more types of support across generations than men to sustain their intergenerational solidarity (Bucx et al., 2012; Kalmijn and De Graff, 2012; Kalmijn and Uunk, 2007; Silverstein et al., 2006). Parenthood also strengthens women's involvement with older generations. Min et al. (2021) found that daughters receive more support than sons following the transition to parenthood. Other research conducted in rural China and the United States also shows that intergenerational support flows following the birth of a son are greater for adult daughters than adult sons (Kalmijn and De Graff, 2012; Silverstein et al., 2006). Such gendered differences confirm the kin-keeper theory, which argues that women are the essential agents of intergenerational solidarity and that men play a secondary role if any (Bucx et al., 2012).

Patrilineal societies emphasize the conventional gender division of labour: Fathers are expected to be a breadwinner. Studies conducted in Hong Kong show that children's future prosperity, including their educational achievement and career success, is mainly seen as the father's responsibility (Chung et al., 2011; Koh et al., 2015). Societies that emphasize filial piety also emphasize parental authority (Hu and Tian, 2018), particularly through patrilineal inheritance rules and clear kinship boundaries and responsibilities (Nauck, 2010). Due to the conventional emphasis on filial piety, young Taiwanese couples are expected to offer seniors financial assistance and help at home (Lin and Yi, 2011). Specifically, sons and their wives carry out more filial duties than the daughters' families (Lee et al., 1994; Lin and Yi, 2011). Upward support typically consists of financial transfers from adult sons and emotional and instrumental supports from daughters-in-law.

The relationship with in-laws also makes a significant impact on the dynamic between husbands and wives. Research in Taiwan shows that for young couples, relationships with husbands' parents take priority over relationships with wives' parents, resulting in more patrilocal co-residence than matrilocal co-residence (Wu and Yi, 2003). However, Yi et al. (2019) recently documented that Taiwanese couples have increasing interactions with maternal in-laws. They found that hostile relations between men and their parents-in-law significantly damaged relations between the two generations.

Data and Variables

Sample and Data

The TYP is a long-term longitudinal study funded and conducted by the Institute of Sociology, Academia Sinica, Taiwan, since 2000. So far, it has consisted of an 18-year longitudinal study with nine survey waves. Th current chapter selects heterosexual, married people (G2) with at least one living parent or parent-in-law (G1) from the 2017 sample, which yielded a final sample of 971 respondents. Most respondents are 30–33 years old. Among all respondents, two-thirds have at least one child, with their firstborn at an average age of five. Table 7.1 contains demographic information for the survey participants.

Table 7.1 Descriptive statistics of the survey sample

Characteristic	Statistics	
Demographic Characteristics	%	N
N=		971
Male	48.7	473
Female	51.3	498
Average education years		15.41 (yr)
Household monthly income (Median)		85,000 N.T.
Homeownership	45.1	438
Child Information		
Number of children (Avg. 0.97, Range: 0–3)		
Childless	34.88	338
1 child	36.95	358
2 children	24.46	237
3 children	3.72	36
The average age of the oldest child		5
Primary Childcare Provider before the 6th month		
Wife	40.88	258
Husband	1.90	12
Paternal grandparents	20.06	127
Maternal grandparents	15.00	95
Other arrangements (Institutional and other relatives)	21.96	139
Intimate Relationship	Avg.	Md
Marriage satisfaction (Range: 1–4)	3.19	3
Marriage conflict (Range: 0–45)	12.98	15

Control Variables: Demographic Characteristics

The control variables are the respondents' gender, education level, monthly household income and homeownership. These data contain 473 male and 498 female respondents. When the respondents were surveyed, they reported being in a heterosexual, married relationship with one or more living parent/parent-in-law. They had an average of 15.41 years of education, which refers to the degree of a high school graduate in Taiwan. The median household income was 85,000

NT$/month, lower than the 2017 national median of 107,715 NT$/month. Given their age, they are still at their early stage of career development.

In addition to education and income, our models treat homeownership as a supplemental indicator for family class status. Research indicates that many young couples in Taiwan do not have children in part because of the soaring price of real estate (Lin and Chang 2016), suggesting homeownership status may affect the personal decision to have children. Therefore, this study includes it as the control variable in our models. Only 45.1 per cent of the respondents own houses or apartments, which is way below the national average of 84.83 per cent homeownership but may reflect their economic condition and the impact of real estate price increases.

Life Transition Measurement: Parenthood Status

More than one-third of our respondents have no child. Having one child is also more common than two, with 36.95 per cent having one child and 28.18 per cent having two or more. The average age of participants' firstborn is around five years old, which means that most families have preschool children. This study focuses on parenthood status. Thus, a respondent was coded as having transitioned to parenthood if they reported having one or more children at the time of the survey (0 = did not have a child, 1 = have one or more children during the survey).

Intergenerational Co-Residence

Parent–child co-residence has been considered an essential factor that strengthens intergenerational support exchanges (Fingerman et al., 2017). Co-residence across generations also serves as an indicator of our respondents' family structure. In 2017, the average household size in Taiwan was 3.07, which indicates that the nuclear family format might still be the most popular size. Patrilocal norm, namely the custom to live with one's father or husband's family after getting married, is part of the mainstream local culture. However, a recent study suggests that a modified patrilocal residence pattern is popular among young Taiwanese couples with children, leading to more frequent exchanges among the three generations (Nauck and Ren, 2018). The original TYP 2017 survey items address patterns of co-residence through enquiring whether respondents live with the paternal grandparents, the maternal grandparents or neither.

Table 7.2 provides detailed information on co-residence patterns. Most respondents reported not living with their children's grandparents

Table 7.2 Descriptive statistics on intergenerational co-residence

	Male	Female	Total	%
Patrilocal				
With both grandparents	154	95	249	
Paternal grandfather (PGP)	11	11	22	
Paternal grandmother (PGM)	38	39	77	
Subtotal	203	145	348	35.84%
Matrilocal				
With both grandparents	17	55	72	
Maternal grandfather (MGP)	3	1	4	
Maternal grandmother (MGM)	6	19	25	
Subtotal	26	75	101	10.40%
Living with both sides	0	0	0	
Living with no G1				
At least one G1 passed away or lost contact	110	168	278	
All four G1 are alive with contact	144	110	254	
Subtotal	244	278	522	53.76%
Total	**473**	**498**	**971**	**100%**

($N = 522$), and no respondents reported residing with both maternal and paternal grandparents. The patrilocal arrangement is three times more common than matrilocal co-residence.

Primary Childcare Provider

To answer how Taiwanese parents manage the care of their newborns, I utilize TYP 2017 survey Question 59 in constructing this new set of dummy variables to identify the primary childcare provider. The original question states, 'Before your child reaches six months of age, who is the major childcare provider on the weekdays, especially during the daytime?' The choices are (1) myself, (2) my spouse, (3) paternal grandparents, (4) maternal grandparents, (5) other relatives, (6) nanny, (7) private childcare centre, (8) public childcare centre and (9) others. I recoded these responses into five new categories: father-care, mothercare, care by paternal grandparents (Paternal GPcare), care by maternal grandparents (Maternal GPcare) and others (items 5,

6, 7, 8 and 9). As shown in Table 7.1, in descending order, responses consisted of mothercare (40.88 per cent), care by paternal grandparents (20.06 per cent), others (primarily institutional care providers; 21.96 per cent) and maternal grandparents (15 per cent). Fathercare consists of 1.9 per cent. In the models, I use institutional care and care by other relatives as the reference group.

Intimate Relationships

Ageing parents provide crucial support for adult children when they establish marriage relations but may also contribute to marital strain. This study uses marital satisfaction and marriage conflict to measure the interaction between adult children's marriage quality and intergenerational exchanges. The former is a standard global indicator that family researchers use to understand married couples' well-being (Fincham and Bradbury, 1987). The latter may address some of the limitations of marital satisfaction as an indicator of marriage quality in Taiwan.

For marriage satisfaction, this study utilizes information from Question 10 of the TYP 2017 survey, which reads, 'In general, are you satisfied with your relationship with your spouse?' The answers are recorded as (1) very unsatisfied, (2) unsatisfied, (3) satisfied and (4) very satisfied. As anticipated, the median of marriage satisfaction is 3 (satisfied).

According to Wu and Yi (2003), Taiwanese respondents are inclined to paint their marriages in favourable terms. The analysis of national survey data showed that 92 per cent of Taiwanese respondents expressed a positive attitude towards their marriage (Wu and Yi, 2003). However, the actual quality of marriage might be concealed, given that most Taiwanese people tend to consider such issues as private and sensitive.

To accommodate the potential invalidity of the variable marriage satisfaction, this study adds nine items from the TYP 2017 survey to take marriage conflict into account. Question 11 asks, 'For the past year, have you had any conflicts with your spouse regarding the nine issues below: house chores, money, relationships with the opposite sex, interactions with your parents, interactions with your parents-in-law, childrearing issues, having a child or not, job, videogames or cellphone usage?' The answers are recoded in an ascending order, ranging from 1 to 5: 1 = never, 2 = seldom, 3 = sometimes, 4 = often and 5 = always. Based on the sum of responses, the total score of marriage conflict ranges from 0 to 45. As shown in Table 7.1, the average score of marriage conflict is 12.98, while the median is 15.

Analytic Plan

Previous literature has indicated that, in patrilineal Taiwan, the relationship between married women and their mothers-in-law (Mil) is the key to couples' marital satisfaction in Taiwan (Kung, 2019). Therefore, this study examines the exchanges with in-laws as well. To further delineate whether such exchange patterns are gendered, I ran separate models for men and women. Insignificant models are not presented. Separate regression models were computed for the three forms of support (financial, instrumental and emotional) received from parents and parents-in-law and provided to male and female adult children. The model details of the three forms of support are explained in the following sections.

Intergenerational Model 1: Financial Support

This study utilizes the information of intergenerational monetary transmission as financial support indicators. The measurement of intergenerational financial support is constructed from Questions 34a and 35a. Q34a of the survey says, 'For the past year, did you offer money/a stipend to your parents/parents-in-law?' Q35b asks, 'For the past year, did you get money from your parents or parents-in-law?' The responses are recoded in an ascending order: 1 = never, 2 = seldom, 3 = sometimes, 4 = often and 5 = very often. Table 7.3 A and B provide the distribution of responses by male and female respondents, respectively. Insignificant models are removed from the table.

Intergenerational Model 2: Instrumental Support

Downward instrumental support was assessed with Q34b, 'In the past year, did you offer help to your parents or parents-in-law? Help with household chores, for example, cleaning, preparation for dinner, shopping, handling small tasks, childcare, or other care work?' Upward instrumental support was assessed with Q35b, 'In the past year, did you get help from your parents or parents-in-law? Help with household chores, for example, cleaning, preparation for dinner, shopping, handling small tasks, childcare, or other care work?' Responses are recorded in an ascending order: 1 = never, 2 = seldom, 3 = sometimes, 4 = often and 5 = very often. The models for instrumental support are all significant and represented in Table 7.4.

Table 7.3 (A) Regression model of intergenerational financial support: G2 male vs. G1

Variables/ Model	Model 1 G1 father ↑ G2 male	Model 2 G1 mother ↑ G2 male	Model 3 G1 FiL ↑ G2 male	Model 4 G1 MiL ↑ G2 male
Education level	−.004(.026)	0.025(0.028)	0.003(0.018)	0.000(0.020)
Household monthly income	0.004**(0.001)	0.002(0.001)	0.003**(0.001)	0.003*(0.001)
Home ownership	0.007(0.125)	0.226(0.132)	−0.024(0.084)	0.017(0.094)
Have child	−0.302(0.156)	−0.274(0.165)	0.030(0.105)	0.075(0.117)
Intergenerational Co-residence (ref. not living with grandparents)				
Patrilocal	0.200(0.134)	0.673***(0.272)	0.106(0.090)	0.153(0.101)
Matrilocal	0.103(0.270)	0.269(0.285)	0.223(0.181)	0.771***(0.203)
Primary Childcare Provider before the 6th month (ref. institutional and other care)				
Father	−0.168(0.557)	−0.349(0.588)	−0.365(0.374)	−0.516(0.418)
Mother	−0.009(0.220)	−0.160(0.232)	0.098(0.148)	0.069(0.165)
Paternal GPcare	0.538*(0.258)	0.671*(0.272)	0.164(0.173)	0.127(0.194)
Maternal GPcare	0.178(0.276)	0.157(0.291)	0.434*(0.185)	0.693***(0.207)

(Continued)

Table 7.3 (A) Regression model of intergenerational financial support: G2 male vs. G1 (Continued)

Variables/ Model	Model 1 G1 father ↓ G2 male	Model 2 G1 mother ↓ G2 male	Model 3 G1 FiL ↓ G2 male	Model 4 G1 MiL ↓ G2 male
Intimate Relationship				
Marriage satisfaction	−0.030(0.111)	−0.165(117)	0.026(0.074)	−0.002(0.083)
Marriage conflict	−0.006(0.007)	−0.012(0.007)	−0.006(0.005)	−0.005(0.005)
Intercept	2.01***(0.568)	2.342***(0.600)	1.031**(0.382)	1.151**(0.427)
Adjusted R-square	0.047***	0.099***	0.030**	0.074***
N=	473	473	473	473

(B) Regression model of intergenerational financial support: G2 female vs. G1

Variables/ Model	Model 1 G1 father ↓ G2 female	Model 2 G1 mother ↓ G2 female	Model 3 G1 MiL ↓ G2 female	Model 4 G1 mother ↓ G2 female	Model 5 G1 FiL ↓ G2 female	Model 6 G1 MiL ↓ G2 female
Education level	−0.034(0.029)	−0.024(0.035)	−0.034(0.032)	0.048*(0.025)	−0.003(0.020)	−0.005(0.021)
Household income	0.004***(0.001)	0.004**(0.001)	0.002(0.001)	−0.001(0.001)	0.001(0.001)	0.001(0.001)

	(1)	(2)	(3)	(4)	(5)	(6)
Home ownership	−0.108(0.101)	−0.025(0.119)	0.058(0.108)	−0.049(0.084)	−0.012(0.067)	−0.062(0.072)
Have child	−0.212(0.128)	−0.109(0.151)	0.338*(0.138)	0.097(0.107)	−0.026(0.085)	−0.043(0.092)
Intergenerational Co-residence (ref. not living with grandparents)						
Patrilocal	0.007(0.118)	0.120(0.139)	0.312*(0.127)	−0.158(0.098)	−0.125(0.078)	−0.132(0.085)
Matrilocal	−0.007(0.148)	0.685***(0.175)	−0.162(0.159)	−0.153(0.123)	−0.213*(0.098)	−0.144(0.106)
Primary Childcare Provider before the 6th month (ref. institutional and other care)						
Father	0.600(0.469)	0.162(0.555)	0.106(0.505)	0.064(0.392)	0.262(0.312)	−0.302(0.338)
Mother	−0.158(0.176)	−0.261(0.208)	−0.260(0.189)	0.430**(0.147)	0.424***(0.117)	0.424***(0.127)
Paternal GPcare	−0.244(0.204)	−0.039(0.241)	0.418(0.220)	−0.015(0.170)	0.019(0.136)	0.040(0.147)
Maternal GPcare	0.335(0.217)	0.685**(0.256)	0.272(0.233)	0.261(0.181)	0.114(0.144)	0.232(0.156)
Intimate Relationship						
Marriage Satisfaction	−0.114(0.084)	0.027(0.099)	0.068(0.090)	0.069(0.070)	−0.036(0.056)	−0.002(0.060)
Marriage conflict	0.004(0.005)	0.007(0.006)	−0.011*(0.006)	0.007(0.004)	0.005(0.004)	0.005(0.004)
Intercept	2.729**(0.564)	2.299***(0.668)	1.707**(0.608)	0.555(0.471)	1.445(0.375)	1.394***(0.406)
Adjusted R-square	0.055***	0.007***	0.061**	0.039**	0.046***	0.029**
N=	498	498	498	498	498	498

***two-tailed sig. alpha < 0.001 **alpha < 0.01 *alpha < 0.05
****two-tailed sig. alpha < 0.001 **alpha < 0.01 *alpha < 0.05

Table 7.4 (A) Regression model of intergenerational instrumental support: G2 male vs. G1

Variables/ Model	Model 1 G1 father → G2 male	Model 2 G1 mother → G2 male	Model 3 G1 FiL → G2 male	Model 4 G1 MiL → G2 male	Model 5 G1Father → G2 male	Model 6 G1 mother → G2 male	Model 7 G1 FiL → G2 male	Model 8 G1 MiL → G2 male
Education level	0.030(0.021)	0.034(0.021)	0.011(0.019)	0.016(0.026)	0.000(0.024)	0.014(0.024)	0.022(0.023)	0.025(0.025)
Household income	0.000(0.001)	0.000(0.001)	0.000(0.001)	0.000(0.001)	0.000(0.001)	0.000(0.001)	0.000(0.001)	0.000(0.001)
Home ownership	−0.237*(0.100)	−0.065(0.102)	−0.126(0.088)	−0.082(0.095)	−0.062(0.116)	−0.053(0.116)	0.444(0.109)	0.001(0.117)
Have child	−1.27(0.125)	−0.145(0.127)	0.046(0.110)	0.029(0.119)	0.450**(0.145)	0.525***(0.144)	0.501***(0.136)	0.611***(0.146)
Intergenerational Co-residence (ref. not living with grandparents)								
Patrilocal	0.810***(0.108)	1.040***(0.109)	0.039(0.095)	0.010(0.102)	0.644***(0.124)	1.145***(0.124)	−0.117(0.117)	−0.171(0.126)
Matrilocal	−0.093(0.216)	0.137(0.219)	0.702***(0.191)	0.739***(0.206)	−0.017(0.250)	−0.022(0.249)	0.665**(0.235)	1.289**(0.253)
Primary Childcare Provider before the 6th month (ref. institutional and other care)								
Fathercare	−0.057(0.446)	−0.157(452)	0.093(0.393)	0.109(0.424)	−0.393(0.516)	−0.417(0.514)	0.981*(0.485)	0.664(0.521)
Mothercare	0.206(0.176)	0.050(0.179)	0.230(0.156)	0.360*(0.168)	−0.006(0.204)	−0.046(0.203)	0.159(0.192)	0.171(0.206)
Paternal GPcare	0.213(0.207)	−0.025(0.209)	0.096(182)	0.117(0.197)	0.590*(0.239)	1.043***(0.238)	0.209(0.225)	0.147(0.242)
Maternal GPcare	0.247(0.221)	0.201(0.224)	0.262(0.195)	0.420(0.210)	−0.057(0.256)	−0.029(0.255)	1.026***(0.240)	1.126***(0.259)
Intimate Relationship								
Marriage satisfaction	0.089(0.089)	0.014(0.090)	0.138(0.078)	0.121(0.084)	0.045(0.103)	−0.020(0.102)	0.097(0.097)	0.045(0.104)
Marriage conflict	−0.008(0.005)	−0.009(0.006)	0.003(0.005)	0.004(0.005)	0.004(0.006)	0.000(0.006)	0.014*(0.006)	0.010(0.006)
Intercept	1.571***(0.456)	1.838***(0.461)	1.147**(0.401)	1.116**(0.433)	1.530**(0.527)	1.893***(0.524)	0.634(0.495)	0.996(0.532)
Adjusted R-square	0.146***	0.174***	0.028*	0.033**	0.136***	0.293***	0.123***	0.172***
N=	473	473	473	473	473	473	473	473

(B) Regression model of intergenerational instrumental support: G2 female vs. G1

Variables/ Model	Model 1 G1 father →	Model 2 G1 mother →	Model 3 G1 FiL →	Model 4 G1 MiL →	Model 5 G1Father →	Model 6 G1 mother →	Model 7 G1 FiL →	Model 8 G1 MiL →
	G2 female	G2 female	G2 female	G2 female	G2 female	G2 female	G2 female	G2 female
Education level	−0.010(0.027)	0.002(0.030)	−0.049(0.028)	−0.044(0.029)	0.010(0.031)	0.065*(0.033)	0.015(0.031)	0.032(0.032)
Household income	0.001(0.001)	0.000(0.001)	−0.001(0.001)	0.001(0.001)	0.003*(0.001)	0.002(0.001)	0.001(0.001)	0.002(0.001)
Home ownership	−0.045(0.094)	−0.122(0.102)	−0.112(0.095)	0.072(0.098)	−0.173(0.107)	−0.174(0.112)	−0.086(0.105)	0.066(0.110)
Have child	−0.187(0.120)	−0.121(0.129)	0.122(0.120)	0.195(0.125)	0.404**(0.136)	0.570***(0.142)	0.507***(0.133)	0.703***(0.140)
Intergenerational Co-residence (ref. not living with grandparents)								
Patrilocal	−0.073(0.110)	−0.052(0.119)	0.745***(0.111)	1.018***(0.115)	0.011(0.125)	−0.207(0.131)	0.513(0.122)	0.979***(0.129)
Matrilocal	0.558***(0.138)	0.975***(0.149)	0.315*(0.139)	−0.351*(0.144)	0.476**(0.157)	1.312***(0.164)	−0.205(0.154)	−0.161(0.161)
Prvimary Childcare Provider before the 6th month (ref. institutional and other care)								
Fathercare	1.154**(0.439)	0.330(0.475)	0.422(0.441)	0.136(0.458)	0.057(0.499)	−0.781(0.521)	−0.324***(0.489)	−0.230(0.513)
Mothercare	0.319(0.164)	0.249(0.178)	−0.006(0.166)	−0.108(0.172)	0.062(0.187)	0.180(0.195)	−0.147(0.183)	−0.132(192)
Paternal GPcare	0.006(0.191)	−0.043(0.206)	−0.238(0.192)	−0.009(0.1990)	−0.256(0.217)	−0.218(0.227)	0.339(0.212)	0.911***(0.223)
Maternal GPcare	0.403*(0.203)	0.418(0.219)	−0.136(0.212)	−0.006(0.212)	0.937***(0.231)	1.161***(0.241)	−0.213(0.226)	−0.029(0.237)
Intimate Relationship								
Marriage satisfaction	−0.073(0.078)	0.022(0.085)	0.112(0.079)	0.136(0.082)	−0.063(0.089)	−0.038(0.093)	−0.118(0.087)	−0.124(0.092)
Marriage conflict	0.001(0.005)	0.004(0.005)	0.004(0.005)	0.000(0.005)	0.003(0.006)	0.001(0.006)	−0.009(0.005)	−0.010(0.006)
Intercept	2.501***(0.528)	2.311***(0.571)	2.583***(0.531)	2.394***(0.552)	1.847**(0.601)	1.331*(0.627)	2.075***(0.588)	1.767***(0.617)
Adjusted R-square	0.056***	0.105***	0.137***	0.197***	0.110***	0.254***	0.106***	0.251***
$N=$	498	498	498	498	498	498	498	498

***two-tailed sig. alpha < 0.001 **alpha < 0.01 *alpha < 0.05
***two-tailed sig. alpha < 0.001 **alpha < 0.01 *alpha < 0.05

Intergenerational Model 3: Emotional Support

Downward emotional support was constructed by Q34c, 'In the past year, did you listen to your parents' or parents-in-law's opinions or problems?' Upward emotional support was constructed by Q35c, 'In the past year, did your parents/parents-in-law listen to your troubles or opinions?' Responses are recoded in an ascending order: 1 = never, 2 = seldom, 3 = sometimes, 4 = often and 5 = very often. Only three male models and two female models are significant and represented in Table 7.5.

Results

Intergenerational Financial Support: Monetary Transmission

Tables 7.3A and B demonstrate the male and female models of intergenerational financial support. Comparing the two tables, the study finds a significant gender effect. Men in the sample provide financial support to their parents and parents-in-law but do not receive it, whereas women report intergenerational monetary transmission in both directions with their parents and parents-in-law. Compared with childless married women, young mothers are more likely to offer money to their mothers-in-law.

Married Men's Intergenerational Financial Support

Table 7.3A shows the support exchange patterns regarding married men. It shows that men in the sample play a significant role as the breadwinner sons. For our male respondents, all provision models are significant, while receiving models are not. Men offer their mothers money at consistently high rates; those with higher income are more likely to provide their fathers money as well. This provider expectation is also a classed phenomenon: with higher household incomes, married men are more likely to offer money to ageing parents (Models 1, 3, 4), except for the transmission with their mothers. Home ownership presents no significant impact on the flow of financial support for adult children of either sex. It shows that, in contemporary Taiwan, the monetary provision from men to the older generation persists as a common practice.

Both co-residence and childcare arrangements promote intergenerational financial support. Comparing Models 1 and 2 with Models 3

Table 7.5 Regression model of intergenerational emotional support

Variables/Model	Model 1 G1 father ↑ G2 male	Model 2 G1 mother ↑ G2 male	Model 3 G1 mother ↑ G2 male	Model 4 G1 MiL ↑ G2 female	Model 5 G1 mother ↓ G2 female
Control Variables					
Education level	0.033(0.020)	0.047*(0.021)	0.051*(0.021)	0.003(0.028)	0.075*(0.001)
Household income	0.002(0.001)	0.000(0.001)	0.001(0.001)	0.000(0.001)	0.001(0.001)
Home ownership	−0.045(0.095)	0.180(0.097)	0.062(0.099)	0.095(0.094)	−0.212*(0.103)
Have child	−0.160(0.118)	−0.349**(0.122)	−0.067(0.124)	0.170(0.120)	0.257(0.131)
Intergenerational Co-residence (ref. not living with grandparents)					
Patrilocal	0.100(0.118)	0.377**(0.122)	0.112(0.107)	0.393***(110)	−0.009(0.121)
Matrilocal	−0.468*(0.204)	−0.387(0.210)	−0.161(0.214)	−0.058(0.139)	0.117(0.152)
Primary Childcare Provider before the 6th month (ref. institutional and other care)					
Fathercare	−0.312(0.422)	−0.433(0.433)	−0.718(0.442)	−0.497(0.441)	−0.400(0.482)
Mothercare	−0.070(0.167)	0.202(0.171)	−0.025(0.175)	−0.178(0.165)	0.043(0.181)
Paternal GPcare	0.137(0.196)	0.291(0.201)	0.232(0.205)	0.057(0.192)	−0.244(0.209)
Maternal GPcare	0.076(0.209)	0.407(0.215)	0.267(0.205)	−0.353(0.203)	0.277(0.222)
Intimate Relationship					
Marriage satisfaction	−0.019(0.084)	−0.017(0.086)	0.014(0.088)	0.026(0.079)	−0.090(0.086)
Marriage conflict	−0.006(0.005)	−0.002(0.005)	0.003(0.005)	−0.002(0.005)	0.012*(0.005)
Intercept	2.015***(0.431)	1.883***(0.442)	1.511**(0.451)	2.145***(0.530)	2.074***(0.579)
Adjusted R-square	0.033**	0.067***	0.031*	0.032**	0.032**
N=	473	473	473	498	498

****two-tailed sig. alpha < 0.001 **alpha < 0.01 *alpha < 0.05

and 4 in Table 7.3A, focusing on the variable of the primary childcare provider, the study shows that grandparents who provide childcare, including maternal and paternal grandparents, are more likely to receive financial resources from men. For example, Model 1 shows a positive association between paternal grandparents as the primary source and the son's financial support to his father ($b = 0.538$, $p = 0.258$, see Table 7.3A). Model 4 shows a similar relationship between maternal grandparent care and men's financial support to their mothers-in-law (Mil) ($b = 0.693$, $p = 0.207$, see Table 7.3A). Co-residence also boosts men's upward financial support, but only for their mothers and mothers-in-law, not for their fathers and fathers-in-law (Fil).

The findings suggest that, in Taiwan, married men do not directly offer monetary resources to show respect to their elders. Rather, monetary resources are a way of collaborating to boost familial resources, expressing their gratitude towards elders' efforts to provide childcare and, to a lesser extent, sharing money within a household in the case of co-residence. This new style of intergenerational financial support aligns with the 'dual filial piety model' (Yeh, 2009, p. 104), in which young Taiwanese couples have embraced 'reciprocal filial piety (Yeh, 2009, p. 112)' over 'authoritative filial piety (Yeh, 2009, p. 115)', especially with their ageing parents and in-laws.

To our surprise, none of the four models of downward economic transmission from the older generation to adult male children are significant; hence, the downward transmission models are not included in Table 7.3A. A unidirectional transmission between married men and their ageing parents in this study suggests adherence to a traditional gender role in which a married man should bring home the bacon, be the breadwinner and be a good son/husband/father. Another possible interpretation is that the wife manages the family's economic assets in Taiwan, not the husband. If there is any financial support among family members, women are the agents who process such support and not men. To verify this inference, I carefully analyse women's financial support models in the next section.

Married Women's Intergenerational Financial Support

In Table 7.3B, Models 1 to 3 reflect women's reports of upward financial support they provide, and Models 4 and 5 reflect their reports of downward financial support they receive. The analysis shows that women with higher educational levels obtain more financial aids from their mothers, which is different from men. While men with a higher household income are more likely to report providing financial support to their parents and their wives' parents, only women's support for their parents responds to income. However, women may be more likely to give their parents financial aid if they have surplus resources due to a higher income because Taiwanese customs do not obligate married daughters to support their parents. Moreover, Model 3 demonstrates that if women have more frequent conflicts in their marriage, they are less likely to provide financial support to their mother-in-law ($b = -0.011$, $p = 0.006$).

Parenthood status predicts upward financial transfers among women, but only to their mothers-in-law, as Model 3 of Table 7.3B shows. Regarding upward provision, parenthood status and co-residence pattern are two crucial factors. Women with children are more likely to provide financial resources to their mother-in-law than other childless, married women. Patrilocal arrangement promotes women's economic provision to their mother-in-law ($b = 0.312$, $p = 0.127$), while matrilocal pattern enhance married women's chance to provide financial aid to their mothers as well ($b = 0.685$, $p = 0.175$). However, whether grandparents provide care, as shown in Model 3, has no effect. This financial support may represent compensation for childcare offered by mothers-in-law. In any case, this monetary transmission from married women to their mothers-in-law aligns with the understanding that both women as playing the collaborating role of kin-keeper and key agent for their nuclear unit.

The female models show that co-residency and childcare are solid indicators for Taiwanese intergenerational financial support. And childcare responsibilities promote intergenerational financial support reciprocally. Model 2 indicates that, while maternal grandparents are the major childcare providers, or when the female respondents choose a matrilocal arrangement, the maternal grandmothers are more likely to receive money from their daughters. Model 5 further shows that women are less likely to obtain financial support from their fathers-in-law if she chooses matrilocal residence. Therefore, I conclude that co-residency would facilitate intergenerational economic exchanges.

In the cases of mothercare, mothers who work as full-time primary childcare takers are more likely to receive financial aid from both their mothers and their in-laws than mothers who are not. Models 4 to 6 of Table 7.3B present an interesting downward transmission pattern. The indicator of childcare demonstrates that young Taiwanese mothers (especially those who are primary childcare takers) are the nexus of intergenerational exchange, including childcare and financial resources, and not their husbands. Men may not report receiving financial support from their elders because they may feel that such support from the seniors to their families accrues only via their wives.

The results suggest that young Taiwanese parents are both modern and conventional in terms of financial support. Young Taiwanese women are the nexus between the two generations, meaning they have control over and the knowledge of family finances. However, that intergenerational transmission is a gendered division of labor at home. Young Taiwanese men are not expected to accept financial support from the older generation; they leave this to their wives.

Intergenerational Instrumental Support

The regression models of instrumental support demonstrate strong intergenerational solidarity in Taiwan. For example, the *R*-square of Model 6 of Table 7.4A indicates that 29.3 per cent of the variance in the frequency of Taiwanese mothers helping their married sons can be predicted by our model. In a society where public childcare facilities are limited, many grandparents (especially grandmothers) have become major childcare providers as women have entered the formal workforce, as our analysis demonstrates.

Married Men's Intergenerational Instrumental Support

The analysis of Table 7.4A illustrates that men's educational level, household income and homeownership do not predict instrumental support exchanges with ageing parents. However, co-residence and childcare arrangements strongly indicate men's reports of intergenerational instrumental support. As with the financial backing, most of the transmission men reported happens in a downward manner.

Models 5 to 8 in Table 7.4A demonstrate that men with children are more likely to receive instrumental support from their parents and their wives' parents, especially when grandparents are the primary caregivers. For example, Models 7 and 8 show that men receive more instrumental help from their parents-in-law if they are fathers of one or more children. Furthermore, such exchanges are enhanced by the arrangement of co-residence. Patrilocal arrangement promotes provision of instrumental support from the paternal side, while matrilocal arrangement prompts provision from the maternal side. In addition, we noticed that men are more likely to obtain instrumental helps from their father-in-law if they have more frequent marriage conflicts ($b = 0.014$, $p = 0.006$).

While fathercare was relatively unusual, those men who provide childcare are more likely to report receiving instrumental support from their fathers-in-law ($b = 0.981$, $p = 0.485$, see Table 7.4A, Model 7), but not from other grandparents. This exchange pattern may suggest a unique kind of kinship between men and their fathers-in-law across marriage and the generations.

Married Women's Intergenerational Instrumental Support

As for women, Table 7.4B confirms that parenthood status facilitates the downward transmission of instrumental support from grandparents for women as it does for men. Intergenerational co-residence increases women's upward provision of instrumental support. Compared to women with other childcare arrangements, women whose children receive fathercare ($b = 1.154$, $p = 0.439$) or care from maternal grandparents are more likely to provide instrumental support to their ageing fathers ($b = 0.403$, $p = 0.203$, see Table 7.4B, Model 1). If one looks closely at Models 1 to 4 in Table 7.4B, co-residency is an essential factor in facilitating upward instrumental support. Matrilocal arrangement increases women's instrumental support of their parents and decreases their instrumental support to their in-laws. The choice to co-reside with the wife's family significantly waives young married women's conventional obligation to offer domestic help and care for their in-laws.

If Taiwanese men with children acquire more help from the older generation, does this pattern also apply to Taiwanese women? Happily, the answer is yes. Table 7.4B shows that young mothers, like young fathers, receive more help from the older generations from all four grandparents (see Table 7.4B, Models 5 to 8) than their childless counterparts. Moreover, they rely heavily on older women to ease their burden of providing childcare. For instance, in Models 5 to 8 in Table 7.4B, the conditions of co-residence and childcare arrangements consistently and significantly promote assistance from the older generation all the time, particularly from grandmothers.

Intergenerational Emotional Support: Listen or Give Advice

Emotional support from significant others and our primary group offers a sense of security, crucial to psychological well-being (Silverstein et al., 2013). Table 7.5 displays five effective models for male (Models 1 to 3) and female respondents (Models 4 and 5).

Men in the sample with higher educational levels report a solid emotional bond with their ageing mothers, as shown in Models 2 and 3 in Table 7.5. However, reciprocal emotional exchanges are not shared with their fathers or in-laws. Ageing mothers play the role of kin-keeper with their adult sons.

The regression coefficient shows that men with children are less likely to give their mothers emotional support than men without ($b = -0.349$, $p = 0.122$). Fathers of preschoolers are exhausted and have no spare time to listen to their ageing mothers. Still, men with patrilocal arrangement are more likely to offer their mothers emotional support ($b = 0.377$, $p = 0.122$, see Table 7.5, Model 2).

On the other hand, Taiwanese women's propensity to provide their elders emotional support did not differ by parenthood status. For women, the effect of education was apparent for downward exchange of emotional support with their ageing mothers ($b = 0.075, p = 0.001$, see Table 7.5, Model 5). Women with patrilocal arrangements were more likely to provide emotional support to their mothers-in-law, but not to other ageing parents, even those of her own. Unlike married men, who seem to have a mutual bond with their mother, married women in Taiwan are more isolated: they are more likely to acquire emotional support from their mothers and offer emotional support to their mothers-in-law. These findings corresponds previous study that married Taiwanese women still feel obligated to provide emotional labour for their in-laws, in order to fulfil their husbands' filial piety responsibility (Kung, 2019). The author considers such practice as a persistence of patriarchal tradition that married man outsource their responsibility of filial piety to their wives.

Finally, it is time to talk about the marriage indicators. Among all models of emotional supports, the female model of emotional support is the only one that keeps marriage indicators accountable. Women who face more conflicts in their marriages are more likely to receive emotional support from their ageing mothers ($b = 0.012$, $p = 0.005$, see Table 7.5, Model 5). This pattern, however, does not imply instrumental or economic supports.

Discussion

This chapter aimed to clarify the association between parenthood status and types of intergenerational support between generations. To this end, I examined whether and to what extent intergenerational financial, instrumental and emotional support differ according to whether respondents have a child.

The analysis of intergenerational exchanges in this chapter presents an interesting cultural change of contemporary East Asian families, confirming the pattern of a 'modified patriarchal society' (Yi and Chang, 2008) and demonstrating how it is practiced in the domestic sphere. Results from the regression analysis indicate that traditional patriarchal norms and egalitarian practices coexist in contemporary Taiwanese families. For instance, both G2 fathers and mothers are more likely than childless ones to receive domestic help from G1 grandparents and in-laws, while G2 mothers are more likely to acquire money from the older generation only when they shoulder the responsibilities of being the primary child caregivers. Such practices reflect the traditional gendered division of labour: The father is the breadwinner who lacks the time and skills needed for childrearing. He receives instrumental help (but not monetary resources or emotional guidance) from the grandparents. These results again confirm the notion that young Taiwanese couples still practice patrilineal family norms, but with some democratic changes.

Another surprising phenomenon is that co-residence and childcare arrangements promote financial and instrumental support between generations. When grandparents are responsible for their grandchildren's care, they tend to offer domestic help and money to their adult children; the same pattern occurs for adult children who co-reside with their ageing parents and in-laws. However, such exchanges are gendered, too. Men receive more instrumental resources but provide one-sided upward financial support. On the contrary, women rarely receive domestic help from fathers-in-law when grandparents take on childcare responsibilities or when they live in patrilocal arrangement. In exchange, women receive financial support from ageing mothers and in-laws for their childrearing duties. Note that reciprocal financial transmissions only befall between G1 and G2 women, which make young married women the key persons who develop mutual bonds across generations, including the relationship with their in-laws. Once again, the models display the reality of the modern patrilineal family in Taiwan, where young mothers are the significant coordinators in the domestic sphere and intergenerational family finance.

Previous research undertaken in various countries has identified various disadvantages of grandparents' care provision, identifying such an arrangement as a risk factor for children's development. However, this chapter suggests that grandparents' provision of childcare facilitates active exchanges between the younger and older generations, especially in promoting the transmission of economic resources and collaborative care work. On the one hand, the widespread practice of grandmothers providing childcare reflects how hard Taiwanese young parents struggle with balancing between work and childcare. On the other hand, this chapter suggests a hidden benefit in that such arrangements bring Taiwanese families closer together through resource exchanges that may improve the lives of all generations involved.

References

Albertini, M., Kohli, M., & Vogel, C. (2007). Intergenerational transfers of time and money in European families: Common patterns—different regimes? *Journal of European Social Policy, 17*(4), 319–334.

Albertini, M., & Radl, J. (2012). Intergenerational transfers and social class: Inter-vivos transfers as means of status reproduction? *Acta Sociologica, 55*(2), 107–123.

Belsky, J., & Rovine, M. (1984). Social-network contact, family support, and the transition to parenthood. *Journal of Marriage and Family, 46*(2), 455–462.

Bengtson, V. L., & Roberts, R. E. L. (1991). Intergenerational solidarity in aging families: An example of formal theory construction. *Journal of Marriage and Family, 53*(4), 856–870.

Birditt, K. S., Brown, E., Orbuch, T. L., & McIlvane, J. M. (2010). Marital conflict behaviors and implications for divorce over 16 years. *Journal of Marriage and Family, 72*(5), 1188–1204.

Bucx, F., van Wel, F., & Knijn, T. (2012). Life-course status and exchanges of support between young adults and parents. *Journal of Marriage and Family, 74*(1), 101–115.

Cherlin, A. J. (2010). *The marriage-go-around: The state of marriage and the family in America today.* New York, NY: Vintage.

Chung, T. K., Yip, A. S., Lok, I. H., & Lee, D. T. (2011). Postnatal depression among Hong Kong Chinese fathers. *Hong Kong Medical Journal, 17*(2), 9–12.

Cong, Z., & Silverstein, M. (2012). Caring for grandchildren and intergenerational support in rural China: A gendered extended family perspective. *Aging and Society, 32*(3), 425–450.

Elder, G. H., Johnson, M. K., & Crosnoe, R. (2003). The emergence and development of life course theory. In J. T. Mortimer & M. J. Shanahan (Eds.), *Handbook of the life course* (pp. 3–19). New York, NY: Springer.

Elder, G. H., Jr. (1985). *Life-course dynamics: Trajectories and transitions, 1968–1980.* Ithaca, NY: Cornell University Press.

Elder, G. H., Jr. (1994). Time, human agency, and social change: Perspectives on the life course. *Social Psychology Quarterly, 57*(1), 4–15.

Fincham, F. D., & Bradbury, T. N. (1987). The assessment of marital quality: A reevaluation. *Journal of Marriage and Family, 49*(4), 797–809.

Fingerman, K. L., Hou, M., Kim, K., & Birditt, K. S. (2017). Coresident and nonresident emerging adults' daily experiences with parents. *Emerging Adulthood, 5*(5), 337–350.

Fingerman, K. L., Miller, L., Birditt, K., & Zarit, S. (2009). Giving to the good and the needy: Parental support of grown children. *Journal of Marriage and Family, 71*(5), 1220–1233.

Frankenberg, E., Lillard, L., & Willis, R. (2002). Patterns of intergenerational transfers in Southeast Asia. *Journal of Marriage and Family, 64*(3), 627–641.

Giarrusso, R., Feng, D., & Bengtson, V. L. (2005). The intergenerational-stake phenomenon over 20 years, in M. Silverstein & K. W. Schaie (Eds.), *Annual review of gerontology and geriatrics, 2004: Focus on intergenerational relations across time and place* (pp. 55–76). New York, NY: Springer.

Grundy, E. (2005). Reciprocity in relationships: Socioeconomic and health influences on intergenerational exchanges between Third Age parents and their adult children in Great Britain. *The British Journal of Sociology, 56*(2), 233–255.

Hansen, K. V. (2005). *Not-so-nuclear families: Class, gender, and networks of care.* New Brunswick, NJ: Rutgers University Press.

Hogg, R., & Worth, A. (2009). What support do parents of young children need? A user-focused study. *Community Practitioner: The Journal of the Community Practitioners' & Health Visitors' Association, 82*(1), 31–33.

Huss, B., & Pollmann-Schult, M. (2020). Relationship satisfaction across the transition to parenthood: The impact of conflict behavior. *Journal of Family Issues, 41*(3), 383–411.

Hu, A., & Tian F. (2018). Still under the ancestors' shadow? Ancestor workshop and family formation in contemporary China. *Demographic Research, 38*(1), 1–36.

Kalmijn, M., & De Graaf, P. M. (2012). Life course changes of children and well-being of parents. *Journal of Marriage and Family, 74*(2), 269–280.

Kalmijn, M., & Uunk, W. (2007). Regional value difference in Europe and social consequences of divorce: A test of the stigmatization hypothesis. *Social Science Research, 36*(2), 447–468.

Kinsella, K. (2000). Demographic dimensions of global aging. *Journal of Family Issues, 21*(5), 541–558.

Kluwer, E. S. (2010). From partnership to parenthood: A review of marital change across the transition to parenthood. *Journal of Family Theory & Review, 2*(2), 105–125.

Knodel, J., & Debavalya, N. (1997). Living arrangements and support among the elderly in Southeast Asia: An introduction. *Asia-Pacific Population Journal, 12*, 5–16.

Koh, Y. W., Lee, A. M., Chan, C. Y., Fong, D. Y. T., Lee, C. P., Leung, K. Y., et al (2015). Survey on examining prevalence of paternal anxiety and its risk factors in the perinatal period in Hong Kong: A longitudinal study. *BMC Public Health*, *15*(1), 1131.

Komter, A. E., & Vollebergh, W. A. M. (2002). Solidarity in Dutch families: Family ties under strain? *Journal of Family Issues*, *23*(2), 171–188.

Kung, H.-M. (2019). Persistence and change in the comparative status of mothers-in-law and daughters-in-law in Taiwanese families: 1979 to 2016. *Journal of Family Issues*, *40*(14), 1937–1962.

Lee, J., & Bauer, J. W. (2013). Motivations for providing and utilizing child care by grandmothers in South Korea. *Journal of Marriage and Family*, *75*(2), 381–402.

Lee, Y.-J., Parish, W.L., & Willis, R.J. (1994). Sons, daughters, and intergenerational support in Taiwan, *American Journal of Sociology*, *99*(4), 1010–1041.

Lin, P.-S., & Chang, C.-O. (2016). "No house no children? Dare not have children after buying a house": The links of house buying on household fertility behavior. *Taiwanese Journal of Sociology*, *59*: 93–138.

Lin, I.-F. & Wu, H.-S. (2014). Intergenerational exchange and expected support among the young-old. *Journal of Marriage and Family*, *76*(2), 261–271.

Lin, J.-P., & Yi, C.-C. (2011). Filial norms and intergenerational support to aging parents in China and Taiwan. *International Journal of Social Welfare*, *20*(1), 109–120.

Macmillan, R., & Copher, R. (2005). Families in the life course: Interdependency of roles, role configurations, and pathways. *Journal of Marriage and Family*, *67*(4), 858–879.

Min, J., Johnson, M. D., Anderson, J. R., & Yurkiw, J. (2021). Support exchanges between adult children and their parents across life transitions. *Journal of Marriage and Family*, 1–26. doi:10.1111/jomf.12787.

Moore, S., & Rosenthal, D. (2016). *Grandparenting: Contemporary perspectives.* Abingdon: Routledge.

Nauck, B. (2010). Intergenerational relationships and female inheritance expectations: Comparative results from eight societies in Asia, Europe, and North America. *Journal of Cross-Cultural Psychology*, *41*(5–6), 690–705.

Nauck, B., & Ren, Q. (2018). Coresidence in the transition to adulthood: The case of the United States, Germany, Taiwan, and Mainland China. *Chinese Sociological Review*, *50*(4), 443–473.

Nomaguchi, K. M., & Milkie, M. A. (2004). Costs and rewards of children: The effects of becoming a parent on adults' lives. *Journal of Marriage and Family*, *65*(2), 356–374.

Rossi, A. S., & Rossi, P. H. (1990). *Of human bonding: Parent-child relations across the life course.* New York, NY: Aldine de Gruyter.

Settersten, R. (2017). *Invitation to the life course: Towards new understandings of later life.* Abingdon: Routledge.

Shih, Y.-P. (2019). Parenting in three-generation Taiwanese families: The dynamics of collaboration and conflicts, in S. L. Blair & R. P. Costa (Eds.), *Transitions into parenthood: Examining the complexities of childrearing. Contemporary perspectives in family research*, Vol. 15, 231–256.

Silverstein, M., & Bengtson, V.L. (1997). Intergenerational solidarity and the structure of adult child-parent relationships in American families. *American Journal of Sociology, 103*(2), 429–460.

Silverstein, M., Cong, Z., & Li, S. (2006). Intergenerational transfers and living arrangements of older people in rural China: Consequences for psychological well-being. *Journals of Gerontology, Psychological Sciences and Social Sciences, Series B, 61*(5), 256–266.

Silverstein, M., Lowenstein, A., Katz, R., Gans, D., Fan, Y.-K., & Oyama, P. (2013). Intergenerational support and the emotional well-being of older Jews and Arabs in Israel. *Journal of Marriage and Family, 75*(4), 950–963.

Wu, M.-Y., & Yi, C.-C. (2003). A marriage is more than a marriage: The impacts of familial factors on marital satisfaction, *Journal of Population Studies. 26*, 71–95.

Yang, H. (1996). The distributive norm of monetary support to older parents: A look at a township in China. *Journal of Marriage and Family, 58*(2), 404–415.

Yeh, K. H. (2009). The dual filial piety model in Chinese culture: Retrospect and prospects. *Indigenous Psychological Research in Chinese Societies, 32*: 101–148.

Yi, C.-C., & Chang, Y.-H. (2008). Fuxi jiating de chixu yu bianqian: Taiwan de jiating shehuixue yanjiu, 1960-2000 [The continuity and change of the patrilineal family] In G.-S. Shieh (Ed.), *Qunxue zhengming: Taiwan shehuixue fazhanshi, 1945-2005 [Interlocution: A thematic history of Taiwanese sociology, 1945–2005]* (pp. 23–73). Taipei: Socio Publishing.

Yi, C.-C., Lin, W.-H., & Ma, J. K.-H. (2019). Marital satisfaction among Taiwanese young married couples: The effects of resources and traditional norms. *Journal of Family Issues, 40*(14), 2015–2043.

Zimmer, Z., Korinek, K., Knodel, J., & Chayovan, N. (2008). Migrant Interactions with elderly parents in rural Cambodia and Thailand. *Journal of Marriage and Family, 70*(3), 585–598.

8

Childcare Arrangements Among Young Parents in Taiwan

Wan-chi Chen and Hao-Chun Cheng

Introduction

Despite some inconsistency in fertility statistics among different institutions, one is not mistaken by saying that Taiwan's fertility rate has been in the lowest-low group in the world for the past ten years.[1] Under the pressure of the low fertility rate, childcare policy has been an important issue in Taiwan in recent years. Along with the trend of increasing female labour participation, the government embarked on several policies or practices in the past two decades.

The first stage is the 'Shechyu Baomu Jhihchih Sitong (Community Babysitter Support System)', launched in 2001. The second stage is the 'Baomu Tuo Yu Guanli Yu Tuo Yu Feiyong Bujhu Shihshih Jihua (Childminder Management and Subsidy Programme)', launched in 2008. The third stage is the programme 'Jiangou Tuo Yu Guanli Jhihdu Shihshih Jihua (Constructing Childcare Service Management System)', launched in 2015 (Wang, 2014). Overall, most of these policies have been attempting to provide parents with infants and toddlers accessible, affordable and accountable childcare service.

Have these efforts been transferred into what Taiwanese parents are in urgent need of? Do parents with infants and toddlers take good advantage of the benefit these policies provide? What are their ideal ways of childcare arrangements? As a matter of fact, the Taiwanese society still does not have a clear picture of how young parents today manage the childcare arrangements or whether their ideal picture of childcare has changed. What is known is that Taiwan, representing the East Asian familial customs, displays a childcare pattern with a large family and kinship sector (Ochiai, 2009). However, there are still many questions left unanswered. Is there any gap between actual and ideal childcare arrangements? Do single-parent families arrange childcare differently from two-parent families? Are childcare expenses a heavy burden for Taiwanese young parents? Do childcare arrangements associate with relationship satisfaction? This study aims to explore these questions.

Relying on the couple dataset gathered from the 2017 TYP data and the spousal data, this study provides a portrait of childcare arrangements among young parents in Taiwan. Several issues have been investigated. Findings are reported around four main themes: (1) the overall profile of childcare arrangement in Taiwan; (2) differences in childcare arrangements by family structure and by education; (3) using the information on the most preferred arrangement of childcare to investigate the ideal-actual mismatch; (4) childcare arrangements and satisfaction to parent–child relationship.

Literature Review

Along with the rapid economic development since the 1960s, Taiwan has gone through social changes as most late-developed countries do, including educational expansion, equalization of educational opportunities for women, and increasing female labour participation.[2] These trends have been followed by more demographic trends, such as delayed marriage, delayed birth and the continuing decline of fertility rate (Lesthaeghe, 2010). As more and more married women choose to engage more in paid work, childcare demand became an increasingly urgent problem. Whether the state should play a role to some extent in sharing childcare responsibilities also becomes an issue to be debated.

Observing the development of family policies in Taiwan enables us to examine the underlying assumption behind each policy (Wang, 2014). The government did not take any role in childcare support until year 2001. Before the millennium, childcare had been regarded as the responsibility of individual families, mainly the parents. In 2001, Community Nanny Support System was introduced, aiming to increase the supply of qualified nannies and provide childcare subsidy for parents. In the following year, the Act of Gender Equality in Employment was enacted and yielded unpaid parental leave in Taiwanese workplace for the first time. A few years later, the Childminder Management and Subsidy Programme launched in 2008, another policy intending to ensure the quality of childcare services and to partly subsidize parents' expenses in outside-of-family childcare. About the same time, paid parental leave began being applied for certain groups (such as teachers and government employees). In year 2012, a new policy 'Parental Subsidy for Unemployed Parents Programme' was put into practice. About the same time, nanny management system expanded the range and included kinship nannies. While most previous policies support dual-career families and thus encourage women's labour market participation, policies after 2012 encourage parents to arrange childcare back into the families – the opposite of defamilialsim. The following section discusses the concepts of defamilialism and familialism in family support policies.

Examining Policies: Defamilialism or Familialism?

In line with the worldwide increase of female labour participation and the decline of fertility rate, the perspective on childcare responsibility is changing and raising numerous debates. Governments all over the industrialized world face the decisions of how their family policies take shape. Scholars identified the trend of defamilialism when the state plays an increasingly larger role in supporting individual families in childcare, usually through providing public care or subsidies (Esping-Andersen, 1999). However, not all family policies necessarily encourage defamilialization. Some policies push the society towards 're-familialism', such as parental subsidies and maternal leaves that encourage mothers to stay home taking care of children (Leira, 2006).

Leitner (2003) distinguishes policies into two dimensions – one is to increase the use of childcare services outside of families (defamilialism); the other is to provide benefits, encouraging parents not to outsource and to take the childcare responsibilities by themselves (familialism). Using this two-by-two categorization, four types of childcare policies have been identified: (1) implicit familialism, (2) defamilialism, (3) optional familialism, (4) explicit familialism. According to Leitner (2003), implicit familialism refers to when countries offer neither defamilialized nor actively familialized supports for caring within family, but it still regards family as the main role of caring in a society. Defamilialism characterizes countries that offer actively defamilialized care policies, such as public childcare institutions. Optional familialism demonstrates that countries offer both strong familialism and defamilialized care policies to people in need. Explicit familialism refers to that the country offers both strong familialized and weak defamilialized childcare policies.

Both optional familialism and explicit familialism regard family as the core of care supports. In other words, these two types of ideology assume that members within families still have the responsibilities to take care of children, and the government should assist its people to fulfilling their family obligations. On the other hand, defamilialism and implicit familialism suggests that the government plays a more active role in providing childcare supports to families with children.

Wang (2014) found Leitner's (2003) categorization extremely useful while examining changes in Taiwan's childcare policies from 2001 to 2012. The author argues that Taiwan has experienced the transformation through implicit familiamlism, defamilialism, optional familialism and in recent years coming to explicit familialism and frame them within the Taiwanese context. Implicit familiamlism, similar to Leitner's definition, refers to the concept that childcare is regarded mainly as family responsibility while the role of government is only supplementary. Defamilialism indicates a process that the government takes an increasingly active role on providing childcare support, such as developing a training system of professional nannies. Optional familialism refers to policies that push mothers back to family; among all policies of familialization, parental leave might be the most important one. As for explicit familialism, it signifies a recent stage that the government came up with more and more policies with familialization effect, such as new strategies encouraging 'kinship relatives as nannies' or different types of parental subsidy.

An and Peng's (2016) comparative study yields to a similar conclusion. They compare childcare policies in Japan, South Korea and Taiwan. Although they found a common pattern towards the increased use of financial support among the three countries over time, this commonality does not mean these three countries' policies are converging. Taiwan has been strengthening familialization by increasing the leave compensation to value time off to provide childcare; Japan values family care; South Korea facilitates the use of market-based care services through policy. This study suggests that the degree of defamilialization is lowest in Taiwan, providing a picture somewhat consistent with Wang's (2014) description on Taiwan's recent development of childcare policies. Outside-of-family childcare services play a minor role in encouraging women to engaged in paid work in Taiwan.

The Missing Role of Grandparents in the Debate

As outlined in the previous sections, it seems that Taiwan's progress in establishing a supportive system of childcare services is not successful. It even lags behind Japan and South Korea. However, if compared with Japan and Korea, female labour participation rate in Taiwan is the highest (An and Peng, 2016). The question becomes, how will this study account for the seeming contradiction between the least defamilialized policies and the highest female labour market participation rate in Taiwan (in the East Asian context)?

Let's rethink the two opposite concepts of familialism and defamilialism (or interchangeably, familization and defamilization; see Lohmann and Zagel, 2016). There are certain assumptions behind these concepts. Most debates about family policies in the Western world revolve around the assumption of a core family: if the policy put more emphasis on family values and stressed family responsibilities in childcare, it tends to push working women back into the families, which is less likely to protect women from an uninterrupted career plan. Nevertheless, if we go beyond the form of core families and extend the meaning of family into kinship, the practices of dual-career family and familialized childcare would become much less incompatible. For example, when grandparents are involved in childcare and mothers remain on the track of uninterrupted career, should we call it a familialization or a defamilialization trend?

East or West, the role of grandparents in childcare is getting more and more attention for the past decade. Analysing European Social Survey data from 23 European countries, Jappens and Van Bavel (2012) find that mothers in more conservative regions are more inclined to use grandparents as the main source of childcare instead of formal alternatives. This study also shows that the availability of formal childcare provisions as a contextual factor matters. The higher the formal childcare coverage rate in a country, the smaller the probability that mothers will count on grandparents as the main source of childcare for their children. Thomese and Liefbroer (2013) focused on the case of Netherlands, reporting that maternal grandparents are more likely to provide childcare than paternal grandparents, and grandmothers were more likely to do so than grandfathers. Analysing two waves of panel data from 10 European countries,

Leopold and Skopek (2014) investigated what factor is associated with the gender gap in grandparenting. They found that the retirement of grandfather significantly increases his share of grandparenting. Regional difference is also an important factor. Controlling for couples' division of paid work, the gender gap in grandparenting was smallest in the north and largest in the south of Europe.

Bringing back focus on Taiwan, it has been reported that care work for young children heavily rely on family and kinship (Ochiai, 2009; Yi, 1994).[3] Almost two-thirds of dual-earner families reported grandparents as the main caregiver of their children under the age of three in 2010 (Tsai, 2014). Panel data of 2,500 seventh graders in 2000 in northern Taiwan show that half of the teenagers were raised in a three-generation household, living with their grandparents (Yi et al., 2006). Co-residence with grandparents as one form of childcare arrangement at families' early stage might well explain why the percentage of teenagers reporting intimacy with grandparents remains high while nuclear families are increasing (Chang et al., 2008). All these studies suggest that grandparenting is a non-negligible part of the picture of childcare arrangements for Taiwanese parents.

Existing Taiwan-related studies which involved the role of grandparents focus mainly on the context of intergenerational relations. The implication of the availability of grandparenting on parents' decision or policy debate is less concerned. Still, there are a few studies on this topic. Drawing on in-depth interview data, Sun (2008) finds that Taiwanese grandparents treat childcare assistance as their moral responsibility. Chang (2015) used a different approach; analysing cross-sectional data, her study finds that the presence of young children is associated with household composition. People with young children are more likely to co-reside with elderly parents or extended kin. Though the direction of causality is unclear. Analysing social attitude survey data, Lin and Yi (2019) found that childcare is considered a family responsibility more than elderly care. It may well account for the prevalence of grandparenting in Taiwan.

Factors Related to Childcare Arrangements

Previous studies give us an overview of childcare arrangements in current Taiwan. The first part highlights that childcare services play a minor role in encouraging women to engage in paid work. The second part calls our attention to the importance of the role of grandparents in childcare support. Now we turn to review what other factors might be related to childcare arrangements.

Krapf (2014) analyses data from Sweden, Finland and Western Germany. The results show that, in Sweden, a country with strong support for dual-earner families, usage was largely independent of mothers' characteristics. However, in Finland and Western Germany, highly educated mothers were found to be more likely to use childcare than less-educated mothers. Using the Generations and Gender Survey data from Russia and selected European countries, Pelikh and Tyndik (2014) obtain a similar conclusion – variations in using childcare services can be partly explained by the age of children and mother's education. The younger the child is, the less likely are the parents to use formal childcare provisions. The higher the mother's education level, the higher the use of formal childcare. Verhoef et al. (2016) use survey data from dual-earner couples in the Netherlands. They found that nonstandard work made couples less likely to use care provided by relatives or friends. In other words, these parents rely on themselves for childcare.

Few studies paid attention to whether family structure (whether they refer to single-parent household or not) is associated with childcare arrangements. Most researchers treat it as control or just a minor explanatory variable. Jappens and Van Bavel (2012) hypothesized that the probability for single mothers to rely on grandparents for childcare would be higher than other parents. Nevertheless, their results show the opposite, meaning that it is significantly lower than non-single mothers. Pelikh and Tyndik (2014) reported that single fathers are less likely to use childcare services, compared with two-parent families (it is not clear why single mothers are not included in the comparison scheme). Krapf (2014) showed that single mothers are more likely to use childcare services, compared to married and cohabiting mothers, but it occurs only in Finland (not in Sweden and Germany). All the above literature focused only on European countries. The most related literature about Taiwan on this issue is the study by Chen (2016), who found that single fathers were more likely to settle in multigenerational living arrangements than single mothers and intact families' parents (probably for the reason of better grandparenting support).

The Gap between the Ideal and the Actual Arrangement

The data used in this study collected 'the most preferred arrangement in childcare' from the respondents, which is a rarely collected piece of information among other research. What is the ideal way of childcare for most parents? Do parents always get to choose what they prefer? There is little understanding of these questions. Through in-depth interviews with several Taiwanese parents, Ou and Hung (2017) try to answer the question, 'what is the best choice of care model?'. The authors pointed out that care arrangements are deeply affected by culture; however, Taiwanese mothers 'struggle with a cultural contradiction between the 'self-interest' of being a working professional and the 'altruism' of being a caregiver' (Ou and Hung, 2017). It implies that it may not be easy for mothers to decide what is the most ideal way of care arrangement.

Wang's (2016) policy evaluation project, which is commissioned by Taiwan's Minister of Health and Welfare, provided some information on the gap between the ideal and the actual arrangements. 'What is your most preferred childcare arrangement?' Through questionnaire survey, the author found that 'parents stay home taking care of the child without working' has the highest frequency (40 per cent or so) among four options.[4] Among those who chose 'parents taking care of the child themselves' as their number one priority, 42 per cent of them arranged otherwise. Among those who chose 'institutional childcare' as their top priority, 68 per cent arranged otherwise. The author concluded that the availability of good quality childcare service may be a crucial factor in accounting for the gap between the ideal and the actual arrangement.

From the literature review above, we get the knowledge that institutional childcare services (especially in public sector) in Taiwan are in deficiency, due to the assumption of familialism by the government. In addition, grandparents seem to play an increasingly important role in childcare in a form that is left out of discussion in previous studies, in the context of a rapidly ageing society. All these features endow Taiwan as the excellent case to study the strategies of child arrangement among parents. In the following section, the authors make a brief description of the Taiwan Youth Project (TYP) survey data and what kind of detailed information it contains.

Data and Method

Data

The analytic data of this chapter are from the TYP survey, which is a longitudinal survey data sponsored and conducted by Academia Sinica, Taiwan. The TYP survey launched in March 2000, when two groups of subjects are in 7th and 9th grades. The follow-up interviews were conducted in 2000 (October), 2001, 2003, 2004 (February and October), 2006, 2008, 2011, 2014 and 2017. In the 2013 survey, the TYP also interviews subjects' spouse. Since then, the TYP collected spousal data in each wave (the interval between subject interviews and spouse interviews is about six months). This study adopts the form of couple data through combining the 2017 subjects data and 2018 spousal data. Regarding the range of the respondents, this study focuses only on parent(s) with at least one child. The number of observations is 663.[5] Among these 663 households, 559 households have husbands' information and 578 households have wives' information. Missing observations of one parent could be due to either single-parent family formation or declining to do the spousal survey.

Variables

The current analyses mainly rely on the information about these young parents' childcare arrangements for the first child, including the type of actual and ideal childcare arrangements (who is the actual main caregiver, who is the ideal main caregiver), whether and how long do they take parental leave for, whether and how much they receive childcare subsidy and monthly childcare expenditure. The phase in need of intensive childcare supports is divided into three stages: 0–6 months old, 6 months to 2 years old and 2–3 years old. The above information for all three stages has been collected in the survey.

Childcare Arrangements

Regarding the type of childcare arrangements, the question is as follows: 'During the day on weekdays (or when you are working), who is the main caregiver of your first child (when he/she was 0–6 month's old, take the first stage for example)?' The information on both the actual and the ideal arrangements have been collected. The original options include self, spouse, paternal grandparents, maternal grandparents, other kinship caregiver, nannies, private daycare center and public daycare center. In most analyses in this chapter, classification is simplified into four categories: (1) parents, (2) kinship caregivers (mostly grandparents), (3) nannies, (4) daycare center. In order to examine whether there is a gender difference in the effect of childcare arrangement on respondent's satisfaction to parent–child relationship, we further separate parents into father and mother based on respondent's gender in the regression models.

Demographic Characteristics and Socio-Economic Backgrounds

In addition to childcare arrangements, we also include respondent's demographic and socio-economic backgrounds into our analysis: highest education level (1 = Junior high school; 2 = High school (including vocational high school); 3 = Some college; 4 = College and above), monthly household income (in NTD),[6] whether the family is intact or not (1 = the respondent is currently married; 0 = the respondent is single or divorced) and the first child's gender (1 = male; 0 = female). Table 8.1 provides descriptive statistics for demographic characteristics of these respondents. The husbands' mean age is 32.9 and the wives' mean age is 31.7. About 4 per cent of the households are single-parent families.

Method

In this chapter, descriptive statistics are adopted to delineate a general picture of actual and ideal childcare arrangement among Taiwanese young couples since there are few studies focusing on this issue. The study presents the distribution of actual and ideal childcare arrangement and the gap between them. It also examines how family structure and parental education are associated with parent's actual and ideal childcare arrangement.

In addition to descriptive statistics, ordinal logistic models also help with examining how actual childcare arrangements are associated with parent's satisfaction to parent–child relationship.[7] Our models include parents' education, family structure, household income and the first child's gender as control variables in the models. Since not every first child reached the age of two or three, the number of observations in models for different stages would not be identical. In order to examine whether there is a gender difference in the effect of

Table 8.1 Descriptive statistics of socioeconomic backgrounds (*n* = 663[a])

	% or mean	S.D.	Min	Max
Husband's age[a]	32.9	2.8	27	45
Wife's age[a]	31.7	2.1	22	48
Husband's highest education level				
Junior high school	3.9%	–	–	–
High school (incl. vocational high school)	19.8%	–	–	–
Some college	24.4%	–	–	–
College and above	24.6%	–	–	–
Graduate school and above	11.5%	–	–	–
Missing	15.8%	–	–	–
Wife's highest education level				
Junior high school	1.8%	–	–	–
High school (incl. vocational high school)	14.5%	–	–	–
Some college	28.7%	–	–	–
College and above	33.6%	–	–	–
Graduate school and above	8.6%	–	–	–
Missing	12.8%	–	–	–
Couple's education (*n* = 482)				
Low: Both parents are high school or below	10.4%	–	–	–
Mid: One of parents is some college	61.4%	–	–	–
High: Both parents are college or above	28.2%	–	–	–
Household income (in NTD)[b]	92,722.3	46,862.9	5,000	200,000
Intact family	96.1%	–	–	–
The first child's gender				
Male	49.3%	–	–	–
Female	50.4%	–	–	–
Missing	0.3%	–	–	–

[a]The number of observations (households) in this study is 663. Notice that the cases will drop for the 2nd and 3rd stages because some respondents' child's age hasn't reached one or two years old. Among these 663 households, 559 households include the husband's information, and 578 households include the wife's information. There are two missing cases in 'husband's age' and one missing value in 'Wife's age'.
[b]The number of nonresponse cases for the variable of household income is 22.

childcare arrangement on respondent's satisfaction to parent–child relationship, the models separate parents into fathers and mothers based on respondent's gender.

Result

The Overall Profile of Childcare Arrangement in Taiwan

The upper part of Figure 8.1 displays the distribution of actual childcare arrangements with the original classification with eight categories. The patterns for all three stages are similar – mother is the most frequent arrangement, paternal grandparents is the second and maternal grandparents is the third most frequent category. In contrast, all outside-of-family options (nannies, private daycare center, public daycare center) have low percentages before the age of three. The only exception is private daycare center at the stage of 2–3 years old, though it is still relatively low (12.3 per cent). The percentage of institutional childcare presented here is obviously much lower than that of Japan and Korea.[8] Comparing different stages, we also observe that the percentage of mother as the caregiver decreases as the child grows older. This decrease is likely due to mothers returning to the workforce.

Next, we simplify the categorization into four types of arrangements (parents, kinship caregiver, nannies, daycare center) and display the distribution in the bottom half of Figure 8.1. Since the majority of 'kinship caregiver' is grandparents, we can conclude that family support has been, and is still, the most important childcare support in the long-term trend of increasing female labour participation in Taiwan. Later we will use this four-category distribution to compare the actual and ideal childcare arrangements.

In addition to the distribution of childcare arrangement in Taiwan, Table 8.2 displays the descriptive statistics of parental leave (in percentage and months), parental subsidy and childcare subsidy (in percentage and the average amount per month) and childcare expenditure (per month) in the three stages, respectively.

Regarding parental leave, about one-fifth of the households (20.8 per cent) reported to take parental leave at the first stage of the child's age. The percentage of taking parental leave drops along with the child's growth, reducing to 11.2 per cent at the second stage and 2 per cent when the child becomes a toddler.

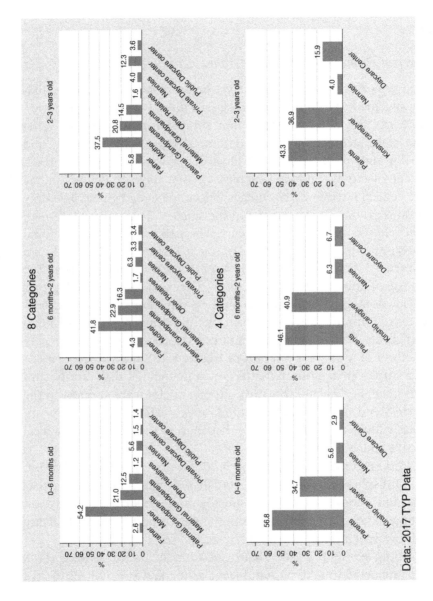

Figure 8.1 The distributions of actual and ideal childcare arrangements

In terms of parental subsidy, more than half of the households receive parental subsidy at the first stage. The average amount for those who obtain parental subsidy is NT$5,808 (~US$200). As the child grows bigger, we observe a significant drop from the second stage to the third stage, which is from 43.6 per cent to 13.8 per cent. This pattern is in line with the fact that parents are more likely to choose to take care of their children by themselves before kids transition to toddlerhood.

The proportion of receiving childcare subsidy shows a similar pattern with that of receiving parental subsidy. Nevertheless, most parents do not receive childcare subsidy: less than 15 per cent of the parents report receiving it at the first stage, and only 4.4 per cent at the third stage. On average, the highest amount of childcare subsidy is at the stage of 2–3 years old, which is approximately NT$3,781.5 per month. The amounts in other two stages are less than NT$3,000 per month.

Table 8.2 also shows that the child expenditure also decreases along with the child's growth, approximately from NT$12,658 per month at the first stage to NT$10,675 at the third stage. Again, there appears a significant drop between the second and the third stage. What is worth

Table 8.2 Descriptive statistics on parental leave, childcare subsidy and childcare expenditure

	0–6 m	6 m–2 yr	2–3 yr
Parental leave (1 = Yes)	20.8%	11.2%	2.0%
Parental leave (Months)[a]	4.8	8.5	7.1
Parental subsidy (1 = Yes)	54.9%	43.6%	13.8%
Parental subsidy (NTD/mo.)[a]	5,808.2	4,317.1	3,620.9
Childcare subsidy (1 = Yes)	11.7%	13.9%	4.4%
Childcare subsidy (NTD/mo.)[a]	2,914.3	3,781.5	2,724.1
Childcare expenditure (NTD/mo.)[a]	12,658.1	12,541.6	10,675.0
Parents	313.8	104.0	145.4
Kinship caregiver	5,100.0	5,100.4	4,467.7
Nanny	17,462.2	17,051.2	12,725.0
Daycare center	13,302.6	12,081.4	7,918.8
Public	10,194.4	8,363.6	6,933.3
Private	16,100.0	15,976.2	8,204.8

[a]Limited to those who answered 'yes' only (i.e., zero has been excluded)

noting is that there is a notable disparity between the amount of childcare subsidy and childcare expenditure. On average, childcare subsidy can only cover one-third of the actual childcare expenditure at best.

Another aspect worth highlighting is the difference in childcare expenditure among various types of arrangements. The option of hiring nanny is the most expensive, compared to other alternatives. The option with the second-highest average expenses is daycare center. Also, the expenditure in the private daycare centers is, of course, higher than the public ones, although the difference decreases at the third stage. Leaving those parents who take care of their child themselves aside, the least costly option is kinship caregiver, which refers to grandparents in most cases. This economic reason might be one of the explanations why grandparent's support in childcare is prevalent in Taiwan.

Differences in Childcare Arrangements by Family Structure and Education

In this subsection, actual childcare arrangements will be shown separately by two factors – family structure and parents' education – to observe whether and how different demographic characteristics are associated with different childcare patterns.

Figure 8.2 displays the distributions of childcare arrangements for two-parent families and single-parent families. As one might expect, the option of parental care for single-parent families is not as available as for two-parent families. The percentages of single parents taking care of the child by themselves are significantly lower than that of two-parent families for all three stages. It is possible that the childcare need is fulfilled mostly by grandparents and nannies. Note that although single parents are less likely to take care of the child themselves, the proportion of sending kids to daycare centers for single parents is less than half of that for parents from intact families at the child's stage of 2–3 years old (7.7 per cent compared to 16.3 per cent). This finding may reflect single parents' disadvantages in financial resource.

Figure 8.3 shows whether and how parental education is related to the pattern of childcare among two-parent families. We divide parental education into three groups: high (both parents have college

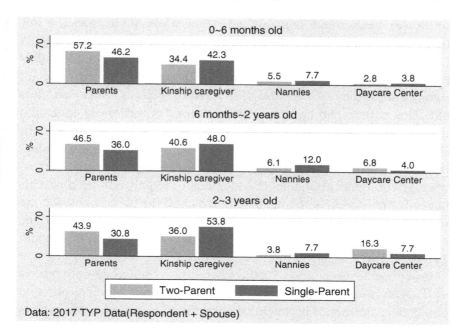

Figure 8.2   Actual childcare arrangements by family structure

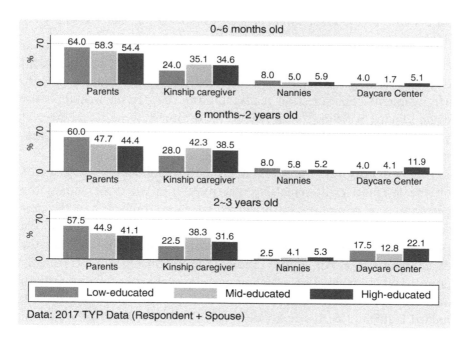

Figure 8.3   Childcare arrangements by parents' education (intact families only)

or above), medium (at least one parent has associate degree) and low (both parents are high school or below). Overall, the percentages taking care of the child themselves are always the lowest for highly educated parents across all three stages, though the difference is not significant for the first two stages, or when the child is under two years old. This pattern can be expected since mothers with more education usually have higher opportunity cost if they exit labour market for childcare. The independence test shows that, when the child reaches the toddler stage, the difference in childcare arrangements for parents with different educational level is significant. Highly educated parents not only are less likely to take care of the child themselves but also are more likely to adopt institutional childcare. This association is in line with some findings from European countries (Krapf, 2014; Pelikh and Tyndik, 2014).

One possible explanation for this phenomenon is that daycare centers in Taiwan usually provide the combined services of childcare and pre-school education. This might be attractive to highly educated parents since these parents usually have a higher expectation of their children and thus are more eager to choose institutional childcare at this stage.

How Close to the Ideal Childcare? Investigating the Ideal-Actual Mismatch

In the 2017 and 2018 TYP surveys, information about parents' ideal childcare arrangements are also collected besides the actual childcare arrangements. The question reads, 'During the day on weekdays (or when you are working), who is your most preferred main caregiver of your child (when your first child was 0–6 months old, take the first stage for example)?'

Figure 8.4 displays the actual and the ideal childcare arrangements on the left and right panels, respectively. For all three stages, the percentage of parental care preferred is always higher than the percentage of parents taking care of the child themselves in reality; the percentage of kinship care preferred is always much lower than the actual percentage. Apparently, though family kinship support (mostly grandparents) is available in supporting childcare for more than one-third of these young parents, the majority of the parents still regard childcare as their own responsibility and wish to take care of the child by themselves.[9]

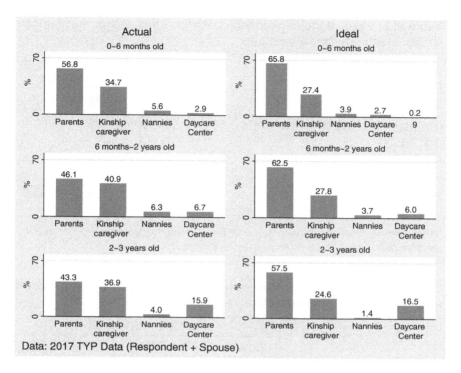

Figure 8.4 Comparing the distributions of actual and ideal childcare arrangements

Next, the study asks, how many parents are not able to arrange childcare exactly as they preferred? These parents are considered as displaying mismatch between ideal and actual arrangements. The left panel of Table 8.3 lists the percentage of ideal-actual mismatch for all families for each stage separately. Overall, about one-fifth to one-fourth of parents are not able to practice their most preferred arrangement of childcare.

Does this proportion of mismatch vary across families with different demographic characteristics? Table 8.3 compares two-parent families and single-parent families, showing that the percentage of mismatch for single parents is significantly higher than that for two-parent families regardless of child's stage. Almost four out of ten single parents have difficulty in realizing their ideal childcare arrangements for their toddlers.

Whether education helps parents match their actual childcare arrangements with the ideals is the next question. To our surprise, the findings presented in Table 8.4 suggest a negative association between

Table 8.3 Percentage of mismatch between ideal and actual childcare arrangements, by family structure

Child's stage	All		Two-parent families		Single-parent families	
	N	%	*N*	%	*N*	%
0–6 months old	660	20.0	635	19.5	25	32.0
6 months–2 years old	645	24.0	621	23.7	24	33.3
2–3 years old	503	24.7	477	23.9	26	38.5

Note: The percentage of mismatch signifies 'how many parents are not able to arrange childcare exactly as they most preferred?'

Table 8.4 Percentage of mismatch between ideal and actual childcare arrangements, by parents' education

Child's stage	Parental education					
	Low		Mid		High	
	N	%	*N*	%	*N*	%
0–6 months old	50	10.0	241	22.4	136	21.3
6 months–2 years old	50	14.0	241	24.1	135	28.2
2–3 years old	40	5.0	195	27.7	95	25.3

Note: The table only includes two-parent families.

parental education and the ideal-actual matching. Parents with higher educational level have lower percentage of having their ideal childcare arrangement realized in all three stages, compared to the least-educated parents.

The education differentials in this ideal-actual mismatch are most obvious when the child is at the toddler stage ($\chi_2^2 = 9.382$; p-value = 0.01). It is highly likely that this ideal-actual mismatch among highly educated parents is because their demand for good-quality institutional childcare service is not met. In order to check this surmise, we look at the distributions of the most preferred childcare arrangements at the stage of toddler by parents' education. It is found that, when only 14.6 per cent of the less-educated parents prefer institutional childcare, the percentage for highly educated parents comes to almost 30 per cent. The result signifies that, though institutional childcare is not favoured by most parents so far, the need for a well-developed system of institutional childcare still deserves the attention of policy-makers in the context of higher education expansion.

Childcare Arrangements and Satisfaction to Parent–Child Relationship

In this subsection, we use ordinal logistic models to explore the relationship between actual childcare arrangements and the satisfaction to parent–child relationship. The focus is the variable of childcare arrangements (five categories: self, spouse, kinship caregiver, nanny and daycare center). Control variables include respondent's gender, education level, household income, family structure and the child's gender. Most coefficients of control variables are not significant at the 0.05 significance level, except for family structure. We found that parents' satisfaction to parent–child relationship in intact families is significantly higher than parents in single-parent families, regardless of child's age and parents' gender (results not shown).

As shown in Panel A of Table 8.5, the help of kinship caregiver significantly elevates their satisfaction to parent–child relationship at the second and third stages by about 58.4 per cent and 125.0 per cent (the coefficients are 0.46 and 0.81; the odd ratios of these two coefficients are 1.584 and 2.248). At the third stage, spousal support that take on work-time childcare responsibilities also has a significant positive effect on parent–child relationship satisfaction (coefficient: 0.76; odds ratio: 2.138).

Considering males and females may have different preferences in childcare arrangements and thus reflecting on their self-evaluation on the satisfaction to parent–child relationship, we separate these two groups in our analysis. Interestingly, we found that the impacts of the childcare arrangements on parents' perceived quality of parent–child relation are different between fathers and mothers. For fathers (see Panel B), childcare arrangements do not play a significant role in predicting the satisfaction to parent–child relationship across these three stages; for mothers (see Panel C), the help of kinship caregiver will significantly elevates their satisfaction to parent–child relationship at the second and third stage by about 84.4 per cent and 133.0 per

Table 8.5 The ordinal logistic regression models: The association of childcare arrangements and parent's satisfaction to parent–child relationship

	0–6 months		6 m–2 yrs		2–3 yrs	
	Coef.	S.E.	Coef.	S.E.	Coef.	S.E.
Panel A. All Parents						
Childcare arrangements						
(Ref. = self)						
Spouse	0.00	0.30	0.54	0.29	0.76*	0.33
Kinship caregiver	0.22	0.23	0.46*	0.23	0.81**	0.26
Nanny	−0.26	0.38	−0.01	0.37	0.51	0.52
Daycare center	−0.17	0.51	−0.07	0.36	0.47	0.31
N	638		623		485	
Log Likelihood	−439.46		−427.87		−331.56	
Panel B. Fathers						
Childcare arrangements						
(Ref. = self)						
Spouse	−0.57	0.84	0.42	0.52	0.79	0.53
Kinship caregiver	−0.58	0.86	0.26	0.52	0.88	0.54
Nanny	−1.11	0.99	−0.08	0.68	0.84	0.87
Daycare center	−0.03	1.17	−0.14	0.70	0.17	0.59
N	307		299		222	
Log Likelihood	−204.80		−199.41		−150.02	
Panel C. Mothers						
Childcare arrangements						
(Ref. = self)						
Spouse	−0.36	0.69	0.91	0.73	0.67	0.67
Kinship caregiver	0.43	0.26	0.61*	0.26	0.85**	0.32
Nanny	−0.02	0.47	0.03	0.48	0.54	0.68
Daycare center	−0.66	0.70	−0.00	0.46	0.80*	0.40
N	331		324		263	
Log Likelihood	−227.49		−222.28		−175.88	

Note: *$p < 0.05$; **$p < 0.01$; ***$p < 0.001$. Respondent's highest education level, household income, intact family, and the first child's gender are controlled in the models.

cent, respectively (the coefficients are 0.61 and 0.85; the odd ratios of these two coefficients are 1.844 and 2.330). In addition, 'Daycare center', compared to 'self', can significantly elevate women's satisfaction to parent–child relationship by about 122.5 per cent as well (the coefficient is 0.80 and the odds ratio is 2.225).

The results indicate that there is a gender difference in the relationship between childcare arrangements and parent's perceived quality of parent–child relationship. Also, it indicates that mothers perceive higher quality of parent–child relationship when other family members or daycare center take the main responsibility of childcare during work time.

Conclusion

In the context of serious policy debate on defamilialism-familialism dilemma, many East Asian countries display a childcare pattern with a large family and kinship sector (Ochiai, 2009), a pattern which is difficult for us to attribute in the spectrum of defamilialism-familialism. Among these East Asian countries, Taiwan demonstrates its uniqueness with an even higher reliance on grandparents' support in childcare. Focusing on childcare arrangements among Taiwanese parents in younger generation, this study yields to several interesting findings, wrapped up in four main themes.

The Overall Profile of Childcare Arrangement in Taiwan

Despite how family policy has been in focus for the past two decades, outside-of-family childcare arrangements occupy only a small share among all types of childcare options, especially before the child age of two (8 per cent, 13 per cent and 20 per cent for the three stages, respectively). In the long-term trend of increasing female labour participation in Taiwan, family support has been, and is still, the most important type of childcare support.

Furthermore, different types of childcare arrangements vary in expenditures. The option of nanny is the most expensive, followed by daycare center. Grandparenting seems to be the most economical choice other than parents taking care of the child by themselves (if we disregard their opportunity costs).

Differences in Childcare Arrangements by Family Structure and by Education

Parents with different demographic characteristics exhibit differences in childcare arrangements. Single parents are much less likely to choose the option of childcare by parent than two-parent families across the child's stage. They are also less likely to adopt institutional childcare when the child becomes a toddler. Kinship support is their main source of support. Other than family structure, parents' education also exhibits some influence. Highly educated parents are significantly more likely to adopt institutional childcare when the child reaches the toddler's age.

How Close to the Ideal Childcare? Investigating the Ideal-Actual Mismatch

For all three stages, the percentage of parents preferring parental care is consistently higher than the percentage of parents taking care of the child themselves in reality; the percentage of preferences for kinship care is always much lower than that of the actual arrangements. What these results may reveal is that though family kinship (mostly grandparents) are available in supporting childcare for more than one-third of these young parents, the majority of the parents still regard childcare as their own responsibility and wish to take care of the child by themselves.

Overall, about one-fifth to one-fourth of parents are not able to practice their most preferred arrangement of childcare. The percentage of mismatch for single parents and parents with more education is significantly higher than that for other parents. For example, almost four out of ten single parents struggle to acquire their preferable childcare supports. More than one-fourth of parents with college degree are unable to practice their most preferred childcare arrangements when the child gets older than six months. This mismatch between the ideal and actual childcare arrangements among highly educated parents is probably because their demands for high-quality institutional childcare service are not met.

Childcare Arrangements and Satisfaction to Parent–Child Relationship

Types of childcare arrangements do not affect fathers' satisfaction of parent–child relationship. However, they are significantly related to mothers' satisfaction. Mothers perceive higher quality of parent–child relationship when kinship caregivers or daycare center take on the responsibility of childcare during the day.

There are substantial findings and important implications in this study, but some limitations persist. First, TYP data only sample senior high school students from Taipei city, New Taipei city and Yilan county at the first wave. Some respondents are in attrition in the past waves. Thus, the results cannot be inferred to the whole population in Taiwan. Second, the survey asked the respondents to pick a single answer for the question 'who is the main caregiver?' for each stage. However, it is possible that some parents adopt multiple types of childcare arrangements at the same time. TYP data do not contain information about more complicated patterns of childcare arrangement. Third, it should be cautioned that, compared with the general population in Taiwan, the TYP sample in this analysis tends to be those who get married and bear children earlier than average.[10] Therefore, the childcare pattern shown in this study may be limited to those who marry and have children at a younger age. It is not surprising that young parents rely more on kinship support because the grandparents of the child tend to be younger, too.

The findings of this chapter yield a few implications. First, the case of Taiwan illustrates that the importance of grandparenting in sharing childcare responsibility has been neglected in the familialism-defamiliamlism policy debate. As Sun's (2008) qualitative study has shown, Taiwanese grandparents see childcare assistance as their moral responsibility. The prevalence of grandparenting we observe in this study might be an adjusted form of familialism that reflects cultural preference and cannot be changed in a short time. Family policies do not have to take either stance. While most parents with children under the age of two in Taiwan do not deem outside-of-family childcare arrangement as ideal, grandparenting subsidy and supporting system might be an effective solution in increasing mothers' flexibility of choice and to encourage female labour participation. Family care with state support could be a compromised strategy.

Second, there's still much room to emphasize father's role in sharing childcare responsibility in Taiwanese society. As one may observe from this study, women are still taking the responsibilities of being the main caregiver in families. Although there have been some reforms in childcare policies, young mothers in Taiwan might still experience the burden of the Second Shift, just as what women in previous cohorts experienced. The finding of fathers being more likely to report father as an ideal caretaker than mothers sheds light on how family policies should provide more incentives and construct a social context that encourage male employees to utilize these childcare policies.

Third, government may have to pay more attention on fulfilling the needs of institutional childcare, particularly for toddlers. When their children reach the age of two, parents with college degrees are more likely than parents without college degrees to favour institutional childcare. This preference might explain why the ideal-actual mismatch in childcare arrangement among highly educated parents is the highest among all. Following the trend of educational expansion, the percentage of college-educated population is increasing; thus, we can expect that the demand for institutional childcare may increase as well. In other words, along with the child getting older, traditional kinship-supported childcare arrangement might not meet Taiwanese parents' needs.

Fourth, there are at least two more reasons for the government to put more effort in providing accessible and affordable childcare services. One is that the gap between the ideal and actual arrangement is much larger for single-parent households than other families. This gap, which reflects their need for support, may be due to the absence of resources and assistance from a second parent in the household. The other reason is that mothers with toddlers experience a higher degree of satisfaction of parent–child relationship when someone else is sharing the childcare responsibility during daytime. Either kinship caregiver or institutional services help improving mothers' subjective well-being.

Notes

1   According to statistics that are derived from the Central Intelligence Agency (CIA), Taiwan's the total fertility rate (TFR) in 2022 is 1.08, which is the 227th of 224 regions and countries (Source: https://www.cia.gov/the-world-factbook/field/total-fertility-rate/country-comparison).

2   During the past five decades, Taiwan has experienced drastic industrialization: the percentage of the agricultural population has declined from 55.57 per cent in 1953 to 4.90 per cent in 2017. At the same time, the percentage of the population in service

industries is increased from 27.0 per cent to 59.30 per cent (Source: Yu and Wang (2009) and the below websites: https://agrstat.coa.gov.tw/sdweb/public/book/Book.-aspx and https://www.dgbas.gov.tw/ct.asp?xItem=42616&ctNode=3102). Meanwhile, there is an elevation of women's human capital as well. The labour force participation rate of female increased from 39.13 per cent in 1978 to 50.92 per cent in 2017; the tertiary enrolment rate of female (among those who aged between 18 and 21) also raised from 12.59 per cent to 89.24 per cent in this period (data source: https://english.moe.gov.tw/cp-28-14508-95005-1.html), whereas the labour force participation rate of male is decreased by 10.83 per cent, and the and the tertiary enrolment rate of male is increased by 61.28 per cent (Source: https://english.-moe.gov.tw/cp-28-14508-95005-1.html and https://shorturl.at/gBJ57).

3   Comparing social networks for childcare and elderly care in six East Asian countries, Korea, China, Taiwan, Thailand, Singapore and Japan, Ochiai (2009) concludes that the most prevalent pattern in Asian societies today is the pattern with a large family and relatives sector and a large market sector. There's cross-country variation, though. The relationship of mutual dependence between family and kinships appears to be stronger in China, Taiwan and Singapore than in Thailand and Korea.

4   The other three options are 'parent working and taking care of the child at the same time', 'kinship relative is the main care giver' and 'outside-of-family childcare'.

5   Since not all of the first child has reached the second or third stage, the sample sizes for childcare arrangements in the latter two stages are smaller than 663.

6   The original variable is categorical, and we treated it as a continuous one by taking the midpoint of each category as the value of respondents within the category. For example, the first category is 'less than 10,000', so we coded it as '5,000' for all respondents in that category.

7   The original categories for parent's satisfaction to parent–child relationship is four categories, which is from 'dissatisfied' (1) to 'satisfied' (4). However, there are no parent reporting that they are 'dissatisfied' in parent–child relationship.

8   In 2017, enrolment rates in institutional care services, 0- to 2-year-olds, are 29.6 per cent in Japan and 56.3 per cent in Korea. The rates for 2-to-3-year-olds are 83.0 in Japan and 93.7 in Korea (OECD, 2019).

9   If we look at fathers' and mothers' answer on the ideal arrangement separately, we got an interesting finding (data not shown in the format of table): Compared with the wives in this survey, the husbands came up with a higher percentage of those who think father is the ideal childcare arrangement across all three stages. For example, 3.3 per cent of wives replied that 'father' is her ideal choice of childcare during the day at the child age of 0–6 months; in contrast, 6.6 per cent of husbands chose this option as his ideal. These gender comparisons give us some reflections: Whose ideal portrait of childcare is more traditional? Who is more constrained by existing stereotype? It might be women, not men!

10   The average ages of first marriage of men and women in 2017 are 33.0 and 30.6, respectively (Minister of Interior, 2020). However, in our analysis, the mean age of fathers with new-born babies or toddlers is 32.9 and that of mothers is 31.9.

References

An, M.-Y., & Peng, I. (2016). Diverging paths? A comparative look at childcare policies in Japan, South Korea and Taiwan. *Social Policy and Administration, 50*(5), 540–558.

Chang, Y.-H. (2015). Childcare needs and household composition: Is household extension a way of seeking childcare support? *Chinese Sociological Review, 47*(4), 343–366.

Chang, Y.-H., Yi, C.-C., & Lin, K.-H. (2008). Kin network and its effect on the psychological wellbeing of the youth: The case of Taiwan. *Journal of Comparative Family Studies, 39*, 19–38.

Chen, W.-C. (2016). The role of grandparents in single-parent families in Taiwan. *Marriage & Family Review, 52*, 41–63.

Esping-Andersen, G. (1999). *Social foundations of postindustrial economies.* New York, NY: Oxford University Press.

Jappens, M., & Van Bavel, J. (2012). Regional family norms and childcare by grandparents in Europe. *Demographic Research, 27*, 85–120.

Krapf, S. (2014). Who uses public childcare for 2-year-old children? Coherent family policies and usage patterns in Sweden, Finland and Western Germany. *International Journal of Social Welfare, 23*(1), 25–40.

Leira, A. (2006). Parenthood change and policy reform in Scandinavia, 1970s–2000s. In A. L. Ellingsæter & A. Leira (Eds.), *Politicising parenthood in Scandinavia: Gender relations in welfare states* (pp. 27–52). Bristol: The Policy Press.

Leitner, S. (2003). Varieties of familialism: The caring function of the family in comparative perspective. *European Societies, 5*(4), 353–375.

Leopold, T., & Skopek, J. (2014). Gender and the division of labor in older couples: How European grandparents share market work and childcare. *Social Forces, 93*(1), 63–91.

Lesthaeghe, R. (2010). The unfolding story of the second demographic transition. *Population and Development Review, 36*, 211–251.

Lin, J.-P., & Yi, C.-C. (2019). Dilemmas of an aging society: Family and state responsibilities for intergenerational care in Taiwan. *Journal of Family Issues, 40*(14), 1912–1936.

Lohmann, H., & Zagel, H. (2016). Family policy in comparative perspective: The concepts and measurement of familization and defamilization. *Journal of European Social Policy, 26*(1), 48–65.

Minister of Interior. (2020). *Median and mean of age at first marriage by gender* [data file]. Retrieved from https://www.ris.gov.tw/info-popudata/app/awFastDownload/file/y4s5-00000.xls/y4s5/00000/

Ochiai, E. (2009). Care diamonds and welfare regimes in East and South-East Asian societies: Bridging family and welfare sociology. *International Journal of Japanese Sociology, 18*(1), 60–78.

Organization for Economic Co-operation and Development (OECD). (2019). *OECD family database: Enrolment in childcare and preschool* [data file]. Retrieved from http://www.oecd.org/social/family/database.htm

Ou, T.-T., & Hung, H.-F. (2017). Zuei Lisiang Jhaogu Anpai? Wunhua Jiehshih Guandian [What is the best choic of care model? A cultural perspective]. *Taiwan Shehueifuli Syueh Kan* [*Taiwanese Journal of Social Welfare*], *13*(2), 1–77.

Pelikh, A., & Tyndik, A. (2014). Preschool services for children: Cross-national analysis of factors affecting use. *International Social Work*, *57*(5), 470–485.

Sun, S. H.-L. (2008). Not just a business transaction: The logic and limits of grandparental childcare assistance in Taiwan. *Childhood: A Global Journal of Child Research*, *15*(2), 203–224.

Thomese, F., & Liefbroer, A. C. (2013). Childcare and child births: The role of grandparents in The Netherlands. *Journal of Marriage and Family*, *75*(2), 403–421.

Tsai, P.-Y. (2014). Difficulties in work-family reconciliation in Taiwan, in M. M. Merviö (ed.), *Contemporary social issues in East Asian societies: Examining the spectrum of public and private spheres* (pp. 164–177). Hershey, PA: Information Science Reference.

Verhoef, M., Roeters, A., & der Lippe, T. (2016). Couples' work schedules and child-care use in The Netherlands. *Journal of Child and Family Studies*, *25*(4), 1119–1130.

Wang, S.-Y. (2014). Menlimenwai Shei Jhaogu, Pingjia Puji Lu Tiaotiao? Taiwan Ying'er Jhaogu Jhengtse Jhih Tijhih Neihan Fensi [The analysis of infant care policies and debates in Taiwan]. *Taiwan: A Radical Quarterly in Social Studies*, *96*, 49–93.

Wang, S.-Y. (2016). *105 Niandu Jiangou Tuo Yu Guanli Jhihdu Shihshih Jihua Jhih Chengsiao Pinggu Fang'an Chengguo Baogao [The 2016 report for the evaluation of the establishment of childcare system]*. Social and Family Affairs Administration (SFAA), Minister of Health and Welfare.

Yi, C.-C. (1994). Childcare arrangements of employed mothers in Taiwan. In E. N. L. Chow & C. W. Berheide (Eds.), *Women, the family, and policy: A global perspective* (pp. 235–254). Albany, NY: State University of New York Press.

Yi, C.-C., Pan, E.-L., Chang, Y.-H., & Chan, C.-W. (2006). Grandparents, Adolescents, and parents: Intergenerational relations of Taiwanese youth. *Journal of Family Issues*, *27*(8), 1042–1067.

Yu, T.-S., & Wang, C.-L. (2009). *Taiwanren Kou Biandong Yu Jingji Fajhan [The demographic change and economic development in Taiwan]*. Taipei: Linking Publishing.

Part V

The Longitudinal Effect From Early Adolescence to Young Adulthood

Parent–Child Relationships From Adolescence to Early Adulthood: The Role of Conceptions of Adulthood

Ju-Ping Lin, Chia-Wen Yu and Chiu-Hua Huang

Introduction

The Dependence Tendency of the Younger Generation in East Asia

Since the 1990s, terms such as 'parasite singles', 'the kangaroo generation' and 'NEET' (Not in Employment, Education or Training) have been used by the mass media of Japan, South Korea and China to address the topic of whether young adults of this generation are refusing to grow up. This topic has aroused heated discussion. Japanese scholar Yamada coins the term 'parasite singles' to refer to the many unmarried adults in Japan who continue to live with their parents. These young adults resemble parasites by living off their parents with low incomes (Yamada, 1999). In South Korea, the term 'kangaroo generation' describes the phenomenon of young adults continuing to receive financial support from their parents. From an economic development perspective, Lee (2010) borrowed the term 'satellite generation' (para. 12), arguing that because the South Korean economy has entered a period of slow growth, finding a job has become challenging for young adults entering the labour market; therefore, their dependence on parents has increased.

Taiwan began promoting education reform in the 1990s. Since then, the number of higher education institutions has increased rapidly. In 2015, the enrolment rate of the college-aged population (20 years old) in Taiwan was 73 per cent, which was the highest among 35 member countries of the Organization for Economic Cooperation and Development (OECD). As the younger generation spends more time in school, they postpone employment and financial independence until later in life. Moreover, the average age at first marriage in Taiwan has been continually increasing, reaching 34.7 and 32.1 years for men and women, respectively, in 2019.

The quote 'At thirty, I stood firm (*san shi er li*)' summarizes traditional age norms in Chinese society. Specifically, the Chinese character '立(*li*)' means to stand firm in society and accomplish certain achievements, such as getting married and advancing in a career. The age norms for life events among people transitioning to adulthood have changed gradually. However, the proportion of unmarried adult children living with their parents has increased over the past two decades in Taiwan. Young adult children who have few siblings and resources are likely to develop 'downward-transfer' interactions with their parents, and they mainly acquire financial assistance from their parents. Also, in the last decade, the representation of the 'downward-transfer' type in intergenerational interaction appears to have grown (Lin, 2012). The old saying 'Storing crops for famine time and rearing children for senior days' was established based on the norms of filial piety in the intergenerational relationships in Chinese families: parents receive support from their adult children during old age in exchange for the support they provided their children earlier in life. The inter-generational relationship between young adults and their parents has transformed into adult children depending on their parents, which differs from intergenerational relationships in traditional Chinese families. Merely exploring this phenomenon from the perspective of socio-economic development or attributing it to the younger genera-tion refusing to grow up is incomprehensible.

Transitions to Adulthood in a Changing Society

Life transitions have become an emergent issue in developmental and family studies. More recently, researchers have focused on transitions from late adolescence to early adulthood (Aquilino, 2006; Arnett, 2000a, 2000b). Because of social changes, the characteristics of and keys to 'becoming an adult – ' including marriage, parenthood, fin-ishing education, and finding employment – can occur at any point from a person's late teens through their mid to late 20s (Arnett, 2015). Arnett (2000a, 2004) analyses the development of young American adults aged 18–25 years and proposed the theory of emerging adult-hood. Arnett coins the term 'emerging adulthood' to describe the stage of having left the dependency of childhood and adolescence but not yet having entered full adulthood (2000a, p. 469). He asserts that emerging adulthood, as a distinct period, isolates young adults from social roles and normative expectations and allows them to explore and develop various possibilities.

The life course is a series of socially defined events and different roles that individuals assume over time (Giele and Elder, 1998). 'Social roles' and 'social relations' are core concepts of the life-course perspective. Research has confirmed that younger generations who grow up in different countries or social cultures develop different conceptions of the transition to adulthood (Arnett and Padilla-Walker, 2015; Piumatti et al., 2016; Tagliabue et al., 2016). In addition, families of varying social classes may provide different resources to their children to facilitate their transition to adulthood (Aquilino, 2006). Overall, families play an essential role in young adults' transition to adulthood. This is particularly true for Chinese families because traditional Chinese culture emphasizes interdependence among family members. However, relevant studies have yet to explore the effect of family relations during adolescence on young adults' conceptions of the transition to adulthood as well as whether their conceptions affect their relationship with their middle-aged or older parents.

The Conception of Adulthood and Parent–Child Relationships

Taiwanese society, which is influenced by traditional Confucian culture, values filial piety and has undergone rapid social and economic changes. By focusing on Taiwanese adults in their 30s, this study investigates the following two questions: (1) What do young adults think about the transition to adulthood? (2) What is the role of young adults' conceptions of the transition to adulthood in the development of their parent–child relationships from adolescence to early adulthood?

Most studies claim that parental roles significantly affect child development. In particular, parent–child relationships are closely related to the attitudes and behaviours of adolescents and young adults (Brenning et al., 2015). According to the concept of solidarity, intergenerational relationships between adult children and parents as a multi-dimensional construct with six elements of solidarity:

structural, associational, affectual, consensual, functional and normative (Bengtson and Roberts, 1991). Therefore, clarifying the correlation between parent–child relationships during adolescence and intergenerational relationships during adulthood may be difficult. This study mainly explores the correlation between parent–child relationships during adolescence and young adults' dependence on their parents. Research has shown that parenting style during adolescence affects the interaction between adult children and their parents (Gillespie, 2020) and that parent–child affection is a key to determining whether intergenerational relationships during adulthood are influenced by parent–child relationships during adolescence (Aquilino, 1997; Lavee et al., 2004; Rossi and Rossi, 1990). Therefore, this study defines parent–child relationships during adolescence as (1) perceptions of parenting behaviours during adolescence and (2) parent–child affection during adolescence. By addressing the tendency of young adults to rely on their parents, this study focuses on support in intergenerational relationships. In terms of adult children's support for their parents, which originates from the Chinese cultural expectation of filial piety, this study mainly analyses the financial support provided by adult children for their older parents.

Based on the cultural and social context of Taiwan, the three main themes this study examines are (1) the conception of adulthood of Taiwanese young adults, (2) the influence of parent–child relationships during adolescence (parenting behaviours, parent–child affection) on young adults' conception of adulthood and (3) the association between relationships with parents during adolescence and young adults' provision of financial support to parents, and the mediating role of the conceptions of the transition to adulthood on their associations.

Background in Theory and Research

Parent–Child Relationships From Adolescence to Early Adulthood

Research on parent–child relationships has long been based on two orientations. One is attention – that is, the parent–child relationship during childhood and adolescence as the beginning of the life development process. The other focuses on the intergenerational relationships between adult children and their parents. Hagestad (1987) referred to these research orientations as the alpha–omega tendency in parent–child research. This research trend has contributed to the lack of research on the correlation between children's early interaction with parents and adults' relationships with their middle-aged or older parents.

To elucidate the parent–child relationship during childhood and adulthood, Rossi and Rossi (1990) demonstrated that the intergenerational relationship between adult children and parents is related to parent–child affection and family cohesion during childhood and adolescence. They assert that the characteristics of early parent–child relationships remain in the relationship between adult children and their middle-aged or older parents. They hypothesize that intergenerational relationships reflect a snowball effect. The life-course perspective posits that the life trajectories of parents and children are intertwined and interrelated throughout the course of life (Elder et al., 2003). The basic assumption of life-course developmental psychology is developmental plasticity and the potential for change and adaptation in life (Baltes, 1987). Therefore, the key questions of the snowball effect are as follows: Under what circumstances does the relationship between parents and adolescents endure to adulthood? In what situations do relationship changes occur?

Whitbeck et al. (1991) found that parenting behaviours, such as harsh discipline, parental monitoring and parental rejection, during childhood have a slight effect on the quality of the contemporary adult child–parent relationship. Adults who perceived early parental rejection were less likely to report close relationships with their parents. Aquilino (1997) used longitudinal data from the National Survey of Families and Households to explore continuity and changes in parent–child interactions from childhood to adulthood. Aquilino discovered that when children enter adulthood, prior emotional closeness between children and parents affect intergenerational relationships. Lavee et al. (2004) conducted a study on families living in a kibbutz and demonstrated that the closer the parent–child relationship during childhood, the stronger the intergenerational emotional connection is during adulthood. In addition, children who experience a positive upbringing and develop an intimate parent–child relationship while growing up tend to stay in close proximity to parents and maintain frequent contact with their parents. Overall, research has reported consistently that parent–child affection in adolescence significantly affects intergenerational relationships in adulthood.

By adopting a retrospective research design, researchers have examined the parent–child interactions during an individual's childhood (Lavee et al., 2004; Rossi and Rossi, 1990; Whitbeck et al., 1991). During interviews, the responses of adult children or parents regarding parent–child interaction during adolescence may be affected by the respondents' current intergenerational relationships. In other words, the reconstruction of past family life experiences may reflect a respondent's perception of the present intergenerational relationships. Therefore, the correlation between early parent–child interaction and intergenerational relationships during adulthood may have been overestimated, which limits the generalizability of research results. Using longitudinal data to analyse the correlation between early parent–child relationships and intergenerational relationships during adulthood is a crucial research orientation for overcoming such limitations.

Transition to Adulthood: A Journey Shared by Parents and Children

Ginott (1969) mentions in his book *Between Parent and Teenager* that teenagers complain about their mothers hovering over them like a helicopter. Cline and Fay (1990) developed the term 'helicopter parenting' to describe parents who overprotect their children or interfere with their lives, and this topic has aroused further discussion. Children born in 1981–2000, who grew up during the boom in digital technologies, are referred to as millennials or Generation Y, and the prevalence of mobile communications during their upbringing contributed to helicopter parenting. Scholar Richard Mullendore referred to mobile phones as 'the world's longest umbilical cord' (as cited in Swann, 2014, para. 3). Traditional Chinese families emphasize interdependence among family members. Parental supervision (*guan*), responsibilities and authority in relation to the child are based on the value of filial piety. A study in Taiwan demonstrated that the parental supervision of recent university graduates has two dimensions: demand and support (Wu, 2013). As their children transition into adulthood, middle-aged parents face a role transition that requires them to change from rearing their children to assisting and supporting their children's independence (Neugarten, 1976). Child and parental development are interrelated. According to the life-course perspective, the transition to adulthood could be traced back to the individuals' upbringing and parent–child relationships during adolescence, which extend to intergenerational relationships with their parents during adulthood. Therefore, this journey was shared by parents and children and should be analysed with a more comprehensive measure.

What Does 'Coming of Age' Mean?

Multiple studies have explored the younger generation's thoughts on their transition to adulthood. Nelson and Luster (2015) comprehensively organized relevant research findings and concluded that the younger generation considers accepting responsibility for oneself, making independent decisions and becoming financially independent to be crucial indicators of transitioning into adulthood, whereas marriage and parenthood are considered negligible indicators. Furthermore, previous research indicated that the younger generation's conception of adulthood may differ among different sociocultural contexts (Arnett and Padilla-Walker, 2015; Piumatti et al., 2016; Tagliabue et al., 2016).

The aforementioned studies conducted in the West, mainly in the United States or Europe, reported that young adults' conception of adulthood seems to reflect individualistic values. Yang (2004), a famous psychologist, argues that current Taiwanese society, having undergone social modernization, is a traditional-modern bicultural society comprising both collectivistic cultural elements (of traditional agricultural societies) and individualistic cultural elements. In terms of youth career development, Westerners value individualism and emphasize individuals' control of their environments and the realization of their potential. Beginning with self-exploration, their goal is to attain self-actualization (Huang, 2005). However, in the context of a bicultural society, the self in the Chinese cultural value system is a 'composite self' that combines the independent, contained self of Western cultures and the self-in-relation of traditional Chinese culture (Lu, 2003). Therefore, the self–other relationship is key to youth development (Yang and Lu, 2008), and the most significant self–other relationship is within the family (Hsu, 2002). Family has a large influence on personal career development. Western parents serve as supporters of their children's career development, whereas Chinese parents have more expectations of their children's roles and obligations. Chinese families believe that children are the continuation of the family lineage and that they should therefore glorify the family name and repay the burden borne by their parents (Lu, 2003). Accordingly, young Taiwanese adults living in a bicultural society may have different conceptions of the transition to adulthood compared with young Western adults. Furthermore, upbringing and parent–child relationships in adolescence are critical factors that might influence young adults' conceptions of the transition to adulthood. Although researchers have examined conceptions of adulthood, relevant studies have rarely explored the effect of family experience during adolescence on young adults' conceptions of the transition to adulthood.

Present Study

Taiwanese society, which is influenced by traditional Confucian culture, values filial piety and has undergone rapid social and economic changes. By focusing on Taiwanese adults in their 30s, this study used panel data to examine the conception of adulthood under a life-course perspective by linking the conception with the parent–child relationship before and after becoming adults, age-wise. The overarching goals of the present study are to (1) explore young adults' conceptions of the transition to adulthood, (2) analyse the influence of parenting behaviours and parent–child affection during adolescence on young adults' conceptions of the transition to adulthood and (3) examine the association between relationships with parents during adolescence and young adults' provision of financial support to their parents, and the mediating role of the conceptions of the transition to adulthood on their associations.

Data and Methods

Data and Sample

Data are obtained from the Taiwan Youth Project (TYP), which is a panel study conducted by the Institute of Sociology at Academia Sinica, Taiwan (Survey Research Data Archive, 2020). The research team investigates influential social contexts, including family, school and youth community, to understand the transition from adolescence to young adulthood from a life-course perspective. This study uses a multistage stratified cluster sampling design. The first stratum is 'county and city', and the second stratum divides the first stratum into two or three strata on the basis of urbanization level. Subsequently, 40 schools were selected from three locations: Taipei City, New Taipei City and Yilan County. In each school, two or three classes in seventh grade (J1 cohort who were 13 years of age in 2000) and ninth grade (J3 cohort who were 15 years of age in 2000) were selected, and all students were asked to complete a questionnaire. For the first survey of the J1 and J3 cohorts, 2,696 and 2,890 students, respectively, were sampled from 81 classes in 40 schools. The sample comprises a total of 5,586 students. The first phase of the project consists of nine waves of adolescent surveys conducted from 2000 to 2009. Phase 2 of the wave 1 adult survey began in 2011; participants were no longer separated into cohorts and were interviewed once every three years (in 2011, 2014 and 2017).

Data on 2,550 adults in this study were obtained from the 2017 TYP (phase 2, wave 3). Because this study focuses on intergenerational relationships, only participants with at least one living parent were included. Furthermore, to analyse the adolescent–parent relationship and parenting behaviour among seniors in high school, data in the phase 1, wave 4, J3 cohort (2003) and the wave 6, J1 cohort (2005) were combined. After excluding participants with missing values, the final sample includes 2,076 participants (1,095 male adults, 981 female adults). The average age of the respondents is 31.33 years.

Measurements

Individual characteristics (phase 2, wave 3, 2017, Table 9.1)

Gender is coded as a dummy variable (0 = female; 1 = male). The sample comprises 47.3 per cent female and 52.7 per cent male. The average years of schooling are 15.73 years. A dummy variable is used for marital status, namely unmarried (including widowed, never married or divorced) and married (including first marriage or remarriage). In the sample, 38 per cent of participants are married. For employment status, we also use a dummy variable, namely unemployed and employed (including full time and part time); 91.1 per cent of participants in the sample are employed.

Young Adults' Conceptions of the Transition to Adulthood (Phase 2, Wave 3, 2017)

Regarding young adults' conceptions of the transition to adulthood, Arnett (2001) proposes criteria for adulthood that reflect independence, interdependence, role transitions, norm compliance, family capacities,

Table 9.1 Description of analytic variables (*N* = 2,076)

	Range	Mean	SD	n	%
Individual Characteristics					
Gender					
Male				1,095	52.7
Female				981	47.3
Education level	9–20	15.73	1.935		
High school and below				266	12.8
College				1,380	66.5
Master's degree and above				430	20.7
Marriage status					
Unmarried				1,287	62.0
Married				789	38.0
Employment status					
Unemployed				185	8.9
Employed (Full time, Part time)				1,891	91.1
Adolescent–Parent Relationships					
Parenting Behaviours					
Positive	1–5	3.39	0.917		
Negative	1–5	1.77	0.719		
Adolescent–Parent Affection	-5.19–12.45	0	2.370		
Young Adults' Financial Support for Parents	1–5	2.76	1.470		

and biological and chronological transitions, which are frequently cited. However, subsequent studies demonstrated through reliability analysis claim that the alpha levels of these subscales are low. Moreover, factor analyses have failed to verify whether the items of each dimension align with the original conceptual framework (Badger et al., 2006; Kins and Beyers, 2010; Nelson and Barry, 2005). Specifically, Mayseless and Scharf (2003) and Sirsch et al. (2009), who conducted studies in different countries, discover that because of differences in cultural and social contexts, the direct application of Arnett's criteria for adulthood without modification may be inappropriate.

This study refers to the emerging adulthood theory proposed by Arnett studies (2001, 2003, 2015) and Chinese norms of adulthood to propose criteria for adulthood. Furthermore, we invited researchers with a background in youth development and family research to a symposium, where they confirmed eight criteria for adulthood. Participants were asked to rate each of the following criteria according to whether they must be achieved before a person can be considered an adult: (a) accept responsibility for the consequences of one's actions, (b) become financially independent from parents, (c) become less self-oriented and develop greater consideration for others, (d) identify personal beliefs and values independently of parents or other influences, (e) have at least one child, (f) get married, (g) finish education and (h) care for ageing parents. Items are rated on a 5-point Likert scale ranging from not at all important (=1) to very important (=5). The higher score indicated greater importance.

Intergenerational Relationships: Young Adults' Financial Support for Parents (Phase 2, Wave 3, 2017)

Young adults' financial support for parents is measured using the following question: 'how frequently did you provide financial support to your own parent(s) in the past year?' Responses are rated from not at all (=1) to very frequently (=5). Higher scores indicate higher levels of financial support provided to parents.

Adolescent–Parent Relationships (Phase 1, J3, Wave 4, 2003 and J1, Wave 6, 2005)

This study defines parent–child relationships during adolescence as (1) perceptions of parenting behaviours during adolescence and (2) parent–child affection during adolescence.

Adolescents' perceptions of their parents' behaviours are measured using four items: responsiveness, monitoring, inconsistency and harshness. The respondents rated each item on a 5-point Likert-type scale ranging from never (=1) to always (=5). An exploratory factor analysis using direct oblimin rotation is conducted to verify the domains of parenting behaviours. Two factors have eigenvalues exceeding 1.0 and explained 69.44 per cent of the variance (Kaiser–Meyer–Olkin (KMO) value $= 0.497, p < 0.001$). The first factor, positive parenting behaviours, accounts for 33.58 per cent of the variance (eigenvalue $= 1.343$, Cronbach's $\alpha = 0.548$). This factor consists of two items: 'your parents knew your whereabouts every day (monitoring)' and 'parents shared their opinions when making a decision related to the family (responsiveness)'.

The other factor, negative parenting behaviours, accounts for 35.86 per cent of the variance (eigenvalue = 1.434, Cronbach's α = 0.540). The factor is composed of two items: 'parents arbitrarily blamed you according to their mood when you made the same mistakes (inconsistency)' and 'hit or spanked you as punishment (harshness)'.

Adolescent–parent affection was measured by the question 'How did you get along with your father/mother in the past year?' The scale includes three items: (a) making your father/mother feel warm, (b) imitating your father/mother and (c) sharing your secrets with your father/mother. Respondents in the wave 4, J3 survey (2003) rated the first two items on a 4-point scale ranging from never (=1) to always (=4), and those in the wave 6, J1 survey (2005) rated the items on a 5-point scale ranging from never (=1) to always (=5). All participants rated the third item on a 4-point scale ranging from never (=1) to always (=4). High scores indicated strong affection between adolescents and their parents. These three questions are standardized into Z scores and summed to create an index of adolescent–parent affection, which has adequate internal consistency (Cronbach's α = 0.701).

Results

Young Adults Conceptions of the Transition to Adulthood

Participants were asked to indicate the importance of eight criteria for adulthood on 5-point scales. Higher scores indicated higher importance. Exploratory factor analysis with direct oblimin rotation revealed two factors with eigenvalues exceeding 1.0 and accounted for 64.76 per cent of the total variance (KMO = 0.777, $p = < 0.001$).

Table 9.2 presents the results of the factor analysis. Two factors were identified in the criteria for adulthood. The first factor, Personality Maturity, accounted for 40.09 per cent of the variance (eigenvalue = 3.207) Personality Maturity and consisted of four items (Cronbach's α = 0.812, see Table 9.2 for individual items and factor loadings). The second factor, Social Role Transition (eigenvalue = 1.973), accounted for 24.67 per cent of the variance and consisted of the other four items (Cronbach's α = 0.800, see Table 9.2 for individual items and factor loadings).

Table 9.2 Factor analysis of the importance of criteria for adulthood
($N = 2,076$)

Items	Factor loading		Communality (h2)
	Factor 1 Personality maturity	Factor 2 Social role transition	
(1) Accept responsibility for the consequences of one's actions	**0.837**	0.054	0.706
(2) Become financially independent from parents	**0.788**	0.209	0.664
(3) Become less self-oriented and develop greater consideration for others	**0.782**	0.092	0.620
(4) Identify personal beliefs and values independently of parents or other influences	**0.746**	0.066	0.562
(5) Have at least one child	−0.033	**0.913**	0.835
(6) Get married	−0.031	**0.897**	0.806
(7) Finish education	0.234	**0.658**	0.488
(8) Care of ageing parents	0.292	**0.645**	0.502
Eigenvalues	3.207	1.973	
Variance Explained (%)	40.09	24.67	
KMO		0.777	
Bartlett's test of sphericity		6,559.090***	

Note: ***$p < 0.001$

Young Taiwanese adults identified Personality Maturity to be an essential marker of adulthood (mean = 4.39; Table 9.3). They wholeheartedly agreed that responsibility, economic independence, consideration of others and independent decision-making are criteria for adulthood. They ascribed relatively less importance to Social Role Transition that satisfies social norms for adult roles and responsibilities (mean = 3.27), among which marriage and parenthood were rated the least crucial criteria for adulthood. The analysis results in Table 9.4 indicate that males ascribed higher importance to Social Role Transitions compared with females ($t = 7.570$; $p < 0.001$). Moreover, respondents with less education valued Social Role

Table 9.3 Importance of criteria for adulthood ($N = 2,076$)

Items	Mean (SD)
Personality Maturity	**4.39(0.632)**
(1) Accept responsibility for the consequences of one's actions	4.72(0.689)
(2) Become financially independent from parents	4.35(0.825)
(3) Become less self-oriented and develop greater consideration for others	4.29(0.849)
(4) Identify personal beliefs and values independently of parents or other influences	4.21(0.801)
Social Role Transition	**3.27(0.931)**
(5) Have at least one child	2.92(1.236)
(6) Get married	2.89(1.256)
(7) Finish education	3.55(1.191)
(8) Care of ageing parents	3.71(1.000)

Transitions more than did respondents with more education ($F = 40.985$; $p < 0.001$), and married people attached greater importance to Personality Maturity and Social Role Transition than did unmarried people ($t = 4.131$, $p < 0.001$; $t = 6.688$, $p < 0.001$). Employment status did not affect young adults' conceptions of the transition to adulthood.

Adolescent–Parent Relationships and Young Adults' Conceptions of the Transition to Adulthood

Multiple regression analyses were conducted to examine the association between adolescent–parent relationships and young adults' conceptions of the transition to adulthood. After all individual characteristics were controlled, adolescent–parent relationships were significantly associated with young adults' conceptions of the transition to adulthood (Table 9.5). Model 1–2 in Table 9.5 presents that the more often parents adopted negative parenting behaviours and the greater the parent–child affection during adolescence, the more likely young adults would agree with the importance of Social Role Transition. However, parenting behaviours and parent–child affection during adolescence had no significant predictive power on young adults' perceived importance of Personality Maturity.

Table 9.4 Comparison of perceived importance of criteria for adulthood by gender, education, marriage status and employment status of young adult (N = 2,076)

Criteria for adulthood	Personality maturity	Social role transition
	M/SD	M/SD
Total	4.39/0.632	3.27/0.931
Gender		
Male	4.38/0.647	3.41/0.977
Female	4.41/0.614	3.11/0.851
t	−0.925	7.570***
Education level		
High school and below	4.39/0.619	3.68/0.885
College	4.39/0.654	3.26/0.927
Master's degree (and above)	4.41/0.565	3.03/0.893
F	0.350	40.985***
post hoc test		1>2>3
Marriage status		
Married	4.46/0.624	3.44/1.000
Unmarried	4.35/0.633	3.16/0.872
t	4.131***	6.688***
Employment status		
Employed	4.40/0.630	3.28/0.931
Unemployed	4.32/0.650	3.16/0.930
t	1.556	1.578

Note: ***p < 0.001

Adolescent–Parent Relationships, Young Adults' Conceptions of the Transition to Adulthood and Intergenerational Relationships

Preliminary Analyses

Multiple regression analyses were performed to examine the association among adolescent–parent relationships, conceptions of the transition to adulthood, and young adults' provision of financial support to their parents (Table 9.5). In Table 9.5, Model 2 indicates that when demographic variables were controlled, the more often parents adopted positive parenting behaviours and the greater the parent–child affection during adolescence, the more likely adult children

Table 9.5 Multiple regression analysis predicting young adults' conceptions of the transition to adulthood and intergenerational relationships (N = 2,076)

| | Conceptions of the transition to adulthood | | Intergenerational relationships | | |
| | Personality maturity | Social role transition | Provide financial support to parents | | |
Model (β)	Model 1-1	Model 1-2	Model 2	Model 3	Model 4
Individual Characteristics					
Gender[a]	−0.012	0.153 ***	0.002	−0.007	−0.006
Education	0.020	−0.194 ***	−0.027	−0.003	−0.017
Marriage status[b]	0.093 ***	0.126 ***	−0.085 ***	−0.083 ***	−0.094 ***
Employment status	0.044 *	0.032	0.155 ***	0.152 ***	0.152 ***
Adolescent–Parent Relationships					
Parenting Behaviours					
Positive	0.014	−0.016	0.055 *		0.056 *
Negative	−0.034	0.060 **	0.036		0.034
Affection	0.015	0.136 ***	0.058 *		0.051 *

Table 9.5 Multiple regression analysis predicting young adults' conceptions of the transition to adulthood and intergenerational relationships (N = 2,076) (Continued)

| | Conceptions of the transition to adulthood | | Intergenerational relationships | | |
| | Personality maturity | Social role transition | Provide financial support to parents | | |
Model (β)	Model 1-1	Model 1-2	Model 2	Model 3	Model 4
Conceptions of the Transition to Adulthood					
Personality Maturity				0.023	0.025
Social Role Transition				0.062 **	0.050 *
F	3.891***	34.512***	12.625***	12.746***	10.664***
R^2	0.013	0.105	0.041	0.036	0.045
Adjusted R^2	0.010	0.102	0.038	0.033	0.040
F Change	1.294	14.080***	7.154***	5.114**	5.779***
Df	3	3	3	2	5

Notes: $^*p < 0.05$, $^{**}p < 0.01$, $^{***}p < 0.001$
[a]Ref = female
[b]Ref = Unmarried
[c]Ref = Unemployed

would provide financial support to their parents. In Model 3, the correlation between young adults' conceptions of the transition to adulthood and the provision of financial support to their parents was analysed. Young adults who expressed greater agreement with the importance of Social Role Transition more frequently provided financial support to their parents. Model 4 was used to examine the association of adolescent–parent relationships, conceptions of the transition to adulthood and young adults' provision of financial support to parents after all individual characteristics were controlled. The more positive parenting behaviours parents adopted, parent–child affection during adolescence and aggregability of young adults with the importance of Social Role Transition, the more frequently they provided financial support to their parents.

Mediation Analysis

To examine the mediating effect of young adults' conceptions of the transition to adulthood in the association between adolescent–parent affection and young adults' financial support for their parents, this study follows the steps enumerated by Baron and Kenny (1986). Mediation analysis is performed (see Table 9.5).

Figure 9.1 illustrates the result of the mediation analysis. The total effect of adolescent–parent affection on young adults' financial support for their parents (Fig. 9.1a) is statistically significant ($\beta = 0.058$, $p < 0.05$). As shown in Fig. 9.1b, the effect of adolescent–parent affection on Social Role Transition ($\beta = 0.136$, $p < 0.001$) is statistically significant as well as the effect of Social Role Transition on young adults' financial support for their parents ($\beta = 0.050$, $p < 0.05$). Finally, the magnitude of the direct effect of adolescent–parent affection on young adults' financial support for their parents when controlling for Social Role Transition (Fig. 9.1b) has decreased ($\beta = 0.051$, $p < 0.05$) compared with the total effect of adolescent–parent affection on young adults' financial support for their parents (Fig. 9.1a), suggesting a partial mediation. Bootstrapping analysis indicates that adolescent–parent affection has exerted an indirect effect on young adults' financial support for their parents through Social Role Transition (indirect estimate $= 0.013$, $p < 0.05$; 95% confidence interval [CI] $= 0.0025$ to 0.0254). In other words, the results from the mediating model indicate that strong affection between adolescents and parents is related to young adults' frequent

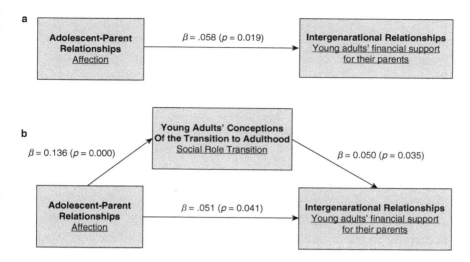

Figure 9.1 Output of mediation analysis.
Note: (a) Illustration of the total effect: Adolescent–parent affection affects young adults' financial support for their parents; **(b)** Illustration of the Mediation Design: Adolescent–parent affection affects young adults' financial support for their parents through Social Role Transition

provision of financial support to their parents through the ascribed importance of Social Role Transition.

Discussion

To address the phenomenon of young East Asian adults' high dependence on their families, this study explores whether the younger generation refuses to grow up based on their conceptions of the transition to adulthood. From a life-course perspective, this study explores the effects of parent–child relationships during adolescence on young adults' conception of the transition to adulthood and the role of such conceptions in the development of parent–child relationships from adolescence to early adulthood. The main findings are as follows.

Young Taiwanese adults aged approximately 30 years believe that the criteria for adulthood can be divided into two dimensions: (1) Personality Maturity, which involves the development of an independent personality, economic independence, self-determination and responsibility for one's behaviour and (2) Social Role Transition, which refers to meeting social expectations and transitioning into adult roles with certain responsibilities (such as completing education, getting married, bearing children and caring ageing parents). Regarding the criteria for adulthood, young adults ascribed more importance to Personality Maturity and less importance to Social Role Transition. Young Taiwanese adults' ratings of criteria for adulthood concur with the conclusion reached by Nelson and Luster (2015) in their comprehensive review of relevant literature. The most crucial criteria were accepting responsibility for oneself, making independent decisions and financial independence. Overall, 30-year-old Taiwanese adults preferred intrinsic, individualistic traits as the criteria for adulthood. They seem to be reluctant to define adulthood according to traditional markers, social culture or life events (such as marriage and parenthood). This finding is consistent with the results of Western research, such as the studies by Arnett (2001) and Arnett and Padilla-Walker (2015).

The results of the present study also accentuate the uniqueness of Chinese society. The quote 'At thirty, I stood firm' reflects traditional age norms for young adults in Chinese society, which include marriage and career development. Regarding the indicators of adulthood, young people in Taiwan ascribed more importance to completing education and becoming financially independent from parents and less importance to getting married and becoming a parent. Compared with women, men placed more emphasis on Social Role Transition and believed that only when a person transitions into adult roles and responsibilities expected by society can the person be considered an adult. This result is attributable to the patrilineal family system in Chinese society, in which men are expected to shoulder the responsibility of family continuity. A relevant study in Taiwan demonstrated that in most three-generation families, older parents live with their sons (Lin, 2012). Compared with women, men tend to attribute the transition to adulthood more to social expectations and family obligations (such as finishing education, getting married, bearing children and caring for ageing parents) in this cultural context.

The results of this study verify that young adults' conceptions of the transition to adulthood are influenced by their parent–child relationships during adolescence. The more frequently negative parenting behaviours were adopted and the stronger parent–child affection was during adolescence, the more importance young adults attached to

Social Role Transition. This result can be explained by the concept of the 'self' in the Chinese cultural value system. Lu (2003) defines the self of Chinese people as the composite self. Parent–child relationships in families are the most crucial self-other relationships and the key to adolescent development. The results regarding the negative parenting behaviours (harshness and inconsistency) perceived by adolescents imply that parent-centred authoritative parenting combined with strong parent–child affection increases children's expectations to fulfil personal role obligations and prompts young adults to identify with markers of adulthood that satisfy society's expectations.

This study confirms the correlation between parent–child relationships and intergenerational relationships during adolescence. The more positive parenting behaviours adopted and parent–child affection shown during a child's adolescence, the more frequently the child provides support to parents during adulthood. The present research results support the hypothesis that intergenerational relationships exhibit a snowball effect (Rossi and Rossi, 1990). Furthermore, through mediation analysis, the results in this study support the mediating effect of young adults' conceptions of the transition to adulthood on the correlation between adolescent–parent relationships and intergenerational relationships during adulthood. Strong parent–child affection during adolescence prompts young adults to recognize Social Role Transition as a significant marker of adulthood and provide financial support for their middle-aged or older parents.

Conclusion

In this study, longitudinal data were used to identify correlations between parent–child relationships in adolescence and adulthood; accordingly, this study explores the transition to adulthood – a journey shared by parents and children. Overall, young adults' conceptions of the transition to adulthood were related to parenting behaviours during their adolescence. As the old saying goes, 'storing crops for famine time and rearing children for senior days', meaning that just as one stores up grain against lean years, parents bring up children for the purpose of being looked after in old age. In this study, the traditional filial obligation in Chinese society was assessed on the basis of the behavioural mechanism of children providing financial support to their parents. According to the responses of 30-year-old adults in Taiwan, in addition to the solid foundation established by early positive parenting behaviours, strong parent–child affection during adolescence is likely to strengthen young adults' identification with social role norms and prompt them to provide intergenerational support. Our findings confirm the importance of cultural norms and suggest that filial obligation recognized by young adults today tends to not only be based on traditional parental authority but also parent–child affection.

This study contributes to a greater understanding of young adults' conceptions of adulthood and provides empirical support for a deeper investigation of how the conception of adulthood mediates the effect of relationship with parents during adolescence on young adults' provision of financial support for parents. According to the concept of solidarity, intergenerational relationships between adult children and parents are multifaceted because parent–child relationships have various aspects (Bengtson and Roberts, 1991). This study mainly focuses on intergenerational support-functional solidarity; future research should elaborate on the other dimensions of intergenerational solidarity (affectual solidarity) to clarify the correlation between parent–child relationships during adolescence and intergenerational relationships during adulthood.

References

Aquilino, W. S. (1997). From adolescent to young adult: A prospective study of parent-child relations during the transition to adulthood. *Journal of Marriage and Family*, *59*(3), 670–686.

Aquilino, W. S. (2006). Family relationships and support systems in emerging adulthood In J. J. Arnett & J. L. Tanner (Eds.), *Emerging adults in America: Coming of age in the 21st century* (pp. 193–217). Washington, DC: American Psychological Association.

Arnett, J. J. (2000a). Emerging adulthood: A theory of development from the late teens through the twenties. *American Psychologist*, *55*(5), 469–480.

Arnett, J. J. (2000b). High hopes in a grim world: Emerging adults' views of their futures and 'Generation X'. *Youth & Society*, *31*(3), 267–286.

Arnett, J. J. (2001). Conceptions of the transition to adulthood: Perspectives from adolescence through midlife. *Journal of Adult Development*, *8*(2), 133–143.

Arnett, J. J. (2003). Conceptions of the transition to adulthood among emerging adults in American ethnic groups. *New Directions for Child and Adolescent Development*, *2003*(100), 63–76.

Arnett, J. J. (2004). *Emerging adulthood: The winding road from the late teens through the twenties*. Oxford: Oxford University Press.

Arnett, J. J. (2015). *Emerging adulthood: The winding road from the late teens through the twenties* (2nd ed.). New York, NY: Oxford University Press.

Arnett, J. J., & Padilla-Walker, L. M. (2015). Brief report: Danish emerging adults' conceptions of adulthood. *Journal of Adolescence, 38*: 39–44.

Badger, S., Nelson, L. J., & Barry, C. M. (2006). Perceptions of the transition to adulthood among Chinese and American emerging adults. *International Journal of Behavioral Development, 30*(1), 84–93.

Baltes, P. B. (1987). Theoretical propositions of life-span developmental psychology: On the dynamics between growth and decline. *Developmental Psychology, 23*(5), 611–626.

Baron, R. M., & Kenny, D. A. (1986). The moderator–mediator variable distinction in social psychological research: Conceptual, strategic, and statistical considerations. *Journal of Personality and Social Psychology, 51*(6), 1173–1182.

Bengtson, V. L., & Roberts, R. E. L. (1991). Intergenerational solidarity in aging families: An example of formal theory construction. *Journal of Marriage and Family, 53*(4), 856–870.

Brenning, K., Soenens, B., Petegem, S. V., & Vansteenkiste, M. (2015). Perceived maternal autonomy support and early adolescent emotion regulation: A longitudinal study. *Social Development, 24*(3), 561–578.

Cline, F., & Fay, J. (1990). *Parenting with love and logic: Teaching children responsibility*. Colorado Springs, CO: Piñon Press.

Elder, G. H. Jr., Johnson, M. K., & Crosnoe, R. (2003). The emergence and development of life course theory. In J. T. Mortimer & M. J. Shanahan (Eds.), *Handbook of the life course* (pp. 3–19). New York, NY: Kluwer Academic/Plenum Publishers.

Giele, J. Z., & Elder, G. H. Jr. (1998). *Methods of life course research: Qualitative and quantitative approaches*. Thousand Oaks, CA: SAGE.

Gillespie, B. J. (2020). Adolescent intergenerational relationship dynamics and leaving and returning to the parental home. *Journal of Marriage and Family, 82*(3), 997–1014.

Ginott, H. G. (1969). *Between parent and teenager*. New York, NY: Scribner.

Hagestad, G. O. (1987). Parent-child relations in later life: Trends and gaps in past research. In J. B. Lancaster, J. Altmann, A. S. Rossi & L. R. Sherrod (Eds.), *Parenting across the life span: Biosocial dimensions* (pp. 405–433). New York, NY: Aldine de Gruyter.

Hsu, L. K. (2002). *Americans and Chinese: Passage to differences* (2nd ed.). Taipei: SMC Publishing Inc.

Huang, K. K. (2005). *Rujia Guansi Jhuyi: Wunhua Fansih Yu Dianfan Chongjian [Confucian relationism: Culture reflections and paradigm reconstruction]*. Taipei: National Taiwan University Press.

Kins, E., & Beyers, W. (2010). Failure to launch, failure to achieve criteria for adulthood?. *Journal of Adolescent Research, 25*(5), 743–777.

Lavee, Y., Katz, R., & Ben-Dror, T. (2004). Parent-child relationships in childhood and adulthood and their effect on marital quality: A comparison of children who remained in close proximity to their parents and those who moved away. *Marriage and Family Review, 36*(3), 95–113.

Lee, Y. M. (19 August 2010). *Nanhan Daishu Zu Jyujyueh Jhangda De Sinshihdai [Kangaroo generation in South Korean: People refuse to grow up]*, Pixnet. Retrieved from https://ymlee.pixnet.net/blog/post/31919829

Lin, J. P. (2012). Taiwan Jiating De Dai Jian Guansi Yu Dai Jian Hudong Leising Jhih Bianchian Chyushih [Intergenerational relations and a typology of inter-generational interaction between adult children and parents: Trends in Taiwanese families]. In C. C. Yi & Y. H. Chang (Eds.), *Social change in Taiwan, 1985–2005: Family and marriage* (pp. 75–124). Taipei: Institute of Sociology, Academia Sinica.

Lu, L. (2003). Defining the self-other relation: The emergence of a composite self. *Indigenous Psychological Research in Chinese Societies, 20*, 139–207.

Mayseless, O., & Scharf, M. (2003). What does it mean to be an adult? The Israeli experience. *New Directions for Child and Adolescent Development, 2003*(100), 5–20.

Nelson, L. J., & Barry, C. M. (2005). Distinguishing features of emerging adulthood: The role of self-classification as an adult. *Journal of Adolescent Research, 20*(2), 242–262.

Nelson, L. J., & Luster, S. (2015). 'Adulthood' by whose definition? The complexity of emerging adults' conceptions of adulthood. In J. J. Arnett (Ed.), *The Oxford handbook of emerging adulthood* (pp. 421–437). New York, NY: Oxford University Press.

Neugarten, B. L. (1976). Adaptation and the life cycle. *The Counseling Psychologist, 6*(1), 16–20.

Piumatti, G., Garro, M., Pipitone, L., Di Vita A. M., & Rabaglietti, E. (2016). North/ South differences among Italian emerging adults regarding criteria deemed important for adulthood and life satisfaction. *Europe's Journal of Psychology, 12*(2), 271–287.

Rossi, A. S., & Rossi, P. H. (1990). *Of human bonding: Parent-child relations across the life course.* New York, NY: Aldine de Gruyter.

Sirsch, U., Dreher, E., Mayr, E., & Willinger, U. (2009). What does it take to be an adult in Austria? Views of adulthood in Austrian adolescents, emerging adults, and adults. *Journal of Adolescent Research, 24*(3), 275–292.

Survey Research Data Archive, SRDA. (2020). *Taiwan youth project* [data file]. Retrieved from https://srda.sinica.edu.tw/browsingbydatatype_result.php? category=surveymethod&type=2&csid=1

Swann, S. (25 June 2014). *Am I a helicopter parent? 5 signs you need to learn to let go a little.* Effingham Herald. Retrieved from https://www.effinghamherald.net/ lifestyle/hot-topics/am-i-a-helicopter-parent-5-signs-you-need-to-learn-to-let-go-a-little/

Tagliabue, S., Crocetti, E., & Lanz, M. (2016). Emerging adulthood features and criteria for adulthood: Variable- and person-centered approaches. *Journal of Youth Studies, 19*(3), 1–15.

Whitbeck, L. B., Simons, R. L., & Conger, R. D. (1991). The effects of early family relationships on contemporary relationships and assistance patterns between adult children and their parents. *Journal of Gerontology, 46*(6), S330–S337.

Wu, M. Y. (2013). The concept of guan in Chinese parent-child relationships. In C. C. Yi (Ed.), *The psychological well-being of East Asian youth: Transition from adolescence to early adulthood.* New York, NY: Springer.

Yamada, M. (1999). *The age of parasite singles.* Tokyo: Chikuma Shinsho Press.

Yang, K. S. (2004). A theoretical and empirical analysis of the Chinese self from the perspective of social and individual orientation. *Indigenous Psychological Research in Chinese Societies, 22*: 11–80.

Yang, K. S., & Lu, L. (2008). *Jhongguoren De Zihwo: Sinlisyueh De Fensi [The Chinese self: Psychological analysis].* Taipei: National Taiwan University Press.

10

Norms and Relations: Developmental Self-Esteem Trajectory and Its Determinants From Adolescence to Adulthood

Yuh-Huey Jou

Introduction

Adolescence and young adulthood are important transitional periods in the process of personal growth. Adolescence connects childhood and adulthood and is a key stage of personality development. Young adults experiment with a variety of new roles about building intimate personal relationships and assuming responsibilities in workplaces. Some studies have argued that self-esteem is a key factor in predicting how youths perform their roles successfully. Self-esteem is the overall affective evaluation and appraisal of one's attitude towards the self, including one's worth, value, competence and importance (Gecas, 1982; Gecas and Schwalbe, 1983; Rosenberg et al., 1995). How it evolves during the early phases of life course is a research issue, and its significance should not be underestimated.

According to life-span theory, the developmental trajectory of self-esteem is likely to be related to changes in resource characteristics, such as increased independence or declined health in late adolescence (Baltes and Eccles, 2005). The gains in available resources in young adulthood may enable individuals to perceive themselves in a more positive way (Heckhausen et al., 1989). Simultaneously, the transition to young adulthood is recognized as a critical time of possessing relative independence for new social roles and self-exploration (Arnett, 2000). Previous studies, however, have used cross-sectional designs, which had some limitations in grasping the individual's growth curves and specifying potential cohort differences, not to mention being easily contaminated by hidden heterogeneity in modelling (Zimmerman et al., 1997).

In this study, I used data from a longitudinal survey conducted by the TYP in Taiwan for 18 years (from 2000 to 2017) to investigate the characteristics of the self-esteem of Taiwanese youth from adolescence to adulthood. The primary purposes of this study are to identify Taiwanese people's different developmental trajectories of self-esteem groups at this stage of transition and to evaluate the influences of cultural, relational and demographic factors operating in the grouping of self-esteem among youths. This study takes a step forward by using panel data alongside a person-centred approach to examine the developmental trajectories of self-esteem among adolescents and young adults.

Developmental Self-Esteem Trajectory From Adolescence to Young Adulthood

In recent years, the availability of longitudinal data sets and the latest methodological advancements have allowed analysis of specific patterns of self-esteem development across the life span (Orth et al., 2012; Trzesniewski et al., 2003a). With regards to the trajectory of self-esteem in the adolescent period, some studies have shown that self-esteem increases over time (Cairns et al., 1990; Pullmann et al., 2009; Robins et al., 2002; Roeser and Eccles, 1998; Twenge and Campbell, 2001), some have shown no change in self-esteem over different stages (Chubb et al., 1997; Young and Mroczek, 2003) and some have even found that self-esteem declines over time (McMullin and Cairney, 2004; Zimmerman et al., 1997). In addition, some academics have reported a curvilinear pattern (Chung et al., 2014; Erol and Orth, 2011; Fan and Yi, 2016; Jou, 2015). A common observation is that during the young adult period, self-esteem is likely to increase (Donnellan et al., 2007; Galambos et al., 2006; Huang, 2010; Orth et al., 2010).

Certain young people look at themselves in such a critical way that their negative perception leads to a decline in self-esteem. Their self-esteem can be challenged by physiological changes, cognitive changes and environmental changes, such as changes in school environments from junior high to high school (Trzesniewski et al., 2003b). With age increasing, the gap between ideal ego and reality ego decreases, which might impact how youths see themselves more unfavourably than favourably.

It is worth noting that the development of self-esteem among young Taiwanese has a close correspondence with their educational stages.

From the first to the third year of junior high school, self-esteem shows a downward trend. After reaching the lowest point in the last year of junior high school (the ninth grade), self-esteem tends to build up when entering high school before it declines again in senior year (Huang, 2002). Self-esteem would gradually improve over the years in college (Hsiao and Su, 2014) but slightly decline after graduation (Jou, 2015). In addition, studies also pointed out that the decline in girls' self-esteem is more observable than that of boys (Fan and Yi, 2016). Maternal support has a considerable influence on early puberty, while paternal support generates substantial effect during the middle and late puberty (Fan and Yi, 2016).

Essentially, self-esteem's development trajectory during adolescence is prone to display an upward trend, despite a few reports about an inverted U-shaped curve or no significant change. These inconsistencies may be due to the use of a single growth trajectory for a collectivity and ignorance of individuals' different trends in development. In short, the pathways of individuals' self-esteem are often not homogeneous. For many youth, self-esteem may show a gradual upward trend, but for some others, it may decline as they grow. Furthermore, it can also be an up-and-down phenomenon. Larger data sets are more helpful with capturing the heterogeneous growth trajectories among youths. To more effectively observe this heterogeneity, a person-centred approach is utilized to analyse the growth trajectories at within-individual and between-individual levels (Wang, 2013).

It is necessary to explore whether the developmental trajectory of self-esteem is homogeneous in the overall sample or is heterogeneous across different groups. To achieve this goal, this study's first steps are to examine the self-esteem characteristics of Taiwanese youth from adolescence to adulthood and to distinguish the developmental trajectories of self-esteem groups at this stage from the person-centred perspective.

Cultural, Relational and Personal Factors of
Self-Esteem Development

Previous research emphasizes that the development of self-esteem varies in association with a number of major factors: cultural norms (filial piety, fraternal respect, being conscientious in deeds and faithful in words and so on), interpersonal relationships (such as parental and peer relationships), personal characteristics (such as gender, physical health, academic achievement and delinquency) and family contexts (such as family socioeconomic status) (Chung et al., 2014; Conger and Donnellan, 2007; Erol and Orth, 2011; Fan and Yi, 2016; Gebauer et al., 2015; Jou, 2015; Orth, 2018). The second goal of this study, thus, is to examine these factors simultaneously with regards to their influences on the trajectory of self-esteem over time.

Cultural Norms

Cultural norms are the shared expectations and rules that guide the behaviours of people within a group or population. These expectations and rules are learned from and reinforced by parents, friends, teachers and others growing up. Confucianism has stressed a set of norms for young people to follow closely. The Analects requires that:

> A student should be filial at home and practice fraternal respect outside. He should be conscientious in deeds and faithful in words. Universally cherishing all of humanity, he should draw close to those who are benevolent. When he has efforts to spare, then he should study the literature.

As of today, these norms still constitute important codes of conduct that is expected of young people. The norm of being conscientious in deeds and faithful in words is similar to the concept of Conscientiousness in the Big Five traits, which refers to how people control, regulate and direct their impulses, and show their sense of responsibility and reliability (Roberts et al., 2009).

Gebauer et al. (2015) have used meta-analysis to explore the relationship between each of the Big Five personality traits (Extraversion, Agreeableness, Neuroticism, Conscientiousness and Openness) and self-esteem both at the individual and the national levels. They found that Extraversion emerged as the strongest predictor of self-esteem at the individual level, followed by Conscientiousness and then Openness. Interestingly, at the national level, the relation between Conscientiousness and self-esteem was the strongest. Taiwan's data in Gebauer et al.'s (2015) study also show that Conscientiousness had the strongest correlation with self-esteem ($r = 0.21$), followed by Extraversion ($r = 0.18$), then Openness ($r = 0.13$), while Neuroticism and Agreeableness were negatively correlated to self-esteem ($r_s = -0.12$, -0.09). This result suggests that for Taiwanese, Conscientiousness as a cultural norm plays a significant role in self-esteem. The present study further explores the influence of conscientious belief on the development trajectory of self-esteem.

Interpersonal Relationships

Social relations are indispensable for the development of children and adolescents (Jou, 2015), and family and peer relationships are particularly critical. Young peoples are most likely to seek support for problem resolutions from their family and friends (Finan et al., 2018). Warm relationships are associated with healthier personalities, including positive self-esteem and emotional stability (Khaleque, 2013; Khaleque and Ali, 2017; Laible and Carlo, 2004). Conversely, social rejection or conflict is linked to anxiety and insecurity, resulting in low self-esteem and poor adjustment (Bagwell et al., 1998; Leary, 2015). This study mainly examines the function of parental and peer relationships on self-esteem trajectories from adolescence into emerging adulthood.

Personal Characteristics and Family Context

Numerous studies of gender differences in self-esteem have shown that male adolescents or young adults have higher self-esteem than females do (Bleidorn et al., 2016; McMullin and Cairney, 2004; Twenge and Campbell, 2001). However, some studies contended that gender differences were small (Orth et al., 2010; Quatman et al., 2001) or even insignificant (Donnellan et al., 2007). Kling et al. (1999) have identified gender role, socialization and cultural emphasis to be accountable for men's higher self-esteem than women's. Boys are expected to develop self-confidence and are more likely to influence others through direct demands, whereas displaying self-confidence or direct expression has traditionally been discouraged for girls. Women and girls consistently report greater dissatisfaction with their appearance and bodies than boys and men do, and negative evaluation of one's attractiveness is tied to lower self-esteem.

Some research suggests that higher self-esteem is associated with better physical health, better academic achievement and less delinquency (Erol and Orth, 2011; Warren et al., 2016; Yang et al., 2019). Those who are healthy tend to have good academic performances; those who exercise high self-control have more confidence in their lives and are more successful in education, work and relationships, which, in turn, accelerates their self-esteem. For instance, Chung et al. (2014)

found that individuals who received better grades showed a greater increase in self-esteem over four years in college. Warren et al. (2016) found that the trajectories of adaptive functioning (including self-esteem, life satisfaction, connections with others and self-reported health) were correlated with adolescent delinquency – adolescents who showed stable adaptive functioning adolescents reported less delinquency.

Socio-economic status (SES) is regarded as an indicator of status within social groups. Elevated self-esteem can originate from a higher SES (Rosenberg and Pearlin, 1978). Recent research also suggests that children from families with higher SES are more likely to have higher self-esteem (Jou, 2015; Orth, 2018) because their parents can provide a better home environment. However, Twenge and Campbell (2002) found that SES has a small but significant relationship with self-esteem in a meta-analysis of 446 samples.

It is worth noting that many studies on the relationship between cultural norms, interpersonal relationships, personal characteristics, and family environment and self-esteem are cross-sectional, which greatly limits the conclusions that can be drawn. Only a few studies have explored the long-term effects of these factors on the development of self-esteem. The research design of this study can provide evidence for these predictors from a longitudinal, trajectory approach.

The Present Study

Using the 2000–2017 TYP longitudinal data, this study explores the developmental curve of the self-esteem of Taiwanese youth from adolescence to adulthood, distinguishes the latent trajectory patterns of their self-esteem development and assesses the influence of a number of important cultural, relational and personal factors on the developmental trajectories of self-esteem patterns. The overall analytical model is shown in Figure 10.1.

Figure 10.1 contains a combination of a continuous latent growth variable for self-esteem at the upper side, η_j (j = intercept (I), linear slope (S) and quadratic slope (Q)) and a latent trajectory categorical variable (C), with K classes, $C_i = (c_1, c_2, \ldots c_K)'$, where $c_i = 1$ if individual i belongs to class k and zero otherwise. Multiple indicators of self-esteem (Y-15, Y-18,... Y-32) were measured during six time stages. On the left side of Figure 10.1, various predictors (cultural

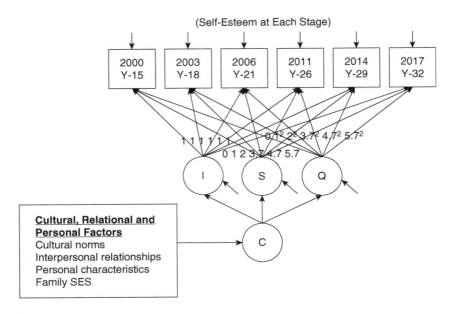

Figure 10.1   Analytical model

norms, interpersonal relationships, personal characteristics and family backgrounds) are set to predict the categorical latent trajectories (*C*), since the model allows the mixing proportions to depend on prior information and/or subject-specific variables.

Since self-esteem were measured at 15, 18, 21, 26, 29 and 32 years old, the linear slope factor loadings of self-esteem at each stage were subtracted by 15 and divided by 3. The factor loadings of the latent growth variable were marked as 1, 1, 1, 1 and 1 for intercept; 0, 1, 2, 3.7, 4.7 and 5.7 for linear slope; 0^2, 1^2, 2^2, 3.7^2, 4.7^2 and 5.7^2 for quadratic slope, respectively.

Data and Method

Data and Sample

The data were derived from a panel study conducted for the Taiwan Youth Project (TYP) by the Institute of Sociology, Academia Sinica, Taiwan. This project completed 12 waves of surveys from 2000 to 2017. A random sample of 2,696 seventh-grade students (first year of junior high school) and 2,890 ninth-grade students (third year of junior high school) as well as one parent per each student and their home class teachers (between 2000 and 2002) were interviewed at the beginning of 2000. Phase I followed them from 2000 to 2009; Phase II continued in 2011, 2014 and 2017 with spouse surveys (see detailed description of this programme at http://www.typ.sinica.edu.tw/).

The sample used for this chapter was based on a survey of ninth-grade students from junior high schools located in three regions of northern Taiwan (Taipei City, Taipei County and Yi-Lan County). The TYP contacted participants in 6 waves from 2000 (n = 2,851; ninth-grade students, approximately 15 years old, Y-15), 2003 (n = 2,072, 18-year-old teenagers, Y-18), 2006 (n = 1,805, 21-year-old adults, Y-21), 2011 (n = 1,536, 26-year-old adults, Y-26), 2014 (n = 1,369, 29-year-old adults, Y-29) and 2017 (n = 1,263, 32-year-old adults, Y-32). Participants who answered in the first wave and the final wave and at least five times in the six-wave questionnaires were selected. The final sample was 1,181 (984 answered all 6 waves) males (53.2 per cent) and females (46.8 per cent) respondents.

Measurement

Self-Esteem

Participants' evaluation of self on the Rosenberg Self-Esteem Scale (Rosenberg, 1965, 1986) was conducted during six waves in 2000, 2003, 2006, 2011, 2014 and 2017. The nine items listed at the end of this section were rated on a 4-point scale: strongly disagree (=1), disagree (=2), agree (=3) and strongly agree (=4). Cronbach's alphas for each wave ranged from 0.77 to 0.86. The degrees of agreement may not be equivalent, so the dichotomized scores were adopted (Chang, 2006). The 'strongly disagree' and 'disagree' were recoded into 0, and the 'strongly agree' and 'agree' 1. The binary scores were summed; the higher scores indicated a higher degree of self-esteem.

1. I have no way to solve some of my own problems. (Reverse scoring)
2. I cannot control what happened to me. (Reverse scoring)
3. I feel powerless when dealing with various problems in my life. (Reverse scoring)
4. I have a positive attitude towards myself.
5. I feel that I'm a person of worth.
6. I am satisfied with myself.
7. I feel I do not have much to be proud of. (Reverse scoring)

8. I certainly feel useless at times. (Reverse scoring)
9. At times, I think I am no good at all. (Reverse scoring)

Cultural Norms: Conscientious Belief
Conscientiousness reflects the disposition to be responsible, organized, hard-working, goal-directed and adhering to norms and rules; it comprises multiple facets, including industriousness, self-control, responsibility, reliability and so on (Roberts et al., 2014). Three items ('responsible for one's own work', 'being able to take care of oneself' and 'becoming a trustworthy person') were measured in 2000 and rated on a 4-point scale, ranging from strongly unimportant ($=1$) to strongly important ($=4$) (Cronbach's alpha = 0.67). A higher score indicates a stronger conscientious belief.

Interpersonal Relationships
Interpersonal relationships were measured in 2000, including parental warmth, parental conflict and class atmosphere. Items of parental warmth and conflictual interactions with father and mother were measured separately.

Three items of warmth ('accepts and cares me', 'asks my opinion on important things' and 'listens to me carefully') and three items of conflict ('loses his/her temper', 'gets angry at me' and 'argues with me because I don't agree with him/her') were rated on a seven-point scale, ranging from never ($=1$) to always ($=7$) (Cronbach's alpha = 0.81–0.86). Maternal and paternal warmth were highly correlated ($r = 0.66$, $p < 0.001$), and so were maternal and paternal conflict ($r = 0.51$, $p < 0.001$). Therefore, I added up the paternal and maternal scores into a new indicator. The same procedure was applied to parental warmth and parental conflict.

Class atmosphere includes the classroom environment, the social climate and the emotional and the physical aspects of the classroom. Five items were measured, such as 'Our classmates are close to each other, just like a family', 'When I need them, my classmates will always help me in time', and 'I don't like to interact with my classmates (reverse)' and so on. Each item was rated on four-point scale (ranging from 1 = strongly disagree to 4 = strongly agree) (Cronbach's alpha = 0.74). A higher score indicated a better class atmosphere.

Personal Characteristics and Family Context
Personal characteristics and family contexts were also measured during the first wave of the survey, including gender, academic performance,

deviant behaviour, health and family SES (parental education and family income). Gender of the adolescent was coded as 1 for female and 0 for male. Participants' academic performances were measured by one item, 'What was your average grade for the last semester?', ranging from very poor (=1) to very good (=5). Delinquency was measured with ten items that asked respondents to indicate whether they did any of the following behaviours in the past 12 months: running away from home, absenteeism, deliberately destroying others' belongings, acting out sexual behaviours, injuring others, blackmailing others, smoking, drinking or chewing betel nuts. Following measurement methods used in other studies (Amato et al., 2016), the ten items listed above were summed and dichotomized (0 = never, 1 = at least once).

Physical health was a self-reported measure, which was rated on a 5-point scale (1 = very poor to 5 = very good), with a higher score indicating better physical health.

There were eight categories of parental education ranging from never being formally educated to having a degree from graduate school. These eight categories were converted into years of education. Because there was high correlation between father's and mother's years of education ($r = 0.65$), I decided to calculate an average of the education years of fathers and mothers for use in models to avoid multiple collinearity.

Monthly family income was measured in 1,000 Taiwanese dollars, the logarithm of which was taken to avoid skewness (the original distribution was 0–800,000).

The summary statistics of participants' gender and family SES variables are presented in Table 10.1, and the means of other major variables are shown in Table 10.2.

Analytic Strategy

Data were analysed using the manual three-step approach of latent trajectory Gaussian mixture model (LT-GMM) with a robust maximum likelihood estimator (Asparouhov and Muthén, 2014; Nylund-Gibson et al., 2014) supported by Mplus 8.0 (Muthén and Muthén, 1998–2017).

In the first step, a latent growth model (LGM) was used to explore participants' overall developmental trajectory under the assumption that the overall sample is homogeneous. The linear

Table 10.1 Gender and family characteristics

	N	**%**	**Missing**
Gender			
Girls	553	46.8	
Boys	628	53.2	
Family income in 2000			
Less than NT30,000	114	12.3	257
NT30,000 – less than 60,000	377	40.8	
NT60,000 – less than 90,000	240	26.0	
NT90,000 – less than 120,000	127	13.8	
More than 120,000	66	7.1	
Father's education			
Less than primary school	5	0.4	48
Primary school	190	16.8	
Junior high school	311	27.5	
Senior or vocational high school	332	29.3	
Junior college	152	13.4	
University	115	10.2	
Graduate school	28	2.5	
Mother's education			
Less than primary school	11	1.0	26
Primary school	281	24.3	
Junior high school	294	25.5	
Senior or vocational high school	383	33.2	
Junior college	110	9.5	
University	68	5.9	
Graduate school	8	0.7	

LGM (0, 1, 2, 3.7, 4.7, 5.7), curve LGM (0^2, 1^2, 2^2, 3.7^2, 4.7^2, 5.7^2), and freely estimated LGM (0, 1, *, *, *, *) were compared. The following criteria were used for evaluating acceptable model fit: comparative fit index (CFI) value greater than or equal to 0.95, root-mean-square error of approximation (RMSEA) (zero indicating perfect fit), and standardized root mean square residual (SRMR) (values less than or equal to 0.06) (West et al., 2012).

Table 10.2 Mean and standard deviation of major variables

	Range	*M*	SD
Conscientious belief at 2000 (Y-15)	1–4	3.5	0.5
Parental warmth at 2000 (Y-15)	1–7	3.8	1.4
Parental conflict at 2000 (Y-15)	1–7	2.6	1.1
Class atmosphere at 2000 (Y-15)	5–20	14.7	2.6
Academic achievement at 2000 (Y-15)	0–5	2.9	1.2
Deviance behaviour at 2000 (Y-15)	0–1	0.4	0.5
Physical health at 2000 (Y-15)	0–5	3.5	1.0
Self-esteem at 2000 (Y-15)	0–9	4.9	2.3
Self-esteem at 2003 (Y-18)	0–9	6.0	2.2
Self-esteem at 2007 (Y-21)	0–9	5.6	2.4
Self-esteem at 2011 (Y-26)	0–9	6.2	2.3
Self-esteem at 2014 (Y-29)	0–9	6.8	2.2
Self-esteem at 2017 (Y-32)	0–9	6.8	2.3

In the second step, a latent class growth analysis (LCGA) was utilized to examine the initial (intercept) and slope mean level of self-esteem in the study sample, with an aim to evaluate whether there was evidence for unobserved heterogeneity in self-esteem change over time. Wickrama et al. (2016) indicate that the lack of significant mean growth and the presence of significant variance in the initial mean level and the slope might be indicative of heterogeneity in growth.

In the third step, self-esteem trajectories were modelled using growth mixture modelling (GMM) following procedures and guidelines set forth by Wickrama et al. (2016). The fits of two to five trajectories of self-esteem were estimated. To determine the optimal number of growth trajectories, both conceptual and statistical considerations were applied. Class size and multiple model fit indices that assessed the solutions' accuracy parsimony (i.e. BIC, ABIC) and reliability (Nylund et al., 2007) were also considered.

Finally, after determining the class number of growth trajectories, the impacts of cultural and contextual factors on self-esteem growth trajectories were examined (Asparouhov and Muthén, 2014). Using the auxiliary option, the optimal number of growth trajectories and the measurement error are fixed and prespecified to the values computed in the second step.

To address the issue of missing data, an expectation-maximization (EM) algorithm was used. This technique is based on an expectation step and a maximization step that are repeated several times until maximum likelihood estimates are obtained (Tzou and Chiang, 2012).

Results

The Developmental Curve of Self-Esteem

The overall developmental trajectory of self-esteem from adolescence to adulthood was investigated on three different models. The results of model fit (Table 10.3) show that the BIC and ABIC of the linear LGM were the highest, and the BIC and adjusted-BIC of the freely estimated LGM were the lowest, indicating that the growth trajectory of youths' self-esteem from the middle school, high school, university to young adult stages had changed unequally. The loadings of the freely estimated LGM are 0, 1, 0.82, 1.55, 2.09 and 2.12; the intercept of self-esteem is 4.93, and its linear growth rate (slope) is 0.89, indicating that self-esteem increases as young people entering adulthood. In addition, there is a significant variance in the initial and slope (2.13 and 0.44, respectively, both $p < 0.001$) of self-esteem, suggesting unobserved heterogeneity exists in the growth of self-esteem over time.

Developmental Trajectory Classes of Self-Esteem

LCGA was used to identify the heterogeneous subgroups of the freely estimated LGM. LCGAs fix within-class variances for growth

Table 10.3 Fit statistics for latent growth modelling (LGM)

Statistic	Number of parameters	BIC	Adj-BIC	CFI	RMSEA	SRMR
Linear growth	11	30,186.654	30,151.714	0.887	0.106	0.084
Curve growth	15	30,191.119	30,143.473	0.897	0.116	0.085
Freely estimated growth	15	30,111.888	30,064.243	0.940	0.089	0.068

parameters at zero, precluding any covariance among the growth parameters; as per Figure 10.1, parameters were all fixed at zero. This particular practice also assumes that all members of particular classes follow the same latent trajectory. The values for the BIC and adj-BIC did not seem to provide a clear conclusion for either the three or four class models. However, an alternative fit index, the Lo–Mendell–Rubin Likelihood Ratio Test (LMR–LRT), showed that the three-class solution ($p = 0.0000$) fit better than the four-class solution ($p = 0.1182$) in the upper part of Table 10.4. Thus, on the basis of on the LMR–LRT, the three-class model is preferred for LCGA.

To determine the optimal number of growth trajectories, GMMs with variance and covariance equality constraints across latent classes were used, in which variance estimates and covariance estimates for within-class growth parameters, and covariance paths among all latent factors were freely estimated but constrained to be equal across

Table 10.4 Fit statistics for latent class growth analysis (LCGA) and growth mixture modelling (GMM)

Statistic	Number of parameters	BIC	Adj-BIC	Entropy	LMR-LRT
LCGA-F2	15	30,247.558	30,199.912	0.860	0.0000
LCGA-F3	18	29,951.120	29,893.946	0.786	0.0000
LCGA-F4	21	29,911.260	29,844.557	0.690	0.1182
LCGA-F5	24	29,870.335	29,794.102	0.704	0.0531
GMM-F2	18	29,905.308	29,848.134	0.841	0.0000
GMM-F3	21	29,851.990	29,785.286	0.788	0.0234
GMM-F4	24	29,838.011	29,761.779	0.794	0.0455
GMM-F5	27	29,856.904	29,771.142	0.754	0.9475

Note: *LCGA*, latent class growth analysis; *GMM*, growth mixture modelling; *F*, freely estimated growth model; *Number*, the number of latent classes.

classes. The model fit (BIC, adj-BIC and entropy) of GMM was better than LCGA. A minimum value for the BIC and adj-BIC was not reached through the five-class model. The LMR–LRT found that the four-class solution ($p = 0.0455$) fit better than the five-class solution ($p = 0.9475$) in the lower part of Table 10.4. Based on the LMR–LRT, the four-class model was chosen for GMM.

The estimated average of the GMM unconditional model is shown in Figure 10.2. The first class is named 'curved and getting better' (comprising 29.5 per cent). Young adults in this group reported the second highest score of self-esteem initially and a gradual rise after entering adulthood. The second class is comprised of participants whose self-esteem showed the highest start that kept increasing, and is labelled 'high and rising' (53.4 per cent). Young adults in the third class reported lower initial scores of self-esteem and maintained lower scores; this class is called 'keeping low and flat' (12.0 per cent). Young adults belonging to the fourth class reported the lowest score of

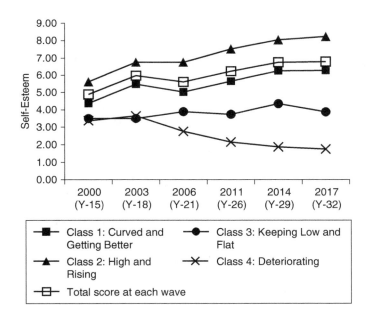

Figure 10.2   Four-class solution of freely estimated GMM.
Note: Class 1: Curved and Getting Better (29.49%),
Class 2: High and Rising (53.39%),
Class 3: Keeping Low and Flat (12.03%),
Class 4: Deteriorating (5.01%)

self-esteem at the outset and grew worse. This class is labelled 'deteriorating' (5.0 per cent).

From the results, it can be found that more than 80 per cent of participants' self-esteem increases over time, while nearly 20 per cent of participants' self-esteem is in decline during their transition to adulthood.

The Effects of Cultural, Relational and Personal Factors

While accounting for classification error, the effects of cultural and contextual factors were evaluated in a multinomial logistic regression displayed in Table 10.5. The results indicate that conscientious belief

Table 10.5 Results of the three-step multivariate multinomial regression for self-esteem growth trajectories

	Curved and getting better [a]		Keeping low and flat		Deteriorating	
	b	s.e.	b	s.e.	b	s.e.
Intercept	−1.14	1.86	1.90	1.27	1.26	0.95
Cultural Norms						
Conscientious belief	0.44	0.37	−0.48*	0.24	−0.40*	0.20
Interpersonal Relationships						
Parental warmth	0.08	0.17	−0.14	0.11	0.04	0.07
Parental conflict	0.35*	0.17	0.12	0.13	0.30***	0.08
Class atmosphere	−0.22***	0.06	0.03	0.05	−0.04	0.04
Personal Characteristics						
Gender (male = 1)	−0.31	0.39	−0.60*	0.27	−0.59**	0.20
Academic achievement	−0.06	0.13	−0.36**	0.11	−0.06	0.08
Delinquency (1 = at least once)	−0.24	0.39	0.53*	0.26	0.28	0.20
Physical health	−0.38*	0.15	−0.40**	0.12	−0.06	0.10
Family SES						
Parents' education	0.08	0.07	0.06	0.04	0.00	0.03
Family income	−0.01	0.09	−0.03	0.07	−0.03	0.05

[a]Ref. = High and Rising.
***$p < 0.001$, **$p < 0.01$, *$p < 0.05$

decreases the likelihood of being in the 'keeping low and flat' and 'deteriorating' groups (-0.48, -0.40, $p_s < 0.05$) when the 'high and rising' group was used as reference group. Those who belonged to 'curved and getting better' or 'keeping low and flat' reported a significantly higher level of parental conflict (0.35, 0.30, $p_s < 0.05$). Those who reported an unpleasant class atmosphere have a higher odd to be placed in the 'curved and getting better' group (-0.22, $p < 0.001$).

There was a lower proportion of males observed in the 'keeping low and flat' and 'deteriorating' groups (-0.60, -0.59, $p_s < 0.05$). The 'keeping low and flat' group reported lower academic performance and more delinquencies when compared to the 'high and rising' group (-0.36, 0.53, $p_s < 0.05$). The 'keeping low and flat' and 'deteriorating' groups appeared to have poorer physical health (-0.38, -0.40, $p_s < 0.05$). However, parental warmth and family SES (parental education and household income) did not carry significant effects.

Discussion and Conclusion

This study endeavours to identify the patterns of developmental self-esteem trajectories and examines the cultural, relational and personal factors affecting the self-esteem trajectories from adolescence to young adulthood. Through an analysis of longitudinal panel data in Taiwan, four patterns of developmental self-esteem trajectory are identified, and the impacts of predictors were recognized.

Compared with linear or curvilinear changes, it is empirically more suitable to describe the developmental self-esteem trajectory via the freely estimated LGM. The growth rate is nonlinear but generally increases during adolescence. Previous studies using long-term data or meta-analyses showed that the developmental self-esteem trajectory has increased from adolescence to adulthood (Galambos et al., 2006; Steiger et al., 2014; von Soest et al., 2016; Wagner et al., 2013). Robins and Trzesniewski (2005) further proposed that in this phase of entering adulthood, the gap between the ideal self and the actual self becomes narrowed, the positive and negative characteristics are integrated, and self-control increases. Thus, the overall sense of self-evaluation and self-worth is enhanced. The results of this study are similar to these studies.

It is worth noting that the developmental self-esteem trajectory of young people in Taiwan is heterogeneous, despite most of them showing progressively higher self-evaluation over time. The results of the GMM show that their trajectory of self-esteem can be clearly divided into four patterns, namely 'curved and getting better', 'high and rising', 'keeping low and flat' and 'deteriorating'. For more than 80 per cent of young people, self-esteem was high during adolescence and increased when they entered adulthood (the proportions of groups 'curved and getting better' and 'high and rising' were 82.9 per cent). On the other hand, less than 20 per cent of them showed low self-esteem during adolescence and a continuous decline when entering adulthood ('keeping low and flat' and 'deteriorating'). Most young people's self-esteem improves as they enter adulthood, while a few people with poor self-evaluation are detected as well. It is crucial to pay attention to the unfavourable experiences and impacts of this smaller subpopulation.

The upward or downward developmental trajectory of self-esteem is accounted for by cultural norms, relationships and personal characteristics. In particular, the influence of conscientious belief on developmental self-esteem trajectory is quite substantial. Those with higher conscientious beliefs not only possess a higher self-esteem during adolescence, they also have experienced an upward trend in later stages. In contrast, those with weaker conscientious beliefs have a lower self-esteem early on, which remains low or declines when entering early adulthood. In sum, the conscientious belief plays a vital role during adolescence and young adulthood. These results echo traditional Confucian norms, which are still important to contemporary Taiwanese young people (Kitayama et al., 2009). Future research on the developmental self-esteem should consider other cultural norms, such as filial piety and fraternal respect, to gain a deeper understanding of the unique meaning and scope of influence of particular cultural norms in a society.

Social relation is another important determinant. Intimacy and connections with parents and class peers appear to enhance personal self-affirmation. On the contrary, if people are alienated from or have conflictual relationships with parents or school peers, they are likely to feel a lack of mutual support and assistance, making them deny others and perceive themselves negatively. These effects not only are prominent among adolescents but also observable on young adults. Their far-reaching impact cannot be ignored.

Consistent with past studies, personal characteristics such as gender, academic performance, delinquency and physical health also have significant influences on the developmental trajectories of self-esteem (Chung et al., 2014; Hsiao and Su, 2014; Jou, 2015; Kling et al., 1999). Participants in the 'keeping low and flat' or 'deteriorating' groups were mostly female. Furthermore, participants in the 'keeping low and flat' group reported lower academic performance, higher rate of delinquency and poor health. In contrast, males are more likely to be in the 'high and rising' group, so do those who have higher academic performance, lower rate of delinquency and better health. Personal characteristics in early adolescence have a profound effect on the development of self-esteem. The results of this study provide supportive evidence for this hypothesis.

Several possible directions for future research are proposed. First, the self-esteem measured in this study is a global self-esteem. Considering the characteristics of Chinese concepts, future research can explore the additional developmental trajectory patterns of specific self-esteems including individual-oriented, relationship-oriented, familistic (group)-oriented and other-oriented self, as was suggested by Yang (2004) for a Chinese cultural context. Second, numerous studies have shown that there is a strong correlation between low self-esteem and depression (Butler et al., 1994; Shahar and Davidson, 2003). The relationship between self-esteem and depression deserves research attention in future studies. Lastly, as individuals grow up, they tend to face more problems related to work, marriage and parenting. How self-esteem evolves and exerts influence on these life domains can be another priority issue in the research agenda of emerging adulthood in Taiwan.

References

Amato, P. R., King, V., & Thorsen, M. L. (2016). Parent–child relationships in stepfather families and adolescent adjustment: A latent class analysis. *Journal of Marriage and Family, 78*(2), 482–497.

Arnett, J. J. (2000). Emerging adulthood: A theory of development from the late teens through the twenties. *American Psychologist, 55*, 469–480.

Asparouhov, T., & Muthén, B. (2014). Auxiliary variables in mixture modeling: Three-step approaches using Mplus. *Structural Equation Modeling: A Multidisciplinary Journal, 21*, 329–341.

Bagwell, C. L., Newcomb, A. F., & Bukowski, W. M. (1998). Preadolescent friendship and peer rejection as predictors of adult adjustment. *Child Development, 69*, 140–153.

Baltes, P. B., & Eccles, J. S. (Eds.). (2005). Theoretical approaches to lifespan development: Interdisciplinary perspectives. *Research in Human Development, 2*(1–2).

Bleidorn, W., Arslan, R. C., Dennissen, J. J. A., Rentfrow, P. J., Gebauer, J. E., Potter, J., et al. (2016). Age and gender differences in self-esteem: A cross-cultural window. *Journal of Personality and Social Psychology, 111*(3), 396–410.

Butler, A. C., Hokanson, J. E., & Flynn, H. A. (1994). A comparison of self-esteem lability and low trait self-esteem as vulnerability factors for depression. *Journal of Personality and Social Psychology, 66*(1), 166–177.

Cairns, E., McWhirter, L., Duffy, U., & Barry, R. (1990). The stability of self-concept in late adolescence: Gender and situational effects. *Personality and Individual Differences, 11*(9), 937–944.

Chang, C. J. (2006). A study of some theoretical foundation and its application on humanities and social sciences scale construction. *Journal of Humanities and Social Sciences, 1*(9), 137–162.

Chubb, N. H., Fertman, C. I., & Ross, J. L. (1997). Adolescent self-esteem and locus of control: A longitudinal study of gender and age differences. *Adolescence, 32*(125), 113–129.

Chung, J. M., Robins, R. W., Trzesniewski, K. H., Noftle, E. E., Roberts, B. W., & Widaman, K. F. (2014). Continuity and change in self-esteem during emerging adulthood. *Journal of Personality and Social Psychology, 106*(3), 469–483.

Conger, R. D., & Donnellan, M. B. (2007). An interactionist perspective on the socioeconomic context of human development. *Annual Review of Psychology, 58*, 175–199.

Donnellan, M. B., Trzesniewski, K. H., Conger, K. J., & Conger, R. D. (2007). A three-wave longitudinal study of self-evaluations during young adulthood. *Journal of Research in Personality, 41*(2), 453–472.

Erol, R. Y., & Orth, U. (2011). Self-esteem development from age 14 to 30 years: A longitudinal study. *Journal of Personality and Social Psychology, 101*(3), 607–619.

Fan, G. H., & Yi, C. C. (2016). Developmental self-esteem trajectories among Taiwanese adolescents: Effects of family and school context. *Taiwanese Journal of Sociology, 60*, 55–98.

Finan, L. J., Ohannessian, C. M., & Gordon, M. S. (2018). Trajectories of depressive symptoms from adolescence to emerging adulthood: The influence of parents, peers, and siblings. *Developmental Psychology, 54*(8), 1555–1567.

Galambos, N. L., Barker, E. T., & Krahn, H. J. (2006). Depression, self-esteem, and anger in emerging adulthood: Seven-year trajectories. *Developmental Psychology, 42*(2), 350–365.

Gebauer, J. E., Sedikides, C., Wagner, J., Bleidorn, W., Rentfrow, P. J., & Gosling, S. D. (2015). Cultural norm fulfillment, interpersonal belonging, or getting ahead? A large-scale cross-cultural test of three perspectives on the function of self-esteem. *Journal of Personality and Social Psychology, 109*(3), 526–548.

Gecas, V. (1982). The self-concept. *Annual Review of Sociology, 8*(1), 1–33.

Gecas, V., & Schwalbe, M. (1983). Beyond the looking-glass self: Social structure and efficacy-based self-esteem. *Social Psychology Quarterly, 46*(2), 77–88.

Heckhausen, J., Dixon, R. A., & Baltes, P. B. (1989). Gains and losses in development throughout adulthood as perceived by different adult age groups. *Developmental Psychology, 25*(1), 109–121.

Hsiao, C. C., & Su, C. J. (2014). Chingshaonian Zihzun Chengjhang Chyushih Ji Siangguan Yingsiang Yinsu Tantao [Discussion of adolescent self-esteem growth and the relevant factors]. *Bulletin of Educational Research, 60*(3), 75–110.

Huang, L. W. (2002). Ziwogainian Jhih Fazhanlicheng: Cong Chingshaonian Chuqi Dao Zhonghouqi De Zhuanbian [The development process of self-concept: The transition from the early to the later stages]. *Paper presented at the 2002 Annual Conference of Taiwanese Sociological association, Taichung, Taiwan.*

Huang, C. (2010). Mean-level change in self-esteem from childhood through adulthood: Meta-analysis of longitudinal studies. *Review of General Psychology, 14*(3), 251–260.

Jou, Y. H. (2015). Chingshaonian Jhih Chengnian Chuchi Chinzihguansi De Bianhua Jichi Yingsiang [Longitudinal effect of parent-child interactions on psychological well-being during the transition from adolescence to young adulthood]. *Chinese Journal of Psychology, 57*(1), 67–89.

Khaleque, A. (2013). Perceived parental warmth, and children's psychological adjustment, and personality dispositions: A meta-analysis. *Journal of Child and Family Studies, 22*(2), 297–306.

Khaleque, A., & Ali, S. (2017). A systematic review of meta-analyses of research on interpersonal acceptance–rejection theory: Constructs and measures. *Journal of Family Theory & Review, 9*(4), 441–458.

Kitayama, S., Park, H., Sevincer, A. T., Karasawa, M., & Uskul, A. K. (2009). A cultural task analysis of implicit independence: Comparing North America, Western Europe, and East Asia. *Journal of Personality and Social Psychology, 97*(2), 236–255.

Kling, K. C., Hyde, J. S., Showers, C. J., & Buswell, B. N. (1999). Gender differences in self-esteem: A meta-analysis. *Psychological Bulletin, 125*(4), 470–500.

Laible, D. J., & Carlo, G. (2004). The differential relations of maternal and paternal support and control to adolescent social competence, self-worth, and sympathy. *Journal of Adolescent Research, 19*(6), 759–782.

Leary, M. R. (2015). Emotional responses to interpersonal rejection. *Dialogues in Clinical Neuroscience, 17*(4), 435–441.

McMullin, J. A., & Cairney, J. (2004). Self-esteem and the intersection of age, class, and gender. *Journal of Aging Studies, 18*(1), 75–90.

Muthén, L. K., & Muthén, B. O. (1998–2017). *Mplus user's guide* (8th ed.). Los Angeles, CA: Muthén & Muthén.

Nylund-Gibson, K., Grimm, R., Quirk, M., & Furlong, M. (2014). A latent transition mixture model using the three-step specification. *Structural Equation Modeling: A Multidisciplinary Journal, 21*(3), 439–454.

Nylund, K. L., Asparouhov, T., & Muthén, B. (2007). Deciding on the number of classes in latent class analysis and growth mixture modeling: A Monte Carlo simulation study. *Structural Equation Modeling: A Multidisciplinary Journal, 14*(4), 535–569.

Orth, U. (2018). The family environment in early childhood has a long-term effect on self-esteem: A longitudinal study from birth to age 27 years. *Journal of Personality and Social Psychology, 114*(4), 637–655.

Orth, U., Robins, R. W., & Widaman, K. F. (2012). Life-span development of self-esteem and its effects on important life outcomes. *Journal of Personality and Social Psychology, 102*(6), 1271–1288.

Orth, U., Trzesniewski, K. H., & Robins, R. W. (2010). Self-esteem development from young adulthood to old age: A cohort-sequential longitudinal study. *Journal of Personality and Social Psychology, 98*(4), 645–658.

Pullmann, H., Allik, J., & Realo, A. (2009). Global self-esteem across the life span: A cross-sectional comparison between representative and self-selected Internet samples. *Experimental Aging Research, 35*(1), 20–44.

Quatman, T., Sampson, K., Robinson, C., & Watson, C. M. (2001). Academic, motivational, and emotional correlates of adolescent dating. *Genetic, Social, and General Psychology Monographs, 127*(2), 211–234.

Roberts, B. W., Jackson, J. J., Fayard, J. V., Edmonds, G., & Meints, J. (2009). Conscientiousness. In M. R. Leary, & R. H. Hoyle (Eds.), *Handbook of individual differences in social behavior* (pp. 369–381). New York, NY: Guilford Press.

Roberts, B. W., Lejuez, C., Krueger, R. F., Richards, J. M., & Hill, P. L. (2014). What is conscientiousness and how can it be assessed?. *Developmental Psychology, 50*(5), 1315–1330.

Robins, R. W., & Trzesniewski, K. H. (2005). Self-esteem development across the lifespan. *Current Directions in Psychological Science, 14*(3), 158–162.

Robins, R. W., Trzesniewski, K. H., Tracy, J. L., Gosling, S. D., & Potter, J. (2002). Global self-esteem across the life span. *Psychology and Aging, 17*(3), 423–434.

Roeser, R. W., & Eccles, J. S. (1998). Adolescents' perceptions of middle school: Relation to longitudinal changes in academic and psychological adjustment. *Journal of Research on Adolescence, 8*(1), 123–158.

Rosenberg, M. (1965). *Society and the adolescent self-image.* Princeton, NJ: Princeton University Press.

Rosenberg, M. (1986). Self-concept from middle childhood through adolescence. In J. Suls & A. G. Greenwald (Eds.), *Psychological perspective on the self* (pp. 182–205). Hillsdale, MI: Erlbaum.

Rosenberg, M., & Pearlin, L. I. (1978). Social class and self-esteem among children and adults. *American Journal of Sociology, 84,* 53–77.

Rosenberg, M., Schooler, C., Schoenbach, C., & Rosenberg, F. (1995). Global self-esteem and specific self-esteem. *American Sociological Review, 60,* 141–156.

Shahar, G., & Davidson, L. (2003). Depressive symptoms erode selfesteem in severe mental illness: A three-wave, cross-lagged study. *Journal of Consulting and Clinical Psychology, 71*(5), 890–900.

von Soest, T., Wichstrøm, L., & Kvalem, I. L. (2016). The development of global and domain-specific self-esteem from age 13 to 31. *Journal of Personality and Social Psychology, 110*(4), 592–608.

Steiger, A., Allemand, M., Robins, R., & Fend, H. (2014). Low and decreasing self-esteem during adolescence predict adult depression two decades later. *Journal of Personality and Social Psychology, 106*(2), 325–338.

Trzesniewski, K. H., Donnellan, M. B., & Robins, R. W. (2003a). Stability of self-esteem across the life span. *Journal of Personality and Social Psychology, 84*(1), 205–220.

Trzesniewski, K. H., Robins, R. W., Roberts, B. W., & Caspi, A. (2003b). Personality and self-esteem development across the life span. *Advances in Cell Aging and Gerontology, 15*, 163–185.

Twenge, J. M., & Campbell, W. K. (2001). Age and birth cohort differences in self-esteem: A cross-temporal meta-analysis. *Personality and Social Psychology Review, 5*(4), 321–344.

Twenge, J. M., & Campbell, W. K. (2002). Self-esteem and socioeconomic status: A meta-analytic review. *Personality and Social Psychology Review, 6*(1), 59–71.

Tzou, H., & Chiang, P.M. (2012). The effects of imputation methods on the detection of differential item functioning. *Psychological Testing, 59*(1), 1–32.

Wagner, J., Lüdtke, O., Jonkmann, K., & Trautwein, U. (2013). Cherish yourself: Longitudinal patterns and conditions of self-esteem change in the transition to young adulthood. *Journal of Personality and Social Psychology, 104*(1), 148–163.

Wang, Y.C. (2013). Application of growth mixture model to heterogeneous trajectories of depressive moods of adolescents: A six-step strategic model development mechanism, *Journal of Educational Research and Development, 9*, 119–148.

Warren, M. T., Laura, W. L., Rote, W. M., & Shubert, J. (2016). Thriving while engaging in risk? Examining trajectories of adaptive functioning, delinquency, and substance use in a nationally representative sample of U.S. adolescents. *Developmental Psychology, 52*(2), 296–310.

West, S. G., Taylor, A. B., & Wu, W. (2012). Model fit and model selection in structural equation modeling. In R. H. Hoyle (Ed.), *Handbook of structural equation modeling* (pp. 209–231). New York, NY: The Guilford Press.

Wickrama, K. A. S., Lee, T. K., O'Neal, C. W., & Lorenz, F. O. (2016). *Higher-order growth curves and mixture modeling with Mplus: A practical guide.* New York, NY: Routledge/Taylor & Francis Group.

Yang, K. S. (2004). A theoretical and empirical analysis of the Chinese self from the perspective of social and individual orientation. *Indigenous Psychological Research in Chinese Societies, 22*, 11–80.

Yang, Q., Tian, L., Huebner, E. S., & Zhu, X. (2019). Relations among academic achievement, self-esteem, and subjective well-being in school among elementary school students: A longitudinal mediation model. *School Psychology Quarterly, 34*(3), 328–340.

Young, J. F., & Mroczek, D. K. (2003). Predicting intraindividual selfconcept trajectories during adolescence. *Journal of Adolescence, 26*, 586–600.

Zimmerman, M. A., Copeland, L. A., Shope, J. T., & Dielman, T. E. (1997). A longitudinal study of self-esteem: Implications for adolescent development. *Journal of Youth and Adolescence, 26*, 117–141.

11

Early Delinquency Trajectory and Developmental Outcomes in Adulthood: Findings From the Taiwan Youth Project

Yi-fu Chen and Chyi-In Wu

Introduction

The continuity of delinquency over the life course has been observed and theorized in current literature. Research has shown the association between early delinquency and adult crime and the risk factors concerning this association (Loeber, 1982; Maughan and Rutter, 1998) and has provided theoretical explanations (Gottfredson and Hirschi, 1990; Moffitt, 1993). Although this early and late continuity of delinquency has been well established, the impact of early delinquency on domains other than crime in adulthood has less been explored in the current literature. Recent work from Kerridge et al. (2020) and Pedersen et al. (2020) explored the impacts of early delinquency on educational attainment and socio-economic status in adulthood. Their works connect types of delinquents with status attainment to show the consequences of early delinquency for certain types of delinquents. These results show a spill-over effect of early delinquency and its heterogeneity. The findings are intriguing; however, the mechanisms behind the link between early delinquency and attainment outcomes have still not been well addressed.

Drawing from the concept of continuity (Schulenberg et al., 2003) and social control theory (Hirschi, 1969; Sampson and Laub, 1993), the current chapter addresses this literature gap by investigating two research questions using the 17-year longitudinal dataset of the Taiwan Youth Project (TYP). We first investigated the types of delinquency in the early lives of the youths. Although types of delinquency have been explored in the current literature, the cases in non-Western countries have less been investigated. Based on their delinquency trajectories across adolescence, we constructed trajectory groups of delinquency among the participants of the TYP. We then connected the trajectory groups with substance use in adulthood based on the ideas of heterotypic continuity and functional discontinuity. Next, we connected the trajectory groups with socio-economic attainment in adulthood. Using social control theory, we explored possible mechanisms that mediated the relationship between early delinquency and socioeconomic attainment in adulthood.

Literature Review

Types of Delinquency and the Empirical Studies in Taiwan

Developmental theories of delinquency were proposed over three decades ago. Both Patterson et al. (1992) and Moffitt (1993) proposed two types in the offending population: Early-onset or life-course-persistent delinquents show their inception of delinquency in late childhood and persist across adulthood, while late-onset or adolescent-limited delinquents show delinquency around mid-adolescence and leave their delinquent career before entering adulthood. During the past decades, the quest to distinguish different types of trajectory groups in populations of offenders has received attention in the literature. Moffitt's (1993, 1997, 2006) theoretical work and several empirical longitudinal studies that followed delineated several trajectory groups in populations of offenders and identified theoretical predictors in offenders' early lives, distinguishing the trajectory groups from each other (Fergusson et al., 2000; Hoeve et al., 2008; Kerridge et al., 2020; Kessler, 2020; Nagin and Land, 1993; Odgers et al., 2008; Piquero and Brezins, 2001; van der Geest et al., 2009; Wiesner and Capaldi, 2003; Wiesner and Silbereisen, 2003). These studies, based on growth mixture modelling (Muthén, 2004; Nagin, 1999, 2005), generally found Moffitt's hypothesized life-course-persistent and adolescent-limited delinquents plus several more trajectory groups that Moffitt had not hypothesized. Furthermore, Jolliffe et al. (2017) reviewed 55 longitudinal studies that tested Moffitt's typology and found support for the typology argument.

Although the findings on types of delinquency abound in different countries and areas, only a few studies were based on non-Western data. Chen et al. (2009) found a three-trajectory model based on four-wave longitudinal data of males aged 13–17 in a Northern city of

Taiwan. The study identified early starters (10.1 per cent of the sample), late starters (55.7 per cent of the sample) and non-offenders (34.1 per cent of the sample) during this age period. Weng (2008) extended Chen et al. (2009) by including data from age 13 to 19 in the analysis. The findings confirmed the previous findings on the early and later starter trajectory groups and identified additional trajectory groups during this age period. With a national representative dataset in Taiwan, Tang (2018) analysed the delinquent trajectories on a sample aged from 13 to 18. The results showed a 4-group model with high constant, low constant, low increasing and high decreasing groups. Although there was consistency in the findings of delinquency groups, the current literature in non-Western countries cannot distinguish the persistent delinquents from the adolescent-limited delinquents since the age ranges in data used in these studies never went beyond adolescence. The current study addressed this literature gap by including delinquency and substance use beyond adolescence. We used the adult data from the TYP to see if the delinquency during early adolescence continued during young adulthood and adulthood in a non-Western society.

Early Delinquency and Its Continuity Across the Life Course

Researchers have consensus about the continuity of delinquent and criminal behaviour over the course. As Nagin and Paternoster (1991) and Sampson and Laub (1992) indicated, the link between early antisocial behaviour and later criminal offending is prominent across studies. Based on arrest data and statistics, Blumstein's research (1986) showed a small group of offenders who kept their criminal career for a long time. Although these people accounted for only 5 per cent of the offender population, they committed 80 per cent of the total offending. Loeber (1982) carefully reviewed existing literature and confirmed the continuity of delinquent and criminal behaviour over time. Like Nagin and Paternoster (1991) and Sampson and Laub (1992), Loeber also noted the link between early delinquency and later criminal offending. These findings have shown the importance of tracing the early experience of offenders.

The studies of the continuity of delinquency, however, failed to consider the heterogeneity in this early-later link. Robins (1978), Loeber and Le Blanc (1990), Sampson and Laub (1992) and Rutter and Rutter (1993) indicated that not all delinquents in early life become criminals in their later life. Life course theories, such as Sampson and Laub's (1993) theory of age-graded informal control and their concept of turning points, emphasized factors that change the developmental trajectories of delinquency and crime over time. Such theories addressed the potential of various types of informal social control (such as employment, military enlistment and marriage) to alter individual delinquent trajectories across time (Laub and Sampson, 2006; Sampson and Laub, 1993; Simons et al., 2002; Warr, 1998). Although it is important for life-course researchers to trace the trajectories of delinquency from early to later life course (Murray et al., 2010), it is equally important to investigate the discontinuity in delinquency over the life course from the turning point perspective.

Moffitt (1993) investigated this heterogeneity and proposed a two-type model of delinquents for explanations. In her theory, we observe the continuity in life-course-persistent delinquents who start their delinquent career early and continue to do so over the life courses; at the same time, discontinuity can be found in the adolescent-limited delinquents who discontinue their delinquency when entering adulthood. The argument has been supported by several empirical studies regarding the continuity and discontinuity of delinquency/offending (Chung et al., 2002a, 2002b; Hoeve et al., 2008; Odgers et al., 2008; van der Geest et al., 2009; Wiesner and Capaldi, 2003). More recent studies have also extended the theory to explain the link between early delinquency and late substance use. For example, Kerridge et al. (2020) used data from a large US general population survey to identify four types of offenders: Adolescent-limited, adult-onset, life-course-persistent and non-offenders. Then, they connected the group membership to substance use in adulthood. The findings showed that people in the offending groups had higher substance use (drugs, cannabis, alcohol and nicotine) than those in the non-offending group in adulthood.

This finding, which has less been shown in previous empirical studies, reflects what Schulenberg et al. (2003) described regarding the types of continuity/discontinuity in behaviours over the life course. The authors distinguished four types of continuity and discontinuity with two dimensions. The descriptive dimension shows the same behaviours over time, while the explanatory dimension shows the same underlying purpose, function, or meaning of behaviours

(Schulenberg et al., 2003). Homotypic continuity refers to the presence of behaviours over the life course; the behaviours perform the same function for the individuals. For example, for life-course-persistent delinquents, the early delinquency and adult crime can be categorized as homotypic continuity since the behaviour and function are consistent over the life course. Heterotypic continuity refers to the presence of the different behaviours over the life course while the underlying purpose remains. In the drug use example, individuals may use marijuana to get thrilling and exciting experiences during adolescence and drive racing cars during adulthood. Although the behaviours are different, they share an underlying reason. Therefore, for life-course-persistent delinquents, high levels of delinquency during adolescence and excessive use of illicit drugs both share underlying reasons, such as impulsivity, low self-control and sensation seeking. For heterotypic continuity, we would expect high levels of early delinquency and substance use in later lives for the life-course-persistent delinquents.

For the adolescent-limited delinquents, we would expect a different type of continuity. Functional discontinuity shows an opposite pattern as shown in heterotypic continuity. The behaviours remain the same over the life course, while the underlying reasons are different. The involvement in substance use during adolescence for the adolescent-limited delinquents may continue using during adulthood. However, the underlying reasons for the behaviour would be different for adolescent-limited delinquents. As Moffitt indicated, adolescent-limited delinquents participate in delinquency (and substance use) due to the maturation gap. Once they reach adulthood, their delinquency would subside. Therefore, their substance use in adulthood could be for recreation and social gathering purposes. We expect the levels of substance use for adolescent-limited delinquents would be lower than that of the other offending group.

Early Delinquency and Developmental Outcomes in Adulthood

In addition to the types and the continuity of delinquency, developmental challenges that are related to increases in delinquency during adolescence connect early delinquency to other domains of their lives in adulthood. In the current study, we mainly focus on the link between early delinquency and socio-economic attainment and the possible mediating role of social bonds and precarious transitions.

Recent studies have shown the negative effects from the types of delinquency perspective. Kerridge et al. (2020) showed that the life-course-persistent delinquents significantly had lower educational attainment and less family income than those in the adolescent-limited and adult-onset groups. Pedersen et al. (2020) investigated Moffitt's 'normal' hypothesis regarding the developmental outcomes of the adolescent-limited group. Moffitt argued that adolescent-limited delinquents would be considered 'normal' since their delinquency is a way of adjustment to the changing environment and a practice of adult roles. Since delinquency abstainers in adolescence do not go through this process, they would face maladjustments when entering adulthood. Pedersen et al. (2020) tested the hypothesis by observing the adolescent abstainers' educational and labour market outcomes when they were in midlife. The results did not support Moffitt's argument. Instead, the adolescent abstainers turned out to be better in educational attainment and earnings than their delinquent counter-parts. To our best knowledge, there has not been an empirical study that tests the hypothesis in a non-Western context. Therefore, the current study investigates the long-term influences of early delin-quency on adulthood socio-economic attainment from the types of delinquency perspective.

Research on those with early puberty has shown that failure to cope with the stress related to changes in physical development and social roles is associated with elevated delinquency during adolescence (Ge et al., 2002; Lynne-Landsman et al., 2010; Shelton and Van Den Bree, 2010) and this in turn influences outcomes in other life domains. Previous research has shown that precarious transitions, such as high school dropouts, early marriage and parenthood, and early school-to-work transitions, impede the bonds to conventional institutions. For example, research on young adults has demonstrated positive associa-tions among high school dropouts, limited post-high school education and later employment opportunities (Gore et al., 2003). The malad-justments that occur during these transitions not only produce the peak in Gottfredson and Hirschi's (1991) bell-shaped age-crime curve and Moffitt's (1993, 2006) observation of increased delinquency during this time, but also hinders the development of conventional social bonds and social skills through the process of cumulative continuity of dis-advantages (Caspi et al., 1987). We would expect that those with high delinquency during adolescence have fewer opportunities to form social bonds with conventional institutions, such as family and schools. This, in turn, hinders their opportunities of pursuing future socio-economic attainment.

In addition to the obstructed opportunities, the precarious transitions also constitute stressful situations that create excessive demands on individuals. Wickrama and colleagues indicated that youths who experienced these excessive demands face challenges in emotional, social and economic responsibilities in adulthood (Wickrama and Bryant, 2003; Wickrama et al., 2005, 2015). These provide further obstacles in getting social resources that would facilitate their career development. Although the adverse effects of precarious transitions on later life chances have been established in the current literature, the influence of early delinquency on precarious transitions has less been addressed. Therefore, it is important to understand whether early delinquency increases the chances of precarious transitions and has adverse impacts on socio-economic attainment during adulthood. The current study investigates this possible mediating process.

In sum, the current study is set to investigate types of delinquents during early adolescence and the consequences of being different delinquent types using a 17-year longitudinal data set. This is one of few studies that explore types of delinquents in a non-Western context and across adolescence and adulthood. On the basis of Nagin's (2005) group-based model, we presented empirical evidence to answer three aforementioned research questions: (1) How many types of delinquents are there in this non-Western sample across early to mid-adolescence? (2) What are the consequences of early delinquency on adult outcomes, such as delinquency, substance use and socio-economic attainment? (3) How do social bonds and precarious transitions mediate the link between early delinquency and socio-economic attainment in adulthood?

Method

Data

We used data from the TYP, a prospective longitudinal survey in northern Taiwan. There were two cohorts of samples in the TYP. The current study used the data from the younger cohort (the J1 cohort) which were recruited when they were 13 years old. The first wave of data collection was in 2000 and continued annually for the next 7 waves. In 2009, the research team conducted interviews for the 9th wave when the youths were 22 years old, which concluded the phase one data collection. After that, the survey was conducted every three years, and three more waves of data were collected in the phase two period. The last data collection was in 2017 when the participants were 30 years old.

In the current study, we used all the phase two data and eight waves of the phase one data. Due to the attrition and missing data, the sample size in each wave varied; the initial sample size was 2,690 at the first wave of data collection. Over 66 per cent of the original sample was re-contacted at the end of phase one data collection. In 2017, 45.5 per cent of the original sample and 66.4 per cent of the initial sample of phase two was re-contacted. To address the attrition and missing data, we conducted two sets of analyses. First, for the missing data in a single wave, a chained equation imputation was used. Second, we calculated the probability of attrition at each wave by conducting a series of logistic regression models. The variables included in the models were based on previous TYP publications (Lin et al., 2009; Lin and Lee, 2013). The inverse of the probabilities were used as weights in the later analyses. To do so, we can take the attrition bias into consideration in our statistical models.

Measures

Delinquency

In each wave, the TYP used different items to assess the delinquency of youths. To provide a valid comparison, we selected the same items across ages of 13–15 to construct the trajectory groups. The items were smoking or drinking, running away from home and hurting someone physically. We dichotomized the scores of the items and then summed the scores to create the delinquency measures. The scores ranged from 0 to 3. We treated the measures as categorical variables in the group-based models. We also used a three-item measure in the age 16 and 18 data collection. In addition to general delinquency, items of physical violence were used to create a violence measure at age 18. At the age of 20 and 22, five items were used to create the delinquency measure, including stealing, smoking or drinking, chewing betel nuts, using illicit drugs and damaging other people's stuff. The items were dichotomized and summed to form the delinquency measures. There were only items of substance use included in the phase two surveys. At ages 24 and 30, respondents reported the number of cigarettes consumed last week, frequency of drinking alcohol and frequency of excessive drinking (4 units or more a day). At age 27, only cigarettes and alcohol use were assessed.

Life-Course Transitions

The respondents reported whether they were full-time students, held full- or part-time jobs, and were self-employed. All the items were dichotomized to form the life-course transition measures.

Social Bonds

Social bonds consist of peer support, perceived parental warmth, family cohesion and economic independence/isolation. Peer support was assessed with five items. The respondents reported levels of support from friends, and the responses were formatted to range from 1 (strongly disagree) to 4 (strongly agree) and were averaged to create the peer support measure. Respondents reported levels of perceived parental warmth for their mothers and fathers based on eight items on the parental warmth scale. The responses ranged from 1 (never) to 5 (always) and were averaged to create the paternal and maternal warmth measures. We then calculated the average score of the two warmth measures to get the parental warmth measure. Family cohesion, in which the respondents indicated the sense of togetherness in the family, was assessed by four items. The responses ranged from 1 (strongly disagree) to 4 (strongly agree) and were summed to form the family cohesion measure. Respondents reported the sources of their daily expenses. We used the information and created a measure called 'on-my-own'. That means the respondents did not receive any money support for daily expenses from anyone but themselves. The measure indicated the economic independence or lack of economic support at the time of data collection.

Socio-Economic Attainment

The socio-economic attainment of the respondents was assessed at the age of 30. Respondents reported their highest educational degree on a 7-point scale (1=elementary school; 7=PhD) and their monthly income from the current job, personal annual income, types of employment, job authority and occupational status. They reported their monthly income (salary and bonus) from the current job on a

22-point scale (1=TWD 4,999 and below; 22=TWD 200,000 and above). Similarly, personal annual income (including salary, gain from investment and other sources of income) was assessed through an open-ended question. We re-coded the answer into 18 categories, ranging from 9,999 and below (=1) to 200,000 and above (=18). Two measures regarding types of employment were created. First, they reported whether they were in non-standard employment (including part-time, temp and short-term contractor) and whether they were self-employed. The second one is job authority, which was assessed by asking how many people were under the supervision of the respondents; a higher score means higher job authority. The respondents were also asked to report the occupation and position of their current job. We coded the responses with ISCO-08 and scored them with ISEI-08 (International Socio-Economic Index of Occupational Status) (Ganzeboom, 2010).

Analytical Strategy

Using a group-based modelling approach (Nagin, 1999, 2005), we first analysed the trajectories of the early delinquency (ages 13–15) and distinguished qualitatively different delinquent groups. After establishing the trajectory groups, a series of ANOVAs or cross-tables was presented to validate the trajectory groups. Next, we presented another set of ANOVAs or cross-tables to delineate the association between the early trajectory groups and the later developmental outcomes. In the final stage, we conducted a regression model for assessing the mediating roles of social bonds and life course transitions. All the analyses were adjusted with the attrition weights to correct possible attrition bias. The group-based modelling was conducted using Mplus 8.4 (Muthén and Muthén, 1998–2017), and the ANOVAs, cross-tabulation analyses, and the regression models were conducted using Stata 17 (StataCorp, 2021).

Result

The Developmental Patterns of Early Delinquency

We first presented cross-tabulation analysis to show the developmental patterns of delinquency across ages 13–15 among the participants. In the analysis, we dichotomized the delinquency measures to

Table 11.1   The developmental patterns of early delinquency

Age 13	Age 14	Age 15	N	%
None	None	None	1541	61.7
None	None	1 or above	350	14.0
None	1 or above	None	102	4.1
None	1 or above	1 or above	105	4.2
1 or above	None	None	137	5.5
1 or above	None	1 or above	103	4.1
1 or above	1 or above	None	42	1.7
1 or above	1 or above	1 or above	117	4.7

Note: The listwise $N=2,497$.

avoid empty cells. Approximately 61.7 per cent of the participants did not engage in any of the delinquent behaviour across ages 13–15, while around 5 per cent of them persistently engaged in the behaviour (see Table 11.1). The percentage of persistent involvement was close to that of Moffitt's theory. Fourteen per cent of the participants showed late involvement. Around a total of 8 per cent (5.5 and 1.7 per cent) of the participants showed a desistant pattern in their delinquency involvement. The rest of the developmental patterns were inconsistent across time, and each of them describes approximately 4 per cent of the participants. In sum, among the TYP participants, about 40 per cent showed some delinquency involvement during the early adolescence. As we can also see, there were different developmental patterns among this 40 per cent. Next, we will explore the possible groups among these developmental patterns.

The Developmental Trajectory in the Early Delinquency

We conducted group-based modelling to find qualitatively distinct trajectory groups. The group-based modelling (Jones et al., 2001; Nagin, 1999, 2005) is a reduced form of the growth mixture modelling (GMM) (Muthén, 2002). In Muthén's GMM, the parameters can be set to random within a group, indicating inter-individual variation. Nagin's procedure, which Muthén calls the latent class growth mixture model (LCGM), assumes the invariant trajectory for people within groups, while Muthén's GMM can free this assumption. We chose Nagin's modelling approach in the current study for a practical reason. Since group-based modelling treats the within-group variation as zero, we expected the analysis to extract as many trajectory groups as possible. In doing so, we would not miss empirically interesting groups. In GMM, we could take the risk of ignoring some theoretically or empirically interesting groups.

Table 11.2 shows the model selection process for deciding the number of trajectory groups. Mplus provides several criteria to guide the selection process, such as Akaike's Information Criterion (AIC), Bayesian Information Criterion (BIC) and Sample-adjusted BIC (ABIC). As suggested by Nylund et al. (2007), relatively small AIC, BIC or ABIC could be an indication of a good model. As shown in Table 11.2, the 4-class model was a good model, although the difference between the 3-class and 4-class models was small. In addition to these criteria, two likelihood ratio tests (Lo–Mendell–Rubin [LMR] and Vuong–Lo–Mendell–Rubin [VLMB]) were shown in the Table 11.2. The significance of the tests ($p < 0.05$) indicated that the K-class model is better than the K-1-class model. According to the tests, the 3-class model showed a better fit than the 4-class model. Therefore, we used the results from the 3-class model for the subsequent analyses.

The results of the 3-class model are presented in Figure 11.1A–C. Figure 11.1A–C showed the model-based probabilities of reporting zero, one, and two or more delinquent behaviour across ages 13–15, respectively. We can see that group one showed the highest probabilities in Figure 11.1A and the lowest probabilities in Figure 11.1B and C. We, therefore, named this group as 'low group,' which comprised 75.6 per cent of the participants. The second group showed a moderate probability of having zero delinquent behaviour (Figure 11.1A) and having one delinquent behaviour (Figure 11.1B); we named this group 'moderate group',

Table 11.2 Model selection process of the group-based modelling

Models	2-Class model	3-Class model	4-Class model
AIC	9044.218	**8979.408**	8948.102
BIC	9090.849	**9043.525**	9029.705
ABIC	9065.431	**9008.575**	8985.224
VLMB LR test	4.146***	**1.314*****	6.78E12
LMR LR test	595.097***	**67.922*****	35.774

Note: ***p<0.001; Model selected in bold.

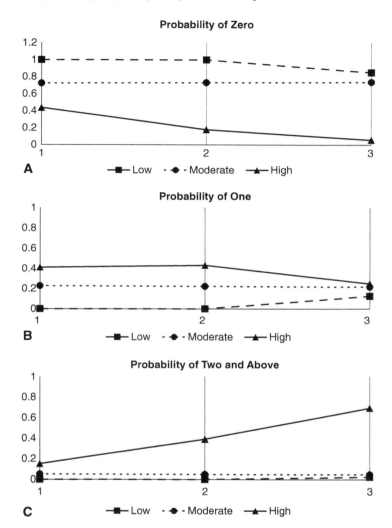

Figure 11.1 (A) Estimated probability of zero delinquency for trajectory groups. (B) Estimated probability of one delinquency for trajectory groups. (C) Estimated probability of two or more delinquency for trajectory groups

and 15.3 per cent of the participants were in this group. Finally, the last group showed the lowest probabilities in Figure 11.1A and the highest probabilities in Figure 11.1B and C. Therefore, we named the group 'high group', which took up 9.1 per cent of the participants. Forty-seven per cent of the participants in the low group were males, while the percentages were 60.7 and 70.7 per cent in the moderate and high group.

The Early Trajectory of the Delinquency and the Continuity of Substance Use

To further validate the three trajectory groups, Table 11.3 presents the percentages of having one or above delinquent behaviour in each trajectory group in early, mid-adolescence and early young adulthood. We also presented the percentage of substance use across ages 24–30. Note that we cannot directly compare these percentages due to the

Table 11.3 The delinquency and substance profile of the early delinquency trajectory groups

	Low (75.6%)	Moderate (15.3%)	High (9.1%)	χ^2
Early adolescence				
Age 13	0%	62.92%	70.48%	–[a]
Age 14	0%	48.18%	82.02%	–[a]
Age 15	18.5%	26.37%	100.00%	681.96***
Mid-adolescence				
Age 16	8.33%	22.83%	55.89%	292.47***
Age 18				
General delinquency	26.2%	42.73%	71.93%	129.799***
Violence	0.02[a]	0.02[a]	0.17[b]	48.18***
Young adulthood				
Age 20	11.72%	25.01%	63.67%	189.67***
Age 22	46.48%	61.70%	81.85%	64.47***
Age 24				
Smoking	13.90%	28.35%	61.67%	147.76***
Drinking	19.32%	26.55%	40.23%	28.45***
Binge drinking	37.90%	44.34%	55.14%	13.01**
Age 27				
Smoking	13.43%	27.24%	55.26%	110.68***
Drinking[b]	2.66	3.27	4.40	10.97***
Age 30				

Table 11.3   The delinquency and substance profile of the early delinquency trajectory groups (Continued)

	Low (75.6%)	Moderate (15.3%)	High (9.1%)	χ^2
Smoking	14.99%	28.51%	53.65%	81.79***
Drinking	52.53%	56.92%	72.27%	15.58***
Binge drinking	28.15%	39.13%	68.20%	43.74***

Note: $N=2,512$ at first wave of data collection; Weighted statistics presented in the table.
[a]Chi-square was too big to show in the table due to the zero cell size.
[b]Means were presented in the table and F test was used.
**$p<0.01$ ***$p<0.001$.

inconsistent items used to create the delinquency measures in each period; instead, we showed the patterns within a given age period.

The first four rows of Table 11.3 present the prevalence rates of delinquency across ages 13–15. The low group showed no delinquency at the age of 13 and 14, and the prevalence rate of the low group at age 15 was 18.5 per cent, which was the lowest among the three trajectory groups. This low group's prevalence rates of delinquency (ages 16, 18, 20 and 22), smoking, and drinking (ages 24, 27 and 30) continued to remain the lowest through mid-adolescence and young adulthood.

In contrast, the high group showed the highest prevalence rates of delinquency during early adolescence. All the participants in the high group had been involved in one or more delinquency at age 15. Between the ages of 16 and 22, the prevalence rates of the high group ranged from 55 to 81 per cent. In addition, the group showed significantly higher levels of violence at age 18 than did the other two groups. The drinking and smoking behaviours in the last three occasions of data collection also showed the same pattern. The prevalence of binge drinking (4 or more units of alcohol consumption on one occasion) was over 55 per cent for the participants in the high group. This shows a possible heterotypic continuity between the early delinquency and adulthood substance use for participants in the high group.

During early adolescence, the prevalence rates of delinquency for the moderate group declined across time. The group continued to have moderate prevalence rates of delinquency among the three groups. The early declining trend of delinquency for this group of participants implies that their involvement in these behaviours could be experimental. However, they continuingly and moderately involved in later lives showed some detrimental effects of this early involvement, such as higher smoking and excessive drinking rates than those in the low group. The moderate group's findings regarding the continuity between early delinquency and adulthood substance use showed a mixed result. The prevalence rate of drinking in the moderate group was lower than that in the high group and slightly higher than that in the low group, which indicates some functional discontinuity for the link between early delinquency and alcohol use. However, the pattern of the smoking behaviour was different. Compared to the low group, the prevalence rate of smoking was doubled in the moderate group, while the rate was halved in the high group. This observation possibly characterizes a heterotypic continuity for the link between early delinquency and smoking.

The results presented in Table 11.3 provide evidence that the trajectory groups have predictive validity for future delinquency and substance use. The high group has a similar developmental pattern in delinquency as the early starters (Patterson et al., 1992) and the life-course persistent delinquents (Moffitt, 1993) do. The low and moderate groups showed some delinquency in mid-adolescence and early adulthood. In addition to differences in rates of delinquency in later lives, further analyses showed no difference in types of delinquency they tended to involve. Both groups could be the 'normative' type in Moffitt's (1993) typology – adolescent-limited delinquents – although the moderate group showed an earlier start in delinquency than did the low group.

The Impacts of the Early Delinquency Trajectory on Life-Course Transitions

After validating the model-based trajectory group with the early and later delinquency/substance use, we moved to the second research question. Table 11.4 presents the results for the effects of delinquency on life-course transitions when being in a given trajectory group. In this section, we focused on the transitions in two periods of time: high school (age 18) and college graduation (age 22).

The first panel in Table 11.4 presented two life-course events at age 18 across three trajectory groups. At the age of 18, almost all the participants in the low and moderate group were in school, while

Table 11.4 The effects of the early delinquent trajectory groups on life-course transitions

	Low	Moderate	High	F/χ^2
Mid-adolescence (Age 18)				
Full-time student	96.5%[a]	95.1%[ab]	75.1%[b]	99.46***
Full- or part-time job	15.4%[a]	20.0%[ab]	41.5%[b]	51.59***
Early adulthood (Age 22)				
Full-time student	76.4%[a]	67.0%[b]	31.7%[c]	107.54***
Full- or part-time job	51.7%[a]	45.2%[ab]	66.8%[b]	17.72***
Self-employment	1.5%	1.0%	4.2%	5.35

Note: Weighted statistics presented in the table; the numbers in the same row with the same superscript do not achieve statistical significance at 0.05 with the Bonferroni post hoc comparison; *$p<0.05$ **$p<0.01$ ***$p<0.001$.

about a quarter of the participants in the high group were not in school. Over 40 per cent of the participants in the high group were involved in the job market at this age, while only 15 per cent in the low group and 20 per cent in the moderate had done so. In other words, during this period, although there were not many differences between the low and moderate groups in life-course transitions, we observed that the participants in the high group showed an early involvement in the job market and an early school-to-work transition.

At age 22, 76.4 per cent of the participants in the low group and 67 per cent in the moderate group remained in school at age 22, meaning they could be pursuing degrees beyond a bachelor's degree, while only 31.7 per cent of the participants in the high group were in school. Overall, over half of the participants in each group had at least a part-time job at this age. Interestingly, we observed a higher percentage of self-employment at this time in the high group than those in the other two groups. The proportion of self-employed participants in this group was about three times more than those in the low and moderate groups. The relatively early out-of-school, school-to-work transitions, and the self-employed experience could constitute a source of stress that influences their future socio-economic outcomes.

The Impacts of the Early Delinquency Trajectory on Social Bonds

Table 11.5 presents the findings of social bonds for each trajectory of delinquent groups. We observed that participants in the high group

Table 11.5 The effects of the early delinquent trajectory groups on social bonds

	Low	Moderate	High	F/χ^2
Mid-adolescence (Age 18)				
Peer support	14.40[a]	14.10[ab]	13.78[b]	6.04**
Parental warmth	26.06[a]	25.31[a]	23.72[b]	15.43***
Family cohesion	11.27[a]	10.70[b]	9.95[c]	19.99***
Young adulthood (Age 24)				
On-my-own	2.4%	2.6%	3.4%	.26
Family cohesion	17.30	17.03	17.25	1.33
Young adulthood (Age 27)				
On-my-own	81.3%[a]	91.7%[b]	82.0%[ab]	9.34**
Family cohesion	13.05[a]	12.64[b]	13.18[ab]	3.35*

Note: Weighted statistics presented in the table; the numbers in the same row with the same superscript do not achieve statistical significance at 0.05 with the Bonferroni post hoc comparison; *$p<0.05$ **$p<0.01$ ***$p<0.001$.

had relatively minor support from peers, parents and family at age 18. However, we did not observe significant differences at age 24. During this period, low proportions of 'on-my-own' in each group showed that the majority of the participants in each group depended on others economically. Young adults in the high group had a slightly higher proportion to be 'on-my-own' than that in the other two groups, although the difference did not reach statistical significance. At age 27, the participants in the moderate group showed a higher proportion (91.7 per cent) of being 'on-my-own' than those in the low and high group. At this age, this means that more participants in the moderate group had achieved economic independence. The participants in this group also reported a lower score in family cohesion than those in the low group.

In sum, we did not observe significant differences among the three trajectory groups in most of the indicators of social bonds, except for those at age 18. This observation supports the immediate effect of early delinquency on social bonds. However, the adverse effect of early delinquency could dissipate as time passes by. The following section discusses our investigation on the influence of social bonds at age 18 on adulthood attainment in the following analyses.

The Impacts of the Early Delinquency Trajectory at Age 30

From a traditional point of view in Taiwanese society, when reaching age 30, a person should be economically and socially independent. We would expect a person to have a career and have achieved at least part of adulthood indices. Therefore, it is a culturally important life stage for these participants. Table 11.6 exhibits the developmental outcomes when the TYP participants were 30 years old.

Overall, we observed few differences in the achievement among the three groups at the age of 30. The participants in the high group had significantly lower education levels than those in the other two groups. They had some vocational school degrees, whereas the participants in the low and moderate groups had some college degrees. The participants in the high group had slightly higher job authority than those in the low group; however, their occupation status was lower than those in the other two groups. Although it did not reach statistical significance, there was a higher proportion of self-employment in the high group than that in the other two groups. When considering their earnings, we did not find any differences in monthly income from the current job and personal income among the three trajectory groups.

In sum, although they had a relatively low educational degree and occupational status, the participants in the high group did earn equally more than those in the other two groups. When considering

Table 11.6 The effects of the early delinquency trajectory groups on socio-economic attainment at age 30

	Low	Moderate	High	F/χ^2
Socio-economic attainment				
Highest educational degree	4.46[a]	4.33[a]	3.21[b]	37.73***
Monthly income from the current job	9.00	8.85	9.20	.33
Personal annual income	17.14	17.56	17.71	2.36
Non-standard Employment	4.1%	3.6%	5.5%	.28
Job authority	.44[a]	.62[ab]	.77[b]	5.55**
Self-employment	12.9%	9.4%	17.7%	.90
Occupational status (ISEI08)	48.41[a]	47.44[a]	42.65[b]	6.05**

Note: Weighted statistics presented in the table; the numbers in the same row with the same superscript do not achieve statistical significance at 0.05 with the Bonferroni post hoc comparison; *$p<0.05$ **$p<0.01$ ***$p<0.001$.

job authority and self-employment, it seems the participants in the high group are slightly inclined to be in higher managerial positions. To explore further, we investigated the occupations with the minor ISCO groups. The participants in the high group had relatively high proportions to be cooks and shop salespersons. It could be that the participants in this group owned shops, food stands or restaurants. For the participants in the low group, high proportions of them were sales and purchasing agents and office clerks. The participants in the moderate group also had a high proportion as salespersons and purchasing agents; however, they were also working as engineering professionals and software developers.

To further investigate the impact of early delinquency on educational and occupational attainment, we conducted a series of regression analyses. The highest degree in education and occupational status – the ISEI-08 score – was regressed on dummy variables of the trajectory group, early transition into work, and family cohesion. The results are presented in Table 11.7.

Panel A of Table 11.7 presents the analyses of early transition and family cohesion (age 18) as predictors of educational and occupational attainment. Compared with the low group, participants in the high group showed significantly lower levels of education at age 30, while there was no significant difference between the low and moderate groups. The effect of the trajectory groups held when introducing early transition into work and family cohesion in the models, favouring that early delinquency has influenced their chances of educational attainment. In addition to the trajectory groups, early transition into work had a negative impact on their educational attainment, while family cohesion at age 18 did not predict the educational attainment at age 30. After introducing early transition into work, the difference in educational attainment between the low and high groups dropped, showing some mediating effect of this early transition. The final model explained about 15 per cent of the total variance in educational attainment.

The second part of analyses in panel A reveals the influences of early delinquency, early transition into work, family cohesion and educational attainment on occupational status. In M1, we observed a significant difference in occupational status between the low and high groups. This difference became non-significant after introducing early transition into work in the model (M2). Early transition into work

Table 11.7 The developmental outcomes at age 30 of the early delinquent trajectory groups and the mediating role of life course transitions and social bonds during late adolescence and young adulthood

	Highest degree in education						Occupational status							
	M1		M2		M3		M1		M2		M3		M4	
Panel A	**Coef**	**SE**	**Coef**	**SE**	**Coef**	**SE**	**Coef**	**SE**	**Coef**	**SE**	**Coef**	**SE**	**Coef**	**SE**
Trajectory groups														
Low (Ref)														
Moderate	−0.07	0.11	0.00	0.11	0.01	0.11	−1.02	1.22	−0.01	1.3	0.05	1.30	−0.19	1.17
High	−1.20***	0.15	−0.82***	0.16	−0.79***	0.16	−6.40***	1.69	−3.19	2.0	−2.92	2.02	0.81	1.82
Transition (age 18)			−1.09***	0.11	−1.08***	0.11			−6.97***	1.3	−6.90***	1.34	−1.33	1.26
Family cohesion (age 18)					0.03	0.02					0.20	0.18	0.08	0.16
Degree in education													5.31***	0.36
Constant	3.95***	0.14	4.39***	0.14	4.11***	0.22	43.88***	1.61	45.68***	1.7	43.44***	2.72	21.52***	2.84
Adjusted R²	0.09***		0.15***		0.15***		0.03***		0.06***		0.06***		0.25***	

(Continued)

Table 11.7 The developmental outcomes at age 30 of the early delinquent trajectory groups and the mediating role of life course transitions and social bonds during late adolescence and young adulthood (Continued)

	Highest degree in education						Occupational status							
	M1		M2		M3		M1		M2		M3		M4	
Panel B	Coef	SE	Coef	SE	Coef	SE	Coef	SE	Coef	SE	Coef	SE	Coef	SE
Trajectory groups														
Low (Ref)														
Moderate	−0.07	0.11	−0.10	0.10	−0.11	0.10	−1.02	1.22	−1.05	1.2	−1.03	1.21	−0.81	1.07
High	−1.20***	0.15	−1.08***	0.14	−1.08***	0.14	−6.40***	1.69	−5.71***	1.6	−5.47***	1.71	0.12	1.54
Transition (across)			−0.57***	0.06	−0.58***	0.06			−2.86***	0.7	−2.89***	0.69	0.30	0.63
Family cohesion (across)					−0.02	0.02					−0.11	0.22	0.03	0.20
Degree in education													5.50***	0.31
Constant	3.95***	0.14	4.34***	0.14	4.71***	0.29	43.88***	1.17	45.76***	1.6	47.52***	3.49	21.49***	3.40
Adjusted R^2	0.09***		0.16***		0.15***		0.03***		0.04***		0.04***		0.26**	

Note: Weights were included in the analysis; Coef=Unstandardized coefficients; SE=Standard errors; All the models included gender, single family, and areas as covariates; ***$p < 0.001$.

showed a significant and negative impact on adulthood occupational status, while early family cohesion did not have a significant effect (M3). This model explained only 6 per cent of the variance in occupational status. The effect of the early transition into work became non-significant after introducing educational attainment in the model (M4). Combined with the results in educational attainment, it seems the early transition into work influenced the chance of getting higher levels of education and in turn influenced their occupational attainment.

Panel B of Table 11.7 includes measures of transitions into work and family cohesion across time. We calculated the number of transitions into work across ages 18 to 22. The variable ranged from 0 to 2. For the family cohesion, we averaged the scores of family cohesion at ages 18, 22 and 24; the reason to use family cohesion was that this was the only social bond measure available across waves. Results came out with significant main effects of the trajectory group on educational and occupational attainment; this main effect remained when the models included the transition variable. The time-averaged measure of family cohesion did not influence the educational and occupational attainment when variables of trajectory groups and transitions were in the model. The results indicated that early transition into work had a greater effect than that of the cross-time measure.

In sum, the regression analysis results showed that the early delinquency had its long-term effect on educational and occupational statuses, and the transition into work at age 18 seems to mediate this effect. The findings support that the adverse effects of early precarious transitions on life chances and early delinquency could be the factors influencing the transitions (see results in Table 11.4).

Discussion

Research of life-course criminology and criminal career has connected early delinquency with later crimes over the life span. The continuity thesis has been supported by past studies with different longitudinal datasets across countries. However, although the evidence abounds, only a few studies show how early delinquency influences other aspects of lives in later life courses. Furthermore, no research has investigated the long-term effects in a non-Western context. To address this literature gap, the current study investigates the long-term influence of early delinquency spanning across 17 years in the TYP sample. We propose three research questions and provide empirical evidence with the TYP data via group-based modelling, a series of ANOVA analyses and regression analyses to answer them.

The group-based modelling identified delinquent trajectory groups across the TYP participants' junior high school years. We observed two trajectory groups in which the youths started their delinquency early with different levels. The youths in the high group, like the early starters in Patterson's typology (1992), showed a high level of involvement in various delinquent activities, while the moderate group showed early but moderate levels of involvement. The youths in the low group started their involvement in delinquency in the last year of their junior high school and continued it later in their lives. However, unlike Moffitt's prediction, we did not find an abstinent group among the TYP youths. We further validated the trajectory groups with data from the later waves. The high group continued their high levels of involvement in delinquency after leaving junior high school, and their involvement in violent behaviour was also the highest among the three groups. We observed this pattern at the age of 30. This group could mimic Moffitt's life-course-persistent delinquents, although the severity of offending was relatively low due to the measures of delinquency used in the current study.

The participants in the low and moderate groups also continued their delinquency in later life course; however, the proportion of violence involvement was relatively low for the two groups. The participants in the low group could mimic Moffitt's adolescent-limited delinquents, also known as the 'normative' type of delinquents (1993). The participants in the moderate group had a similar pattern to those in the low group, although their proportion of involvement was higher than that in the low group. In sum, the trajectory groups identified in the TYP sample show similar patterns in the past literature with some variations (Chen et al., 2009; Weng, 2008). However, these studies only identified the trajectory groups based on data from ages 13 to 18. The current study extends the past literature by including data during the early adulthood to validate the early trajectory groups.

In the ANOVA analyses, we observed a continuity between early delinquency and substance use across mid-adolescence to early adulthood. The moderate and high groups showed a continuity in substance use across life courses, and the high group itself showed a relatively high prevalence rate in drinking and smoking and the highest binge drinking rate. We found this pattern similar to the heterotypic continuity described in Schulenberg et al. (2003). The moderate group, compared to the low group, showed continuity in smoking and early delinquency and a discontinuity in drinking and early delinquency. The different patterns shown in smoking and drinking could be the underlying reason for tobacco and alcohol use being different for the participants in the moderate group. Future studies may explore this topic to extend our understanding of this long-term effect.

We further presented the trajectory group differences in life-course transitions and social support across mid-adolescence to early adulthood and socio-economic attainment in adulthood. The early delinquency influenced the education and occupation achievement of the participants in the high group. However, the differences revealed the carry-over effect of the early education outcomes. The participants in the high group were less likely to stay in school and more likely to make a school-to-work transition during mid-adolescence and early adulthood. When they did, those in the high group tended to attend vocational or technical school. This explains why the average education levels at age 30 for participants in the high group were about some vocational school degree. The educational outcomes, in turn, influenced their occupational attainment. The participants in the high group tended to be owners of shops, food stands or restaurants, considering the high proportion of self-employment in this group. Therefore, even though they showed some disadvantages in educational and occupational outcomes, the participants in the high group earned a similar level of income as those in the other two groups. In sum, although they showed high levels of delinquency in early and mid-adolescence, the participants in the high group turned out to be fine in their adulthood, except for educational degrees and occupational status.

The participants in the low and moderate groups did not differ in most of the indicators of life-course transitions and socio-economic attainment across mid-adolescence to early adulthood and in their 30s. As we mentioned earlier, the participants in the two groups could be the 'normative' type of delinquents in Moffitt's (1993) typology. Therefore, the early delinquency could be a form of 'trying to be adults' and would not influence them in later life courses. However, we observed that the moderate group participants showed less support from their family and were more likely to be 'on-my-own' during early adulthood than those in the low group did. It could be why they experienced a higher level of substance use in young adulthood and at the age of 30.

We investigated our third research question with a series of regression models. The main effects of early delinquency on educational and occupational attainment were mediated by the early transition into work. The finding indicated the importance of life-course transition during the early stage of the life course. Furthermore, the effects of early transition into work and the early out-of-school transition (found in ANOVA analyses) showed the adverse influence of the early disruption in education careers on adulthood socioeconomic status. This finding supported the argument of precarious transitions in the current literature. However, we did not find the effects of early and time-averaged social bonds on adulthood socio-economic status in the presence of the precarious transition and early delinquency. It could be that social bonds work on other life domains, such as psychological well-being and health. We will leave the exploration to future studies.

Before we conclude our discussion, a few limitations need to be addressed. First, we still need to be cautious regarding the research findings due to the attrition rate in the TYP study and the possible selection bias. Although we addressed this issue by using propensity scores of attrition as weights in the analyses, we still did not know the levels of delinquency of those dropping out of the study. Therefore, there could be more trajectory groups than we found in the current study. Second, the inconsistency of the delinquency measure across waves could limit the validity of the trajectory groups. The TYP team asked participants' delinquency in almost the first nine waves of the data collection; however, the items were inconsistent across waves. Therefore, to form a meaningful comparison, we used only four items from the 8-item scale at the first wave of data collection. Although we tried to cover the diversity of offences in the item selection, the delinquency measure used in the current study could limit the numbers of the trajectory groups. Besides, the TYP data contained few items to measure serious offences. We observed a high offence group mimicking Moffitt's life-course delinquents; however, the seriousness of the offences was relatively low. Therefore, the readers should be cautious about the research findings.

Despite the limitations, the findings of the current study extend our understanding regarding the trajectory groups and the effects of early delinquency on later life-course outcomes. Previous studies have focused on the continuity and heterogeneity of delinquency across a limited period. In addition to investigating the early delinquency and the trajectory groups, we present the relationships between early delinquent trajectories and later delinquency and substance use. We extended the study period in the delinquency literature in Taiwan into young adulthood. Furthermore, we extended the existing literature by investigating the effects of early delinquency on adulthood socio-economic attainment. Those with high levels of delinquency during adolescence did experience a short-term disadvantage and took a hit in their educational levels. As we have seen, at the age of 30, they had lower educational degrees and less prestigious occupations than their counterparts who had relatively low levels of delinquency during adolescence. However, most of them found a way to establish their own careers. Therefore, when comparing income earned at age 30 across groups, there was no significant difference. The participants in the high group turned out to be fine in terms of earning. Therefore, we conclude this chapter with the following sentence: Early delinquency is not destiny.

References

Blumstein, A., Cohen, J., Both J. A., & Visher, C. A. (1986). *Criminal careers and career criminals* (*Vol. 1*). Washington, DC: National Academy Press.

Caspi, A., Elder, G. H., & Bem, D. J. (1987). Moving against the world: Life-course patterns of explosive children. *Developmental Psychology, 23*(2), 308–313.

Chen, Y., Wu, C., & Lin, K. (2009). The dynamic relationships between parenting and adolescent delinquency: A group-based model approach. *Crime and Criminal Justice International, 12*, 59–100.

Chung, I.-J., Hawkins, J. D., Gilchrist, L. D., Hill, K. G., & Nagin, D. S. (2002a). Identifying and predicting offending trajectories among poor children. *Social Service Review, 76*(4), 663–685.

Chung, I.-J., Hawkins, J. D., Gilchrist, L. D., Hill, K. G., & Nagin, D. S. (2002b). Childhood predictors of offense trajectories. *Journal of Research in Crime and Delinquency, 39*(1), 60–90.

Fergusson, D. M., Horwood, L. J., & Nagin, D. S. (2000). Offending trajectories in a New Zealand birth cohort. *Criminology, 38*(2), 525–551.

Ganzeboom, H. B. G. (2010). *International standard classification of occupations.* ISCO-08. With ISEI-08 scores. http://www.harryganzeboom.nl/isco08/isco08_with_isei.pdf

Ge, X., Brody, G. H., Conger, R. D., Simons, R. L., & Murry, V. M. (2002). Contextual amplification of pubertal transition effects on deviant peer affiliation and externalizing behavior among African American children. *Developmental Psychology*, *38*(1), 42–54.

Gore, S., Kadish, S. J., & Aseltine, R. H. (2003). Career centered high school education and post-high school career adaptation. *American Journal of Community Psychology*, *32*(1–2), 77–88.

Gottfredson, M. R., & Hirschi, T. (1990). *A general theory of crime*. Stanford, CA: Stanford University Press.

Hirschi, T. (1969). *Causes of delinquency*. Berkeley, CA: University of California Press.

Hoeve, M., Blokland, A., Dubas, J. S., Loeber, R., Gerris, J. R. M., & van der Laan, P. H. (2008). Trajectories of delinquency and parenting styles. *Journal of Abnormal Child Psychology*, *36*(2), 223–235.

Jolliffe, D., Farrington, D. P., Piquero, A. R., Loeber, R., & Hill, K. G. (2017). Systematic review of early risk factors for life-course-persistent, adolescence-limited, and late-onset offenders in prospective longitudinal studies. *Aggression and Violent Behavior*, *33*, 15–23.

Jones, B. L., Nagin, D. S. & Roeder, K. (2001). A SAS procedure based on mixture models for estimating developmental trajectories. *Sociological Methods and Research*, *29*(3), 374–393.

Kerridge, B. T., Chou, S. P., Huang, B., & Harford, T. C. (2020). Sociodemographic characteristics, adverse childhood experiences and substance use and psychiatric disorders among adolescent-limited, adult-onset, life-course-persistent offenders and non-offenders in a general population survey. *Crime and Delinquency*, *66*(12), 1729–1753.

Kessler, G. (2020). Delinquency in emerging adulthood: Insights into trajectories of young adults in a German sample and implications for measuring continuity of offending. *Journal of Developmental and Life-Course Criminology*, *6*(4), 424–447.

Laub, J. H., & Sampson, R. J. (2006). *Shared beginnings, divergent lives: Delinquent boys to age 70*. Cambridge, MA: Harvard University Press.

Lin, K., & Lee, C. (2013). The attrition trajectory analysis. *Paper presented at the 5th conference on Taiwan youth Project, Taipei, 28–29 November*.

Lin, K., Lin, D., & Hsieh, P. (2009). The attrition analysis of the Taiwan youth Project. *Paper presented at the 3rd youth conference of Taiwan youth Project, Taipei, 4–5 December*.

Loeber, R. (1982). The stability of antisocial and delinquent child behavior: A review. *Child Development*, *53*(6), 1431–1446.

Loeber, R., & Le Blanc, M. (1990). Toward a developmental criminology. In M. Tonry & N. Morris (Eds.), *Crime and justice*. Chicago, IL: University of Chicago Press.

Lynne-Landsman, S. D., Graber, J. A., & Andrews, J. A. (2010). Do trajectories of household risk in childhood moderate pubertal timing effects on substance initiation in middle school?. *Developmental Psychology*, *46*(4), 853–868.

Maughan, B., & Rutter, M. (1998). Continuities and discontinuities in antisocial behavior from childhood to adult life. *Advances in Clinical Child Psychology, 20,* 1–47.

Moffitt, T. E. (1993). Adolescent-limited and life-course-persistent antisocial behavior: A developmental taxonomy. *Psychological Review, 100*(4), 301–326.

Moffitt, T. E. (1997). Adolescence-limited and life-course-persistent offending: A complementary pair of developmental theories. In T. P. Thornberry (Ed.), *Developmental theories of crime and delinquency.* Piscataway, NJ: Transaction Publishers.

Moffitt, T. E. (2006). Life-course persistent versus adolescence-limited antisocial behavior. In D. Cicchetti & D. Cohen (Eds.), *Developmental psychopathology* (2nd ed., pp. 570–598). New York, NY: John Wiley.

Murray, J., Irving, B., Farrington, D. P., Colman, I., & Bloxsom, C. A. (2010). Very early predictors of conduct problems and crime: Results from a national cohort study. *Journal of Child Psychology and Psychiatry, 51*(11), 1198–1207.

Muthén, B. O. (2002). Second-generation structural equation modeling with a combination of categorical and continuous latent variables. In L. M. Collins & A. G. Sayer (Eds.), *New methods for the analysis of change.* Washington, DC: American Psychological Association.

Muthén, B. O. (2004). Latent variable analysis: Growth mixture modeling and related techniques for longitudinal data. In D. Kaplan (Ed.), *Handbook of quantitative methodology for the social sciences* (pp. 345–368). Newbury Park, CA: SAGE Publications.

Muthén, L. K., & Muthén, B. O. (1998–2017) *Mplus user's guide* (8th ed.). Los Angeles, CA: Muthén and Muthén.

Nagin, D. S. (1999). Analyzing developmental trajectories: A semiparametric, group-based approach. *Psychological Methods, 4*(2), 139.

Nagin, D. S. (2005). *Group-based modeling of development.* Cambridge, MA: Harvard University Press.

Nagin, D. S., & Land, K. C. (1993). Age, criminal careers, and population heterogeneity: Specification and estimation of a nonparametric, mixed Poisson model. *Criminology, 31*(3), 327–362.

Nagin, D. S., & Paternoster, R. (1991). On the relationship of past to future participation in delinquency. *Criminology, 29*(2), 163–189.

Nylund, K. L., Asparouhov, T., & Muthén, B. O. (2007). Deciding on the number of classes in latent class analysis and growth mixture modeling: A Monte Carlo simulation study. *Structural Equation Modeling: A Multidisciplinary Journal, 14*(4), 535–569.

Odgers, C. L., Moffitt, T. E., Broadbent, J. M., Dicson, N., Hancox, R. J., Harrington, H., et al. (2008). Female and male antisocial trajectories: From childhood origins to adult outcomes. *Development and Psychopathology, 20*(2), 673–716.

Patterson, G. R., Reid, J. B., & Dishion, T. J. (1992). *Antisocial boys.* Eugene, OR: Castalia.

Pedersen, W., Hart, R. K., Moffitt, T. E., & von Soest, T. (2020). Delinquency abstainers in adolescence and educational and labor market outcomes in midlife: A population-based 25-year longitudinal study. *Developmental Psychology*, *56*(11), 2167–2176.

Piquero, A. R., & Brezins, T. (2001). Testing Moffitt's account of adolescence-limited delinquency. *Criminology*, *39*(2), 353–370.

Robins, L. N. (1978). Study childhood predictors of adult antisocial behavior: Replications from longitudinal studies. *Psychological Medicine*, *8*(4), 611–622.

Rutter, M., & Rutter, M. (1993). *Developing minds: Challenge and continuity across the life span*. London: Penguin Books Ltd.

Sampson, R. J., & Laub, J. H. (1992). Crime and deviance in the life course. *Annual Review of Sociology*, *18*(1), 63–84.

Sampson, R. J., & Laub, J. H. (1993). *Crime in the making: Pathways and turning points through life*. Cambridge, MA: Harvard University Press.

Schulenberg, J. E., Maggs, J. L., & O'Malley, P. M. (2003). How and why the understanding of developmental continuity and discontinuity is important: The sample case of long-term consequences of adolescent substance use. In J. T. Mortimer & M. J. Shanahan (Eds.), *Handbook of the life course* (pp. 413–436). New York, NY: Kluwer Academic/Plenum Publishers.

Shelton, K. H., & Van Den Bree, M. B. (2010). The moderating effects of pubertal timing on the longitudinal associations between parent–child relationship quality and adolescent substance use. *Journal of Research on Adolescence*, *20*(4), 1044–1064.

Simons, R. L., Stewart, E., Gordon, L. C., Conger, R. D., & Elder, G. H. Jr. (2002). A test of life-course explanations for stability and change in antisocial behavior from adolescence to young adulthood. *Criminology*, *40*(2), 401–433.

StataCorp. (2021). *Stata statistical software: Release 17*. College Station, TX: StataCorp LLC.

Tang, M.-C. (2018). *Heterogeneous trajectories of deviant behaviors: The influences of perceived social support and personal characteristics*. Master's thesis. Taipei: National Taiwan Normal University.

van der Geest, V., Blokland, A., & Bijleveld, C. (2009). Delinquent developmental in a sample of high-risk youth: Shape, content, and predictors of delinquent trajectories from age 12 to 32. *Journal of Research in Crime and Delinquency*, *46*(2), 111–143.

Warr, M. (1998). Life-course transitions and desistance from crime. *Criminology*, *36*(2), 183–216.

Weng, G. (2008). *Research of deviant peers, negative emotions, and efficacy impact on the juvenile delinquency development*. Master's thesis. Chiayi: National Chung Cheng University.

Wickrama, K. K. A. S., & Bryant, C. M. (2003). Community context of social resources and adolescent mental health. *Journal of Marriage and Family*, *65*(4), 850–866.

Wickrama, K. K. A. S., Lee, T. K., O'Neal, C. W., & Kwon, J. A. (2015). Stress and resource pathways connecting early socioeconomic adversity to young adults' physical health risk. *Journal of Youth and Adolescence*, *44*(5), 1109–1124.

Wickrama, K. K. A. S., Merten, M. J., & Elder, G. H. Jr. (2005). Community influence on adolescent precocious development: Racial differences and mental health consequences. *Journal of Community Psychology, 33*(6), 639–653.

Wiesner, M., & Capaldi, D. M. (2003). Relations of childhood and adolescent factors to offending trajectories of young men. *Journal of Research in Crime and Delinquency, 40*(3), 231–262.

Wiesner, M., & Silbereisen, R. K. (2003). Trajectories of delinquent behavior in adolescence and their covariates: Relations with initial and time-averaged factors. *Journal of Adolescence, 26*(6), 753–771.

Part VI

Transition to Adulthood in Japan, South Korea and China

12

School-to-Work Transition Among High School Students in Japan: School-mediated System and Labour Market Outcomes

Hiroshi Ishida

Introduction

The topics of economic gaps and social inequality have received renowned attention in the 1990s in Japan (Chiavacci, 2008; Ishida and Miwa, 2009, 2011; Ishida and Slater, 2009; Ohtake, 2005; Ohtake and Saito, 1998; Sato, 2000; Tachibanaki, 1998). Labour economist Yuji Genda's *A Nagging Sense of Job Insecurity* (2005) documented the increased uncertainty and decreased job security which were widespread among the younger generation in Japan. To maintain the employment security of the older generation, the younger Japanese generation was deprived of favourable employment and promotion opportunities. Indeed, there is a clear increase both in the unemployment rate among youth and in the proportion of young people who are engaged in non-standard forms of employment, such as part-time and non-regular work (Kosugi, 2003, 2005, 2010; Tarohmaru, 2006). Thus, there is the emergence of an increased differentiation among the younger population, beginning in the 1990s.

Entry into the labour market marks the beginning of the differentiation of youth, and the school-to-work transition is the key process sorting young people into differential positions. The transition from school to work is particularly relevant in Japan because of the emphasis on long-term employment and internal promotion among large Japanese companies (Koike, 1988; Sugayama, 2011). There is a strong impact of the entry positions on the subsequent life courses and occupational trajectories (Ishida, 1993; Kondo, 2007).

This study examines the process of obtaining a job after school, and how it is related to social inequality. I will examine the activities leading to a job and their impact on the outcomes of the job search. In examining the process of transition from school to work, I will focus on the role played by school institutions in matching students and jobs. Japanese schools have been well known for their active role in mediating the job-matching process (Brinton, 2010; Chiavacci, 2005; Oshima, 2012). Recent observations by the Japanese mass media and academic fields alike emphasize changes in the process of this transition in Japan. Some argue that the traditional assistance provided by schools has disappeared, and individual students are left alone to find their own strategies in the job search. The key terms among the proponents of change are individual choice and responsibility. With the influence of neo-liberal thinking, individual youth are expected to take the initiative in their job search, without relying on the existing institutions, and at the same time they are expected to take full responsibility of the outcomes of their search.

Honda (2005) claims that around the mid-1990s, the school-mediated transition to work which is characteristic of Japanese society began to crumble and threatened to collapse. Schools were no longer equipped to assist students. In addition to the macro-economic condition, Honda blames the school-mediated transition for the deterioration of employment opportunities among the young people and claims that schools should no longer act as a mediator. The school-mediated job search system deprives students of the freedom and responsibility to choose their occupational destiny. Honda (2005, 2009) concludes that schools failed to impart skills that are relevant to occupational success, and that employers bore the cost of training students with necessary skills. Schools focused on establishing long-term relationships with employers at the expense of preparing high school students for long-term occupational careers. Students concentrated on receiving good grades and attendance records which led to recommendations from their school to advantageous companies. However, they were deprived of the opportunity to acquire occupational skills which are necessary for obtaining long-term occupational careers.

These claims regarding significant changes regarding the role of school often require heavy qualifications. Other recent studies do not support the idea of the breakdown of the school-mediated transition to the workforce (Brinton, 2010; Ishida, 2014; Ogawa, 2021). Schools continue to aid students, and the breakdown of school-mediated transition is greatly overestimated. I argue that the process of obtaining a job is embedded in the existing institutions, and further that those institutions, namely schools, can help alleviate the formation of social inequality. The apparent changes that are often emphasized in the media are not accurately representative of the underlying mechanism.

Transition From School to Work

Japan has been praised for its low level of youth unemployment and the smooth transition from school to work up until the mid-1990s. Japanese students have been generally successful in moving into the labour market in an orderly fashion, immediately following school graduation. The main reason for this successful transition was ascribed to the active role played by schools in the process of matching students and jobs. The prototype of the school-mediated transition originated in the 1950s (Kariya et al., 2000; Sugayama, 2011) and was firmly established in the 1980s (Kariya, 1991).

Table 12.1 shows the result of a survey conducted in the late-1980s by the National Institute of Employment and Occupational Research (Koyo Shokugyo Sogo Kenkyusho, 1989). Cross-national comparisons highlight the distinctive characteristics of the Japanese transition from school to work. It shows cross-national differences in the methods used for finding jobs after school completion. In Japan, the overwhelming majority of students used the school placement office. In the US and Britain, advertisements and personal contacts were the most popular methods. The cross-national difference is especially striking among high school students.

There are several features which characterize the school-to-work transition among Japanese high school students (Brinton, 2010; Kariya, 1991; Kariya and Rosenbaum, 1987, 1995; Rosenbaum et al., 1990; Rosenbaum and Kariya, 1989):

1. The schedule is highly regulated by the rules set forth by the government. The schedule regarding the transition begins in the middle of the senior year and continues until the graduation date in March. The Japanese academic year begins in April and ends in March. The job search takes

Table 12.1 Methods used for searching jobs by education for three countries (multiple answers)

	Relatives	Friends	Booklets magazines	Ads	Public offices	Schools	Private agencies	Other
Japan								
Secondary education	22.4	11.7	4.9	6.6	4.5	62.6	0.9	3.7
Higher education	25.1	15.8	19.5	13.0	4.0	59.6	3.4	11.6
United States								
Secondary education	41.1	35.5	0.0	45.8	15.7	13.8	8.4	30.1
Higher education	38.4	36.1	0.0	56.2	16.4	46.6	14.6	27.4
Britain								
Secondary education	37.6	29.8	0.0	48.7	15.2	42.3	25.9	12.1
Higher education	18.1	25.0	0.0	68.1	14.7	36.2	21.6	11.2

Source: National Institute of Employment and Occupational Research (Koyo Shokugyo Sogo Kenkyusho). *Seishonen no Shokugyo Tekiyo nikansuru Kokusai Hikaku Kenkyu* (International Comparative Study of Occupational Adjustment of Young People) (Tokyo: Koyo Shokugyo Sogo Kenkyusho, 1989).

place while students are still in school. Furthermore, important dates are determined in advance. For example, every year, June 20th is designated as the starting date for employers to submit hiring forms to the Public Employment Security Office, the agency under the Ministry of Health, Labour, and Welfare. Employers must fill out the hiring forms if they are interested in hiring high school seniors who are expected to graduate the following spring. The Public Employment Security Office checks the hiring forms to ensure they comply with regulations prescribed by the Labour Standard Law. These forms are forwarded from the Public Employment Office to high schools beginning July 1st. High schools match students to employers and submit recommendation forms to employers beginning September 5. Interviews and the formal screening process of job candidates cannot begin until September 16; employers are prohibited from engaging in any recruiting activities until that date to avoid pre-selection by employers.

2. The opportunities of employment differ depending on the high school.
   The opportunities of employment for high school students are determined by which high school the students happen to attend, because the job openings are not equally distributed among different schools. Employers are allowed to designate the schools to which the job announcements are sent from the Public Employment Office. In order words, it is not a system that allows individual students to apply to a company, but rather a system in which students must apply through schools. Thus, if the school where students attend does not receive a job opening announcement, he/she does not have a chance to be hired by this company.

3. Students can only apply to one company at a time.
   Students can only apply to one company at a time, at least in the first round of applications. To assure fairness among students, and to make sure that a particular student does not receive multiple offers, schools regulate the application process. Because students can only apply to companies through their school's recommendation, schools are able to regulate the process and use the 'one-student-one-company' allocation rule. For this system to work, when a student is offered a job by the recommended company, he/she is expected to accept the offer.

4. Schools select students who can apply to particular companies.
   Schools select among students usually based on meritocratic criteria to determine which student is recommended to a particular company. Since it is possible that many students are interested in the same company, schools must have a selection procedure to restrict the candidates. In selecting the nominees, schools normally use grades and attendance records.

5. There is a long-term relationship between employers and schools.
   There is a long-term relationship between particular employers and particular high schools, due to the repeated transaction of recommendation and hiring. Some employers are willing to hire students from the same high school repeatedly and ask the high schools to recommend the students to them. In return for job openings, high schools try to make sure to recommend students every year. Because of the long-term relationship, employers value the recommendations highly and almost always hire students recommended by the schools. In return, high schools do not recommend students who do not meet employers' specifications, even though that may mean not recommending any students in a particular year.
6. The job search process is completed before graduation.
   Most students who intended to work after graduation complete the job search process while still in school, and they begin their employment immediately following the school graduation on April 1st. Unlike other industrial nations where the job search process of many young people continues after school graduation, Japanese students know their destinations prior to the completion of education.

This is a very intriguing system which has been in place for quite a long time, its historical origins set in the late 1940s (Kariya et al., 2000; Sugayama, 2011). Recently, however, the school-mediated system has been subject to criticism. Hori (2016) claims that the practice of delegated selection by schools and long-term relationship between employers and schools was not as widespread as earlier studies (e.g. Kariya, 1991) indicated. There were also regional variations in the practice of school mediation. Otawa (2014) argues that the assistance provided by schools was characterized as 'school-led selection and allocation' in the 1980s but it has now changed to 'student-centred support' which emphasizes consultation with students rather than allocation of students. Hori (2016) shows that high schools characterized by 'student-centred support' are mostly found in metropolitan areas and are not widely spread across the nation.

In this study, I concentrate on the question of whether this kind of school-mediated system still exists in contemporary Japan, and whether the system makes a difference in the outcomes (that is, the kinds of jobs students obtain). Before presenting empirical findings, I will first provide some background information.

Figure 12.1 shows the trends of destinations of high school graduates (percentage by destinations after high school graduation).

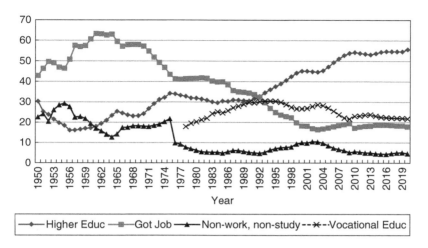

Figure 12.1 Destinations of high school graduates, 1950–2020
Source: Ministry of Education, *Gakko Kihon Chosa* [School Basic Surveys] (Tokyo: Ministry of Education, various years)

Obtaining a job following high school graduation constituted the most popular destination until the 1980s. However, the rate has declined sharply due to the expansion of the higher education sector during the 1990s, and today about 20 per cent of high school graduates obtain full-time jobs and move directly into the labour market. Figure 12.2 presents the ratios of job openings to job applicants for high school graduates. If the ratio is 1.0, this means that the number of job openings is equal to the number of job applicants, and ratios greater than 1 mean that there are more job openings than applicants. Although the ratios over this period are all greater than 1, the ratio has always been below 2 since the mid-1990s except for the last four years, reflecting the economic downturn.

It is therefore true that the number and proportion of high school students who go through the school-mediated job search process have been decreasing, and the labour market for high school graduates has been stagnating from the mid-1990s to early part of 2010s. However, this does not necessarily mean that the school-mediated process has completely broken down, or that the advantages associated with the school-mediated process have disappeared. I will argue that high school students continue to use school-mediated process to find first jobs, and that the labour market benefits of school-mediated transition persist.

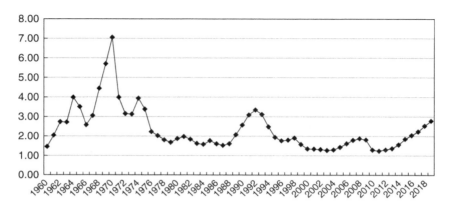

Figure 12.2   Rate of job openings to job applicants for high school graduates 1955–2019
Source: Shokugyo Anteikyoku, Ministry of Health, Labor, and Welfare, *Shinki Gakusotsusha no Rodo Shijyo* [Labor Market of New Graduates] (Tokyo: Ministry of Health, Labor, and Welfare, various years)

Data and Variables

The dataset for this study comes from the Japanese Life Course Panel Surveys (JLPS). The JLPS is a panel study which follows up young people who were aged 20–34 in 2007 (the youth sample) and the middle-aged who were 35–40 in 2007 (the middle-aged sample) in Japan. The first wave of the JLPS was conducted between January and April of 2007. The youth and middle-aged samples were drawn from the population using the electoral and resident registries so that they are representative of the respective age groups in the population. The questionnaires were sent by mail to those who agreed to take part in the first and follow-up surveys. The staff from a professional survey organization picked up the questionnaires at a later date. The response rate for the youth sample was 35 per cent, with 3,367 responses, and the response rate for the middle-aged sample was 40 per cent, with 1,433 responses. The JLPSs have been conducted every year since 2007, and the retention rates have been about 80 per cent for the youth sample and 87 per cent for the middle-aged sample (see Ishida et al., 2008, 2009, and Yamamoto and Ishida 2010 for details of the JLPS).

The supplementary sample was added in 2011 to compensate for the attrition in the original sample drawn in 2007. The respondents were drawn from the same population and with the same method as the 2007 respondents. However, the questionnaires were sent and returned by mail, not collected by the staff from a survey organization due to financial reasons. The response rate for the youth sample was 32 per cent, with 710 responses, and the response rate for the middle-aged sample was 31 per cent, with 253 responses. These respondents have been followed up every year since 2011.

In 2019 the refresh youth sample aged 20–31 in 2019 was added because the original respondents were already 32–52 in 2019. The refresh sample allows us to compare the youth aged 20–31 in 2007 and 2019. The sampling methods were identical to the 2007 survey, and the questionnaires were sent by mail and collected by the staff from a professional survey organization at a later date. The response rate for the refresh sample was 31 per cent, with 2049 responses. These respondents have been followed up every year since 2019.

My analyses targeted respondents who graduated from high school and began employment because I focused on the transition from high school to work. Those who went on for further education (technical schools, junior colleges and universities) were excluded from the analyses. The respondents in the 2007 original survey, the 2011 supplementary survey and the 2019 refresh survey were combined. There were 1,855 high school graduates with valid responses to the school mediation question.

The use of the school-mediated job search is the main independent variable. It was determined by the following survey question: 'how did you get to know your first job?' The following responses were coded as school mediation: 'through teachers at schools where you graduated (including school recommendation)'. The proportion represents those who found their first job through schools.

There are four outcome variables: the timing of the start of the first job, whether the first job was something the respondent desired, the firm size of the first job and the employment status of the first job. The survey did not ask the question of entry wages. Respondents who began working immediately following school graduation were given the score of 1 and zero otherwise. Over 85 per cent of the respondents began working immediately after graduation. Respondents who never worked after school graduation were excluded from the analysis. Respondents were asked if their first job was the job which they had desired before they started working. Those who replied positively to this question were given a score of 1 and 0 otherwise. About one half of the respondents had a score of 1. The firm size of the first place of employment was classified into two groups: (1) large firms with 300 or more employees and the public sector and (2) small firms which employed less than 300 employees. About 40 per cent of respondents worked in large firms. Finally, the employment status of the first job was classified into two groups: (1) regular employment and (2) non-regular employment. Regular employment includes managers and owners, employees working full-time, and self-employed and family workers. Non-regular employment includes those who worked part-time, temporary staff, contract workers and those with side jobs. About 80 per cent of the respondents had regular employment.

Several control variables are used in my analyses. Two demographic variables, gender of the respondent and birth cohort, are included. The respondents were divided into three cohorts: those born between 1987 and 1998 (those who were aged 20–31 in 2019), those born between 1975 and 1986 (those who were aged 20–31 in 2007) and those born between 1966 and 1974 (those who were aged 32–40 in 2007). The comparison of the first two cohorts implies the change among the same age group (aged 21–31) between 2007 and 2019.

Five variables are introduced as social backgrounds. The father's and the mother's education take the score of 1 when the respondents' fathers and mothers attended institutions of higher education (both junior colleges and universities) and 0 otherwise. Dummy variables indicating missing on the father's and the mother's education are also included. The living standard when the respondents were 15 years old takes the value from 1 poor to 5 wealthy. The number of books at home is used as a measure of cultural resources at home. The atmosphere at home captures how warm the home environment was when the respondent was growing up and takes the values of 1 'not warm', 2 'if anything, not warm', 3 'if anything, warm' and 4 'warm atmosphere'. Finally, two school characteristics are introduced as control. The type of high school where the respondent attended is classified into two groups: (1) academic high schools and (2) vocational and other high schools. High school grade is used as a control variable, classified as either above average or otherwise. The statistical methods used in this paper are cross-tabulation, ordinary least-square regression and logistic regression.

Findings

Figure 12.3 shows the percentage of high school graduates who used schools to obtain their first job after high school by birth cohort. There are slight variations in the percentage by cohort: 51 per cent of high school graduates in the youngest birth cohort (born from 1987 to 1998) which corresponds to the refresh youth sample (respondents aged 20–31 in 2019), 40 per cent in the 1975–1986 birth cohort (respondents aged 20–31 in 2007) and 46 per cent in the 1966–1974 birth cohort (respondents aged 32–40 in 2007). Even among the youngest cohort, the majority of high school graduates still relied on schools in their job search. The evidence is not consistent with the claim that the school-mediated job search has completely disappeared in recent times.

We next examine the outcomes of the job search and observe whether there were any differences between school-mediated searches and non-mediated searches. The first outcome examined is whether high school graduates were able to start working immediately following graduation. Figure 12.4 shows that 97–99 per cent of those

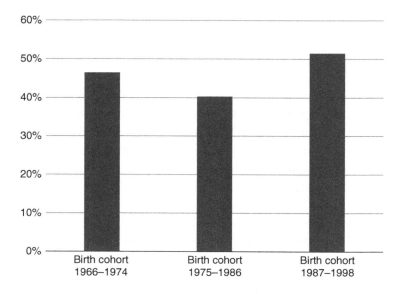

Figure 12.3 School mediation rate among high school graduates by birth cohort (%)

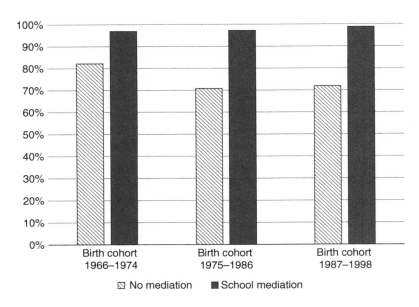

Figure 12.4   School mediation and the timing of start of first job

who found their first jobs through school started working on April 1st, immediately following graduation, while the percentages for those who found their first jobs without the assistance of school are much less: 71 per cent for the two youngest samples and 82 per cent for the middle-aged sample. Schools seem to help the smooth transition to work among high school students.

The second outcome is whether the respondent's first job was his or her preference (Figure 12.5). The majority (51 per cent of the youngest cohort, 59 per cent of the next youngest cohort and 57 per cent of the middle-aged cohort) of those who found their first jobs through school reported that their jobs were their first preference. The percentage is much smaller for those who did not use the school to find their first jobs.

Two other types of outcomes are considered. Figure 12.6 shows the firm size of the first job. The percentage of those who found their first jobs in large firms (those with more than 300 employees) and the public sector is clearly different between graduates who used the school to find jobs and those who did not. The percentage of those who worked in large firms and the public sector are at least 15 per cent higher among students who used school assistance.

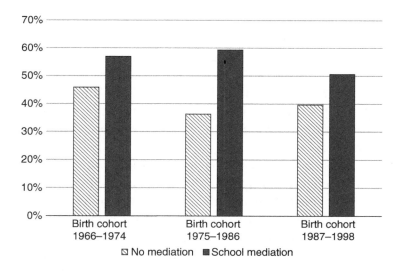

Figure 12.5 School mediation and whether the first job was first preference

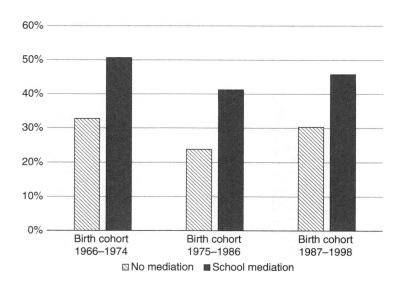

Figure 12.6 School mediation and firm size (percentage worked in large firms and public sector)

Finally, the percentage of those who found full-time regular employment is shown according to whether the respondent used the school to find a job or not (Figure 12.7). Among the middle-aged sample, the difference is 25 per cent. However, among the two youngest cohorts, school mediation made a large difference. If high school graduates did not use the school mediation process, their chances of finding a regular job were greatly reduced by more than 40 per cent to 50 per cent.

All these results lead us to conclude that school mediation offers significantly better job opportunities in contemporary Japan. The effects of school mediation are still apparent even among the youngest cohort, and there is no clear sign of the effects being reduced in the recent period. Although the effects of school mediation on four outcomes are striking, there is the possibility that those who used school mediation are already specific kinds of people. For example, if students who used school mediation are those who were more able and had good grades, and if students who did not use school mediation are those who were not successful in academic work, then the effect of school mediation is likely to be overestimated. The effect may simply reflect the fact that students who used school mediation were able students to begin with and that it is not the school mediation which

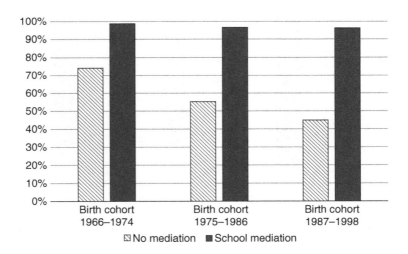

Figure 12.7 School mediation and employment status (percentage of students who obtained regular employment)

produced the apparent effect. Since school grades are used as one of the important criteria for internal selection of students, we must consider the possibility that the academic achievement of students is responsible for the effect of school mediation.

Figure 12.8 shows the relationship between school grades and the use of school mediation. It is indeed the case that students with above-average grades are more likely to use school mediation in their job search than those with lower grades.

Another confounding factor which we need to take into account is school types. If the students from a particular type of school are more likely to use school mediation than those from other types of school, then the effect of mediation is likely to be overestimated by the effect of school types. Figure 12.9 shows the relationship between school types and the use of school mediation. Students from vocational schools are more likely to use school-mediated placement than those from academic schools, probably because vocational schools tend to have stronger long-term linkages with particular employers than academic schools. This difference is more pronounced among high school graduates who left school in recent periods.

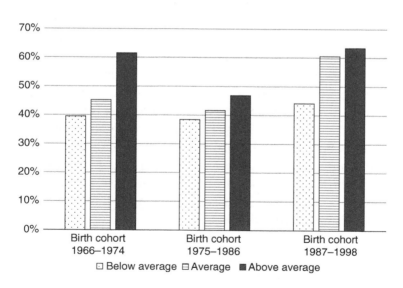

Figure 12.8 School mediation rate and high school grade by birth cohort

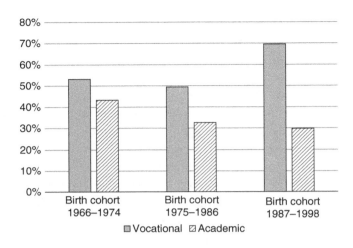

Figure 12.9 School mediation rate and high school types by birth cohort

I now address the question about the apparent effect of school mediation can be explained by school grades and school types. To do this, I examine the effect of school mediation after controlling for (1) gender and cohort, (2) gender, cohort and social background and (3) all variables including school type and school grade. These factors are assumed to be causally prior to school mediation. By controlling for these factors, we can estimate the net causal effect of school mediation.

Figure 12.10 presents the effects of school mediation on the timing of obtaining first jobs after various controls are introduced. The results are based on running a series of OLS regression without and with different control variables. I show the results of combing three birth cohorts because the results are consistent across three cohorts. The bars indicate the difference in the percentage of high school graduates who obtained their first job immediately following graduation between those who used mediation and those who did not. When there is no control, the difference is about 22 per cent: students who found their first jobs through school mediation are 22 per cent more likely to start working immediately after graduation than those who found jobs without the assistance of school. The effects of school mediation hardly change after the introduction of various controls. Even after controlling for all the causally prior variables, the difference is 19 per cent.

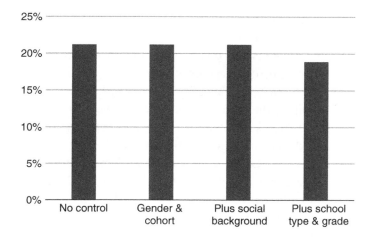

Figure 12.10 Effect of school mediation on the timing of first job after various control

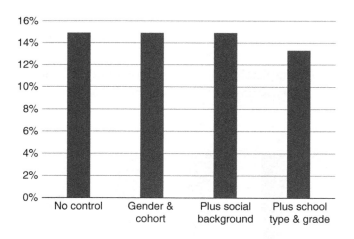

Figure 12.11 Effect of school mediation on first job preference after various control

Figure 12.11 shows the effect of school mediation on whether the first jobs were the students' first preference. The effect of school mediation hardly changes from 15 per cent with no control to 13 per cent with all control variables. The effect of school mediation on the first job preference appears to be smaller than its effect on the timing of starting the first job, but it is still significant and does not change by the introduction of controls.

Figure 12.12 presents the effect of school mediation on firm size. When there is no control, the school mediation increases the chances of being employed in large firms by 18 per cent, while after all variables are controlled, the same chances are 13 per cent. Although the magnitude of the effects is not substantial, these effects are statistically significant, and do not change greatly even with controls.

Figure 12.13 presents the effects of school mediation on employment status. The effect is substantial when compared with the effect on firm size: school mediation increases the chances of regular employment by 36 per cent when there is no control and by 34 per cent when all the variables are controlled. Again, the size of the effect does not change very much after the introduction of control variables.

All these figures indicate that the effects of school mediation are largely independent of gender, cohort, school type and most importantly, school grade. Although students with good grades are more likely to use school mediation, the benefits of school mediation are apparent both for students with good grades and those without good grades.

We cannot completely rule out the possibility of unobserved heterogeneity between students who used mediation and those who did

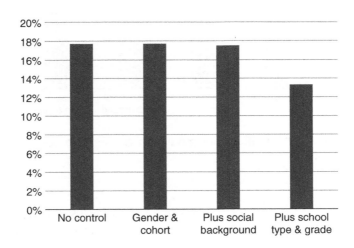

Figure 12.12   Effect of school mediation on firm size after various control

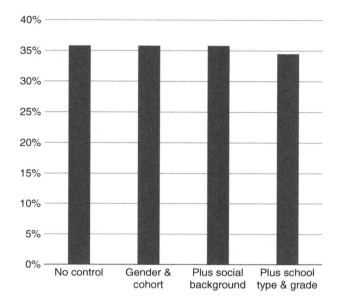

Figure 12.13 Effect of school mediation on employment status after various control

not. However, at least drawing from the measurements available in the survey, the effects of school mediation are robust and are not greatly affected by factors which are causally prior to school mediation.

Finally, I consider the question of who actually uses the school-mediated search. In particular, I examine whether the use of the school-mediated job search is related to students' social backgrounds. Figure 12.14 presents the results of running the logistic regression of the use of school mediation on a range of social background variables. The dots indicate the estimates (log odds ratios), and the lines indicate the 95 per cent confidence interval. None of the social background variables exert significant effects at 5 per cent significance level. The effect of living standard when the respondent was 15 years old is significant at 10 per cent level: the higher the economic well-being, the lower the likelihood of using the school-mediated placement. Students from economically advantaged families may have familial resources to assist students and are less likely to use the assistance from schools than those from economically disadvantaged families. Therefore, the access of school-mediated assistance appears

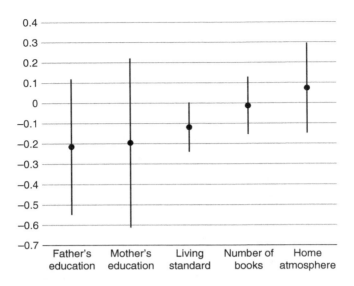

Figure 12.14   Social background and the use of school mediation

to be open to everyone regardless of social background. High schools, which mediate the job-matching process among students, are indeed providing assistance to all high school graduates including those from less advantaged families, and possibly alleviating the negative consequences associated with coming from disadvantaged backgrounds.

Conclusions

This study examined the process of the transition from high school to work among young Japanese people. It focused on the role of schools in shaping the unequal distribution of the outcomes of their first jobs. Previous studies pointed out that Japanese schools played an active role in mediating the job-matching process among students. However, some recent observations by the Japanese mass media and academics emphasized changes in the process of transition in Japan. Some argue that the traditional assistance provided by schools has disappeared and that schools are no longer able to influence the outcomes of the job search. Schools are unable to assist students in providing favourable job outcomes when the students leave school. Without institutional support, students are left with harsh labour market conditions and suffer from deteriorating employment opportunities.

These recent remarks are empirically evaluated by this study. The evidence of this study suggests that Japanese schools continue to play an active role in matching students to jobs, and that there is no apparent decline in the use of the school-mediated system or the effects of using such a system. The idea of the breakdown of the school-mediated transition to work does not receive much empirical support.

Critics of the school-mediated system claim that schools should not adopt the responsibility of placing students because they interfere with the notions of individual freedom and responsibility. However, these critics do not fully recognize the fact that the students coming from less advantaged social origins are those who benefit most from the school-mediated system because the access to the assistance provided by school is not restricted by social backgrounds. Dismantling the system will further disadvantage those who are already underprivileged in society.

In conclusion, I would like to stress the importance of the role played by institutions in understanding the transition experienced by Japanese youth. Institutions such as schools have the potential for affecting the life opportunities of the individual at particular transitional stages, breaking the cycle of cumulative disadvantages. The proportion of high school graduates who directly move into the labour market after graduation has been shrinking since the 1980s and stayed at about 18 per cent in the 2000s. They are clearly the socially disadvantaged minority who have limited educational resources. It is possible that Japanese schools have contributed to alleviating the reproduction of social inequality and acted as a safety net for the socially disadvantaged. Only through recognizing the role played by institutions are we able to understand the mechanisms through which social inequality is produced and reproduced in Japanese society.

Acknowledgements

This research was supported by Grant-in-Aid for Scientific Research (S) (grant numbers 18103003 and 22223005) and Specially Promoted Research (grant numbers 25000001 and 18H05204) from the Japan Society for the Promotion of Science. The research support in conducting the panel surveys is obtained from the Institute of Social Science, University of Tokyo and The Outsourcing, Inc. The permission to use the panel data is obtained from the Management Committee of the Japanese Life Course Panel Surveys. An earlier version of this study appeared as the Panel Survey Project Discussion Paper Series, Institute of Social Science, University of Tokyo.

References

Brinton, M. C. (2010). *Lost in transition: Youth, work, and instability in postindustrial Japan.* Cambridge: Cambridge University Press.

Chiavacci, D. (2005). Transition from university to work under transformation: The changing role of institutional and alumni networks in contemporary Japan. *Social Science Japan Journal*, *8*(1), 19–41.

Chiavacci, D. (2008). From class struggle to general middle class society to divided society. *Social Science Japan Journal*, *11*(1), 5–27.

Genda, Y. (2005). *A nagging sense of job insecurity: The new reality facing Japanese youth.* Tokyo: International House Press.

Honda, Y. (2005). *Wakamono to Shigoto: 'Gakkō Keiyu no Shūshoku' o Koete [Young people and employment in Japan: Beyond the 'school-mediated job search'].* Tokyo: University of Tokyo Press.

Honda, Y. (2009). *Kyoiku no Shokugyoteki Igi [Occupational significance of education].* Tokyo: Chikuma Shobo.

Hori, Y. (2016). *Koko Shushoku Shido no Shakaigaku [Sociology of occupational guidance in high school].* Tokyo: Keiso Shobo.

Ishida, H. (1993). *Social mobility in contemporary Japan.* Stanford, CA: Stanford University Press.

Ishida, H., & Miwa, S. (2009). "Kaiso Ido karamita Nihon Shakai" [Class mobility and Japanese society]. Shakaigaku Hyoron [Japanese Sociological Review], *59*(4), 648–662.

Ishida, H., & Miwa, S. (2011). Jyoso Howaitokara no Saiseisan [Reproduction of upper white-collar class]. In H. Ishida, H. Kondo & K. Nakao (Eds.), *Gendai no Kaiso Shakai 2 [Contemporary stratified society 2]* (pp. 21–35). Tokyo: University of Tokyo Press.

Ishida, H., Miwa, S., & Murakami, A. (2009). Hatarakikata to Raifusutairu no Henka nikansuru Zenkokuchosa (JLPS) 2008 nimiru Gendai Nihonjin no Raifusutairu to Ishiki [Japanese Life Course Panel Survey 2008 and life styles and opinions of Japanese people]. *Chuo Chosaho [Central Research Report]*, *616*, 1–7.

Ishida, H., Miwa, S., & Ohshima, M. (2008). Tokyo Daigaku Shakai Kagaku Kenkyusho no Paneru Chosa Nituite [On the panel survey of the Institute of Social Sciences, University of Tokyo: Results from the Japanese Life Course Panel Survey 2007]. *Chuo Chosaho [Central Research Report]*, *604*, 1–7.

Ishida, H., & Slater, D. (Eds). (2009). *Social class in contemporary Japan.* London: Routledge.

Ishida, K. (2014). Gakkokara Shokugyo eno Iko niokeru Seidoteki Renketsu Kouka no Saikento [Reconsidering the "institutional linkage" effect in the school to work transition process in Japan: A trend analysis on the first job turnover]. Kyoiku Shakaigaku Kenkyu [The Journal of Educational Sociology], *94*, 325–344.

Kariya, T. (1991). *Gakko Shokugyo Senbatsu no Shakaigaku [Sociology of schools, occupation, and selection].* Tokyo: University of Tokyo Press.

Kariya, T., & Rosenbaum, J. E. (1987). Self-selection in Japanese junior high schools: A longitudinal study of students' educational plans. *Sociology of Education*, *60*(3), 168–180.

Kariya, T., & Rosenbaum, J. E. (1995). Institutional linkages between education and work as Quasi-internal labor markets. *Research in Social Stratification and Mobility*, *14*, 99–134.

Kariya, T., Sugayama, S., & Ishida, H. (2000). *Gakko, Shokuan to Rodoshijyo [Schools, public employment offices, and the labor market]*. Tokyo: University of Tokyo Press.

Koike, K. (1988). *Understanding industrial relations in Japan*. London: Macmillan.

Kondo, A. (2007). Does the first job really matter? State dependency in employment status in Japan. *Journal of Japanese and International Economies*, *21*(3), 379–402.

Kosugi, R. (2003). *Furita toiu Ikikata [Freeter as a way of life]*. Tokyo: Keiso Shobo.

Kosugi, R. (Ed.) (2005). *Furita to Nito [Freeter and NEET]*. Tokyo: Keiso Shobo.

Kosugi, R. (2010). *Wakamono to Shoki Kyaria [Youth and early career]*. Tokyo: Keiso Shobo.

Koyo Shokugyo Sogo Kenkyusho [National Institute of Employment and Occupational Research]. (1989). *Seishonen no Shokugyo Tekiyo nikansuru Kokusai Hikaku Kenkyu [International comparative study of occupational adjustment of young people]*. Tokyo: National Institute of Employment and Occupational Research.

Ogawa, K. (2021). Gakko Keiyu no Shushoku no Kibo to Koka no Susei [Trends in the size and impact of school-mediated employment]. In T. Nakamura, S. Miwa & H. Ishida (Eds.), *Shoshi Korei Shakai no Kaiso Kozo 1 Jinsei Shoki no Kaiso Kozo [The structure of social stratification in the aged society with low fertility. 1. The structure of social stratification in the early stage of life]* (pp. 119–132). Tokyo: University of Tokyo Press.

Ohtake, F. (2005). *Nihon no Fubyodo [Japan's inequality]*. Tokyo: Nihon Keizai Shinbunsha.

Ohtake, F., & Saito, M. (1998). Population aging and consumption inequality in Japan. *Review of Income and Wealth*, *44*(3), 361–381.

Oshima, M. (2012). *Daigaku Shushokubu ni Dekirukoto [Things that can be done by college placement offices]*. Tokyo: Keiso Shobo.

Otawa, N. (2014). *Kokosei Bunka no Shakaigaku [Sociology of high school student culture]*. Tokyo: Yushindo.

Rosenbaum, J. E., & Kariya, T. (1989). From high school to work: Market and institutional mechanisms in Japan. *American Journal of Sociology*, *94*(6), 1334–1365.

Rosenbaum, J. E., Kariya, T., Settersten, R., & Maier, T. (1990). Market and network theories of the transition from high school to work: Their application to industrialized societies. *Annual Review of Sociology*, *16*, 263–299.

Sato, T. (2000). *Fubyodo Shakai Nihon [Japan as an unequal society]*. Tokyo: Chuokoronsha.

Sugayama, S. (2011). *'Shusha Shakai' no Tanjyo [The birth of a society based on entry firm]*. Nagoya: University of Nagoya Press.

Tachibanaki, T. (1998). *Nihon no Keizai Kakusa [Japan's economic inequality].* Tokyo: Iwanami Shoten.

Tarohmaru, H. (2006). *Furita to Nito no Shakaigaku [Sociology of freeter and neet].* Kyoto: Sekai Shisosha.

Yamamoto, K., & Ishida, H. (2010). *Hatarakikata to Raifukosu no Henka nikansuru Zenkoku Chosa no Keppyobunrui to Kaishujyokyo nikannsuru Shoshihyo no Kento [Final disposition codes and survey outcome rates for Japanese Life Course Panel Survey (JLPS)].* Panel survey project discussion paper series no. 34. Tokyo: Institute of Social Science, University of Tokyo.

13

No More Gender Gaps? Gendered Employment Patterns of Young College Graduates in South Korea Since 2000

Min Young Song and Ki-Soo Eun

Introduction

South Korea (hereafter Korea) is well known for its late but successful industrialization. Remarkable economic growth in the 1970s and 1980s ushered the country into the Organisation for Economic Co-operation and Development (OECD) in 1996. Since then, however, Korea has witnessed fundamental post-industrial changes to social institutions and the lives of individuals. In particular, two major shifts within the labour market created new conditions for young people transitioning to adulthood.

First of all, sluggish economic growth and neoliberal labour reform made the job market ever more competitive. This phenomenon is often found in post-industrial countries but is especially prominent in Korea, where there is strong dualism in the labour market (Ahn et al., 2019). Labour market dualism divides workers into primary and secondary workforces, limiting mobility and creating gaps in working conditions between them. In Korea, gaps between the labour markets, segmented according to firm size and employment type, emerged with the growth of conglomerates in the 1970s and 1980s and deepened with the spread of non-standard employment in the 1990s and 2000s (Lee, 2016; Song, 2014). Labour market dualism combined with the expansion of higher education has created excessive supply in the primary labour market and a supply shortage in the secondary labour market. This job market mismatch became further entrenched in Korea after the financial crisis in 1997, with large firms minimizing new hiring in permanent positions and job seekers becoming more reluctant to start a career at small-medium firms (Ahn et al., 2019).

Against this backdrop, the so-called millennial generation entered the labour market. They were born since the demographic shift in the 1980s when a two-child norm emerged in Korea – the total fertility rate dropped from 6.0 births per woman in 1960 to 4.1 in 1973 and 2.1 in 1983 (OECD, 2021a) – alongside the weakening of son preference. In addition, they were the first generation to achieve gender equality in education: the tertiary education rate of women aged 25–34 increased from 23.8 per cent in 1995, 50.9 per cent in 2005, and 75.7 per cent in 2018, overtaking men, who went from 33.6 per cent, 50.8 per cent and 63.8 per cent (OECD, 2021b). Given these distinctive demographic and educational trends, the millennial generation developed new ideas in gender roles: compared to older generations, they are more supportive of the egalitarian idea that men and women should contribute equally to the household economy, as well as care of the family (Song, 2011). With these intertwined changes in population, education and family values, a growing number of highly educated women joined the labour market since 2000, transforming the gender and educational composition of the labour force.

In this context, what changes have occurred in the employment patterns of young adults in Korea? This chapter provides one answer to this question, focusing on gender differences in the employment patterns of young college graduates who made the transition to adulthood from 2000. Drawing on nationally representative large-scale longitudinal data collected every year since 1998, we explore the patterns of first employment and career interruption of young college graduates. To explain, we construct survival-time datasets and examine gender differences in the instantaneous probabilities of college graduates getting a non-part-time job and leaving the labour market in their 20s and 30s. In doing so, we compare those born in the 1980s with those born in the 1970s to identify changes in the patterns of young adults' employment during the period in which Korea entered the post-industrial era.

This chapter comprises five sections. In the next section, we give an overview of the labour market structure of Korea, where we review the existing literature on labour market dualism, educational advancement, and policy responses since 2000. We also examine recent statistics to view gender employment gaps in Korea today from a comparative perspective. Next, the data and methods section outlines the data and our methodology. After assessing the representativeness of the data, we explain our analytic sample and survival-time datasets in detail. The results of our analysis are then presented via an overall analysis of the employment patterns and two subsections, where we plot the hazard rates of getting a non-part-time job and leaving the labour market, respectively, by birth cohort and gender. Finally, the conclusion summarizes our findings and concludes by discussing the implications of our study.

Labour Market Structure in the Post-Industrial Era in South Korea

Cross-national diversity of social institutions is often examined from a regime perspective accompanied by typology. For example, Esping-Andersen (1990) categorizes European capitalist countries as social democratic regimes, liberal regimes and conservative corporatist regimes. His later work discusses East Asian capitalist countries. Japan, for instance, is viewed as a conservative corporatist regime that provides labour market insiders with a higher level of social protection but offers outsiders lower-level social protection. Furthermore, the country is labelled as a 'variant' of the conservative corporatist regime because the position of individual workers in the labour market is decided by firm size, unlike European regimes of the same kind, where positions are primarily dependent on occupation (Esping-Andersen, 1997).

Despite some criticism of this classification (Estévez-Abe and Naldini, 2016), it is undeniable that Japan has some important characteristics in common with European conservative corporatist regimes, which are also shared by Korea (Peng, 2012), namely dualism in the labour market. In Korea, firm size emerged as a key factor in labour market inequalities during industrialization where the state mobilized economic resources on behalf of a handful of conglomerates in the 1970s. With the success of industrialization in the 1980s, gaps in working conditions between firms of different sizes grew, partly because workers at large firms were better organized to claim their share than those at small-medium firms.

In the late 1990s, Korea faced global pressure to implement neoliberal labour reform. Despite much resistance, it was pushed through as part of the bailout programme of the International Monetary Fund (IMF) after the financial crisis of 1997. The reforms created a massive number of non-standard jobs, expanding the size of the secondary labour market and further weakening working conditions for precarious workers, thereby deepening dualism in the labour market. In response, the Korean government strengthened social protection programmes. This effort largely failed, however, as most non-standard workers were excluded from the programmes mainly based on social insurance principles (Lee, 2016; Song, 2014; Yang, 2017; Yoon, 2019), whereby benefits are paid in line with contributions (taxes). For example, in 2019, only 43.1 per cent of non-standard workers were covered by employment insurance compared with 84.8 per cent of standard workers (Kim, 2020, pp. 23–26).

On the other hand, higher education has expanded to a great extent. The enrolment rate of the population aged 18–21 in tertiary education doubled every decade between 1980 and 2000 (from 11.4 per cent to 23.6 per cent and then 52.5 per cent); since 2010, about seven out of ten high school graduates have gone on to attend college (Statistics Korea, 2021). In other words, the vast majority of the population born in Korea since 1980 has received higher education. The entrance of these highly educated people into the labour market transformed the workforce, particularly the female workforce. Women born in the 1980s are not only as highly educated as men, but in the wave of globalization, they have also been influenced by individualism and feminism. Their college experiences inspired them to question traditional gender roles and prioritize their careers over marriage or motherhood (Kim et al., 2019, p. 3). In response, the Korean government improved maternity and parental leave and public childcare provision (Song, 2012). These were part of pronatalist but also women-friendly employment policies, including the creation of quality part-time jobs in the public sector and incentives for similar in the private sector, the introduction of flexible working and affirmative action (Song, 2016).

Despite the educational advancement and the policy support of the state, Korean women are significantly underemployed, especially those of childbearing age. This is often seen to result from gendered dualism in the labour market, which puts women in precarious employment and excludes them from opportunities to take child-related leave. In 2019, for example, half of women employees (50.5 per cent) were in non-standard employment, compared with one-third of men (34.5 per cent), and 55.6 per cent of non-standard workers had been employed less than one year by their current employers (Kim, 2020, pp. 6, 23–26). These women in non-standard employment and on short-term contracts can rarely access paid child-related leave because the entitlement to the benefit is given only if workers have been covered by employment insurance for at least 180 days (Kim, 2020). In addition, employers can refuse to grant leaves at their discretion if employees have been working for them for less than a year (Korean Ministry of Employment and Labor, 2021).

Korean women's low uptake of child-related leave is reflected in Figure 13.1. In this figure, the category 'zero hours actually worked per week' refers to those who are employed but on leave, holidays or in training/education (ILOSTAT, 2021b). In 2019, this accounted for only 2.1 per cent of women workers in Korea, compared with 18.5 per cent in Sweden, 15.5 per cent in France, 13.5 per cent in Germany and 12.9 per cent in the United Kingdom. Figure 13.1 also shows that flexible working hour systems are not properly implemented in Korea. Only 20.9 per cent of Korean female workers worked less than 30 hours per week, compared with 37.4 per cent of Japanese, 33.1 per cent of German and 33.9 per cent of British women workers.

Unsuccessful or incomplete implementation of women-friendly employment policies is reflected in the frequency of underemployment and career breaks among women of childbearing age. In 2018, 65.4 per cent of Korean women aged 25–54 were employed, compared with 86.8 per cent of Korean men (ILOSTAT, 2021a), drawing a prominent M-curve for age-employment profiles rarely seen in other OECD member countries (OECD Family Database, 2019). Interestingly, this tendency is more pronounced among the highly educated than the less educated in Korea. As seen in Figure 13.2, European countries have substantial employment gaps between genders for the population with primary education but not for those with tertiary education. Korea shows a markedly different pattern. In 2018, highly educated women aged between 25 and 34 were employed at a similar rate (69.5 per cent) to their male counterparts (75.6 per cent) in Korea as in other countries. Unlike other countries, however, Korea saw larger gender employment gaps for the highly educated than the less educated among the population aged 35 or older. Specifically, Korean women aged between 35 and 44, many of whom would have children below school age, were about 30 per cent less employed (62.1 per cent) than men (93 per cent). In other words, the highly educated population held a more pronounced M-curve for women's age-specific

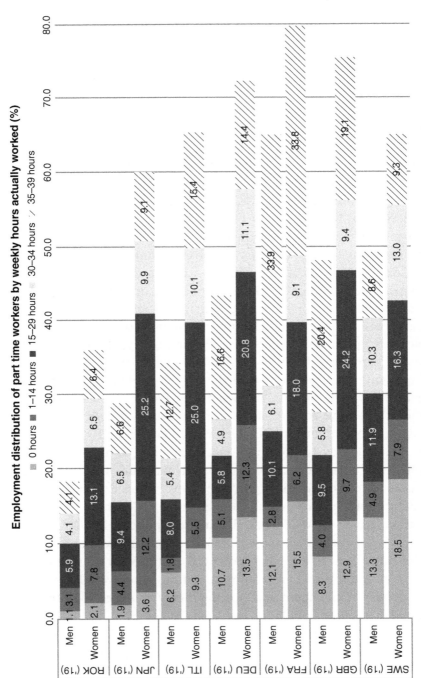

Figure 13.1   Share of employees working fewer than 40 hours per week by gender (%), 2019, selected countries

Source: ILOSTAT (2021) Employees by sex and weekly hours actually worked (thousands) – Annual. (https://www.ilo.org/shinyapps/bulkexplorer40/?lang=en&segment=indicator&id=EES_TEES_SEX_HOW_NB_A) (Accessed on 30 October 2021).

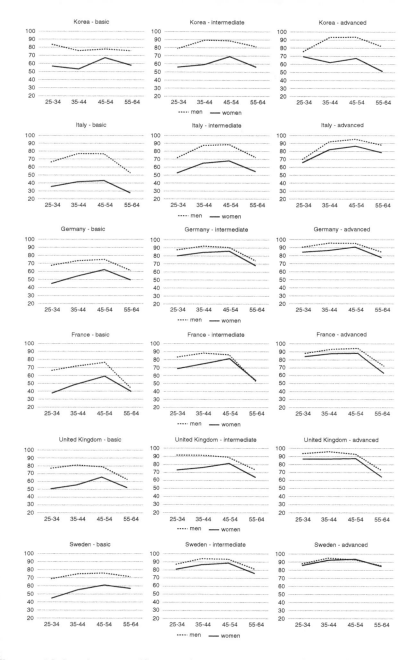

Figure 13.2 Age-specific employment rates by level of educational attainment and gender (%), 2018, selected countries. Notes: Level of educational attainment is defined as follows, based on ISCED-11: 'Basic' refers to 1. Primary education, and 2. Lower secondary education; 'Intermediate' refers to 3. Upper secondary education, and 4. Post-secondary non-tertiary education; 'Advanced' refers to 5. Short-cycle tertiary education, 6. Bachelor's degree or equivalent level, 7. Master's or equivalent level, and 8. Doctoral degree or equivalent level
Source: ILOSTAT (2021) Employment-to-population ratio by sex, age and education – Annual (https://www.ilo.org/shinyapps/bulkexplorer40/?lang=en&segment=indicator&id=EES_TEES_SEX_HOW_NB_A). (Accessed on 30 October 2021).

employment rates and larger gender gaps in overall employment rates than the less educated population in Korea.

However, Figure 13.2 uses cross-sectional data, which provide only a snapshot of the employment status of multiple groups of people at one point in time. Strictly speaking, the lower employment rate of women aged 35–44 compared with that of women aged 25–34 cannot be confirmed evidence of a career break, as there is insufficient information on either the past employment status of the former or the future employment status of the latter. In other words, an investigation into a career interruption requires longitudinal data that provide information on changes in individuals' employment status over multiple points in time.

Data and Methods

This chapter analyses large-scale longitudinal data from the Korean Labor and Income Panel Study (KLIPS) (Korea Labor Institute, 2020). Since 1998, KLIPS has surveyed panel household members aged 15 or older on their economic activities every year. KLIPS draws on three samples. The first sample in 1998 (subsequently referred to as 'the 1998 sample') selected 5,000 original panel households from urban areas through two-stage cluster systematic sampling. The second and third samples were introduced in 2009 ('the 2009 sample') and 2018 ('the 2018 sample'). Unlike the first sample, these two revised samples used probability proportionate sampling and selected panel households from both urban and rural areas.

Drawing on all three KLIPS samples, we plotted tertiary education rates for the population aged 25–34 in Figure 13.3 and age-employment profiles by educational level in Figure 13.4. The figures show similar patterns of young people's education and employment to those seen in the OECD and ILO statistics from the previous section. First, the tertiary education rates of the young female population have become higher than those of their male counterparts since 2005 (see Figure 13.3). Second, regardless of birth cohort, the gender gap among the highly educated kept growing after their late 20s, whereas the gap between less-educated men and women began to decrease in their mid-30s (see Figure 13.4).

Confirming the representativeness of data from KLIPS, our study selected an analytic sample from the original panel household members

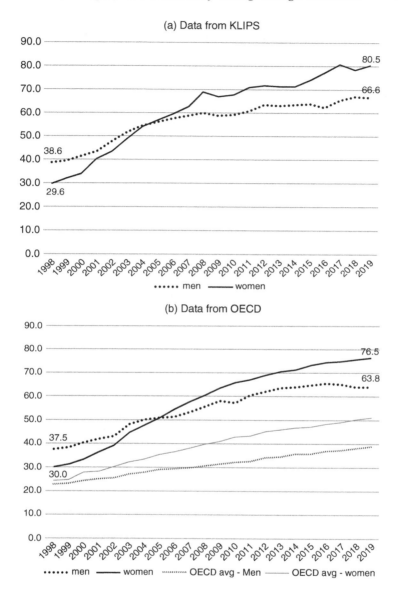

Figure 13.3 Tertiary education rates of the South Korean population aged 25–34 by gender, 1998–2019. Note: Cross-sectional weights are applied to data from KLIPS as follows: the 1998 sample weights to data between 1998 and 2008; the 2009 sample weights to data between 2009 and 2017; and the 2018 sample weights to data between 2018 and 2019 *Data:* KLIPS 1998–2019. All cases (16,869 men and 17,871 women) and observations (*n* = 302,148)

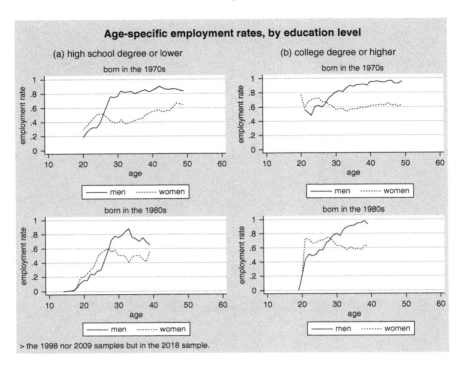

Figure 13.4   Age-specific employment rates of the South Korean population born in the 1970s and the 1980s by education level, birth cohort and gender. Note: Longitudinal weights are applied as follows: the 1998 sample weights to all cases in the 1998 sample; the 2009 sample weights to cases not in the 1998 sample but in the 2009 sample; and the 2018 sample weights to cases neither in the 1998 nor 2009 samples but in the 2018 sample
Data: KLIPS 1998–2019. The sample of those born in the 1970s without a college degree comprises 3,940 cases (1,962 men and 1,978 women) and 29,803 observations; the sample of those born in the 1980s without a college degree comprises 3,510 cases (1,803 men and 1,707 women) and 23,160 observations; the sample of those born in the 1970s with a college or higher degree comprises 3,712 cases (1,901 men and 1,811 women) and 31,625 observations; and the sample of those born in the 1980s with a college or higher degree comprises 3,176 cases (1,520 men and 1,656 women) and 17,483 observations.

of the 1998 sample. This oldest sample represents only the urban population but offers longer observation periods than the other two samples. Using time-varying information about each respondent's educational attainments, we created a new variable measuring the year of college graduation: *t*. If a respondent's highest level of education completed was high school until $t - 1$ but changed to a two-year college or a four-year university in t, the respondent's year of receiving a college degree is t. Based on this information and respondents' age, we selected those who were born between 1975 and 1989 and graduated from college between 1999 and 2018 in their 20s. We then categorized them into three cohorts born in 1975–1979, 1980–1984 and 1985–1989.

Using this analytic sample, we constructed two survival-time datasets. The first one follows changes from un(der)employment to first employment, while the second one from employment to non-employment. To measure these changes, we used information about working statuses (whether or not a respondent is involved in economic activity, including unpaid work for a family business at the time of each survey) and working hours (average weekly hours actually worked during the three months preceding each survey). We excluded part-time work from our definition of first employment, given that many college students work part-time before graduation. We referred to the OECD in defining part-time work: working under 30 hours per week (OECD, 2007, p. 575). Accordingly, we defined un(der)employment as 'not working or working under 30 hours per week' and employment as 'working 30 or more hours per week', while non-employment denotes those not working among the population as a whole.

Based on these definitions, we included respondents who were un(der)employed one year before college graduation in the first survival-time dataset. This dataset has two main variables. The first variable 'survival' indicates a respondent survived or failed to survive, where 'survival' refers to remaining un(der)employed and 'failure' to getting a non-part-time job, at a given time. The second variable 'time' indicates years of job search, which was set to start in the year before college graduation and continued until respondents got a non-part-time job. According to these premises, three types of cases were right-censored, or excluded, from our analytic sample. The first type is the cases where a respondent turned 40 years old or remained un(der) employed over nine years, regardless of employment status; the second type describes cases where information was missing in a certain year due to absence from the survey; finally, the third type refers to respondents who reached the last survey in 2018 before becoming employed or spending nine years in un(der)employment. These are all subsequently referred to as 'lost cases'.

Meanwhile, we included respondents in our second dataset once they got their first non-part-time job. Respondents stayed in the second dataset until they left the labour market. Put differently, 'survival' refers to remaining employed, while 'failure' denotes becoming not-employed. In the second dataset, 'time' was measured by years of employment, which began with our cases being employed and ended with cases leaving the labour market. Conditions for right-censoring are the same as those in the first dataset.

As a result, our first dataset comprised a total of 634 cases (328 men and 306 women) and 1,927 observations, while our second dataset comprised 622 cases (315 men and 307 women) and 3,638 observations. Table 13.A1 and Table 13.A2 present the structure of the two datasets, while Table 13.1 summarizes the characteristics of our analytic sample cases. Compulsory military service delayed the timing of men's college graduation compared with women. The mean of college graduation year was 2000 for women and 2003 for men in the 1975–1979 cohort. This three-year gender gap persisted in the younger cohorts. The average year of college graduation for the 1980–1984 cohort was 2005 for women and 2008 for men, and for the 1985–1989 cohort it was 2010 for women and 2013 for men. Due to the timing of the surveys, the mean age at college graduation was older for the 1975–1979 cohort (especially women) than for the other two cohorts. It was 23.3 for women and 25.2 for men in the 1975–1979 cohort, in comparison to 22.0–22.1 for women and 24.6–24.8 for men in the

Table 13.1 Characteristics of the analytic sample for the survival-time analysis

		1975–79 cohort		1980–84 cohort		1985–89 cohort	
		Men	**Women**	**Men**	**Women**	**Men**	**Women**
Dataset 1	(*N* of cases)	96	54	140	137	92	115
College graduation	year (mean)	2003	2002	2008	2005	2013	2010
	age (mean)	25.2	23.3	24.8	22	24.6	22.1
Years of job search (mean)		2.1	1.9	2.1	1.9	2.3	2.0
Dataset 2	(*N* of cases)	98	78	136	125	81	104

Table 13.1   Characteristics of the analytic sample for the survival-time analysis (Continued)

		1975–79 cohort		1980–84 cohort		1985–89 cohort	
		Men	**Women**	**Men**	**Women**	**Men**	**Women**
College graduation	year (mean)	2003	2001	2008	2005	2013	2010
First employment	year (mean)	2004	2002	2008	2005	2013	2011
	age (mean)	26.7	23.9	26.6	23.5	26.1	23.8
Years in the labour market (mean)		5.9	4.4	5.7	4.4	4.1	4.1

Data: KLIPS 1998–2019. The 1998 sample. No weight is applied.

1980s cohorts. In addition, men tended to spend longer time on job searching than women in all three cohorts. The mean years of job search were 2.1–2.3 for men, compared with 1.9–2.0 for women.

Although the timing of college graduation for men was considerably delayed, men tended to stay in the labour market longer than women once getting their first non-part-time job. The mean years of employment before leaving the labour market were 5.7–5.9 for men, compared with 4.4 years for women, in the 1975–1979 cohort and the 1980–1984 cohort. Meanwhile, the mean years spent in the labour market by the 1985–1989 cohort were shorter than the two older cohorts: 4.1 years for both men and women. There was no gender difference because this youngest cohort contains fewer male cases and a shorter observation period.

Drawing on these two datasets, we conducted a survival-time analysis. Specifically, we estimated the hazard rate – that is, 'the conditional probability that an event will occur at a particular time to a particular individual, given that the individual is at risk at that time' (Allison, 2014, p. 8) – using STATA SE version 16 and the smoothing kernel technique. In doing so, we applied longitudinal weights to our cases to deal with the issue of panel attrition. In particular, weights provided in the year before college graduation were applied to the cases in the first dataset (concerning the timing of first employment), while weights given in the year of getting the first non-part-time job were applied to the cases in the second dataset (concerning the timing of a career break).

Results

*Patterns of College Graduates' First Employment
and Career Breaks*

This section presents results from our analysis of the patterns of college graduates' first employment and career breaks. Figure 13.5 plots the hazard rate of un(der)employed college graduates getting a first non-part-time job at each point in time for nine years of job search, which is assumed to begin one year before college graduation. Meanwhile, Figure 13.6 describes the hazard rate of employed college graduates leaving the labour market at each point in time for nine years starting from the year of first employment. Both figures present cohort differences within each gender as well as gender differences within each cohort. Our focus is to examine how the patterns change over cohort within each gender and how gender gaps in the patterns changed over cohort.

*Hazard Rates of Un(der)employed College Graduates
Getting A First Non-Part-Time Job*

Figure 13.5 plots the hazard rates of college graduates getting their first non-part-time job by gender and birth cohort. Overall, the curves show two tendencies. First, younger cohorts peak at a later point in time. Second, men, compared with women, have higher and more conspicuous peaks. In Figures 13.5A and B, we examine how the patterns change across cohorts within each gender, thereby identifying how gender gaps in the patterns change across cohorts.

In Figure 13.5A, we first look at when men and women reach their peaks by cohort. The 1975–1979 cohort men peaked in *time 2* (at 38 per cent), which means their rate of getting a non-part-time job was the highest in the second year of their job search. Subsequently, the 1980–1984 cohort reached their peak in *time 4* (at 42 per cent) and the 1985–1989 cohort in *time 7* (at 38 per cent). On the other hand, women's rates of getting a non-part-time job peaked in *time 2* (at 28 per cent) in the 1975–1979 cohort, in *time 3* (at 36 per cent) in the 1980–1984 cohort and in *time 3* (at 30 per cent) in the 1985–1989 cohort.

Let us look at changes in women's hazard rates in more detail. Compared with women in the 1975–1979 cohort, women born in the 1980s had a higher hazard rate at every point in time, except for *time 1*,

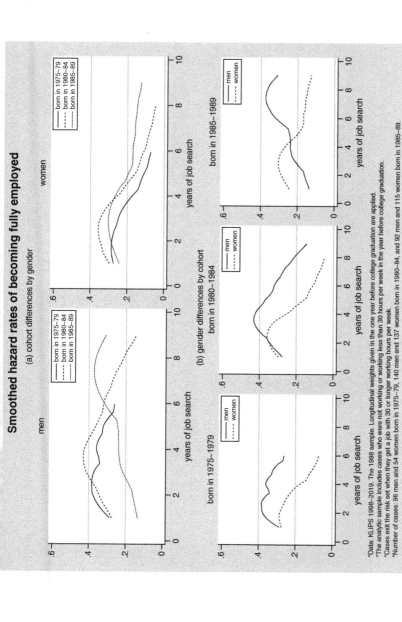

Figure 13.5 Patterns of college graduates' first employment over time: smoothed hazard rates of getting a non-part time job by gender and birth cohort. Note: The analytic sample includes cases who were not working or were working fewer than 30 hours per week one year before college graduation: 96 men and 54 women born in 1975–1979, 140 men and 137 women born in 1980–1984, and 92 men and 115 women born in 1985–1989

Data: KLIPS 1998–2019. The 1998 sample. Longitudinal weights given in the year before college graduation are applied.

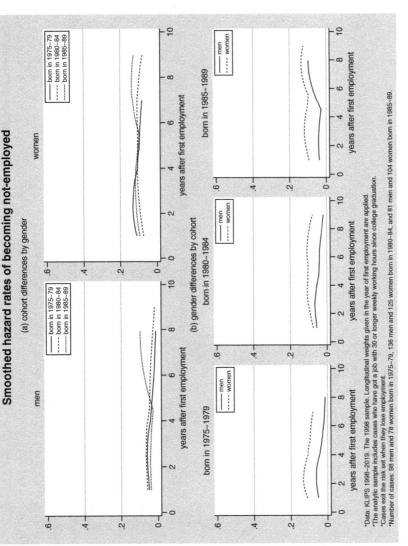

Figure 13.6 Patterns of college graduates' career break over time: smoothed hazard rates of leaving the labour market by gender and birth cohort. Note: The analytic sample includes cases recruited in a job with 30 or more weekly working hours following college graduation: 98 men and 78 women born in 1975–1979, 136 men and 125 women born in 1980–1984, and 81 men and 104 women born in 1985–1989

Data: KLIPS 1998–2019. The 1998 sample. Longitudinal weights given in the year of first employment are applied.

where the 1985–1989 cohort had the lowest hazard rate among the three cohorts. Women in the 1985–1989 cohort were less likely to be employed than the 1980–1984 cohort women for the first four years of their job search; however, their hazard rates surpass their predecessors' from *time 5* onwards. In brief, women's labour market participation has substantially increased among those born in the 1980s, although the timing is delayed, compared with those born in the 1970s.

The progress made by women born in the 1980s has led to substantial changes in gender gaps across cohorts. As seen in Figure 13.5B, women never had a higher hazard rate than men at any point in time within the 1975–1979 cohort; however, women's hazard rates became slightly higher than men's rates until *time 2* in the 1980–1984 cohort. Since then, the 1980–1984 cohort have maintained smaller gender gaps than their predecessors: in *time 4*, for example, women's hazard rate was 20 percentage points lower than men's rate in the 1975–1979 cohort but reduced to only 14 percentage points lower than men's in the 1980–1984 cohort. Although these cohorts have seen a rapid drop in hazard rates for women much earlier than for men, Figure 13.5B suggests that college graduates born in the 1980s experienced a substantial decrease in the gender gap in Korea's labour market entrance.

Hazard Rates of Employed College Graduates Leaving the Labour Market

Now we examine patterns of career interruption. Figure 13.6 contains curves for the hazard rates of employed college graduates leaving the labour market. Unlike in Figure 13.5, we can barely see a peak in the curves in Figure 13.6, nor can we see significant cohort differences in the curves for both genders. In other words, both men and women have similar rates of career break throughout employment, and this tendency has not changed much across cohorts.

In Figure 13.6A, we look at cohort differences by gender in the hazard rates of leaving the labour market. Other than the sudden increase in the curves for the 1985–1989 cohort men since *time 5*, which is attributed to lost cases, men's hazard rates were under 7 per cent throughout the years after first employment in all cohorts. On the other hand, women were more prone to the risk of a career break. Their hazard rates were above 7 per cent at all times in all three cohorts.

During the first four years of employment, the 1980–84 cohort women left the labour market at a lower rate than their predecessors; however, their hazard rates were sustained at 10 per cent between *time 3* and *time 7*, while the 1975–1979 cohort women experienced a slight but continuous decrease during employment. Moreover, there has been a retreat from the progress made in the early years of employment: compared with those in the 1980–1984 cohort, women in the 1985–1989 cohort had higher rates of leaving the labour market in the years after first employment. That is to say, it is hard to confirm a trend towards fewer career breaks among young, highly-educated women in Korea.

As both genders have seen little change in the patterns of career breaks across time and cohorts, the tendency of large gender gaps in the hazard rates of leaving the labour market continued. Figure 13.6B reveals that women had significantly higher hazard rates than men throughout the years of employment in all three cohorts. We can see more than twice the hazard rates for women than men at every point in time in the 1975–1979 cohort. Compared to their predecessors, the 1980–1984 cohort had smaller gender gaps at most times. They were no exception to the pattern of growing gender gaps over time, however, as women's hazard rates remained constant and men's rates decreased. Furthermore, the 1985–1989 cohort showed even larger gender gaps than the 1975–1979 cohort until *time 5*, when men's hazard rate took a jump due to the issue of lost cases. This suggests that a revolution of women's economic empowerment has not yet been completed in Korea, although we need more time to confirm this pattern of the youngest cohort's career interruption.

Conclusion

This chapter aimed to understand how post-industrial changes in the labour market have affected the landscape of youth employment since 2000. Rather than using cross-sectional data limited to the analysis of differences between groups at one point in time, it analyses large-scale longitudinal data to detect changes in employment status within a group over time and compare the employment patterns of different groups. Focusing on gender gaps, it examines the hazard rates of first employment and career breaks before the age of 40 for college gradu-ates born in the 1980s, compared with those born in the late 1970s. In other words, it examines how men and women's employment status changed over time within each birth cohort and, as a result, how gender gaps in employment patterns changed across the three birth cohorts.

Our findings are summarized as follows. On the one hand, the financial crisis in 1997 reinforced dualism in the labour market and exacerbated the mismatch in the youth job market, thereby postponing the timing of first employment, especially for men. On the other hand, changing ideas about gender roles increased the entrance of highly educated women into the labour market, transforming the gender composition of the highly educated workforce and reducing gender gaps in the patterns of college graduates' first employment. Despite the Korean government's endeavours in introducing some work–family policies that attempted to keep women in the workforce after having children, gendered dualism in the labour market made it difficult to implement the policies. As a result, little improvement has been made in the high rate of career breaks among highly educated women, which is in marked contrast to the progress made in labour market entrance.

Our findings show that Korean college graduates no longer face substantial gender gaps in terms of labour market entrance. At the same time, however, gender gaps in the workforce retention rate strongly persist despite the advancement in women's education and work-family policies. This incomplete progress in women's labour market participation is embedded in gendered dualism in the labour market. Excluding the majority of women from employment protection (Kim et al., 2019), the dual labour market reproduces gender discrimination in the process of promotion, training, job assignment and compensation (Choi and Bang, 2018; Kim and Oh, 2019; Lee, 2015; Yoon, 2020). An imbalance between social institutions, including education, the welfare state, the family and the labour market, has resulted in many social problems such as low fertility in Korea. If we acknowledge that the advancement made in education and the welfare state cannot retreat, we may need to make corresponding changes in the family and the labour market. Traditional family values and gender norms may no longer provide a plausible explanation for the ongoing pattern of career interruption among women of childbearing age, given the influence of individualism and feminism on highly educated women since 2000. It seems more likely that they leave the labour market not because of family-related reasons but because of reasons in the labour market itself. With that being said, it is time to pay more attention to labour market structure in order to complete the gender revolution in Korea.

References

Ahn, J., Oh S., & Choi, S. (2019). *Nodongsijang Ijung-Gujowa Cheongnyeon Iljali (I) [Labour market dualism and youth employment (I)]*. Sejong City: Korea Labor Institute. (in Korean).

Allison, P. D. (2014). Event history and survival analysis. In *Series: Quantitative applications in the social sciences* (2nd ed., Vol. 46). Los Angeles, CA: SAGE.

Choi, S., & Bang, H. (2018). *Saeng-Aejugie Ttaleun Seongbyeol Imgeum Gyeogcha - Gyeolhongwa Chulsan-Ui Yeonghyang-Eul Jungsim-Eulo [Life cycle and gender pay gaps: Effects of marriage and childbirth]*. Sejong City: Korea Labor Institute. (in Korean).

Esping-Andersen, G. (1990). *The three worlds of welfare capitalism*. Cambridge: Polity Press.

Esping-Andersen, G. (1997). Hybrid or unique? The Japanese welfare state between Europe and America. *Journal of European Social Policy, 7*(3), 179–189.

Estévez-Abe, M., & Naldini, M. (2016). Politics of defamilialization: A comparison of Italy, Japan, Korea and Spain. *Journal of European Social Policy, 26*(4), 327–343.

ILOSTAT. (2021a). *Employment-to-population ratio by sex, age and education (%) – Annual* [data file]. Retrieved 30 October 2021, from https://www.ilo.org/shinyapps/bulkexplorer40/?lang=en&segment=indicator&id=EES_TEES_SEX_HOW_NB_A

ILOSTAT. (2021b). *Employees by sex and weekly hours actually worked (thousands) – Annual* [data file]. Retrieved 30 October 2021, from https://www.ilo.org/shinyapps/bulkexplorer40/?lang=en&segment=indicator&id=EES_TEES_SEX_HOW_NB_A

Kim, H. (2020). Korea country note. In A. Koslowski, S. Blum, I. Dobrotić, G. Kaufman & P. Moss (Eds.), *International review of leave policies and research 2020* (pp. 365–372).

Kim, Y. (2020). *Bijeong-Gyujig Gyumowa Siltae: Tong-Gyecheong 'Gyeongjehwal-dong-Ingujosa Bugajosa' (2020.8) Gyeolgwa [The size and conditions of non-standard workers: Analysis of statistics Korea's economically active population survey in 2020]*, KLSI Issue Paper, 139. (in Korean).

Kim, E., Lee, S., & Kwon, H. (2019). Wigi Sog Nodongsijang Jin-Ib Sedaeui Nodong-Idong-Eul Tonghae Bon Wigi Hu Hangug Yeoseongnodongsijang [Women labor market structure reflected in labor mobility of women who entered labor market during the economic crisis]. *Journal of Korean Women's Studies, 35*(1), 1–37. (in Korean).

Kim, C., & Oh, B. (2019). Gyeonglyeogdanjeol Ijeon Yeoseong-Eun Chabyeolbadji Anhneunga? Daejol 20dae Cheongnyeoncheung-Ui Jol-Eob Jighu Seongbyeol Sodeuggyeogcha Bunseog [No gender discrimination before career disruption? Gender earnings gap at the early stage of work career among college graduates in South Korea]. *Korean Journal of Sociology, 53*(1), 167–204. (in Korean).

Korea Labor Institute. (2020). *Korean labor and income panel study, 1–22 wave* [data file]. Retrieved 12 October 2020, from https://www.kli.re.kr/klips_eng/index.do

Korean Ministry of Employment and Labor. (2021). *Jeongchaeg Jalyo > Dae-sangjabyeol Jeongchaeg > Yeoseong > Moseongboho Yug-Ajiwon [Policy* materials: *Female employment policies]*. Retrieved 9 April 2021, from http://www.moel.go.kr/policy/policyinfo/woman/list.do (in Korean).

Lee, S.-M. (2015). Oehwan-Wigi Ihu Nodongsijang-Ui Seongbulpyeongdeung: Nodong-Gyeonglyeog Mich Imgeum Gwejeog-Ui Seongbyeol Chaileul Jungsim-Eulo [Gender inequality in the labor market after the financial crisis – focused on the gender differences in work career and wage]. *Journal of Korean Women's Studies*, *31*(2), 91–129. (in Korean).

Lee, S. S. Y. (2016). Institutional legacy of state corporatism in de-industrial labour markets: A comparative study of Japan, South Korea and Taiwan. *Socio-Economic Review*, *14*(1), 73–95.

OECD. (2007). *Glossary of statistical terms*. Retrieved 22 January 2021, from https://stats.oecd.org/glossary/index.htm

OECD. (2021a). *Fertility rates' (indicator)*. Retrieved 22 January 2021, from https://doi.org/10.1787/8272fb01-en

OECD. (2021b). *Population with tertiary education (indicator)*. Retrieved 21 January 2021, from https://doi.org/10.1787/0b8f90e9-en

OECD Family Database. (2019). *LMF1.4: Employment profiles over the life-course*. Retrieved 2 August 2021, from https://www.oecd.org/els/soc/LMF_1_4_Employment_profiles_over_life_course.pdf

Peng, I. (2012). Economic dualization in Japan and Korea. In P. Emmenegger, S. Häusermann, B. Palier & M. Seeleib-Kaiser (Eds.), *The age of dualization: The changing face of inequality in deindustrializing societies* (pp. 226–249). New York, NY: Oxford University Press.

Song, M. Y. (2011). From demographic to normative individualization: A comparative study of family values in Korea and Japan. *Korean Journal of Sociology*, *45*(6), 153–174.

Song, J. (2012). The politics of family policies in Korea. *Korea Observer*, *43*(2), 209–231.

Song, J. (2014). *Inequality in the workplace: Labor market reform in Japan and Korea*. New York, NY: Cornell University Press.

Song, J. (2016). Activating women in the labor market: The development of South Korea's female-friendly employment and labor market policies. *Korea Observer*, *47*(3), 559–596.

Statistics Korea. (2021). *Chwihaglyul Mich Jinhaglyul [Enrolment rates in education]*. Retrieved 29 August 2021, from https://www.index.go.kr/potal/main/EachDtlPageDetail.do?idx_cd=1520 (in Korean).

Yang, J.-J. (2017). *The political economy of the small welfare state in South Korea*. Cambridge: Cambridge University Press.

Yoon, H. (2019). *Hangug Bogjiguggaui Giwongwa Gwejeog [The origin and development trajectory of the welfare state of South Korea]*. Seoul: Saho-pyeonglon Academy. (in Korean).

Yoon, J. (2020). Yeoseong Imgeum Geunlojaui Jigjang Nae Seongchabyeol Insig-E Gwanhan Yeongu -Gieob Teugseong-Gwa Goyonghyeongtaeleul Jungsim-Eulo [Female workers' perceptions of gender discrimination in the workplace]. *Issues in Feminism*, *20*(1), 37–81. (in Korean).

Appendix

Table 13.A1 Structure of the survival-time dataset 1 concerning the timing of first employment

Birth cohort	Years of job search	Men			Women		
		Remaining un(der)-employed (N)	Becoming employed (N)	Lost cases (N)	Remaining un(der)-employed (N)	Becoming employed (N)	Lost cases (N)
1975–79	1	96	39	4	54	37	2
	2	53	23	6	15	6	1
	3	24	15	0	8	2	1
	4	9	1	0	–	–	–
	5	8	2	1	–	–	–
	6	5	3	0	5	1	0
	7	–	–	–	–	–	–
	8	–	–	–	–	–	–
	9	2	0	2	4	0	4
1980–84	1	140	59	10	137	72	5
	2	71	35	2	60	30	5
	3	34	15	0	25	8	4
	4	19	6	2	13	3	1
	5	11	3	1	9	2	3
	6	7	5	0	–	–	–

7	–	–	–	–	–	–
8	–	–	–	4	1	1
9	2	1	1	2	0	2
1985–89 1	92	38	5	115	64	7
2	49	17	3	44	16	4
3	29	8	0	24	9	0
4	21	3	4	15	4	0
5	14	6	4	11	4	0
6	4	1	1	7	1	0
7	–	–	–	6	0	2
8	2	1	0	4	0	2
9	1	1	0	2	1	1

Notes: (1) 'Remaining un(der)employed' means 'not working or working fewer than 30 hours per week one year before college graduation'; (2) 'Becoming employed' means 'getting a job with 30 or more working hours per week'; (3) 'Lost cases' refers to cases right censored for the following reasons: turning 40 years old, having spent nine years in the dataset, missing the survey of the year, or reaching the last survey (in 2018) before spending nine years in the dataset; (4) '-' means no observation available.
Data: KLIPS 1998–2019. The 1998 sample. No weight is applied.

Table 13.A2 Structure of the survival-time dataset 2 concerning the timing of career break

Birth cohort	Years after first employment	Men			Women		
		Remaining employed (N)	Becoming not-employed (N)	Lost cases (N)	Remaining employed (N)	Becoming not-employed (N)	Lost cases (N)
1975–79	1	98	9	5	78	11	4
	2	84	5	3	63	16	3
	3	76	5	8	44	6	3
	4	63	2	1	35	1	2
	5	60	3	4	32	2	1
	6	53	0	2	29	4	0
	7	-	-	-	25	4	0
	8	51	2	2	21	0	3
	9	47	0	47	18	0	18
1980–84	1	136	14	8	125	20	8
	2	114	6	9	97	13	8
	3	99	4	7	76	9	3
	4	88	3	1	64	8	6
	5	84	4	5	50	4	2
	6	75	3	2	44	5	0

7	70	2	7	39	3	2
8	61	2	6	34	5	2
9	53	2	51	27	4	23
1985–89	81	7	7	104	14	8
2	67	10	7	82	14	5
3	50	4	6	63	7	7
4	40	1	7	49	3	3
5	32	1	5	43	3	8
6	26	0	9	32	3	3
7	17	1	6	26	3	10
8	10	1	2	13	2	1
9	7	0	7	10	3	7

Notes: (1) 'Remaining employed' means 'working 30 or more hours per week'; (2) 'Leaving the labour market' means 'becoming not engaged in economic activity'; (3) 'Lost cases' refers to cases right censored for the following reasons: turning 40 years old, having spent nine years in the dataset, missing the survey of the year or reaching the last survey (in 2018) before spending nine years in the dataset; (4) '-' means no observation available.

Data: KLIPS 1998–2019. The 1998 sample. No weight is applied.

14

Who Rises Higher in First Job Attainment? Trends and Patterns of School-to-Work Transition in Hong Kong[1]

Xiaogang Wu and Maocan Guo

Introduction

The relationship between education and first occupation is an important issue in social stratification research. Over the past few decades, scholars have increasingly focused on cross-national differences between education and first jobs (DiPrete et al., 2017; Geber, 2003; Kerckhoff, 2001; Müller and Gangl, 2003; Shavit and Müller, 1998). Comparative studies on school-to-work transitions have shown considerable variation across countries in the impact of education on labour market entry outcomes. It is also widely accepted that such a variation largely reflects institutional differences in the education system, particularly in terms of educational tracking and vocational specificity, meaning the extent to which education provides students with occupational skills and the specificity of those skills (Kerckhoff, 2001; Shavit et al., 2007; Shavit and Müller, 1998).

Cross-national comparisons further suggest that the institutional context of the labour market moderates how the educational system affects the transition from school to work (Breen, 2005). In particular, labour market coordination *per se* affects the matching between education and the first occupation (Andersen and Van de Werfhorst, 2010; Bol and Van de Werfhorst, 2011).

While these studies highlight how nation-specific institutional features of the education system and labour market shape the link between education and first occupation, the fact that this link may be influenced by the expansion of the educational system has been largely ignored. Despite the fact that educational expansion has occurred in many societies, few studies have shown how it affects the transition process from school to work (see Arum and Hout, 1998, for a discussion).

This chapter studies how educational expansion changes the association between education and first occupation in Hong Kong, paying special attention to the changing educational and occupational opportunity structure. We first describe the context of educational expansion, labour market restructuring, and occupational gender segregation in Hong Kong, and derive two hypotheses. We then introduce the data and methodology, after which we move on to show how the school-to-work transition varies by birth cohort and gender. Finally, we discuss the implications of our findings for understanding social mobility and political dynamics among the youth in Hong Kong.

Educational Expansion and School-to-Work Transition in Hong Kong

Over the past few decades, educational opportunities for Hong Kong's youth have increased dramatically (Sweeting, 2004, 2007). The government made primary education free and compulsory in 1971, and then followed up with the first three years of secondary education in 1978 (Pong and Post, 1991; Post, 1994). According to the government's Education Commission (1984, p. 21), the net enrolment rate in high school reached 84.60 per cent in 1983.

The growth of higher education, however, was rather slow until the mid-1980s. In the early 1980s, less than 2 per cent of school-age youth had access to university education (Post, 2003, p. 550), with a 12.79 per cent gross enrolment rate in tertiary education in 1984 (UNESCO, 2021). The first wave of higher education expansion in Hong Kong began in 1988, when Governor Sir David Wilson initiated an increase in college enrolment to 14.5 per cent of the population ages 17–20 by 1995 (Ahrens, 2019). In 1989, the target was increased to 18 per cent by 1995, aiming to triple the 6 per cent enrolment rate of 1988 (Educational Commission, 1988). As shown in Figure 14.1A, this new target quickly increased the number of first-year first-degree under-graduate intake places from 5,397 in 1987–1988 to 14,253 in 1994–1995 (UGC, 2021), with an average annual growth rate of 23.4 per cent over seven years.

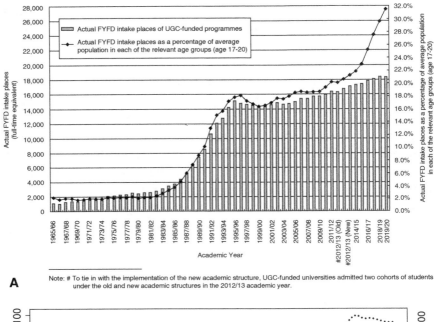

A

Note: # To tie in with the implementation of the new academic structure, UGC-funded universities admitted two cohorts of students under the old and new academic structures in the 2012/13 academic year.

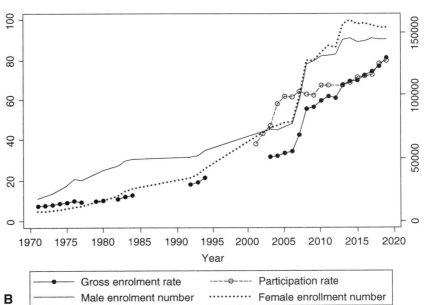

B

Figure 14.1   (**A**) Actual first-year-first-degree (FYFD) intake places of UGC-funded programmers, 1965–2019 academic years, (**B**) expansion of tertiary education in Hong Kong, 1971–2019
Source: University Grants Committee (UGC) (2021), UNESCO (2021), World Bank (2021), Committee on Self-financing Post-secondary Education (2021).

The second wave of higher education expansion in Hong Kong began in 2001. In 2000, considering that Hong Kong's tertiary education participation rate was much lower than that of many developed countries and major cities in Asia, Hong Kong's first Chief Executive, Tung Chee-Hwa, proposed to double the rate to 60 per cent within ten years (Tung, 2000). To achieve this goal, the Hong Kong government encouraged universities to provide self-funded sub-degrees, usually under by auspices of the continuing education programmes, to 15 per cent of the 17- to 20-year-old population. The subsequent development of the privatized market for self-financing sub-degrees has directly contributed to the rapid development of higher education in Hong Kong in the early 21st century. According to the Committee on Self-financing Post-secondary Education (2021), the participation rate of sub-degrees increased from 15.4 per cent in 2001 to 45.4 per cent in 2019, and the number of self-financing sub-degree places increased more than 13-fold from 2,468 in 2001 to 32,589 in 2013. Meanwhile, as shown in Figure 14.1A, actual UGC-funded (publicly funded) first-year first-degree enrolment remained virtually unchanged through 2010 and increased only modestly in subsequent years.

Thus, the second wave of higher education expansion is essentially characterized by the marketization of sub-degrees and non-subsidized programs (including top-up degrees, associate degrees, advanced diplomas and certificate programmes) since 2001 (Ho et al., 2017; O'Sullivan and Tsang, 2015). Figure 14.1B shows the general trend of higher education expansion in Hong Kong. According to statistics of UNESCO (2021), the gross enrolment rate in tertiary education increased from 10.1 per cent in 1980 to 21.5 per cent in 1994, and further from 31.8 per cent in 2003 to 81.0 per cent in 2019. The tertiary education participation rate has also increased rapidly. Within six years, it rose from 37.9 per cent in 2001 to 61.4 per cent in 2006, meeting Tung's policy goal (Committee on Self-financing Post-secondary Education, 2021). In 2019, that participation rate hit 80 per cent. As a result of the dramatic expansion of higher education, Hong Kong's overall educational attainment has risen. According to the latest official data (Census and Statistics Department, 2020), 33.9 per cent of the population ages 15 or above completed tertiary education in 2019, up from 19.5 per cent in 2001. Figure 14.1B also shows the number of tertiary enrolments by gender over time. Consistent with patterns in mainland China and elsewhere (Buchmann et al.,

2008; Buchmann and Hannum, 2001; Lavely et al., 1990; Wu, 2010a, 2012), the male advantage over females in higher education fades over the course of educational expansion and reverses afterwards, here significantly around 2005.

Along with the government-led expansion of higher education (Post, 1994, 2003, 2010), Hong Kong has witnessed structural changes in its economy and labour market employment (Lui, 2009, 2015; Meyer, 2008; Zhao et al., 2004). Table 14.1 presents the percentage of employment by industry and occupation based on consistent official statistics from 1995 to 2019. The first panel shows that while the percentage of employees in industries such as construction and transportation changes only slightly, it declines substantially in industries such as manufacturing, and increases moderately in industries including public administration and finance, insurance and business services. As Figure 14.2A shows, the share of employment in manufacturing shrank from 18.4 per cent in 1995 to 2.7 per cent in 2019, but the share of employment in public administration, social and personal services increased from 21.0 per cent in 1995 to 28.7 per cent in 2019, and the share of employment in finance grew from 11.8 per cent in 1995 to 21.7 per cent in 2019.

The second panel continues to demonstrate changes in the occupational structure. The share of managers and administrators increases only slightly from 8.5 per cent in 1995 to 11.0 per cent in 2019, as does the share of professionals in the labour market, which increases from 4.9 per cent in 1995 to 7.9 per cent in 2019. In contrast, as shown in Figure 14.2B, there is a moderate increase in the proportion of associate professionals, from 13.5 per cent in 1995 to 21.7 per cent in 2019. The shares of service and sales workers, and workers in elementary occupations in the labour market have both increased only slightly since the mid-1990s, but the share of those employed as clerks, craftsmen, and plant and production workers decreased by about 6 per cent in magnitude. Overall, these figures suggest that the structure of Hong Kong's labour market has shifted over the past 25 years: the pace of change has been only moderate in industries such as public administration and finance, business services and in occupations such as managers and professionals, but there has been a substantial reduction in manufacturing jobs and a significant increase in the proportion of associate professionals.

In this sense, compared to the huge changes in the structure of educational opportunities, the structure of labour market opportunities

Table 14.1   Percentage of employment by industry and occupation in Hong Kong, official statistics 1995–2019

Variables %	1995	1999	2003	2007	2011	2015	2019
Industry							
Manufacturing	18.40	11.37	8.42	5.81	3.72	3.01	2.69
Construction	7.89	9.22	8.17	7.89	7.75	8.39	8.77
Trade, wholesale, retail, food and accommodation services	28.39	30.05	30.83	32.83	31.22	29.29	25.89
Transportation, storage, courier, information and communications	11.28	10.91	10.77	10.68	12.14	12.05	11.64
Financing, insurance, real estate, professional and business services	11.76	14.06	14.68	15.73	18.90	19.88	21.69
Public administration, social and personal services	20.99	23.55	26.38	26.44	25.60	26.72	28.67
Others	1.28	0.85	0.74	0.62	0.67	0.67	0.66
Occupation							
Managers and administrators	8.52	7.80	8.49	10.08	10.70	10.86	11.00
Professionals	4.85	5.41	6.36	6.91	6.86	8.04	7.91
Associate professionals	13.47	16.88	18.30	19.30	19.89	19.71	21.72
Clerical support workers	18.59	18.25	16.54	15.66	14.11	13.79	12.53
Service and sales workers	14.07	14.16	15.08	15.40	16.61	16.46	16.07
Craft and related workers	11.88	10.53	8.48	7.51	6.97	6.61	6.13
Plant, production and assemblers	11.05	8.34	7.31	6.25	5.06	4.64	4.35
Elementary occupations	17.10	18.36	19.21	18.73	19.68	19.80	20.20
Others	0.47	0.27	0.22	0.15	0.12	0.09	0.10

Source: Figures are calculated based on 1996–2020 *Hong Kong Annual Digest of Statistics* (Census and Statistics Department of Hong Kong SAR Government, 1994–2020). The coding of occupation has only been consistent since 1993.

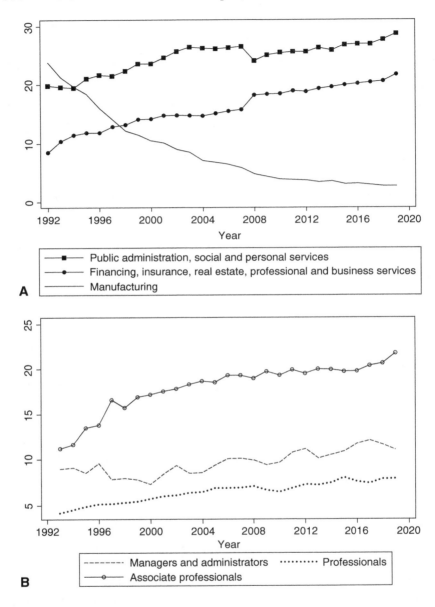

Figure 14.2 **(A)** Percentage of employment by industry in Hong Kong, 1993–2019, **(B)** Percentage of employment by occupation in Hong Kong, 1993–2019
Source: Census and Statistics Department of Hong Kong SAR Government (1994–2020).

has been changing at a relatively slow pace, especially in managerial and professional jobs. Thus, while higher educational expansion has supplied a mass of college graduates in a short period of time, the labour market has not provided an equivalent number of desirable jobs. In other words, the large supply of university graduates following the expansion has made the labour market more competitive, and the supply of skilled labour has largely outstripped the demand. Given that the structure of the labour market has changed little over the past three decades, the increased supply of workers with higher education tends to lower the price of education (Lui, 1994), and only a relatively small number of college graduates will now be able to seize 'good' job opportunities.

Moreover, similar to other societies experiencing dramatic educational expansion, such as mainland China (Guo, 2021), the dramatic increase in first-year first degree places in the first wave of higher education expansion and the dramatic increase in sub-degree holders in the second wave tend to reduce the relative 'quality' of the post-expansion cohort, implying that the signalling value of university certificates is declining (Wong, 2019). If schools do not compensate for the decline in cohort quality by providing a better education, then educational credentials as a signalling device can indicate a decline in the capacity and productivity of the post-expansion cohort, which can also lead to a decline in returns to education. In other words, a certain percentage of post-expansion college graduates are only 'equivalent' to pre-expansion high school graduates. As a result, the jobs available to them may be less prestigious, which puts further downward pressure on the labour market returns to higher education.

Due to the two effects mentioned above (pricing effect and signalling effect), we can test the following hypothesis:

Hypothesis 1: The association between higher education and first job occupational status tends to be lower among younger cohorts.

While Hypothesis 1 predicts that higher education expansion tends to negatively affect the association between university education and first jobs, this negative effect holds only at the aggregate level and may be compensated differently for different social groups. One notable phenomenon during higher education expansion in Hong Kong is the reversed gender gap: girls have outnumbered boys in attending not only upper-secondary school (Pong and Post, 1991) but also college (Figure 14.1B). To understand the positioning of females in the labour market in the context of the reversed gender gap in education, Table 14.2 presents the proportion of females employed in various industries in Hong Kong from 1995 to 2019.

Table 14.2 Percentage of female employment by industry in Hong Kong, official statistics 1995–2019

Variables %	1995	1999	2003	2007	2011	2015	2019
Manufacturing	43.71	42.71	42.23	41.98	37.90	38.11	37.95
Construction	3.08	5.72	7.27	7.64	8.64	9.97	11.28
Electricity, gas and waste management	11.53	12.50	14.87	19.43	20.05	20.89	21.93
Trade, wholesale, retail, food and accommodation services	44.40	46.44	49.51	51.25	51.97	52.13	52.59
Import/export trade and wholesale				47.59	47.54	47.58	47.36
Retail				59.09	61.07	60.18	60.70
Accommodation and food services				52.54	52.56	53.27	54.30
Transportation, storage, courier, communications	33.80	34.22	35.66	33.67	34.40	34.37	35.20
Transportation, storage				33.64	34.49	34.76	35.07
Information and communications				33.73	34.24	33.73	35.42
Financing, insurance, real estate, professional and business services	42.74	42.58	42.74	47.96	48.31	49.21	49.14
Financing and insurance				53.21	51.45	51.51	51.00
Real estate				34.33	37.66	39.21	43.91
Professional and business services				49.68	50.29	51.36	49.81
Public administration, civil services	31.42	33.04	33.81	33.96	35.35	37.02	38.43
Social and personal services	56.20	60.16	63.31	64.26	64.27	65.01	65.78
Total	43.37	45.01	47.80	49.31	49.52	49.74	50.36

Source: Figures are calculated based on 1996–2020 *Hong Kong Annual Digest of Statistics* (Census and Statistics Department of Hong Kong SAR Government, 1994–2020). Consistent information has only been available since 1993.

As in other societies around the world (Cech, 2013; Reskin and Hartman, 1986; Weeden, 1998), occupations in Hong Kong are also highly gender segregated: women are less likely to be concentrated in industries such as manufacturing, construction, electricity, transportation and civil services, but more likely to be concentrated in industries such as retail trade, accommodation and restaurants, and social and personal services.

Over time, however, women are more likely to become civil servants and professionals in finance and business services: the share of women in public administration increased from 31.4 per cent in 1995 to 38.4 per cent in 2019, and the share of women working in finance, insurance, real estate, professional and business services increased from 42.7 per cent in 1985 to 49.1 per cent in 2019. The increase in the share of women in professional jobs is mainly due to a significant increase in the share of women in real estate, from 34.3 per cent in 1995 to 43.9 per cent in 2019. The share of women in finance and insurance, however, decreased slightly from 53.2 per cent in 2004 to 51.0 per cent in 2019. At the same time, women's share of manufacturing jobs declined, from 43.7 per cent in 1995 to 38.0 per cent in 2019. Their share in industries including retails, food and accommodation services, social and personal services are increased. Therefore, similar to the trend in 1991–1996 (Ngo, 2000), both processes of desegregation and re-segregation have taken place in the occupational structure since the mid-1990s.

Figure 14.3 summarizes the trends in occupational gender segregation in Hong Kong since 1993, based on available official statistics. Clearly, as the gender gap in higher education reverses, there are increasing job opportunities for women to become managers in the public sector and professionals in finance, insurance, real estate and business services. The link between higher education and managerial/professional occupations tends to strengthen among women as more and more highly educated women enter the labour market.

Previous research has found that gender inequality in earnings tends to disappear after controlling for women's compatibility with paid work in 1996 (Cheung, 2002). Similarly, we expect that the gender gap in occupational status in the first job tends to disappear or even reverse, especially among the highly educated. Therefore, we propose the following hypothesis to test:

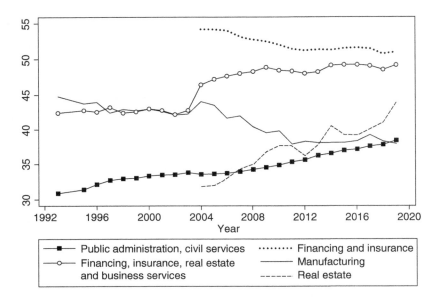

Figure 14.3 Percentage of female employment by industry in Hong Kong, 1993–2019
Source: Census and Statistics Department of Hong Kong SAR Government (1994–2020).

Hypothesis 2: The gender gap in first job occupational status tends to diminish or even be reversed across cohorts among those with higher education.

Data, Variables and Methods

Data

This chapter uses data from the 2011 Hong Kong Panel Study of Social Dynamics (HKPSSD). The HKPSSD is the first household panel study in Hong Kong that aims to track social and economic changes and their impact on individuals (Wu, 2016). It collects a wealth of information on household background, such as household economic activities and parents' education and occupation, as well as individual characteristics, such as education, employment and occupation, and social activities. For this study, although multiple waves of the survey have information on respondents' first jobs in Hong Kong, only the first wave provided detailed categories of first jobs that could generate the ISEI (International Socioeconomic Index, see Ganzeboom et al., 1992) of first jobs.[2] Therefore, this study uses data from the first wave only.

The first wave of the HKPSSD yielded a representative sample of over 3,214 Hong Kong households with 7,218 respondents ages 15 or older and 958 children under age 15. In our analysis, the sample is restricted to those born from 1950 to 1989 that have first job information, which leaves a subsample of 3,049 cases.

Variables

To understand how school-to-work transition patterns change over time in Hong Kong, we distinguish four birth cohorts based on year of birth: 1950–1959, 1960–1969, 1970–1979 and 1980–1989. In public narratives, these birth cohorts are commonly referred to as the 'post-1950s', 'post-1960s', 'post-1970s' and 'post-1980s' generations (Lam-Knott, 2018; Wong et al., 2018). Here, special attention is paid to the post-1980s generation,[3] which are found to have many career-related issues (Yip et al., 2011) and rise as a political force (Lau, 2014) in Hong Kong.

The dependent variable is the respondent's first occupational status. It is first measured by a continuous ISEI score, which is widely used in the literature of comparative stratification research. It is also measured by a six-category occupation code (Wu, 2010b). Specifically, we recode respondents' first occupation into the following categories: manage/professional=6, associate professional=5, clerk=4, service worker=3, skilled worker=2, and unskilled worker=1. Here we do not use the classic EGP class scheme (Erikson et al., 1979) to measure occupational status, as the percentage of self-employed (IVb & IVc) and agricultural workers (VIIb) is quite low in Hong Kong. In the first wave, they only account for 1.1 per cent of those with first job information (33 cases).

Independent variables include gender, education and parental background. Following standard procedures in the literature, we use the CASMIN (Comparative Analysis of Social Mobility in Industrial Nations) educational schema (Kerckhoff et al., 2002) to measure education but recode it as a dummy variable to indicate whether the respondent had a traditional, academically-oriented university education (3b) at the time of his or her first job.[4] Parental background can be measured by multiple indicators. In this study, we use only parental education, which is also a dummy variable to show whether the highest level of education of the respondent's parents have a higher tertiary education(university=1, lower=0).[5] Finally, to keep the model concise, we only include immigration status as a control variable, which is an important dimension of occupational status attainment in Hong Kong (Peng, 2021; Zhang and Ye, 2018). It is a dummy variable (yes=1) indicating whether the respondent was an immigrant to Hong Kong at the time of his or her first job.

Table 14.3 presents summary statistics for the dependent and independent variables. It shows that fewer women than men enter their first job for those born before 1980, but the proportion of women exceeds that of men for those born in the 1980s. Across birth cohorts, the proportion of workers with a university degree at the time of their first job increases substantially: for those born in the 1960s, only 7.58 per cent of workers come from a four-year college, but that number jumps to 21.49 per cent for those born in the 1970s and 26.20 per cent for those born in the 1980s. However, the percentage of parents who have a college degree at the time of their first job does not change much. At the same time, there are fewer immigrants in younger cohorts.

Regarding the distribution of first jobs, overall, the percentage of managers, professionals and associate professionals, or 'middle class' occupations in Hong Kong, essentially increase from 7.5 per cent for those born in the 1950s to 20.6 per cent for those born in the 1970s and 21.5 per cent for those born in the 1980s. However, among those with a university degree, a lower percentage of university-educated workers now have a 'middle class' occupation as a first job: the percentage declines from 69.7 per cent for those born in the 1950s to 57.4 per cent for those born in the 1980s. This decline is particularly pronounced for achieving a managerial or professional position in the first job among those with a university education. Specifically, the percentage is declining from more than 45 per cent for the pre-1980 birth cohorts to about 30 per cent for those born in the 1980s. In contrast, the proportion of individuals with university degrees who become associate professionals is increasing, from less than 20 per cent for the pre-1980 birth cohorts to 27.9 per cent for those born in the 1980s.

Table 14.3 Summary statistics by cohort, HKPSSD 2011

Variables	Total	1950–1959	1960–1969	1970–1979	1980–1989
Male %	49.12	48.26	49.01	46.45	53.66
University %	13.94	3.06	7.58	21.49	26.20
Parental education (university) %	3.73	3.12	2.89	5.23	3.79
Immigrant%	29.46	41.58	28.66	25.76	20.59
First job ISEI[a]	36.39	31.00	36.55	40.15	39.19
	(11.84)	(10.81)	(11.37)	(11.90)	(11.15)
First occupation overall %					
Manager/ professional	7.11	3.42	5.33	11.44	8.68
Associate professional	7.86	4.05	6.54	9.11	12.81
Clerk	23.97	12.74	24.75	33.20	24.88
Service worker	23.91	14.27	22.24	24.08	37.75
Skilled worker	21.75	39.33	23.86	13.66	7.59
Unskilled worker	15.40	26.19	17.28	8.52	8.29
Among university graduates %					
Manager/ professional	39.79	52.27	46.24	45.59	29.47
Associate professional	22.19	17.45	19.72	18.22	27.92
Clerk	26.71	23.74	21.19	30.02	25.99
Service worker	9.64	-	9.65	4.11	16.62
Skilled worker	1.67	6.53	3.19	2.05	-
Unskilled worker	-	-	-	-	-
N	3,049	825	960	680	584

Note: Data are weighted.
[a]Reported are means. Standard deviations in parentheses.

Methods

Because our dependent variables are both continuous and ordinal, we first use OLS regression and ordered logit models to estimate the determinants of first job ISEI and occupational status, respectively. To further empirically measure the association between university education and first job, as well as the possible variation in the magnitude and/or pattern of this association across birth cohorts, we conduct our analysis using a Stereotyped Ordered Regression (SOR) model (see also Wu and Treiman, 2007, for an example).

The SOR model is simply a reparameterization of the multinomial logit model, but it has two desirable properties. First, it does not assume strict ordering among values of the dependent variable but instead estimates a scaling metric for it that considers the effects of individual-level covariates (DiPrete, 1990). Second, it can specify association parameters measuring the association between dependent and independent variables using Goodman's (1979) Row and Column models. In our study, we use Goodman's Row and Columns model 2 (RC2) as a constraint to measure the association between university education and first job occupational status.

The SOR model can be defined as:

$$\log\left(\frac{P(Y=j)}{P(Y=j')}\right) = \text{logit}\left(\frac{\pi_j}{\pi_{j'}}\right) = \alpha_j - \alpha_{j'} + \left(\varphi_j - \varphi_{j'}\right) \sum_{k=1}^{K} \beta_k X_k$$

where Y is the first occupation with categories $j = 1$ to 6, α_j represents the constrained intercept parameters, φ_j represents the scaling metric for the dependent variable (occupation j), X_k represents independent variables, and the β_k are the effect parameters of the independent variables. Hence, the effect of one unit change in X_k on the log odds of being in one occupational destination j versus another j' is captured by $(\varphi_j - \varphi_{j'}) \beta_k$ rather than by β_k as in a standard multinomial logit model. To identify the model, we need to impose some restrictions on φ_j so that $\sum \varphi_j = 0$ and $\sum \varphi_j^2 = 1$.

In the framework of the SOR model, Goodman's (1979) RC2 model can be written as:

$$\text{logit}\left(\frac{\pi_j}{\pi_{j'}}\right) = \alpha_j - \alpha_{j'} + \left(\varphi_j - \varphi_{j'}\right)\mu\sigma_i$$

University education is treated as a covariate in the SOR model, except that it also needs to be rescaled by σ_i, and the effect of university education on first occupation is expressed by a single parameter μ. Likewise, to identify the model, the same restrictions have to be imposed on σ_i so that $\sum \sigma_i = 0$ and $\sum \sigma_i^2 = 1$.

We can estimate models that incorporate covariates intervening between university education and first occupation, and allow the association parameter μ to co-vary with one or more of them, such as birth cohorts in this study:

$$\text{logit}\left(\frac{\pi_j}{\pi_{j'}}\right) = \alpha_j - \alpha_{j'} + \left(\varphi_j - \varphi_{j'}\right)\left(\mu_0 + \sum_{t=1}^{T} \mu_t X_t\right)\sigma_i$$

$$+ \left(\varphi_j - \varphi_{j'}\right)\sum_{k=1}^{K} \beta_k X_k$$

where μ_0 is the basic association parameter and the μ_t represents the effects of covariates X_t on the association. All the above models can be estimated iteratively by using Stata command *mclest* developed by Hendrickx (2004).

Results

Table 14.4 shows the results of OLS regressions of the determinants of first job ISEI by birth cohort. Panel A does not consider the inter-action effect between gender and university education, while Panel B does. Comparing the models, we find that the association between university education and a good first job is decreasing across birth cohorts. As shown in Panel A, net of other factors, the ISEI for first jobs is on average 16.1 points higher for university-educated workers than for those without a university degree, but this advantage declines monotonically from 26.1 points for those born in the 1950s to 12.7 points for those born in the 1980s. This finding supports Hypothesis 1. In the meantime, while the effect of parental education is not signif-icant among those born before 1980, it becomes positively significant among the post-80s generation: all else being equal, the advantage of having a parent with a university degree averages 8.5 points on the ISEI for a first job. Moreover, Panel A results show that the disad-vantage of being a Hong Kong immigrant gradually disappears in first job ISEI: controlling for other factors, immigrants born before 1980 have on average about 5–6 points lower ISEI for their first job than Hong Kong natives, while among those born after 1980, this differ-ence becomes insignificant, albeit with a negative coefficient.

With respect to the effect of gender, surprisingly, Panel A shows that men do not have an advantage over women in first job ISEI. Across birth cohorts, while men's average first job ISEI is significantly higher than women's by 1.7 points ($p = 0.063$) for the cohort of the 1950s when controlling for other factors, the male advantage dimin-ishes among those born in 1960–1979, and becomes reversed among

Table 14.4 OLS estimates of the determinants of first job ISEI, HKPSSD 2011

Variables	Panel A: Without interaction terms					Panel B: With interaction terms				
	Total	1950–1959	1960–1969	1970–1979	1980–1989	Total	1950–1959	1960–1969	1970–1979	1980–1989
Male	−0.437	1.713[+]	−0.254	−1.390	−2.949***	−1.170*	1.628[+]	−0.529	−2.713**	−4.785***
	(0.448)	(0.919)	(0.781)	(0.967)	(0.889)	(0.464)	(0.927)	(0.806)	(1.035)	(0.916)
University	16.110***	26.126***	19.761***	15.259***	12.699***	13.082***	23.798***	16.809***	11.543***	9.320***
	(0.856)	(3.076)	(1.700)	(1.489)	(1.330)	(0.967)	(4.798)	(1.990)	(1.588)	(1.516)
Parental education	3.560**	0.674	2.952	2.493	8.462***	2.954*	0.969	2.367	1.040	7.555**
	(1.173)	(2.005)	(3.008)	(1.447)	(2.368)	(1.197)	(2.128)	(2.858)	(1.767)	(2.296)
Immigrant	−4.776***	−6.117***	−5.055***	−5.179***	−1.179	−4.731***	−6.104***	−5.066***	−5.184***	−0.789
	(0.481)	(0.906)	(0.778)	(1.118)	(0.973)	(0.478)	(0.908)	(0.778)	(1.108)	(0.944)
Male* University						5.826***	3.405	4.585	7.037**	8.116**
						(1.560)	(6.066)	(3.078)	(2.688)	(2.579)
Cohort[a]										
1960–1969	3.676***					3.649***				
	(0.625)					(0.621)				
1970–1979	5.405***					5.369***				
	(0.704)					(0.698)				
1980–1989	2.864***					3.101***				
	(0.673)					(0.664)				
Constant	33.666***	33.029***	37.093***	39.847***	37.663***	33.989***	33.053***	37.234***	40.461***	38.613***
	(0.613)	(0.990)	(0.588)	(0.624)	(0.739)	(0.614)	(0.991)	(0.591)	(0.615)	(0.743)
R-squared	0.327	0.261	0.246	0.335	0.343	0.334	0.262	0.248	0.347	0.365
N	2,534	640	813	575	506	2,534	640	813	575	506

Notes: Robust standard errors in parentheses. Data are weighted.
***$p<0.001$, **$p<0.01$, *$p<0.05$, [+]$p<0.1$ (two-tailed).
[a]Refer to '1950–1959.'

the post-1980s generation: others being equal, women's average first job ISEI is nearly 3 points higher than men's.

Panel B further illustrates how the relationship between gender and first job varies by university education. By additionally including an interaction term between gender and university education, we find that, overall, the interaction term is significant and positive. All else being equal, the gender gap in ISEI for first job is 4.66 (5.83–1.17) points for the university-educated, but −1.17 points for those without a university degree. Across birth cohorts, the interaction effect is positive for the cohorts of 1970s and 1980s. Controlling for other factors, the mean first job ISEI is 4.38 (7.04–2.71) and 3.43 (8.12–4.79) points higher for men than for women in the cohorts of 1970s and 1980s, respectively, but among those without a college degree, men born in the 1970s and 1980s have lower ISEI means for their first job than women (2.71 and 4.79 points, respectively).

Figure 14.4 intuitively illustrates the pattern. By plotting the predicted mean first job ISEI based on models in Panel B, it shows that across birth cohorts, the male advantage in first job ISEI tends to

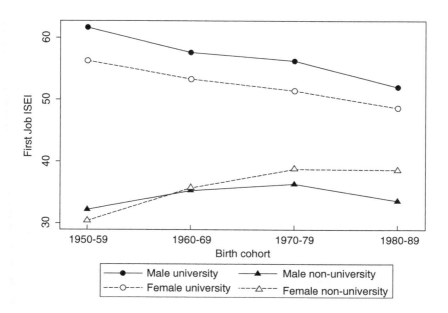

Figure 14.4   Predicted mean first job ISEI, by gender and education

decrease among those with a university education; among those without a university degree, the gender gap is even reversed and female even enjoy some advantage, especially in the post-1980s generation. Overall, this pattern lends support for Hypothesis 2.

These patterns have been consistent if first job status is measured categorically. In addition to the analysis of the first job ISEI, we also run a set of logit models on the determinants of first job occupational status. To facilitate interpretation, Table 14.5 reports the marginal effects rather than the coefficients of the logit models, as marginal effects can be compared across models (Karlson et al., 2013). In Panel A, first job occupational categories are recoded as a dummy variable indicating whether the respondent is a manager or a professional, or an elite in Hong Kong (Wong and Koo, 2016). In Panel B, they are recoded to reflect the 'middle-class' occupations (Wu, 2010b): managers, professionals and associate professionals.[6] The first column of Table 14.4 reports the estimated marginal effects for the entire sample. It shows that men, university degree holders and children having a university-educated father or mother are more likely to obtain a managerial/professional position in their first job. Conversely, immigrants tend to have a lower probability of becoming a manager or professional in their first job. The next four models show the estimation results by birth cohort. They show that although the marginal effect of university education on first job attainment is positively significant, its magnitude is monotonically decreasing across generations, again supporting Hypothesis 1. All else being equal, those with a university degree among the cohort of the 1950s are 43.0 per cent more likely to be a manager or professional in their first job than those without a university degree, but that number changes to 25.9 per cent among the cohort of the 1980s.

Panel B of Table 14.5 shows a similar pattern. Others being equal, university-educated individuals are on average 49.6 per cent more likely to land a middle-class first job than those without a university degree. Across generations, the marginal effect of university education on getting a middle-class first job also declines monotonically. Controlling for other factors, the probability of finding a middle-class first job for those with a university education is 60.0 per cent higher than those without a university degree among the cohort of the 1950s, but the figure becomes 49.1 per cent among the cohort of the 1980s.

Table 14.5 Marginal effects of the logit model estimates of the determinants of first job occupational status, HKPSSD 2011

Variables	Panel A: Manager/Professional vs. Others					Panel B: Manager/Professional/Associate professional vs. Others				
	Total	1950–1959	1960–1969	1970–1979	1980–1989	Total	1950–1959	1960–1969	1970–1979	1980–1989
Male	0.016**	0.004	0.008	0.030[+]	0.024	0.024	−0.011	0.008	0.045	0.058
	(0.006)	(0.011)	(0.009)	(0.017)	(0.017)	(0.014)	(0.019)	(0.021)	(0.034)	(0.039)
University	0.343***	0.430***	0.397***	0.368***	0.259***	0.496***	0.600***	0.529***	0.516***	0.491***
	(0.036)	(0.124)	(0.072)	(0.053)	(0.047)	(0.033)	(0.131)	(0.067)	(0.052)	(0.053)
Parental education	0.046*	0.030	0.004	0.107	0.059	0.082	−0.008	0.124	0.104	0.140
	(0.023)	(0.038)	(0.022)	(0.072)	(0.054)	(0.046)	(0.040)	(0.120)	(0.099)	(0.115)
Immigrant	−0.014*	−0.011	−0.022*	−0.011	0.001	−0.050***	−0.049**	−0.082***	−0.054	0.030
	(0.006)	(0.011)	(0.008)	(0.017)	(0.014)	(0.014)	(0.019)	(0.021)	(0.036)	(0.055)
Cohort[a]										
1960–1969	−0.005					0.017				
	(0.008)					(0.020)				
1970–1979	−0.003					0.027				
	(0.008)					(0.022)				
1980–1989	−0.017**					0.015				
	(0.007)					(0.024)				
Log likelihood	−518.5	−88.27	−121.8	−178.4	−124.5	−978.4	−169	−258.7	−287.8	−253.1
Pseudo R-squared	0.352	0.242	0.336	0.385	0.335	0.254	0.164	0.211	0.289	0.248
N	2,858	738	907	647	566	2,858	738	907	647	566

Notes: Robust standard errors in parentheses. Data are weighted.
*** $p < 0.001$, ** $p < 0.01$, * $p < 0.05$, + $p < 0.1$ (two-tailed).
[a] Refer to '1950–1959'.

Consistent with the results in Table 14.4, the effect of university education on first job occupational status is decreasing.

While Table 14.5 uses occupational dummies as the dependent variables, Table 14.6 treats first job occupational status as an ordinal variable. The conventional ordered logit model shows that university degree holders and individuals with a university-educated father or mother tend to rank higher in the first job occupational category, while men and immigrants tend to rank lower, as shown in Model 1A. Model 1B further shows that the interaction effect between gender and university education is positively significant, indicating that university-educated men tend to have a better first job status than university-educated women, but non-university-educated women tend to have a better first job status than non-university-educated men.

Unlike the ordered logit model, the SOR model does not assume a specific order of occupational categories, but it does assume that occupational categories can be ranked; scaling of categories is one of the results of the analysis. Model 2A shows that without assuming the order of the first job occupational categories, the direction of the effects of covariates (β parameters) is the same as in Model 1A. Again, men tend to have a lower likelihood of obtaining a higher ranked first job. In addition, by using the restriction that the first category is fixed to 0 and the last category is fixed to 1, the estimated scaling rank (φ parameters) is the same as we recode. Differences between φ scale values suggest how the logit of one occupation versus another is affected by covariates in the model. The largest impact of covariates on the logit between adjacent categories is for service workers versus skilled workers, with a difference of 0.53 (0.567–0.040) between the scale values. The smallest impact is on skilled workers versus unskilled workers, a difference of only 0.04. Finally, the μ parameters indicate the degree of influence of university education on first job. Using Goodman's RC2 model, the overall association between university education and first job is positively significant (9.973). However, consistent with our first hypothesis, across birth cohorts, the magnitude of the association is monotonically declining. The impact of having a university education rather than a non-university education on the logit of being a manager or professional rather than an associate professional is 1.68 [(1–0.832)*9.973] for the cohort of the 1950s, 1.45 [(1–0.832)*(9.973–1.361)] for the cohort of the 1960s, 1.25 [(1–0.832)

Table 14.6 Coefficients of ordered logit model and stereotyped ordered regression model estimates of the determinants of first job occupational status, HKPSSD 2011

Variables[a]	Ordered logit		Stereotyped ordered logit	
	Model 1A	Model 1B	Model 2A	Model 2B
Effects of covariates (β)				
Male	−0.654***	−0.833***	−1.448***	−1.565***
	(0.078)	(0.084)	(0.133)	(0.142)
University	2.977***	2.326***		
	(0.142)	(0.163)		
Parental education	0.817**	0.804**	0.963*	0.997*
	(0.269)	(0.251)	(0.461)	(0.466)
Immigrant	−0.905***	−0.903***	−1.284***	−1.357***
	(0.083)	(0.082)	(0.142)	(0.149)
Male*University		1.318***		2.185***
		(0.248)		(0.651)
First job occupational scaling metric (φ)				
Manager/professional			1.000	1.000
Associate professional			0.832	0.806
Clerk			0.721	0.690
Service worker			0.567	0.532
Skilled worker			0.040	0.039
Unskilled worker			0.000	0.000
Education-first job association (μ)				
Overall association			9.973***	8.470***
			(0.499)	(0.565)
Association*1960–1969			−1.361***	−1.420***
			(0.169)	(0.177)
Association*1970–1979			−2.523***	−2.623***
			(0.197)	(0.206)
Association*1980–1989			−2.848***	−2.930***
			(0.214)	(0.223)
Log likelihood	−4589	−4589	−4218	−4213
Pseudo R2	0.112	0.112	0.176	0.177
N	2,858	2,858	17,148	17,148

Notes: Standard errors in parentheses.
***$p<0.001$, **$p<0.01$, *$p<0.05$, +$p<0.1$ (two-tailed).
[a]Parameters for the intercepts are omitted to conserve space. No standard errors for scaling parameters.

*(9.973–2.523)] for the cohort of 1970s and 1.20 [(1–0.832) *(9.973–2.848)] for the cohort of 1980s. Similarly, the impact of having a university education rather than a non-university education on the logit of being a manager or professional rather than a clerk is 2.78 for the cohort of the 1950s, 2.40 for the cohort of the 1960s, 2.08 for the cohort of the 1970s and 1.99 for the cohort of the 1980s. Figure 14.5 visually depicts these predicted logit values. It shows that the association between university education and first job is declining across generations.

Model 2B additionally includes the interaction term between gender and university education in the SOR model. It turns out that the coefficient of the interaction term is positively significant. Again, university-educated men tend to have a higher probability (with a logit of 2.185–1.565) of getting a better first job than university-educated women, but among those without a university education, women's probability of getting a better first job is higher than men's (with a logit of −1.565). Other results are similar to those shown in Model 2A.

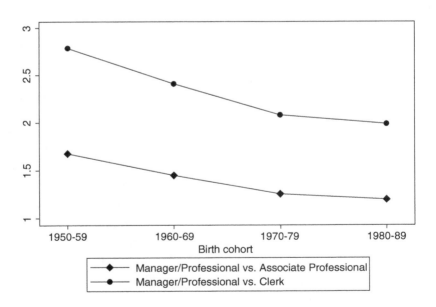

Figure 14.5   Predicted logit for University vs. Non-University education for selected first job occupational categories

Conclusion and Dicussion

This chapter examines the trends and patterns of school-to-transition in Hong Kong. Using data from the 2011 wave of Hong Kong Panel Study of Social Dynamics, we find that while university qualifications confer higher returns to first job occupational status, such returns tend to decline monotonically across birth cohorts. In addition, the male advantage over females in first job occupational status tends to diminish across cohorts among those with university degrees, but reverses among those with non-university degrees, and this reversed gender gap is widening across cohorts. Finally, results of the Stereotyped Order Regression model suggest that the association parameter between higher education and first occupation is declining across cohorts, suggesting that a university degree has become less effective than before as a determinant of first occupation for younger generations.

These results highlight how structural changes in both the education system and labour market have affected the school–work linkage in Hong Kong. Government-led educational expansion since the late 1980s, particularly since 2001, has dramatically increased tertiary education enrolment among younger cohorts in a short period of time (Post, 2010). At the same time, with the s structural changes in the economy of Hong Kong (Lui, 2015; Meyer, 2008), new elite and middle-class jobs have been created at a much slower pace, leading to downward pressure on young adults' first job occupational status. Consequently, the over-supply of highly educated workers has significantly reduced the first job ISEI and occupational status for younger cohorts, especially the post-1980s generation. Among them, however, with the gender gap in higher education reversing under the recent expansion, women have increasing labour market opportunities to obtain better jobs, such as becoming managers and professionals. Thus, structural changes in the education system and labour market have strengthened the link between higher education and first occupation for women, which is rarely seen elsewhere.

In sum, higher education expansion in Hong Kong, coupled with the restructuring of the economy, has made the transition to work more precarious for younger cohorts (see also Wu, 2010b). In particular, it is increasingly difficult for those with higher education to obtain elite or middle-class jobs in the post-1980s generation. Thus, as

Wu (2010b, p. 40) puts it, the key problem for Hong Kong youths nowadays is the 'increasingly bumpy transition from school to work'.

Recent research suggests that younger generations in Hong Kong enjoy less equality of opportunity in terms of social mobility than their predecessors, and that they feel depressed and frustrated about their mobility prospects (Chan et al., 1995; Wong and Koo, 2016). Indeed, self-reported happiness is lower among young people with higher levels of education (Kühner et al., 2021). Several studies have discussed the changing patterns of youth identity politics in Hong Kong (Lam-Knott, 2018; Lau, 2014; Lui, 2007; So and Ip, 2019), arguing that a major reason for the rise of the post-1980s generation as a political force is that they are affected by declining social and occupational mobility. Along this line, our research suggests that educational expansion may be a contributing factor to the growing political discontent and activism of younger generations as the association between higher education and first jobs declines among the post-1980s generation.

Finally, our study contributes to the general literature on school-to-work transitions in two ways. First, we move beyond the institutional perspective of school-to-work transitions by bringing back a structural perspective. The Hong Kong case shows that structural changes in the education system and labour market can independently affect the link between education and first occupation. Second, our findings emphasize how government-led educational expansion in Hong Kong moderates the impact of education on first jobs. Because educational expansion leads to institutional and structural changes in the education system and labour market, future comparative studies of school-to-work transitions cannot ignore this integral component of the school–work relationship.

Notes

1   This research was supported by the Center for Applied Social and Economic Research (CASER) at NYU Shanghai. The HKPSSD data collection was conducted by the Center for Applied Social and Economic Research (CASER) at the Hong Kong University of Science and Technology (HKUST), with funding support from the RGC Central Policy Unit's Strategic Public Policy Research Funding Scheme (HKUST6001-SPPR-08). Direct all correspondence to Xiaogang Wu (xw29@nyu.edu) or Maocan Guo (mcguo@nyu.edu), NYU Shanghai Center for Applied Social and Economic Research (CASER), 1555 Century Avenue, Pudong, Shanghai 200122, China.

2   For each job, the respondent is asked to identify the broad occupational category it falls into, and provide a verbal description of such details as the job title, rank and daily duties. A three-digit ISCO88 code is assigned to each job according to its detailed verbal description. ISEI is generated based on the three-digit ISCO88 code using the Stata command *iscogen* (Jann, 2019). For details of the construction of the ISCO88 code and the HKPSSD project in general, see Wu (2016).

3   Lam-Knott (2018 shows that the definition of the post-1980s generation could include a political dimension: only those born in the 1980s and politically involved can be considered as post-1980s. Here we only define the generations through birth cohorts.

4   We have also tried to use a broader definition of higher education (including lower tertiary education such as non-degree post-secondary education, three-year junior college, and community college) as a dummy variable. The results are similar.

5   We also tried using parental ISEI instead and the results are similar (available upon request). Sensitivity test further shows that the main patterns do not change whether we use parental education or parental ISEI or both to measure parental background.

6   Similar to Table 14.4, we have estimated models with the interaction terms between gender and university education, but sensitivity test shows that the interaction effects are insignificant. Therefore, we do not include them in the results in Table 14.5.

References

Ahrens, K. (2019). *Addresses by the Hong Kong governors and the Hong Kong special administrative region Chief executives 1984–2018 corpus.* Research Centre for Professional Communication in English, The Hong Kong Polytechnic University. http://rcpce.engl.polyu.edu.hk/politicalspeeches/hkpa.html.

Andersen, R., & Van de Werfhorst, H. G. (2010). Education and occupational status in 14 countries: The role of educational institutions and labour market coordination. *British Journal of Sociology, 61*, 336–355.

Arum, R., & Hout, M. (1998). The early returns: The transition from school to work in the United States. In Y. Shavit & W. Müller (Eds.), *From school to work: A comparative study of educational qualifications and occupational destinations* (pp. 417–510). Oxford: Clarendon Press.

Bol, T. & Van de Werfhorst, H. G. (2011). Signals and closure by degrees: The education effect across 15 European countries. *Research in Social Stratification and Mobility, 29*, 119–132.

Breen, R. (2005). Explaining cross-national variation in youth unemployment: Market and institutional factors. *European Sociological Review, 21*(2), 125–134.

Buchmann, C., DiPrete, D. A., & McDaniel, A. (2008). Gender inequalities in education. *Annual Review of Sociology, 34*(1), 319–337.

Buchmann, C., & Hannum, E. (2001). Education and stratification in developing countries: A review of theories and research. *Annual Review of Sociology, 27*(1), 77–102.

Cech, E. A. (2013). The self-expressive edge of occupational sex segregation. *American Journal of Sociology, 119*(3), 747–789.

Census and Statistics Department of Hong Kong SAR Government. (1994–2020). *Hong Kong annual digest of statistics.* https://www.censtatd.gov.hk/en/EIndexbySubject.html?pcode=B1010003&scode=460#section1.

Chan, T. W., Lui, T. L., & Wong, T. W. P. (1995). A comparative analysis of social mobility in Hong Kong. *European Sociological Review, 11*(2), 135–155.

Cheung, C.-K. (2002). Gender differences in participation and earnings in Hong Kong. *Journal of Contemporary Asia, 32*(1, 69–90.

Committee on Self-financing Post-secondary Education. (2021). *Participation rate of post-secondary education.* https://www.cspe.edu.hk/en/Statistics.page#chart-participation-tbl.

DiPrete, T. A. (1990). Adding covariates to loglinear models for the study of social mobility. *American Sociological Review, 55*(5), 757–773.

DiPrete, T. A., Bol, T., Eller, C. C., & Van de Werfhorst, H. G. (2017). School-to-Work linkages in the United States, Germany, and France. *American Journal of Sociology, 122*(6), 1869–1938.

Education Commission of Hong Kong. (1984). *Education commission report No. 1.* https://www.e-c.edu.hk/doc/en/publications_and_related_documents/education_reports/ecr1_e.pdf.

Education Commission of Hong Kong. (1988). *Education commission report No. 3.* https://www.e-.edu.hk/doc/tc/publications_and_related_documents/education_reports/ecr3_c.pdf.

Erikson, R., Goldthorpe, J. H., & Portocarero, L. (1979). Intergenerational class mobility in three Western European societies: England, France and Sweden. *The British Journal of Sociology, 30*(4), 415.

Ganzeboom, H. B. G., De Graaf, P. M., & Treiman, D. J. (1992). A standard international socio-economic index of occupational status. *Social Science Research, 21*, 1–56.

Geber, T. (2003). Loosening links? School-to-work transitions and institutional change in Russia since 1970. *Social Forces, 82*(1), 241–276.

Goodman, L. A. (1979). Multiplicative models for the analysis of occupational mobility tables and other kinds of cross-classification tables. *American Journal of Sociology, 84*(4), 804–819.

Guo, M. (2021). Understanding the consequence of higher educational expansion in China: A double-treatment perspective. *Chinese Sociological Review*, 1–26.

Hendrickx, J. (2004). *MCL: Stata module to estimate multinomial conditional logit models.* https://econpapers.repec.org/software/bocbocode/s423101.htm.

Ho, E. S. C., Wong, R. S. K., Keung, C. P. C. and Sum, K. W. (2017). Analyzing Hong Kong adolescents' expectations for pursuing higher education from PISA. *Jiaoyu Xuebao (Education Journal), 45*(1), 47–69.

Jann, B. (2019). *ISCOGEN: Stata module to translate ISCO codes.* http://ideas.repec.org/c/boc/bocode/s458665.html.

Karlson, K. B., Anders H., & Richard B. (2013). Comparing regression coefficients between same-sample nested models using logit and probit: A new method. *Sociological Methodology*, *42*(1), 286–313.

Kerckhoff, A. C. (2001). Education and social stratification processes in comparative perspectives. *Sociology of Education*, *74*, 3–18.

Kerckhoff, A. C., Ezell, E. D. and Brown, J. S. (2002). Toward an improved measure of educational attainment in social stratification research. *Social Science Research*, *31*, 99–123.

Kühner, S., Jiang, J., Wen, Z., & Lau, M. (2021). Labour market experience, educational attainment and self-reported happiness: Crowding-out amongst young people in Hong Kong. *Journal of Education and Work*, *34*(3), 1–17.

Lam-Knott, S. (2018). Anti-hierarchical activism in Hong Kong: The post-80s youth. *Social Movement Studies*, *17*(4), 464–470.

Lau, C. H. M. (2014). Political participation of the post-80s generation: Their protest activities and social movement in recent years in Hong Kong. In J. Y. S. Cheng (ed.), *New trends of political participation in Hong Kong* (pp. 387–416). Hong Kong: City University Press.

Lavely, W., Xiao, Z., Li, B., & Freedman, R. (1990). The rise in female education in China: National and regional patterns. *The China Quarterly*, *121*, 61–93.

Lui, H. K. (1994). The expansion of tertiary education in Hong Kong. *Higher Education Review*, *27*(1), 23–33.

Lui, T. L. (2007). *Sidai Xianggangren [four Generations of Hongkongers]*. Hong Kong: Step Forward Multimedia Company.

Lui, T. L. (2009). Hong Kong's changing opportunity structures: Political concerns and sociological observations. *Social Transformation in Chinese Societies*, *5*, 141–163.

Lui, T. L. (2015). *Xianggang moshi: Cong xianzaishi dao guoqushi [Hong Kong model: From present Tense to past tense]*. Hong Kong: Chung Hwa Book.

Meyer, D. R. (2008). Structural changes in the economy of Hong Kong since 1997. *The China Review*, *8*(1), 7–29.

Müller, W., & Gangl, M. (2003). *Transitions from education to work in europe: The integration of youth into EU labor markets*. Oxford: Oxford University Press.

Ngo, H. Y. (2000). Trends in occupational sex segregation in Hong Kong. *International Journal of Human Resource Management*, *11*(2), 251–263.

O'Sullivan, M., & Tsang, M. Y. H. (2015). Educational inequalities in higher education in Hong Kong. *Inter-Asia Cultural Studies*, *16*(3), 454–469.

Peng, Y. (2021). From migrant student to migrant employee: Three models of the school-to-work transition of mainland Chinese in Hong Kong. *Population, Space and Place*, *26*(4), e2283.

Pong, S. L., & Post, D. (1991). Trends in gender and family background effects on school attainment: The case of Hong Kong. *British Journal of Sociology*, *42*(2), 249–271.

Post, D. (1994). Educational stratification, school expansion, and public policy in Hong Kong. *Sociology of Education*, *67*(2), 21–138.

Post, D. (2003). Hong Kong higher education, 1981–2001: Public policy and re-emergent social stratification. *Oxford Review of Education, 29*(4), 545–570.

Post, D. (2010). Postsecondary educational expansion and social integration in Hong Kong. In E. Hannum, H. Park & Y. G. Butler (Eds.), *Globalization, changing demographics, and educational challenges in East Asia. Research in the sociology of education* (*Vol. 17*, pp. 231–269). Bingley: Emerald Group Publishing Limited.

Reskin, B., & Hartman, H. (1986). *Women's work, men's work: Sex segregation on the job.* Washington: National Academy Press.

Shavit, Y., Arum, R., & Gamoran, A. (2007). *Stratification in higher education: A comparative study.* Stanford, CA: Stanford University Press.

Shavit, Y., & Müller, W. (Eds.) (1998). *From school to work: A comparative study of educational qualifications and occupational destinations.* Oxford: Clarendon.

So, A. Y., & Ip, P. L. (2019). Civic localism, anti-mainland localism, and independence: The changing pattern of identity politics in Hong Kong special administrative region. *Asian Education and Development Studies, 9*(2), 255–267.

Sweeting, A. (2004). *Education in Hong Kong, 1941 to 2001: Visions and revisions.* Hong Kong: Hong Kong University Press.

Sweeting, A. (2007). Education in Hong Kong: Histories, mysteries and myths. *History of Education, 36*(1), 89–108.

Tung, C. H. (2000). *The policy address 2000.* https://www.policyaddress.gov.hk/pa00/pa00_e.htm.

United Nations Educational Scientific, and Cultural Organization (UNESCO). (2021). *Welcome to UIS.Stat.* http://data.uis.unesco.org/.

University Grants Committee (UGC). (2021). *Student (full-time equivalent): First-year-first-degree students (from 1965/66).* https://cdcf.ugc.edu.hk/cdcf/searchStatSiteReport.action#.

Weeden, K. A. (1998). Revisiting occupational sex segregation in the United States, 1910–1990: Results from a log-linear approach. *Demography, 35*(4), 475–487.

Wong, Y.-L. (2019). Angels falling from Grace? The rectification experiences of middle-class community-college students in Hong Kong. *Studies in Higher Education, 44*(8), 1303–1315.

Wong, Y. L., & Koo, A. (2016). Is Hong Kong no longer a land of opportunities after the 1997 handover? A comparison of patterns of social mobility between 1989 and 2007. *Asian Journal of Social Science, 44*(4–5), 516–545.

Wong, K. T. W., Zheng, V., & Wan, P. S. (2018). The political trust of the post-80s and post-90s generations in Hong Kong: Age and cohort effects. *Modern China Studies, 25*(1), 1–24.

World Bank. (2021). *World Bank open data: Indicators.* https://data.worldbank.org/indicator.

Wu, X. (2010a). Economic transition, school expansion and educational inequality in China, 1990–2000. *Research in Social Stratification and Mobility, 28*(1), 91–108.

Wu, X. (2010b). *Hong Kong's post-80s generation: Profiles and predicaments.* https://www.pico.gov.hk/doc/en/research_reports/HK per cent27s per cent20Post per cent2080s per cent20Generation per cent20- per cent20Profiles per cent20and per cent20Predicaments.pdf.

Wu, Y. (2012). Gender gap in educational attainment in urban and rural China. *Journal of Sociology (Shehui)*, *32*(4), 112–137.

Wu, X. (2016). Hong Kong panel study of social dynamics (HKPSSD): Research designs and data overview. *Chinese Sociological Review*, *48*(2), 162–184.

Wu, X., & Treiman, D. J. (2007). Inequality and equality under Chinese socialism: The Hukou system and intergenerational occupational mobility. *American Journal of Sociology*, *113*(2), 415–445.

Yip, S. F., Wong, W. C., Law, Y. W. and Fu, K. W. (2011). *A study on understanding our younger generation* [online]. Hong Kong: Central Policy Unit Publication. https://www.pico.gov.hk/doc/en/research_reports/A_study_on_understanding_our_young_generation.pdf.

Zhang, Z., & Ye, H. (2018). Mode of migration, age at arrival, and occupational attainment of immigrants from mainland China to Hong Kong. *Chinese Sociological Review*, *50*(1), 83–112.

Zhao, X., Zhang, L., & Kelvin, S. T. O. (2004). Income inequalities under economic restructuring in Hong Kong. *Asian Survey*, *44*(3), 442–473.

Index

A

Academic community, 19–20
Act of Gender Equality in Employment, 211
Adolescence, 3, 5, 10, 166
  developmental self-esteem trajectory, 266–284
  family cohesion, 53
  family conflict, 66
  parental divorce in, 62
  parent-child relationships, 66, 241–262
  self-esteem development, 17
Adolescent–parent affection, 252
Adulthood
  adolescence to early, 241–262
  conceptions of, 241–262
  criteria for, 254 (table)
  defined, 3
  developmental self-esteem trajectory, 266–284
  early delinquency trajectory/ developmental outcomes, 289–315
  factor analysis of, 253 (table)
  parent-child relationships, 243–244
  transitions to, 3–5, 9–10, 242–243
Ageing, 182, 184
Agreeableness, 269
Ajzen, I., 28
Akaike's Information Criterion (AIC), 300
Allen, G., 74
Altruism, 183, 184, 217
ANOVAs, 298
Aquilino, W. S., 245

Arnett, J. J., 242, 249, 260
Arocho, R., 33
Attewell, P., 130
Average Treatment Effect on the Threated (ATT), 107, 116
Axinn, W. G., 84

B

Baomu Tuo Yu Guanli Yu Tuo Yu Feiyong Bujhu Shihshih Jihua, 210
Baron, R. M., 258
Bayesian Information Criterion (BIC), 300
Becker, G., 60, 157
Berk, S. F., 158
Between Parent and Teenager, 246
Big-class concepts, 134
Big Five personality traits, 269
Blumstein, A., 291
Bootstrapping analysis, 258

C

Campbell, W. K., 271
Capital mobility, 126
Catholicism, 43
CFI. *See* Comparative fitness index (CFI)
Chang, Y, -H., 215
Cheung, S. Y., 128
Chien, Y.-N., 100
Childbirth, 65, 69
  cohabitation and, 175
  low acceptance of, 71
Childcare arrangements, 16, 17, 210
  data, 218
  defamilialism, 212–213

demographic characteristics, 219
expenditure, 223, 223 (table)
factors, 215–216
familialism, 212–213
family structure and education,
    224–226, 225 (figure), 232
financial support, 205
by grandmothers, 185
grandparents, missing role of,
    214–215
ideal-actual mismatch, 226–229, 227
    (figure), 228 (table), 232
ideal and actual arrangement, 217
instrumental support, 205
method, 219–221, 220 (table)
parent-child relationship, 229–231,
    230 (table), 232–234
socio-economic backgrounds, 219
subsidy, 223, 223 (table)
in Taiwan, 221–224, 222 (figure), 223
    (table), 231
variables, 218–219
Child-minder Management and Subsidy
    Programme, 211
China, 7, 126, 183, 241
composite self, 247
income, 142
intergenerational relationships, 242
outward-oriented investment, 147
Christianity, 43
Chung, J. M., 270
Classroom environment, 274
Cline, F., 246
Cohabitation, 27, 28, 157
domestic labour arrangements, 162
in Taiwan, 175
unmarried, 175
College degree, 126
College education, 128
College majors, 129, 144
Community Nanny Support System,
    211
Comparative Analysis of Social
    Mobility in Industrial Nations
    (CASMIN), 383
Comparative fitness index (CFI), 140,
    276
Competitive educational system, 5–6
Confucianism, 5, 269

Conscientiousness, 269, 274
Control variables, 108–110
balancing of, 110–113, 110 (table)–
    111 (table)
high school grade, 332
intergenerational support, 188–189
school-to-work transition, 332
Co-residence, 16
financial support, 200, 205
with grandparents, 215
instrumental support, 205
intergenerational, 189–190, 190
    (table)
matrilocal, 187
patrilocal, 187
unmarried, 176
Credential inflation, 128
Credentialism, 101
Crissey, S. R., 33
Cross-national difference, 325
Cross-national diversity, 349
Cross-sectional regression, 101
Cross-tabulation analysis, 298
Cultural norms, 53, 269–270
conscientious belief, 274
early marriage, 70–72
education, 32
no intention of marriage, 83–84
persistent, 6–9, 8 (table)

D
Dating experiences, 33–34
Defamilialism, 212–213
Delaying marriage, 4, 14, 28
emotional factors, 80–81
gender equality, 53
gender role attitudes, 53
insufficient economic resources, 81–82
singlehood, 79
social norms, 32
in Taiwan, 53
Delinquency, 275. *See also* Early
    delinquency trajectory/
    developmental outcomes
adolescence, 290
continuity of, 291
early trajectory of, 302–304
inception of, 290
measures, 296–297

prevalence rates of, 303
spill-over effect of, 289
substance profile and, 302 (table)
types of, 289
Denmark, 28
Dependence tendency, 241–242
Dependent variables, 35, 383, 386, 392
continuous and ordinal, 385
housework, 165
linear probability model (LPM), 47
Depressive symptoms, 100, 101
index of, 106, 112
NEET on, 113–117, 114 (figure), 115
(table)
Descriptive analysis, 106
Descriptive statistics, 37 (table)–40
(table), 42–44
balancing of control variables and,
110–113, 110 (table)–111 (table)
childcare expenditure, 223, 223 (table)
childcare subsidy, 223, 223 (table)
domestic labor involvement, 166–167
intergenerational co-residence, 190
(table)
intergenerational support, 188 (table)
on parental leave, 223, 223 (table)
socioeconomic backgrounds, 219, 220
(table)
Deteriorating, 281
Developmental self-esteem trajectory, 266
adolescence to young adulthood,
267–268
analytic strategy, 275–278
classes of, 278–281, 279 (table), 280
(figure)
cultural norms, 269–270
data and sample, 272–273
developmental curve of, 278, 278
(table)
interpersonal relationships, 270
measurement, 273–275
personal characteristics and family
context, 270–271
present study, 271–272, 272 (figure)
Difference-In-Differences Propensity
Score Matching (DID-PSM),
107–108, 116
subgroup-specific effects of, 118
(table)

Divorce, 7, 14, 47, 53
early marriage, 41
parental, 61, 72
Domestic labor involvement, 155–157
competing hypotheses, 155
descriptive statistics, 166–167
household labour, 157–158
housework distribution, 159–163
housework patterns, in Taiwan,
158–159
institution perspectives, 156
methodological issues, 163–164
methods, 164–166
multivariate analysis, 167–174, 168
(table)–170 (table), 172 (table)–
173 (table)
partnership status and parenthood,
159–163
selection perspective, 155
Domínguez-Folgueras, M., 162
Downward-transfer interactions, 242
Dual filial piety model, 200

E
Early career, 127–130
Early delinquency trajectory/
developmental outcomes, 289
in adulthood, 293–295
at age 30, 307–311
analytical strategy, 298
continuity across the life course,
291–293
continuity of substance use, 302–304
data, 295–295
developmental patterns of, 298–299,
299 (table)
developmental trajectory in, 299–302
life-course transitions, 297, 304–305
measures, 296–297
social bonds, 297, 305–306
socio-economic attainment, 297–298
types of, 290–291
Early marriage, 14, 60
conforming to cultural norms, 70–72
divorce risk for, 41
emotional factors, 76–78, 78–79
likelihood of, 32, 52
normative factors, 78–79
similar age marriage, 42

structural factors, 72–76, 78–79
Taiwan, 29
United States, 29
East Asia, 3, 4, 9, 65
  adulthood in, 10
  childcare, 185
  competitive educational system, 5–6
  persistent cultural norms, 6–9, 8
    (table)
  unemployment, 99
  young parents in, 16
Economic autonomy, 86
Economic gaps, 323
Economic independence, 4, 8, 87
Economic stability, 42
Educational attainment, 50, 109
  age-specific employment rates, 353
    (figure)
  delinquency on, 289
Educational expansion, 127–130
Educational system
  childcare arrangements, 224–226, 225
    (figure)
  competitive, 5–6
  criteria for adulthood, 255 (table)
  leaving, 101–102
Education credential, 130
Education status, 63–64
  early marriage, 75–76, 75 (table)
Education-to-work transitions, 99–122
Emerging adulthood, 10, 28, 133, 242
  marriage intention, 14, 30
Emotional factors, 65–67
  delaying marriage, 80–81
  early marriage, 76–78
  love impulse, 77–78
  no intention of marriage, 84–86
  romantic experience, 77–78
  strained family relationships, 76–77
Emotional support, 198
  intergenerational, 185–186
Empirical strategy, 47
Employment
  criteria for adulthood, 255 (table)
  Hong Kong, 377 (table)
  non-regular, 332
  opportunities of, 327
  regular, 332
  school-mediated transition, 324

in 2011, 133 (figure)
in 2017, 134 (figure)
women-friendly, 351
Endogenous selection bias, 133
Epanechnikov kernel matching, 108
Esping-Andersen, G., 349
Expectation-maximization (EM)
  algorithm, 278
Explicit familialism, 212, 213
Extraversion, 269

F
Familialism, 212–213
Family
  background factors, 34
  characteristics, 276 (table)
  childcare arrangements, 224–226, 225
    (figure)
  children educational attainment, 31
  China, 247
  cohesion, 41, 51, 109
  conventional norms, 182
  disharmony, 84–85
  disruption, 61
  formation, 12, 28
  functions, deficiency of, 72–74
  income, 50, 275
  intactness, 109
  legacy, 182
  non-intact, 32
  policies, 211
  relationships, 61
  well-being, 7
Family context, 274–275
Fathers-in-law (Fil), 200
Fay, J., 246
Fertility, 27, 53, 157
  first marriage, 28
  inconsistency in, 210
  South Korea, 348
  Taiwan, 8 (table)
Financial support, 192
  intergenerational, 183–184
Finland, 216
Firm-level characteristics, 131
  effects on income, 142–145, 143
    (table)–144 (table)
First job, 127
Fishbein, M., 28

Fit statistics
  growth mixture modelling (GMM),
    279 (table)
  latent class growth analysis (LCGA),
    279 (table)
  latent growth modelling (LGM), 278,
    278 (table)
France, 28
Fryer, D., 102
Fukuda, S., 82
Functional discontinuity, 293

G
Gebauer, J. E., 269
Gecas, V., 33
Gender
  age-specific employment rates, 353
    (figure)
  characteristics, 276 (table)
  criteria for adulthood, 255 (table)
  individual and family characteristics
    by, 168 (table)–170 (table)
  intergenerational support and,
    186–187
Gender differences, 33, 51
  in self-esteem, 270
Gender equality, 32, 65
Gender gap, 87
  in grandparenting, 215
Gerber, T., 128
Germany, 351
  longitudinal quantitative study, 186
Ginott, H. G., 246
GMM. *See* Growth mixture modelling
  (GMM)
Goodman, L. A., 386
Gottfredson, M. R., 294
Grandchild. *See* Intergenerational
  support
Grandparenting
  childcare arrangements, 231
  gender gap in, 215
  missing role of, 214–215
  prevalence of, 233
  in Taiwan, 215
Grounded theory, 69
Growth mixture modelling (GMM), 277
  early delinquency trajectory, 299
  fit statistics, 279 (table)

four-class solution of, 280 (figure)
  stimated average of, 280
  variance and covariance equality, 279
Guo, M., 18, 19
Guzzo, K. B., 29

H
Hagestad, G. O., 244
Health and happiness, 106
  NEET, 113–117, 114 (figure), 115
    (table)
Helicopter parenting, 246
Hellevik, O., 47
Heterogeneity, 121, 266
  delinquency, 289
Heterotypic continuity, 293
Hirschi, T., 294
Homotypic continuity, 293
Honda, Y., 324
Hong Kong, 13, 183
  cross-national comparisons, 372
  data, 382–383
  educational expansion, 372–383
  employment, 377 (table), 378 (figure)
  female employment, 380 (table), 382
    (figure)
  first-year-first-degree (FYFD), 374
    (figure)
  intergenerational support, 187
  logit model and stereotyped ordered
    regression model, 393 (table)
  marginal effects of, 391 (table)
  methods, 385–387
  middle-class occupations, 19, 390
  OLS regressions, 387, 388 (table)
  predicted logit for university *vs.* non-
    university education, 394 (figure)
  predicted mean first job ISEI, 389
    (figure)
  school-to-work transition, 18,
    373–383
  statistics by cohort, 385 (table)
  variables, 383–387
Hong Kong Panel Study of Social
  Dynamics (HKPSSD), 382
Hori, Y., 328
Horizontal stratification, 128
Household labour
  allocation of, 155

individual and family effects on, 172
  (table)–173 (table)
neo-economic approach, 157
resource/exchange perspectives, 157
selection and institution processes, 156
time availability, 157
Housework patterns, in Taiwan,
  158–159
distribution of, 159–163
Huang, L.-W., 100
Human capital, 130, 157
Hung, H. -F., 217
Hurdle race, 145–148

I

Ideal-actual mismatch, 226–229, 227
  (figure), 228 (table), 232
Ideological factors, 64–65
IMF. *See* International Monetary Fund
  (IMF)
Implicit familialism, 212
Income, effects on, 142–145, 143
  (table)–144 (table)
Incomplete institutionalization, 161
Independent variables, 383
In-depth interviews, 68–69
Index of depression symptoms, 106, 112
Indonesia, 184
Industrialization, 347
Inequality, 18
Instrumental support, 192, 196 (table)–
  197 (table)
intergenerational, 184–185
Intergenerational co-residence, 189–190,
  190 (table)
Intergenerational emotional support,
  185–186, 204
Intergenerational financial support,
  183–184
married men's, 198–200, 199 (table)
married women's, 200–202
Intergenerational instrumental support,
  184–185
married men's, 202–203
married women's, 203
Intergenerational relationships, 242
Intergenerational support, 181
analytic plan, 192–198, 193 (table)–
  197 (table)

control variables, 188–189
demographic characteristics, 188–189
emotional support, 185–186
financial support, 183–184, 198–202,
  199 (table)
gender and, 186–187
instrumental support, 184–185,
  202–204
intergenerational co-residence,
  189–190
intimate relationships, 191
life transition measurement, 189
monetary transmission, 198–202, 199
  (table)
parenthood status and, 182–186, 189
primary childcare provider, 190–191
sample and data, 187–191, 188 (table),
  190 (table)
Internal labor market, 130–132
International Monetary Fund (IMF),
  349
International socio-economic index
  (ISEI), 135, 145
J1 and J3 groups, 135 (figure)
seemingly unrelated regression (SUR)
  model, 138, 139 (table), 141
  (table)
Interpersonal relationships, 270
developmental self-esteem trajectory,
  274
Interviewees
fertile status of, 75 (table)
marital status of, 68, 68 (table), 75
  (table)
social demographic characteristics of,
  93 (table)–95 (table)
Intimate relationships, 191
Inverse probability of treatment
  weighting (IPTW), 163, 164
IPTW. *See* Inverse probability of
  treatment weighting (IPTW)
Italy, 162

J

Jahoda, M., 102
Japan, 7, 13, 147
childcare policies in, 213
family care, 213
high school students in, 323–343

income, 142
inequality, 18
parasite singles, 241
school-to-work transition, 323–343
Japanese Life Course Panel Surveys
 (JLPS), 330
Jappens, M., 214
Jiangou Tuo Yu Guanli Jhihdu
 Shihshih Jihua, 210
JLPS. *See* Japanese Life Course Panel
 Surveys (JLPS)
Joblessness, 99, 102
Job search process, 328

K
Kamp Dush, C. M., 33
Kangaroo generation, 241
Keeley, M. C., 31
Keeping low and flat, 280 (figure), 284
Kenny, D. A., 258
Kerridge, B. T., 289, 294
Kinship caregiver, 221, 229
Kling, K. C., 270
KLIPS. *See* Korean Labor and Income
 Panel Study (KLIPS)
Knowledge-based economy, 128
Korean Labor and Income Panel Study
 (KLIPS), 354
Krapf, S., 216

L
Labour market, 7, 12, 14, 19, 60, 102,
 126, 241
 dualism, 347
 internal, 130–132
 Japan, 325
 millennial generation, 348
 NEET, 103
 outcomes, 323–343
 secondary, 350
 South Korea, 349–354
Labour Standard Law, 327
Latent class growth analysis (LCGA), 277
 fit statistics, 279 (table)
 heterogeneous subgroups, 278
Latent class growth mixture model
 (LCGM), 299
Latent growth model (LGM), 275
 fit statistics for, 278, 278 (table)

Latent trajectory Gaussian mixture
 model (LT-GMM), 275
Laub, J. H., 291
Lavee, Y., 245
LCGA. *See* Latent class growth analysis
 (LCGA)
Leaving education, 101–102, 104
 in Taiwan, 112
Le Blanc, M., 291
Lechner, M., 108
Leitner, S., 212
Leopold, T., 215
Liberality, 32
Liefbroer, A. C., 214
Life-course transitions, 292, 297
 early delinquent trajectory groups,
 305 (table)
Likelihood ratio statistics, 140
Linear probability model (LPM), 47
Lin, J. P., 100
Lin, W.-S., 215
Liu, J.-T., 100
Living together, 32
Local culture, 183
Loeber, R., 291
Lohmann, H., 214
Lo–Mendell–Rubin Likelihood Ratio
 Test (LMR–LRT), 279
Lost generation, 18
Love impulse, 77–78
LPM. *See* Linear probability model
 (LPM)
Lu, L., 261
Luster, S., 247

M
Manning, W. D., 27, 29
Marriage, 12
 characteristics, for married, 44–47, 45
 (table)–46 (table)
 Chinese societies, 59
 consensus between the couple, 81
 criteria for adulthood, 255 (table)
 data source, 34–35
 descriptive statistics, 37 (table)–40
 (table), 42–44
 desire to, 33–34, 48–52, 48 (table)–49
 (table)
 empirical strategy, 47

financial constraints, 14
freedom and affection, 85–86
intention, 14, 27–54
no intention of, 82–87
objective quality of, 42
postconception, 70–71
probability of, 30–32, 48–52, 48
  (table)–49 (table)
subjective quality of, 42
subsequent, 27–54
Taiwan, 7, 8 (table), 27–54
variables, 35–42
Marxist approach, 132
Mate selection, 59
Maximum likelihood estimation, 138
M-curve, for age-employment profiles,
  351
Mean deviation, 277 (table)
Mediation analysis, 258–259, 259
  (figure)
Meier, A., 74
Men, 18, 43, 174
  first marriage, 60
  intergenerational financial support,
    198–200
  intergenerational instrumental
    support, 202–203
  Taiwan, 63
Middle-class position
  data and methods, 132–138, 133
    (figure)–135 (figure), 137 (table)
  educational expansion, 127–130
  effects on income, 142–145, 143
    (table)–144 (table)
  firm characteristics, 130–132
  internal labor market, 130–132
  occupational status, 127–130
  results and analysis, 138–142, 139
    (table), 141 (table)
  sectors, 130–132
Millennial generation, 348
Model selection process, 300, 300 (table)
Model fit statistics, 140
Modified patriarchal society, 205
Moffitt, T. E., 290, 292, 294
Monetary transmission, 198–202, 199
  (table)
Motherhood, 15, 160, 174
  housework, 175

Mothers-in-law (Mil), 200
Mplus 8.4, 298
Mullendore, R., 246
Multiple regression analyses, 254, 256
  (table)–257 (table)
Multi-stage stratified cluster sampling, 35
Multivariate analysis, domestic labor
  involvement, 167–174, 168 (table)–
  170 (table), 172 (table)–173 (table)
Multivariate multinomial regression,
  281 (table)

N
A Nagging Sense of Job Insecurity, 323
Nagin, D. S., 291
National Institute of Employment and
  Occupational Research, 325
National Longitudinal Survey of Youth
  1997 cohort (NSLY97), 33
Nelson, L. J., 247
Neoliberal economy, 5
Neoliberal transition, 126
Nepal, 29
Netherlands, 214
Neuroticism, 269
Non-intact family, 32
Non-physical attractiveness, 33
Non-regular employment, 332
Nordenmark, M., 102
Normative factors, 64–65
  early marriage, 78–79
  no intention of marriage, 86–87
Not in Employment, Education or
  Training (NEET), 241
  on depressive symptoms, 113–117,
    114 (figure), 115 (table)
  health and happiness, 113–117, 114
    (figure), 115 (table)
  leaving education, 120
  negative effects of, 103
  prevalence of, 99
  short-term effects of, 101
  subgroup-specific effects of, 118
    (table)
  treatment variable, 105
  vs. job neglects, 121
  vs. psychological well-being, 102–104
NVivo software, 69
Nylund, K. L., 300

O

Occupational status, 127–130
  effects on income, 142–145, 143
    (table)–144 (table)
  measurement of, 134
  residuals, 138
One-student-one-company allocation
    rule, 327
On-my-own, 297
Openness, 269
Oppenheimer, V. K., 31, 50
Optional familialism, 212, 213
Ordinal logistic regression models, 230
    (table)
Organisation for Economic
    Co-operation and Development
    (OECD), 27, 241, 347
Otawa, N., 328
Outcome variables
  happiness, 106
  index of depressive symptoms, 106
  self-rated health, 106
Ou, T.-T., 217

P

Padilla-Walker, L. M., 260
Pan, E., 34
Parasite singles, 8, 241
Parental relationships, 61
Parental Subsidy for Unemployed
    Parents Programme, 212
Parental supervision, 246
Parent-child co-residence, 189
Parent-child relationships, 61, 66
  adolescence to early adulthood, 244–246
  adolescent-parent relationships,
    251–252, 254
  childcare arrangements, 229–231, 230
    (table), 232–234
  coming of age, 247–248
  conception of adulthood and,
    243–244
  data and sample, 248–249
  dependence tendency of, 241–242
  individual characteristics, 249
  intergenerational relationships, 251
  mediation analysis, 258–259
  preliminary analyses, 255–258
  present study, 248

  transitions to adulthood, 242–243,
    246–247
  young adults' conceptions of,
    249–251, 252–254, 253 (table)–
    254 (table)
Parenthood, 4, 15, 16, 155
  gender display, 162
  independent variable, 165
  individual and family characteristics
    by, 168 (table)–170 (table)
  intergenerational support and,
    182–186, 189
  responsibilities and behaviours, 162
  temporal ordering of, 163
  transition to, 181
Parenting, helicopter, 246
Partnership, 155, 156
  distribution of, 159–163
  independent variable, 165
  individual and family characteristics
    by, 168 (table)–170 (table)
  temporal ordering of, 163
Paternoster, R., 291
Patrilineal societies, 187
Patterson, G. R., 290
Pedersen, W., 289, 294
Pelikh, A., 216
Peng, I., 213
Persistent cultural norms, 6–9, 8 (table)
Personal characteristics, 274–275
Personality Maturity, 254
Physical attractiveness, 33
Physical health, 270, 275
Postconception marriage, 70–71
Postsecondary education, 133
Pregnancy
  premarital, 51, 75
  unmarried, 28
Pre-marital cohabitation, 7
Premarital conception, 42
Premarital pregnancy, 51, 75
Premarital sex, 51
Primary childcare provider, 190–191
Psychological well-being, 99
  control variables, 108–110
  data and sample, 104–105, 105 (table)
  Difference-In-Differences Propensity
    Score Matching (DID-PSM),
    107–108

leaving education and, 101–102
outcome variables, 106–107
treatment variable, 105–106
vs. NEET, 102–104, 121
Public Employment Security Office,
327
Public university, 142

R
Rational choice, 60
Re-familialism, 212
Regional difference, 215
Regression analysis, 30
Regression model, 14, 166, 192
intergenerational emotional support,
199 (table)
intergenerational instrumental
support, 196 (table)–197 (table)
intergenerational financial support,
193 (table)–195 (table)
Regular employment, 332
Religion, 33, 41
Reproductive intention, 71–72
Richards, M., 34
Robins, L. N., 291
Romantic experience, 77–78
absence of, 80
Root-mean-square error of
approximation (RMSEA), 140, 276
Rosenberg Self-Esteem Scale, 273
Rossi, A. S., 245
Rossi, P. H., 245
Russia, 216
Rutter, M., 291–292

S
Sampson, R. J., 291
Satellite generation, 241
Scholarship, 182
School-mediated system, 323–343
School-to-work transition, 15, 323–325
confounding factor, 337
critics of, 343
data and variables, 330–332
destinations of high school graduates,
329 (figure)
employment, opportunities of, 327
employment status, 336 (figure)
Hong Kong, 18, 372–396

job openings to job applicants, for
high school graduates, 330
(figure)
job opportunities, 336
job search process, 328
long-term relationship, 328
methods, 325, 326 (table)
schedule, 325–327
school mediation, 333 (figure)–341
(figure)
social background, 342 (figure)
students, 327
Schulenberg, J. E., 292
Seemingly unrelated regression (SUR)
model, 138
Seff, M., 33
Self-confidence, 270
Self-esteem, 266. *See also*
Developmental self-esteem
trajectory
Self-rated health, 106
SES. *See* Socio-economic status (SES)
Shechyu Baomu Jhihchih Sitong, 210
Shotgun marriage, 47, 52, 70–71
Signaling theory, 129
Singapore, 183
Singlehood, 69, 80
delaying marriage, 79
Skopek, J., 215
Social bonds, 297
early delinquent trajectory groups,
306 (table)
Social control theory, 289, 290
Social inequality, 99, 323, 324
Social mobility, 126
Social relations, 243, 283
Social roles, 243
Social Role Transition, 259
Social stratification, 183
Socio-economic attainment, 297–298
at age 30, 307 (table)
Socio-economic status (SES), 271
delinquency on, 289
Solidarity
elements of, 243–244
intergenerational, 181–206
South Korea, 7, 13
age-specific employment rates, 356
(figure)

childcare policies in, 213
compulsory military service, 358
data and methods, 354–359, 355
    (figure)–356 (figure), 358 (table)–
    359 (table)
economic growth in, 347
employed college graduates leaving,
    363–364
fertility rate, 348
first employment and career breaks, 360
gender employment gaps in, 348
income, 142
intergenerational instrumental
    support, 185
kangaroo generation, 241
Korean Labor and Income Panel
    Study (KLIPS), 354
labour market structure in, 349–354,
    352 (figure)–353 (figure)
lost cases, 357
market-based care services, 213
survival-time analysis, 358, 358
    (table), 368–372
tertiary education rates of, 355 (figure)
two-child norm, 348
un(der)employed college graduates,
    360–363
un(der)employment, 357
young college graduates, 347–365
Spain, 162
Spousal survey (2013–2018), 12–13
Standard deviation, 277 (table)
Standardized root mean square residual
    (SRMR), 276
Stereotyped Ordered Regression (SOR),
    385, 386
Strandh, M., 102
Structural factors
    early marriage, 78–79
    economic condition, 64
    education status, 63–64, 75–76, 75
        (table)
    family functions, deficiency of, 72–74
    family status, 61–62
    individual resources, 62–64, 63 (figure)
    no intention of marriage, 86–87
Student-centred support, 328
Subgroup-specific analyses, 117–119,
    118 (table), 121
Suitable partner, 80
Sun, S. H.-L., 215, 233

Super-competitive educational system, 6
Sweden, 216, 351
Symptom Checklist-90-Revised (SCL-
    90-R), 106

T
Taipei City, 50
Taiwan, 7
    ageing issues, 182
    birth rate, 182
    childcare arrangements. *See* Childcare
        arrangements
    childcare policies in, 213
    cohabitation rate, 28
    crude marriage rate, 8 (table)
    delinquency, 290–291
    domestic labor involvement of,
        155–177
    economic turmoil, 99
    emotional support, 181–206
    fertility rate, 210
    financial support, 181–206
    first marriage, 8 (table)
    gender role attitudes in, 65
    housework patterns in, 158–159
    instrumental support, 181–206
    knowledge-based economy, 128
    leaving education in, 112
    marriage intention, 27–54
    marrying early/remaining single in,
        59–89
    middle-class position, 126–148
    NEET, 102
    subsequent marriage in, 27–54
    total fertility rate in, 8 (table)
    unemployment, 99
    young parents in, 16
Taiwan Social Change Survey (TSCS),
    100
Taiwan Youth Project (TYP), 10, 29,
    35, 67, 100, 132, 164
    childcare arrangements, 218
    developmental self-esteem trajectory,
        272
    early delinquency trajectory/
        developmental outcomes,
        289–315
    intergenerational support, 181, 187
    marital status of, 67, 67 (table)
    multi-stage stratified cluster sampling,
        35

NEET, 119
parent-child relationships, 248
phase I survey (2000–2009), 11
phase II survey (2011–2020), 12
spousal survey (2013–2018), 12–13
valuable panel dataset, 19
Tasker, F., 34
Thomese, F., 214
Thornton, A., 84
Tiger son, 7
Transition to adulthood, 3–5
marriage, 64
norms and resources, 9–10
Treatment variable, 105–106
Tsai, S.-L., 100
Tsou, M.-W., 100
Tung Chee-Hwa, 375
Twenge, J. M., 271
Tyndik, A., 216
TYP. *See* Taiwan Youth Project (TYP)

U
Unemployment, 99, 105, 147
Japan, 325
United Kingdom, 147, 351
United States, 28, 29, 65, 129
early marriage in, 29
intergenerational support, 186
longitudinal interview study, 186
Unmarried pregnancy, 28

V
Van Bavel, J., 214
Variables, 41–42
childcare arrangements, 218–219
definitions of, 58 (table)
demographic characteristics, 219
dependent, 35, 48
independent, 36
mean and standard deviation of, 277
(table)
outcome, 106–107
socio-economic backgrounds, 219
treatment, 105–106
Verhoef, M., 216

W
Wang, Y.-C.L., 100, 213
Weberian approach, 132

Welfare regime, 183
Western Germany, 216
Western model, 9
Whitbeck, L. B., 245
Wickrama, K. K. A. S., 277
Witteveen, D., 130
Women, 31, 44
domestic work, 158
economic autonomy, 65
fertility, 27
first marriage, 27
housework, 155
intergenerational financial support,
200–202
intergenerational instrumental
support, 203
intergenerational support, 186
labour market, 60
NEET, 112
patrilocal arrangement, 201
probability of marriage, 50
South Korea, 351, 352 (figure)
Wu, X., 17, 18

Y
Yang, C.-L., 28
Yang, K. S., 247, 284
Yi, C. C., 14, 100, 187, 215
Young adults, 3, 9, 16
cohabitation, 175
delaying marriage, 81
developmental trajectory of, 10
educational status, 75
family disharmony, 84
family structure transitions, 61
marriage, 30, 31
parental divorce, 62
pregnancy and childbirth after
marriage, 65
reproductive intention, 71
social behaviours, 17
in Taiwan, 126–148
transition to adulthood, 252–254

Z
Zagel, H., 214
Zero delinquency, 300, 301
(figure)
Zimmerman, M. A., 158